LIFE AFTER POLITICS

GEOFF MULGAN is the Director of the independent think-tank, Demos.

LIFE AFTER POLITICS

New Thinking For The Twenty-First Century

Edited by
GEOFF MULGAN

FontanaPress
An Imprint of HarperCollins*Publishers*

Fontana Press
An imprint of HarperCollins*Publishers*,
77–85 Fulham Palace Road
Hammersmith, London W6 8JB

A Fontana Press Original 1997
3 5 7 9 8 6 4

A catalogue record for this book is available from the British Library

ISBN 0 00 638755 1

Set in Postscript Meridien by
Rowland Phototypesetting Ltd
Bury St Edmunds, Suffolk

All the articles in this book were first published, some in more extended form, by the independent think tank Demos.

Printed and bound in Great Britain by
Clays Ltd, St Ives plc

CONTENTS

Business, Technology and the Future

ACKNOWLEDGEMENTS

The material in this book has been abridged from the following publications, all of which are available from Demos:

Zygmunt Bauman, *Alone Again: Ethics after Certainty*; Vincent Cable, *The World's New Fissures*; Helen Wilkinson, *No Turning Back: Generations and the genderquake*; David Cannon, 'The postmodern work ethic' in *The Time Squeeze*, Demos Quarterly 5; Peter Singer, *How are we to live? Ethics in an age of self-interest*, a Demos Millennium Lecture; Roger Scruton, *Animal Rights and Wrongs*; Philip Dodd, *The Battle Over Britain*; Howard Gardner, 'Opening Minds' in *Opening Minds*, Demos Quarterly 1; David Hargreaves, *The Mosaic of Learning*; Douglas Hague, *Transforming the Dinosaurs*; Ken Worpole and Liz Greenhalgh, *The Freedom of the City*; Geoff Mulgan and Helen Wilkinson, 'Well-being and time' in *The Time Squeeze*, Demos Quarterly 5; Geoff Mulgan and Charles Leadbeater, 'The end of unemployment' in *The end of unemployment: Bringing work to life*, Demos Quarterly 2; Amitai Etzioni, *The Parenting Deficit*; Helen Wilkinson and Geoff Mulgan, *Freedom's Children: Work, relationships and politics for 18–34 year olds in Britain today*; Andrew Adonis and Geoff Mulgan 'Back to Greece' in *Lean Democracy*, Demos Quarterly 3; Charles Leadbeater and Geoff Mulgan 'Lean democracy and the leadership vacuum' in *Lean Democracy*, Demos Quarterly 3; Perri 6, 'Governing by cultures' in *Missionary Government*, Demos Quarterly 6; Michael Power, *The Audit Explosion*; Robin Murray and Geoff Mulgan, *Reconnecting Taxation*; Robert Cooper, *The Postmodern State and the World Order*; John Gray, *After Social Democracy*; Bob Tyrrell, 'The shapers of things to come' in *The Return of the Local*, Demos Quarterly 9; Ivan Briscoe and Geoff Mulgan, *The Society of Networks*; John Ashworth and Helena Cronin, 'Darwinism and the social sciences', Demos Quarterly 10; James

Woudhuysen, 'Before we rush to declare a new era', *Liberation Technology*, Demos Quarterly 4; Charles Hampden-Turner, 'Masters of the infinite game' in *The Age of Asia: Learning from the sunrise societies*, Demos Quarterly 6; Samuel Brittan, 'Darwinian psychology, political economy and the problem of groups', Demos Quarterly 10.

* * *

The editor would like to thank all of the contributors to this volume, many of whom were prepared to sweat over many drafts and accept unreasonable demands with good humour. I would also like to thank the literally hundreds of other people who have taken part in Demos conferences, seminars and discussions, and contributed, either directly or indirectly, to the ideas in this book.

In addition, credit is due to Joanna Wade and Debbie Porter who have ably run the Demos publishing team, and to Toby Mundy at HarperCollins who has been an exemplary editor, always helpful and full of suggestions, while also keeping a firm grip.

GEOFF MULGAN
October 1996

Introduction

GEOFF MULGAN

There can't have been many times in human history when so many problems have demanded fresh ideas and new thinking. Some of them arise from the sheer novelty of a global market which has for the first time brought billions more within its ambit, and in which technologies, organizations and cultures compete, collide and mingle into bewildering new forms. Some are problems of failure, above all perhaps the problems of protecting the natural environment from an often ravenous industrial machine. Others arise from new knowledge – like the ethical issues thrown up by our new understanding of the human genome. And others, like the pressures on the welfare state that inevitably arise from an ageing population (and less inevitably from high unemployment), or the new divisions that have accompanied the shift to a society based ever more on information, are rooted in structural problems.

You might expect that politics would be at the forefront of the search for new solutions. All of these challenges are, above all, collective ones, that aren't easily susceptible to individual choice and individual action. But instead of being at the cutting edge, it is an odd characteristic of our times that all too often politics today feels like a backwater, a declining industry struggling to keep up, rather than a place of imagination and energy.

Behind this gap, between what politics could be and what it is, lies the most striking paradox of modern democracy. Around the world there has never before been such a wide acceptance of the central idea that underpins the culture of democracy – the belief in people's capacity to govern themselves. Modern citizens simply take it for granted that they have a right to run their own lives, to have a say on how decisions are made, and to create their own meanings. Today, from Vladivostok to the Transvaal, democracy has become the official creed of the majority of countries, including many that were until recently despotic, and democratic ideas have permeated education and work, home and culture, in ways that would have been unthinkable even a few decades ago.

Yet despite this unprecedented strength, in other respects democracy looks remarkably weak. In its old heartlands, the central institutions of formal democracy – parliaments and governments, parties and elections – seem tired, even archaic. Governments appear short of legitimacy, unable to inspire, to raise taxes, to run services, or to muster commitment. We know that we need politics – to resolve the big conflicts of interest, and lend direction to complex societies, but we now seem to feel almost congenitally uncomfortable with the ways in which it is organized. It is not that, as in previous times, there is a competing system that promises to make things work better than democracy. Today even Russian communists and Italian fascists claim to support its basic principles. It is rather that it seems to be lagging behind the new world that is evolving around it.

This clash between the culture of democracy and its forms is one of the central issues of our time. It is why we chose the name 'demos', the Greek root of the word democracy, which means the people gathered together. For it posed the question: how can the 'demos' in all its forms be defined, organized, and given expression, in a world that is vastly different from the one in which the nineteenth-century nation-states began setting up their parliaments and parties, shaping the architectures of their politics?

One response is simply to celebrate its apparent decay. It is said that the decline of traditional politics means that we are growing up beyond the crude illusions of party loyalty. No longer do people subscribe to the naive fantasy that governments can engineer a better world. The residue of monarchies, and the childlike faith that leaders have the power to right all wrongs, is being left behind.

For others the new politics of single issue campaigns and self-help offers a superior alternative to the old. It is plural, alive, dynamic and in touch with feelings, unlike the sterile and one-dimensional politics of manifestos and legislative programmes.

There is something to be said for these views. For in part our problems are effects of the maturing of a democratic culture, which is bursting out from the constraints into which it was forced. We are indeed breaking away from the legacies of monarchy and absolutism and recognising more clearly that power is not just something concentrated amongst a few leaders. The great richness of communication brought about this century, not least by the liberation of women, is multiplying the numbers of 'demoses', the places for dialogue and deliberation by people with the confidence to express their own views and interests.

But it would be wrong to be too sanguine. If the core institutions don't work, if the old institutions of democracy are simply neglected rather than replaced, the costs may be high. For all the defects of politics, there is still no other dominant source of leadership in modern societies. Power may have passed to the media, to global finance, even to individual consumers, but often their influence turns out to be negative (a capacity to block things) or constrained (a power to choose between options determined by others) rather than a positive capacity to achieve change. A society without a healthy politics may find it harder legitimately to act in the long-term interests of future generations, for example by investing in education or promoting the environment at the cost of current consumption. Immediate self-interest tends to fill the vacuum that is left when the politics of common purposes disappears. Chronic social ills like long-term unemployment and poor education go unremedied. A spiral can set in as political failure prompts further disconnection from the system which in turn further undermines the capacity of governments to be effective and legitimate.

Moreover as globalization dramatically recasts the landscape of the world's power, for the first time bringing billions into an open global market and rupturing and recasting traditionally enclosed cultures, it may well be that politics becomes far more, not less, important, as a way to solve problems and as a means of providing security and a stable sense of belonging.

This collection is both about understanding this new environment and about responding to it. It is in this sense acutely political, even though little of it falls into the now largely bankrupt boxes of left and right that we inherited from the French revolution. It is concerned with the world of solutions, rather than just describing problems. It is concerned with judgements, rather than detached commentary. In it there is a wide diversity of styles and approaches, covering everything from schools to taxes, lifestyles to administrative mechanisms.

But there are, nevertheless, consistent themes. Many of them fit well with what Italo Calvino described (in his *Memos for the Millennium*) as the essential qualities of the coming era, an era of swiftness and lightness, exactitude and multiplicity, that may contrast sharply with the slow, heavy, standardizing bluntness of so much government and administration this century.

Ten themes in particular stand out.

The first is a slow shift in the goals of politics, away from quantity and towards quality. For much of this century the main goals of policy were economic growth and a reasonable distribution of welfare, defined primarily in economic terms. Growth took over from military prowess as the main measure of political achievement. But today it is not enough simply to accumulate more. There is an abundance of evidence that economic growth on its own does not necessarily translate into a better quality of life, welfare or happiness. Environmental awareness of how the world works has rendered obsolete many of the old categories; nature was one kind of asset that economists were never much good at measuring. Nor is politics simply about the distribution of welfare in narrowly economic terms: as important is the distribution of status, of work and of respect, all things which governments are rather less able to deliver. In some respects this shift towards a greater concern for the quality of life is a measure of the success of economics: most people (at least in the industrialized world) are not starving, homeless or wanting in necessities. Success means that attention can turn elsewhere. But the shift is also a symptom of the distortions that an overly narrow economic approach has brought to human decision-making. This is why public concerns for good work, free time, sustainable environments and better relationships are now apparent all around the policy world, albeit in ways that the policy professionals, with their focus on quantities, throughputs and delivered programmes, find extraordinarily hard to understand.

The second theme concerns globalization. We now have a borderless world in goods and services, technologies and television programmes. There are still very real limits to globalization: even the largest multinationals tend to keep a strong national base, and it is only in the last twenty years that levels of trade and flows of money, people and technology have risen again above the levels of 1913. But globalization is now stretching the fabric of daily life, and remaking the terms of political relations and of locality beyond anything known in the past. It is greatly increasing the capacity not only of private firms and organized crime, but also (surprisingly perhaps) of governments. It provides a new backdrop in which we have to think far more rigorously about how different systems interconnect: industries and environments, educational systems and political ones. Action on one point in the system can have unpredictable and even damaging impacts elsewhere. This is very difficult for governments to grasp, since they prefer to focus on only a handful of indicators, and since few are well designed for a systemic view of the world, a view which grasps how things connect rather than how they are separate. But fortunately globalization also has one other side; it is reshaping the marketplace for ideas, rendering it more open, and more rapid. Few policies can ever be imported wholesale. But more than ever before there is a global trade in which welfare ideas can be imported from Singapore or Malaysia, crime policies from America, cultural policies from Australia, pensions policies from Latin America.

The third theme is diversity. Most of our political traditions have been built on an assumption of homogeneity: the idea that there is a single public, a single nation, or a possibility of generalizing the experiences of one particular class. Across the world this assumption is breaking down. In most societies there are now many more ways of life, many more different sets of values in contention. In the face of this change, two dangerous errors have become common. One is the belief that it is possible to return to an earlier homogeneity, a single language, a single set of values, or a single ethnic mix, to be enforced by government from on high. In fact the world is mongrel, impure and in many respects all the better for that. The other mistake is to believe that there is no limit to this diversity, that societies can cohere without any agreed values, frameworks for how to discuss and argue and allocate, when in fact any community requires some baseline of shared commitments.

The fourth theme is that we live in an age of technology. There are more scientists at work than ever before, and, according to one estimate, more hours of scientific work being done in a single year now than in the whole of human history up to the 1960s. We should not be surprised that new technologies are pouring out of the world's laboratories and throwing up dramatic new challenges in many fields: from the power of IT to reshape governments and businesses to the potential of genetic knowledge to reshape the ways in which we think about human nature, criminality or education.

So far we have experienced just a small proportion of the

big changes that are likely to flow from information technologies (it is worth remembering that it took over fifty years for the car and electricity to have the full impact on the way we live). The key point is that technology is no longer something separate to be considered in a box labelled 'technology policy'. Instead it is part of the environment of every policy field, part of the fabric of life.

The fifth theme is the reimagination of the state. We have grown up with governments that cling to themselves the monopolies of power: not only physical violence, but also the capacity to tax, to pass laws. Today this is changing. The primary long-term reason is that states are no longer so clearly defined by their sovereignty over physical space and their military capacity to defend it. With this historic shift away from a system of states governed by war, the primacy of one level (usually the national) disappears, and instead many different levels of governance, from the transnational to the local, can compete for loyalty, resources and power. But as significant is the sense that states have fallen behind in terms of their capacities and competences, so that we now need nothing less than revolutions to bring them up to date, to help them break free from their twin scleroses: the external one of being locked into big interest groups (like the defence industries or farmers) and the internal one of being locked into stultifyingly bureaucratic ways of working.

The sixth theme is learning. When information and knowledge have become the primary base of the economy, every society needs to worry far more than in the past about its systems of learning. Knowledge industries are now essential to manufacturing and services, and such things as creativity and imagination have become vital economic tools to be nurtured. As a result schools and colleges are no longer just machines for keeping children out of trouble, or preparing them for repetitive menial tasks. Instead they have to prefigure and reflect the best of the emerging society, not the leftovers of the old. Indeed, every institution needs to be able to learn and adapt, to mobilize the 'gold' in the heads of its employees and stakeholders, if it is not to be overtaken, to lose trust and legitimacy.

The seventh theme concerns gender. One of the greatest changes of this century has been that in the relations between men and women. In part this is an economic shift, about the huge movement of women into the workplace, into careers and the professions. In part it is a cultural shift, as the old bases of masculinity in the army and manufacturing decline in significance and as more feminine styles gain greater prominence. In part, too, it is a shift in how we think about the relations between home and work, families and industries, the public and the private. In historical terms this 'genderquake' is still only in its infancy. But its reverberations will be with us for a long time to come.

The eighth theme concerns one of the oldest issues of politics: the balance between the whole and the parts, between the needs of society and the needs of individuals. Having achieved a massive increase in personal freedoms we now understand better that cults of individual freedom can degenerate into childish selfishness. Healthy societies need a sense of interconnectedness and interdependence. They need to understand that a proper sense of individuality encompasses all the many roles in which we are linked to each other – as parents and patients, citizens and consumers, workers and friends. Sometimes these connections are summed up in the word community, although often this gives a misleadingly static flavour to what can be a very dynamic property, and to issues that are now becoming as important for the firm as for the neighbourhood.

Ninth, our relationship to time is changing fast. In part this is because time is becoming far more visible as a resource; as something valuable to be conserved and used well. The big questions of time politics – how work is distributed between the overworked and the underworked, how families achieve a balance between the needs of parenting and those of the workplace – all of these are set to be critical issues in the years ahead. But time is also becoming important because we are becoming more aware of the timeframes within which we operate. The two dominant decision-making techniques of the West, the election and the consumer market, are notoriously short-term. Information technologies are accelerating the pace at which decisions can be made, at which knowledge and emotions travel the world and the pace at which things become obsolete. Yet all societies depend on a capacity to act in the long-term interest – to take actions today that may not bear fruit for decades, or even centuries. This capacity can be embedded deep in families, in personal choices, in institutions that see themselves as part of an historical continuum. Some nations still seem to be good at thinking far into the future. But many have been harmed by the 'bias against the future' that is written into so many systems, and by the telescoping of time horizons in institutions as diverse as universities and banks (which is in part an effect of accelerating information flows, and in part due to conscious policy choices).

Finally, there is the question of trust. Many Western societies are now suffering acute crises of trust, not only in government and politics, but also in many other central institutions. A growing body of thinkers now argues that societal success rests on trust and sociability, on people's capacity to shape their world and to work with others. This is what lies behind successful markets as well as successful democracies. Both can be undermined by crude statist and market ideas which take these social bases for granted. A new cluster of ideas derived from economic sociology, anthropology, psychology and history is giving substance to these insights. It is concerned with the soft as well as hard dimensions of human interactions: the networks that form at local level; what prompts people to trust each other; what makes them cooperate or compete and, crucially, what makes them fulfilled. In other words, our political perspectives are taking us back to the quality and nature of social relationships.

The implication of this last point is vital. For many of our most apparently intractable problems – crime, governmental failure, under-investment – are at root problems of relationships. Even the most apparently economic issues – such as unemployment – turn out on closer inspection to be as much about values and politics, about the willingness of the unemployed to work and the willingess of those with jobs to share with them.

Unfortunately they cannot be tackled head on. For they depend in turn on the existence of legitimate authorities with the power and support to solve them. They depend on an effective demos, able to make collective decisions and put them into practice. This is why the current failure of politics is so important. It condemns societies to gridlock. It condemns them to underperformance.

The immediate context for all of this is an ideological vacuum. Britain, like a number of other Western societies, is now struggling to find a new direction in the wake of two exhausted political projects. The first is social democracy – that combination of faith in government, moderately egalitarian welfare and the mixed economy. By historical standards it had a good run. But by the 1970s and 1980s it was losing the capacity to legitimate further rises in taxation, the capacity to run public industries well and its skill at keeping the industrial peace. Its successor was Thatcherism, a bold project of national renewal which tackled head on many deep structural problems, but then ran out of steam, oddly enough in a wave of rising inflation and public spending. Neither now appears to have the potential to regenerate itself. Neither can restore confidence, or rebuild the legitimacy of institutions. Often things harden before they break apart. In Britain the left hardened into Bennism just before it crumbled. The right hardened into Thatcherism just before it was overtaken by events.

Today we are thinking in the echo of these crashes, the end of the old polarities of left and right, capital and labour. We are thinking in a time of unprecedented possibilities to remake institutions and relationships.

It is my hope that this collection will give a sense of the excitement that those involved in thinking through these questions have experienced. There is a ferment, a passion, a sense of thinking on the edge, that contrasts with the stasis and stagnation of much of our political culture, still content to recycle eighteenth- and nineteenth-century ideas for want of anything better to offer. Instead, this book brings together work from across boundaries, frontiers and disciplines, work that is syncretic and creative and that points the way not just to a richer sense of life *after* politics, but also to a new, more confident politics for the century ahead.

BELIEFS, VALUES AND IDENTITIES

Commentators often write as if the truly powerful drivers of change are all impersonal ones: the power of the market, of new technologies or new production systems is seen as the origin of less obvious changes in family life or public attitudes. But there is just as much evidence that the opposite is true. Few of the genuinely historic changes of the last century can be understood if we ignore the influence of changes in human values. The rising attachments to autonomy, to democracy, to consumption, to the environment have all been as much causes as consequences of change, not least because they have found such rapid expression through the marketplace or the ballot box.

It is easy to understand why their significance is often downplayed. Whereas economic and technological factors are hard and quantifiable, values and attitudes are seen as soft and probably indefinable.

But it is no longer excusable to see them as secondary. As we move into the new millennium public values are becoming more, not less, integral to processes of change. We can see this even in foreign affairs where domestic public opinion has become a more important and often less predictable force than ever before. We can see it in the economy where changing attitudes to the future or to time have a direct bearing on investment patterns or preparedness to work (and where, as a result, economics has been floundering in its attempts to understand such phenomena as savings behaviour or unemployment). And we can see it in politics itself where a growing gulf has become apparent between the core values of many of the main political parties and those of their electorates, and where the relative obsolescence of the older ideologies has cast attention far more onto moral and ethical issues.

This section presents a series of views both of how beliefs and values are changing in the advanced industrialized societies and of what this implies for how we organize life and politics. Each essay offers a different set of insights into the hugely complex processes of changing values and ethical principles.

Helen Wilkinson describes the continuing rise of autonomy, the 'genderquake' that has accompanied feminism and women's growing power in the economy, and the breakdown of traditional forms of authority. She shows why in so many societies quite new problems are coming into view – not only those of achieving further steps towards genuine equality for women, but also measures to prevent some groups of men from falling too far behind, whether in terms of schooling or jobs. Vincent Cable shows how in place of the old left-right divide there is emerging a new axis of identity politics, which ranges from exclusive identities based on nation, ethnicity or religion, towards the more inclusive, universalist principles of the Enlightenment. This is becoming one of the most bitterly fought divides everywhere, from arguments about trade in the US and France, to the campaigns of the BJP in India or Farrakhanites in the US inner city.

These shifts in values are also calling into question older fixed identities. Philip Dodd shows how much of the inherited package of ideas that defined Britishness is being bypassed and losing its relevance – and why the British need to recreate another identity as an outward-looking nation, at ease importing and exporting people, goods and ideas. In the essays on ethics Zygmunt Bauman argues that more than ever we have to make our own meanings, Peter Singer connects current ethical arguments to the wider interests of the world and the environment and Roger Scruton shows why, even though animals do not have rights, we nevertheless have important obligations towards them.

In a democratic era values are the starting point for any credible politics. It is in the realm of values that politics has lost its way, its capacity to speak directly to people's cares and emotions. And it is in the realm of values and ethics that we need to find new foundations for life after politics.

1

Alone Again

Ethics after Certainty

ZYGMUNT BAUMAN

The great Danish theologian, Knud Logstrup, mused: 'It is a characteristic of human life that we mutually trust each other ... Only because of some special circumstance do we ever distrust a stranger in advance ... Initially we believe one another's word; initially we trust one another.' Not so another religious philosopher, Leon Shestov, a Russian refugee and professor at the Sorbonne: '*Homo homini lupus* is one of the most steadfast maxims of eternal morality. In each of our neighbours we fear a wolf ... We are so poor, so weak, so easily ruined and destroyed! How can we help being afraid! ... We see danger, danger only ...'

Surely, Logstrup and Shestov cannot both be right. Or can they? Logstrup was born and died in tranquil, serene, peaceful Copenhagen, where the royals bicycled the streets together with their subjects. Shestov was hunted down and refused university posts by the tsarist regime for being born in the wrong faith, then hunted down and exiled by the anti-tsarist revolution for professing the wrong faith, then drank his fill from the bitter chalice of exile in a foreign country ... The two wise men reported two stridently different experiences. Their generalizations contradicted each other, but so did the lives they generalized from.

And this seems to apply to all of us. We generalize from what we see. Whenever we say 'people are what they are', what we mean is the people we meet; people shaped and moved and guided by the world we together happen to inhabit. And people treated like wolves tend to become wolf-like; people treated with trust tend to become trustworthy. What we think of each other does matter.

Today there is a desperate search for foundations for morality. Some seek it in business ethics or government. But in both those cases the dominance of rules and an instrumental rationality means that morality tends to be neutralized. For the employee the key is to follow procedures not to act with judgement.

But if our life experience shapes our moral outlook, it is hard not to be concerned that today our dominant experience stems from the dissipation of the once solid and relatively lasting frames in which the concerns and efforts of most individuals were inscribed. Jobs, once seen as 'for life', are more often that not now temporary and may disappear virtually without notice, together with the factories or offices or bank branches which offered them. The skills which the jobs required are ageing fast, turning overnight from assets into liabilities. Being prudent and provident, thinking of the future, becomes ever more difficult, as there is little sense in accumulating skills for which tomorrow there may be no demand, or saving money which tomorrow may lose much of its purchasing power. At the moment young men and women enter the game of life, none can tell what the rules of the game will be like in the future. Their only certainty is that the rules will change many times over before the game is finished.

What most of us learn from our experience now, is that all forms in the world around us, however solid they may seem, are not immune to change; that things burst into attention without warning and then disappear or sink into oblivion without trace; that what is all the rage today becomes the butt of ridicule tomorrow; that what is vaunted and recommended and hammered home today is treated with disdain tomorrow (if it's still remembered); that, on the whole, time is cut into episodes – each with a beginning and an end but without prehistory or future; that there is little or no logical connection between the episodes, even their succession looking suspiciously coincidental, contingent and random; and that since they come from nowhere, episodes go by and away without leaving lasting consequences.

Our response to this is to avoid commitment. 'I do not want to get involved' is what we say more often than not to silence inchoate emotions and nip in the bud the shoots of a deeper, intimate human relationship of the 'for richer for poorer, till death us do part' kind. Ever more ingenious locks, bolts and burglar alarms are one of the few growth industries – not just for their genuine or putative practical uses, but for their symbolic value. Inwardly, they mark the boundary of the hermitage where we won't be disturbed, while outwardly they communicate our decision: 'For all I care, outside could be a wasteland.'

All around us are signs of a moral gap: in business, in government, in politics and in daily life. We are being told repeatedly by many on both left and right that the *community* is the most likely candidate to fill the gap. Yet modernity spent most of its time and a lot of its energy on fighting communities – those larger than life groupings into which people are born, only to be held inside them for the rest of their lives by the dead hand of tradition strengthened by collective surveillance and blackmail. From the Enlightenment on, it has been seen as a common-sensical truth that human emancipation, the releasing of genuine human potential, required that the bounds of communities should be broken and individuals set free from the circumstances of their birth. We seem to have come full circle now. The idea of community has been recovered from the cold storage where modernity bent on boundless humanity confined it, and restored to a genuine or imaginary past glory. It is on the community that many hopes bereaved by bankrupt or discredited institutions now focus. What had been once rejected as a constraint is now hailed as the 'enabling capacity'. What was once seen as an obstacle on the road to full humanity, is now praised as its necessary condition. Humanity, we are told, comes in many forms and shapes, and thanks to communities, traditions and cultures, the inherited forms of life are here to see to it that this is the case.

The argument about the supremacy of supposedly 'natural' community in the life of the individual runs as follows: each one of us is born into a certain tradition and language, which decides what to see before we begin to look, what to say before we learn to speak, what to consider important before we start weighing things against each other, and how to conduct ourselves before we start pondering the choices. Thus in order to know what we are, to understand ourselves, we must fathom and consciously embrace that tradition; and in order to be ourselves, to keep our identity intact and waterproof, we must support that tradition with all our heart. In fact, we owe it our complete loyalty; and we ought to offer its demands an unquestionable priority whenever loyalty calls in that society of multiple loyalties clash.

The argument, as it were, reverses the true order of things. Traditions do not 'exist' by themselves and independently of what we think and do; they are daily reinvented by our dedication, our selective memory and selective seeing, our way of behaving '*as if*' they defined our conduct. The communities are *postulated*; and the meaning of their being 'real' is that many people, in unison, follow that postulate. The call to give the 'community of belonging' our prime and undivided loyalty, the demand to consider ourselves the community member first, and all the rest later, is precisely the way to make community a 'reality', to split the larger society into little enclaves which eye each other with suspicion and keep at a distance from each other. And because these communities, unlike modern nations well entrenched in the coercive and educational institutions of the nation-state, do not have many legs to stand on except our individual loyalties, they require an unusually intense emotional dedication and shrill, vociferous and spectacular declarations of faith;

and they scent in the half-hearted, lukewarm and undecided fringes the most mortal of dangers.

So there is another contradiction between the 'community narrative' and the true state of affairs it narrates. The siren song of community is all about the warmth of togetherness, mutual understanding and love; such a relief from the cold, harsh and lonely life of competition and continuous uncertainty. Community advertises itself as the cosy home amidst a hostile and dangerous city; it draws profusely, overtly or obliquely, on the very contemporary image of the sharp divide between the fortified and electronically protected homestead and the street full of knife-carrying strangers, the wasteland subjected to a chary 'neighbourhood watch'. Community seduces its proselytes with the promise of freedom from fear and the tranquillity of *chez soi*. But again, the reality is all too often the opposite. Given the endemic brittleness of foundations, community can ill afford anything but full and militant dedication to the cause; its self-appointed guardians are day and night on the lookout, searching for real or putative traitors, turncoats or just the half-hearted and irresolute. Independence is frowned upon, dissent hounded down, disloyalty persecuted. Pressure to keep the intended flock in the fold is unrelenting; the craved-for cosiness of belonging is offered at the price of unfreedom.

The overall effect of all this is yet another case of the by now familiar tendency to expropriate the individual's moral responsibility. It is now the community, or rather the self-proclaimed wardens of its purity, who draw the boundaries of moral obligations, divide good from evil, and for better or worse dictate the definition of moral conduct. The paramount concern of their moral legislation is to keep the division between 'us' and 'them' watertight; not so much to promote moral standards, as to install *double* standards (as the French say, *deux poids, deux mesures*) – one for 'us', another reserved for the treatment of 'them'.

Moral life is a life of continuous uncertainty, and it takes a lot of strength and resilience and an ability to withstand pressures to be a moral person. Moral responsibility is *unconditional* and in principle *infinite* – and thus one can recognize a moral person by their never quenched dissatisfaction with their moral performance; the gnawing suspicion that they were not moral enough.

On the other hand, a society that engages its members, as the *polis* did, in the different yet imperative task of caring for, and running common affairs so that the common life could observe the standards of justice and prudence – such a society requires neither disciplined subjects nor satisfaction-seeking consumers of socially provided services, but rather tenacious and sometimes obstinate, but always responsible, citizens. To be responsible does not mean to follow the rules; it may often require us to disregard the rules or to act in a way the rules do not warrant. Only such responsibility makes the citizen into that basis on which can be built a human community resourceful and thoughtful enough to cope with the present challenges.

Conceivably . . . And no more than that, since no guarantee is given that such a community will indeed be built, and since there are no foolproof methods to make sure that it is. In fact, the only assurance is the relentless effort of the builders. What may help in this effort is the awareness of the intimate connection (not contradiction!) between autonomous, morally self-sustained and self-governed (often therefore unwieldy and awkward) citizens and a fully-fledged, self-reflective and self-correcting political community. They can only come together; neither is thinkable without the other.

2

Identity Politics

VINCENT CABLE

Political debate has traditionally been expressed in terms of 'left' and 'right'. Since this dichotomy came to be used throughout the Western, post-Enlightenment, world there have been many nuances and national variations, and many disagreements about the relationship between ends and means. But party systems and policy argument have been dominated by the tension between these two ideologically distinct views of the world.

The vernacular may have varied from place to place but politics had a common language. In the very different conditions of peasant, industrializing and post-industrial societies, it was possible to create allegiances around notions of equality, class solidarity and a belief in the capacity of the state to plan, create and distribute wealth: the left. Countervailing forces unified the right; a belief in private property rights, individual opportunity and markets.

The weakening of the left and the near hegemony of the ideas of the right in the wake of the Cold War have radically changed the picture. To be sure, the issue is not conclusively resolved. Social democratic parties continue to win elections (in Sweden; perhaps in Britain). Communists rule in China and may perhaps do so again in Russia. But they do so within a consensus which accepts some form of capitalism and the limitations of the state.

If left *v* right is no longer the dominant dialectic, what could replace it? Is there another organizing principle emerging? The argument advanced here is that there is: one based on the alternative political possibilities created by movements concerned with cultural identity or what is sometimes called 'the politics of the soil'.[1]

The underlying assumption is that politics is, and will continue to be, organized around competing ideas. Some might find that difficult to swallow. They see elections as a competition between Tweedledum and Tweedledee, between rival media managers and spin doctors: all form and no substance. But few who have lived through the Thatcher or Reagan years, or seen the aftermath of the Cold War, imagine that deep down politics is about anything other than different ideas about the way society should be organized. The important question is not whether ideas are important but rather which ideas are decisive at any particular time.

The thesis advanced here is that as the old division between left and right fades a new one is appearing, based on the different ways in which people define their identity. Most of us feel the need for an identity: a sense of belonging to groups which are larger than our family and smaller than the world; not just being part of society (in general) but part of a tighter group. For the most part, at least in the more settled Western democracies like Britain, identity is something personal, multidimensional and essentially nonpolitical. We belong to our country, our town, our neighbourhood, our firm, our profession, our church and possibly our party. At various times in history, however – notably in the racialism and extreme nationalism of the 1930s – we have seen the unifying but destructive potential of exclusive cultural identity when harnessed to politics.

Now again there are special reasons why cultural identity – whether based on religion, language, race, region, nation, clan or tribe – is gaining greater importance. The irony of the situation is captured by Michael Ignatieff: 'the more evident our common needs become, the more brutal becomes the human insistence on the claims of difference. The centripetal forces of need, labour and science, which are pulling us together as a species are counterbalanced by centrifugal forces, the claims of tribe, race, section, region and nation, pulling us apart.'[2]

The nature of this shift can be expressed in a semiformal way through a two-dimensional representation of the forces which drive political movements and parties (Figure 1). Of course, reality is more complex. But as a simplification of the complex reality it is useful to think of an interplay between two sets of ideas or political forces. Traditionally we have tended to categorize political forces in terms of a tension between left and right: different views of the world concerning equality, the role of the public sector and the class loyalty owed to capital or labour. Although those concerns are still with us they are now less polarized and we have a second dimension related to cultural identity.

What this new dimension captures are two, quite different, views of how society should be organized. At one pole are people who define their own and other people's identity in exclusive, closed terms. For racists, religious fundamentalists or nationalists, cultural identity is of all-embracing importance. For them, identity isn't something to be easily cast off or acquired: nothing so straightforward as getting a new passport. Identity provides a powerful social bond and a link between one generation and the next.

Nor is it a private matter. It demands public recognition and respect and has to be defended against outsiders. It is not sufficient that *Satanic Verses* should be read by non-believers in private or that brown and black Europeans should be good citizens or that abortion be left to the conscience of an individual woman. The very existence of alien people and practices is offensive and a threat to identity.

At the other pole are people whose overriding commitment is to individual choice in personal mores and lifestyles. This is the Western liberal tradition. Cultural identity is flexible, multiple or essentially superficial, summed up in the sentiment that 'we are all the same under the skin' (or the veil).

There may also be a sense of society, whether local, national or global, but the boundaries are open and flexible.

These are, of course, caricatures. What is important is the tension between the two ideas, the balance of the two forces, which defines how a country's politics will evolve.

It is not that racism or nationalism or religious fundamentalism will triumph; rather that these 'identity' concerns will define the terms of political debate.

In practice, left-right politics and the politics of identity coexist and interact. Political ideas and movements are best understood in terms of these two dimensions rather than one; from them we can produce several archetypes.

One archetype is the combination of left-wing ideas with those of individual choice in matters of cultural identity. There have long been mainstream democratic socialists who have fought as vigorously for individuals struggling against ethnic discrimination and for freedom of personal belief and freedom of sexual preference as they have fought against a free-for-all in the economic marketplace. There are still many heirs to a tradition which has tried, sometimes with difficulty, to reconcile a commitment to personal liberties with a belief in the need for collective action and social cooperation; we call this *communitarianism.*

But the same leftist ideas have often been suffused with concerns about cultural identity. Colonial liberation movements have often been of this form, for example in Zimbabwe, Burma, Ghana, Vietnam and elsewhere, although others like the ANC in South Africa have been more consciously pluralist. Some of the separatist movements in Western democracies have also tried to link socialism with a form of separatist national identity: the Parti Québecois, Welsh and Scottish nationalism and the leading parties in the Basque country. Kurdish separatists and Iranian Mujaheddin try to blend socialism and nationalism. The cocktail often has murderous forms: the 'red-brown' phenomenon of interwar fascism, Milosevic's regime in Serbia and the Khmer Rouge. Their common ideas could perhaps be generically called

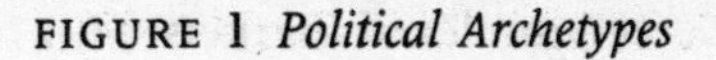

FIGURE 1 *Political Archetypes*

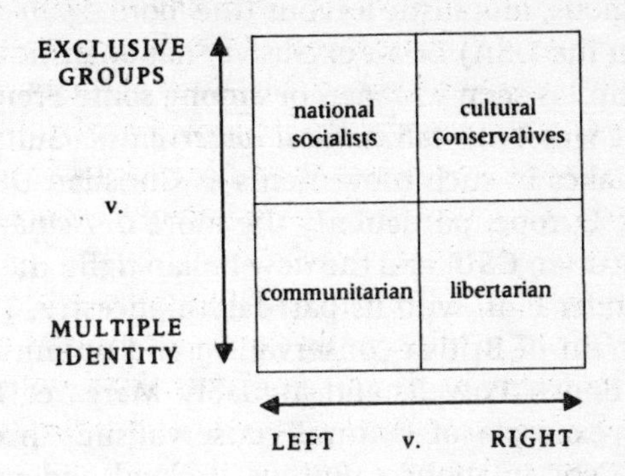

national socialism, a term with unhappy associations but not necessarily pejorative in itself.

On the right there is an intellectual tradition of *libertarianism* which champions the idea of individual liberties and choice across the board. Libertarians do not distinguish between the economic, social and cultural liberties of the individual; freedom is the overriding concern. Yegor Gaidar's Russia's Choice and FIDESZ in Hungary reflect this philosophy, which is common in post-communist Eastern Europe, at least among the young and educated. John Major could reasonably claim to identify with the same strand of thinking. He identifies with the market-reforming radicalism of his predecessor but has a record also of supporting the personal freedoms of racial minorities and gays. Newt Gingrich has tried to construct a libertarian platform in the USA (with some difficulty, in the face of the religious fundamentalism of much of the American 'right'). But libertarians are not necessarily drawn from the political right; Labour's Bob Hawke and Paul Keating in Australia pioneered market reform in Australia while also challenging old racial and cultural prejudices and enhancing personal freedoms. Roy Jenkins, when a Labour minister, championed libertarian ideas in this broad sense in Britain.

Others combine a belief in the economics of markets with strong religious, moralistic fervour (the 'born again' Christian coalition in the USA) or an exclusive, nationalistic approach to capitalism (as seen in Japan or among some French Gaullists); what we could call *cultural conservatives*. Cultural conservatism takes in such movements as Christian Democracy in Catholic Europe, particularly the more muscular variants like the Bavarian CSU, and the new Italian right, the National Alliance under Fini, with its part-fascist ancestry. The ultra-patriotic strain of British conservatism and unionism which produced Enoch Powell, and arguably Margaret Thatcher, is another example of cultural conservatism. Three major 'identity' preoccupations – Europe, Ireland and non-white immigration, brought together through British nationalism – have coexisted with an otherwise unwavering attachment to the logic of market forces on a global scale.

Today, no one captures the flavour of 'cultural capitalism' more eloquently than Mr Pat Buchanan: clearly on the right – and deeply hostile even to the attenuated welfare system of the US – but drawing on the deep prejudices of the 'conservatisms of the heart': race, religion, English language and patriotism.

While we have identified four archetypes and examples of each, reality is a good deal messier. Most movements, like most individuals, are not easy to pigeonhole and the emphasis changes over time in response to events. Nonetheless, the archetypes are useful in helping to construct a picture of the dominant themes and tensions running through political life. In Britain it is still broadly true that the left-right dichotomy holds as a definition of parties and of the underlying debate, which is predominantly about the balancing of market economics and social justice. But Britain may be unusual: traditions die very hard. And arguably, even in Britain, the really important debate does not correspond to the outward form but to the internal tensions within the two leading parties, notably over Europe and potentially over Scotland.

Elsewhere, identity concerns have become dominant, not

subsidiary, and the underlying political dialectic is better understood in other terms than left and right. In France, the left is weaker than it has been for decades and the real battle is between the more libertarian strains of French political thinking and cultural conservatism. In Italy, by contrast, it is the communitarian forces of the former communists and their allies who are pitched against the cultural conservatives of the regional parties and former fascists. Indian politics has produced a broad if loose consensus for liberalization embracing even radical communists (the CPI (M)) but also a deep split between secular parties and those of the Hindu, and nationalist, BJP. Turkish democracy has produced a similar configuration where old (and very bitter) divisions between left and right are being superseded by alignments reflecting the political influence of Islam and also Kurdish identity. In the Islamic world, more generally, questions of identity dominate in the form of struggles between national socialist groups like Ba'ath, or the now somewhat decayed revolutionary regimes of Algeria and Egypt, and the cultural conservatives of Islamic fundamentalism. In Russia, the comically named Liberal Democrats are one expression of a new politics in which xenophobia, ethnicity and even religion play a central role.

It is not that the politics of identity is new or that the left-right polarity has totally disappeared. It is rather that the emphasis has shifted, and in a radical way. There are now many countries where political movements drawing on 'identity' issues are powerful and, in much of Eastern Europe, the Middle East, Asia and Africa these are probably dominant. There are also a few exceptions where identity concerns do not loom large. Brazil has the largest African population outside Africa but this has never been a major political issue (although there is a growing black consciousness movement).

In the West, parties generally retain the formal structures, and some of the language, of left *v* right. But there are strong crosscurrents. These may come from culturally based, regional separatism (Canada, Belgium and, to a lesser degree,

Italy, Spain and Britain); from racism and anti-immigrant agitation (France, Germany, Austria, Switzerland and to a lesser degree in the USA), or out of debates over the loss of national identity through regional integration (Canada, UK, France, Denmark, Norway). Many of these identity concerns are handled within established party structures but there has also been a general rise in support for parties which fall outside the left-right divide to levels not seen since the 1930s. And in some cases – Canada and Belgium; to a degree in Spain and Italy – the old party structures have largely collapsed under the strain.

It is probable that, in time, a clearer pattern will emerge with two new poles dominating as left and right once did. The communitarian and national socialist positions seem, at least at present, the weakest. They both, in different ways, draw upon a socialist tradition which has been badly battered by the dramatic failure of communism and the gradual loss of support and motivation of democratic socialist parties in Germany, Sweden, France, Italy, the UK and elsewhere. Unless the left can find a new source of energy, moral conviction and intellectual credibility, only two serious contenders for political power will remain: the libertarian right and the cultural conservatives.

In this sense we perhaps need to look to East and Southeast Asia for a glimpse of the future. The most violent ideological encounters of the Cold War took place in Asia, not in Europe: the birth of communist China (and Taiwan), and the Korean and Vietnam wars. Yet this history has largely been left behind. Except in the bizarre world of North Korea, there is now a strong consensus for some form of capitalism (even when, as in China and Vietnam, it is called something else). It has been brilliantly successful – from Japan to Singapore through Korea, Taiwan, Malaysia, Thailand, Indonesia and now China.

Yet, it is precisely this consensual, and successful, approach to economics, blending capitalism with judicious use of the powers of the state to provide a background of financial and political stability and good infrastructure, which has highlighted – not banished – the 'identity' dimension of political life. The one major debate which has implicitly run through Japanese politics, and which is now formalized in the emerging two-party system, is how far to compromise a fierce sense of Japanese national identity with the homogenizing demands of a global capitalist system. The 'insider capitalism' of Japan, and the issue of how far to give ground to outsiders, also has echoes in South Korea, Thailand, Indonesia and, now, China.

Within these countries, moreover, cultural identity, not class, is the main divide. Beneath the cosmopolitan veneer and prosperity of Singapore there is an almost paranoid fear of the potentially divisive forces of race and religion. In Malaysia and Indonesia these forces – Islam and other faiths; Malay and Chinese ethnicity – are potentially very divisive. The underlying tension running through all these societies – which may well collectively dominate the world economy in the next century – is between the libertarians who want to free the individual and the cultural conservatives who cling to traditional cultural identity.

Not just individual countries but the world could become polarized in this way, Such a future has been foreseen in Michel Albert's *Capitalisme contre Capitalisme* where three different cultural strands of the private enterprise system – the Anglo-Saxon; the Rhenish or West European; and the East Asian – compete within a global arena.[3]

The categorization may be crude and there are other candidates. But less polemical sources also attest to the major cultural differences (and potential divisions) between the various segments of a superficially 'globalized' capitalist world.

The immediate reason for the emergence of political forces outside the traditional left-right divide is disillusionment with that tradition. The left is in disarray throughout the world, associated with what is seen as a failed project: the collapse of communism and the great difficulties encountered in managing welfare-state social democracies. After the triumphalism of the Reagan/Thatcher years, right-wing parties are also finding the going difficult. All are finding that the End of History, in Fukuyama's phase, has not ended cyclical and structural problems in capitalist economies. And none has found an easy way to reconcile their dual mandate: to conserve tradition and promote stability on the one hand and on the other to allow the creative destruction of market competition. A vacuum has been created for new political forces to enter.

If one, dominant, factor has shaped the new politics it is the phenomenon loosely called 'globalization'.

Identities have been traditionally defined in national terms. While much violence has been done in the name of nation states, they have also bound together disparate peoples and submerged divisive identities. But a powerful mixture of technology and economics is now dissolving some of those bonds. All but the strongest and most clearly defined national identities are being undermined by the phenomenon of globalization: the spreading through efficient global communications systems of information and ideas; global capital markets; easier travel and trade; and the organization of business by corporations which can operate globally and respond to the demands of shareholders of no particular domicile. This is what Richard O'Brien calls the End of Geography.[4]

It is no longer obvious what it means to describe the Midland Bank or ICL as British (or for that matter companies called British Petroleum, British Airways, British Gas and British Telecom). Honda and Ford cars are the product of specialization among many economies. Their workers and customers may be better served but their identity is blurred. The recipients of Star, BBC and CNN satellite television have their eyes opened to a cosmopolitan – albeit largely Western – perspective on the world. Nevertheless, the trend to global integration is clear. The globalization process is complex; it may be reversible in part; national governments do retain powerful policy levers (like immigration control); and 'multinational' companies are stubbornly 'national' in many respects.[5]

In such an increasingly globalized environment people react in quite different ways. Many individuals – in rich and poor countries – respond positively to the freedoms, opportunities and choices opened up by the wider horizons of global business and communications. Many can readily understand the economic logic of global specialization, relishing the chances to sample a multiplicity of experiences and identifying strongly with role models offered by international TV, music and sport.

But others feel threatened by the loss of security, stability, and traditional values. They need to identify with a recognizable, settled value system which gives their lives meaning and dignity. This reaction can be explicitly cultural. The French resistance to the attempt during the GATT negotiations to open up the European market for films to greater competition from Hollywood – *Germinal* versus *Jurassic Park* – was at least superficially such a response (there were also protectionist vested interests). There has similarly been a strong reaction against 'cultural pollution' in China, Vietnam and India directed against Western media and consumer goods.

The reaction is also economic. The French concern over 'delocalization' expresses the fear that greater global competition will sweep away not merely jobs, particularly in agriculture, but a traditional way of life. Sir James Goldsmith's *La Piège* (The Trap) achieved best-seller status, defending French agriculture (and European producers generally) against the perceived threat to national identity from global competition. The defence of Japanese and Korean rice farming from import competition was conducted in terms of the threat to a whole way of life. Public reactions to the European 'threat' to British fishing have been similar. Cultural sensitivity, broadly defined, is becoming a major item on the international economic agenda.[6]

In a world where capital seems to have no fixed abode and

financial flows are largely beyond the physical control of national governments, many of the traditional levers of economic policy no longer work. Government's role increasingly appears limited to building market credibility and confidence. When governments of once powerful nation-states helplessly wring their hands and use global markets as alibis for inactivity, it would be surprising if many people did not start to question what these nation-states exist for.

The threat to cultural identity posed by global economic integration comes variously from trade, from mobile capital, and from the free flow of ideas and images. But it also comes from migrant labour. Immigration has provided much of the emotional fuel behind new extremist movements in Germany, Austria, France and Belgium. The American nativism of Pat Buchanan and others, directed at the influx of Hispanics and Asians, and invoking a spectre of non-white and non-English-speaking states, is a movement which has perhaps yet to reach its full potential. The disparity in wages between rich and poor countries and the growing ease and speed of international travel provides the basis for constant migration pressure, or at least the fear of it.

These specific challenges combine to generate deeper uncertainties about what nations actually exist for. The nation-state is being weakened from above by the forces of globalization and from below by groups and regions which no longer identify with it. In Britain the strains and uncertainties have been apparent in the long, agonizing debate about Europe, and the threat Europe poses, for some, to British national identity. The process of erosion has gone further for Belgium or Canada, both of which have shorter, less resonant histories, porous borders, minimal real economic sovereignty and strong culturally defined minorities. There, a divisive politics of identity has largely taken over. For many other nation-states cobbled together by departing colonial powers a few decades ago, the claims of loyalty to the nation-state are becoming weaker still.

There are particular problems in the formerly communist

east, where the sudden opening up to global markets and communications comes on top of what was essentially the break-up of an empire. People are being required to establish a new identity: to define, often from scratch, where they belong. As long as Yugoslavia or the Soviet Union existed it was not necessary for Bosnian Serbs to decide whether they were primarily Bosnians or primarily Serbs, or for Crimeans to decide if they were Russians or Ukrainians. Now they are being forced to choose as economic globalization further erodes the tenuous ties which have held together these and other multicultural nation-states.

A second major influence has been the 'liberalization revolution' in economic thinking and organization which has run in parallel with globalization and is closely related to it. The collapse of the communist system in the USSR was not just an isolated event but the culmination of a process which has destroyed the credibility of a whole political philosophy. Systems based on state control, central planning and public ownership have been shown not to work, their flaws magnified by the demands of today's information and communications technology.

Everywhere countries are purging themselves of these ideological remnants. There is a broad consensus (despite disagreements over time scales) that immersion in the cold bath of market economics is necessary for the substantial number of countries which have a large dead weight of loss-making and protected industries, established when socialist planning was seen as a precondition for modernity and progress. While the early pioneers of liberalization were dogmatic and insensitive (like Mrs Thatcher) or brutal (like General Pinochet), in few parts of the world, now, is the basic framework of capitalist organization, and the underlying economic logic of the price mechanism, seriously in dispute.

But the liberalization revolution is also a painful affair. While poor people may benefit from the lower inflation and greater economic dynamism that may come from liberalization, much hurt, dislocation and inequality – even if temporary – is resulting from privatization, market deregulation, accelerated economic change and restructuring. In developing countries, powerful demographic pressures and urbanization are being piled on top of adjustments that would be difficult and painful in any event. Radical transformation is already creating deep resentment, particularly in former communist countries, and could still take decades to complete.

Anger and frustration at the pain of liberalization would once have found an outlet in parties of the left. Indeed, in some cases – in Russia, Poland, Lithuania and Venezuela – parties of the left have apparently staged a comeback as a reaction to the process of liberalization (though they seem to have no alternative agenda). In other cases – Chile's Christian Democrats, for example – a sophisticated approach to liberalization is being evolved which sweetens the pill of market reform with antipoverty programmes and safety-net provisions. Some countries may in this way be able to manage the liberalization revolution within the traditional political structures.

But the libertarian ideas associated with market economics pose a deeper challenge to many societies, and one which strikes at the heart of their sense of identity. Liberalization is in danger of being seen not just as painful and difficult but as ethically shallow, or offensive. In the semiliberalized, semicapitalist economies of Russia (and the rest of the former USSR), China and India, the dividing lines between entrepreneurial endeavour, corruption and outright gangsterism are very indistinct. The rapid erosion of family support systems and/or state provision is exposing large numbers in many countries to as harsh an environment as Britain in the time of Dickens, but without the values and institutions of private charity. 'Freedom of choice' has often been seen as an alibi for the commercial exploitation of every human perversion. Amid the money-making and prodigious growth of the new China, pre-communist pornography, prostitution, drugs, gambling, and racketeering have returned. Nearer home, the emergence (or re-emergence) of real poverty and social breakdown alongside acquisitiveness in Western societies has stirred moral disquiet. Consumer and producer choice introduced into a vacuum of values, without rules or self-restraint, appears as crude materialism and selfishness, alien to what are often seen as traditional social values.

Lying behind the principles of liberal market economics is a framework of ethical thinking which was carefully set out by Adam Smith, David Hume and others.[7] Some of the more thoughtful contemporary writers of economic history, like Douglass North, have underlined the importance of law and institutions. However, the libertarian revolution, which has swept through most parts of the world, has lacked a moral foundation. Loss of security and livelihoods has produced an angry backlash against liberalization (and in many cases its association with the West). There has been a retreat to traditional values and loyalties to be found in religious, tribal and national identities.

Both liberalization and globalization together have accelerated economic and social change and undercut the social-class base around which traditional left-right politics was organized. In Western societies, deindustrialization is sweeping away the settled industrial working-class communities which formed the heartland of left-wing parties. New jobs are being created in services, many part-time, and on a self-employed or transitory basis. Even where trades unions have not been systematically weakened – as in the UK and USA – they have steadily lost membership. Moreover, they are now increasingly called upon to address individual grievances rather than collective action. The association of work, community and politics is being severed at a serious cost for American Democrats, British Labour and the German SPD.

At the same time, the no less settled 'bourgeois', middle-class base of the traditional parties of the right is being undermined by the deskilling of many clerical jobs, the 'downsizing' of middle management, competition within the professions and the struggle of small businesses and family farmers to survive.

Social changes are taking place throughout the Western world which make traditional politics hard to sustain. Galbraith's *Culture of Contentment* described a two thirds/one third society in which a relatively 'contented' majority confronted an unskilled, alienated underclass which provides neither the numerical support nor the discipline and motivation to sustain a left-wing majority.[8] In response, French socialists and American Democrats have embraced the 'middle class' only to discover the difficulties of matching their own communitarian tradition to the libertarian agendas of their new supporters. As the French socialists have already discovered, such support is extremely fickle.

There is little prospect of traditional class-based left-right politics being created in those societies which have not yet arrived at the post-industrial stage. The principal targets of Eastern Europe's liberalizers are the heavily unionized, protected, loss-making industries and collective farms, many of which are now being swept away. In newly industrializing countries there are groups of strongly organized workers: the Brazilian Workers Party; Korean steelworkers; the CPI (M) in India. But these are pockets, often a 'labour aristocracy' in a larger, rapidly multiplying, mostly underemployed labour force with a weak sense of solidarity and open to competing pulls on its loyalties. The big cities of the Third World have rarely – Calcutta excepted – served as a cradle for Western-style class-based politics. Indeed, identity politics in some form has flourished more readily; in particular, the rise of Islamic fundamentalism owes much to the pool of unemployed youth in the slums of Cairo, Algiers, Khartoum and Teheran.

One of the strengths of those trying to cultivate the 'politics of the soil' is that they inherit well fertilized ground.

In many countries, ethnic hatreds draw on real experience of past suffering – from Yugoslavia's wartime atrocities and the Indian partition to Ireland's interminable Troubles and the massacres of Armenians, Jews, Palestinians, Kurds, Indonesian Chinese, Tutsis and Ibos. Some grievances have fermented for generations or even centuries. History has dissolved into legend and myth. The parties to the Yugoslav wars draw on long folk memories: the Serbs not just of Nazi but of Ottoman atrocities; and Croats of the partition of the Roman Empire which left them on the western side of a historic dividing line. The Georgian civil war was started under a President who insisted that today's citizens must trace back their family ancestry a thousand years. For the Protestants of Ulster, Cromwell and King William could have been alive yesterday. The Indian BJP seeks to remedy the injustices wrought by the Moghul Emperors. In some cases, distant history provides alibis for today's politics; Israeli territorial expansionists in Likud establish their case from the Old Testament's treatment of Judea and Samaria; the advocates of apartheid found inspiration in the Book of Genesis. In Iran, Sudan and Saudi Arabia (and, if fundamentalists have their way, many other Muslim countries) daily social, economic and political life is governed by texts a thousand years old. In that most modern of societies, the USA, black politics is framed by the psychological legacy of slavery.

Often, the 'history' thus invoked bears no more relation to reality than the Norse myths which inspired the Nazis' Teutonic fantasies. The Hindutva of the 'Hindu fundamentalists' is a total negation of an ancient religion long recognized for its eclecticism and toleration as is the newly 'militant' Buddhism of neighbouring Sri Lanka and Bhutan. Modern Islamic fundamentalism bears little resemblance to the traditions of early Islamic civilization, characterized by the open-minded and cultured traditions of Moorish Spain and medieval Baghdad and Palestine. Real or imagined, the history is believed.

And as some cultural identities are moulded and politicized by prejudices drawn from the past, others, in turn, are triggered. Until the creation of Israel, the Sephardic Jews of North

Africa lived in reasonable harmony with their Arab neighbours. Greeks have lived in the Caucasus since 500 years before Aristotle, but have now been pushed out by tribal warfare and pulled out by a new Panhellenism. Germans lived for 500 years in the East until the upheavals of the former Soviet Union and the attractions of the mother country lured them back. The Egyptian Copts, who survived centuries of upheaval, are now threatened by their previously tolerant Muslim neighbours. Cultures which coexisted for centuries now find it impossible.

It cannot be coincidental that so many historically based claims on identity have re-emerged so strongly and in so many places within such a short space of time.

The shift to identity politics is not preordained. In the future, as in the past, the possibility of a major shift in the nature of politics will hinge on unpredictable events. For example if a Christian fundamentalist were to win the US Presidency; if German xenophobia were to take serious hold; if an Algerian religious fundamentalist regime flooded Southern Europe with refugees; if an aggressively assertive anti-Western leadership were to emerge in Japan, or China; if Yeltsin were to be succeeded by Zhirinovsky.

All are hypothetical but plausible discontinuities which could radically change the nature of political debate way beyond these countries' frontiers. And all would give the politics of identity a new impetus.

Even without dramatic events and in established relatively placid Western democracies the politics of identity is nevertheless increasingly being felt. The outward form of parties and their political rhetoric may not change much; but the issues which politicians are required to address, and which create resonance with others, are changing. American Presidential candidates schooled to occupy the high ground of foreign affairs and ideological debate find themselves mired in questions of personal and religious morality (abortion) or nationalism in relation to immigration and trade. A German provincial election in early 1995 featured a 'left' party (the

SPD) attacking (ethnic German) immigrants, blaming them for unemployment, and a 'right' party (the CDU) proposing a further surrender of German sovereignty to the EU. British politics too, is being drawn into debates which have little or nothing to do with left and right as traditionally understood.

The politics of identity is potentially very divisive. But it can be managed in more or less destructive ways. Most Western countries are experimenting with some form of political devolution, to create or reflect a sense of local and regional identity. Most are also trying different approaches to accommodating varied forms of ethnicity. There are no definitive solutions. But there are some plausible role models; Holland is the European country which perhaps best manages to allow the expression of various religions, racial and national identities within an open, outward looking and yet cohesive society: it therefore suggests that some common elements in the successful management of identity politics are a sense of multiple (rather than exclusive) identity; the use of the principle of subsidiarity to diffuse power and decision-making downwards; the security of a legal framework and a sense of order as an antidote to common passions and populism; and a striving for a sense of 'fairness' and nondiscrimination in the availability of economic opportunities. And since the growth of identity politics is in large part a reaction to the impersonal, distant, alienating forces of globalization, one necessary antidote will be a sense that rules and order are no less relevant at global than at national level.

3

No Turning Back

Generations and the Genderquake

HELEN WILKINSON

In recent years traditional definitions of what it means to be a man or a woman have been worn away with almost bewildering speed. Even many of the feminist arguments of the 1960s and 1970s now seem antiquated as the focus of attention shifts to girls outperforming boys in school, the shifting balance of sexual harassment, or the continuing rise of women breadwinners. And if gender politics in the 1980s was dominated by Margaret Thatcher, a woman who often acted more like a man, gender politics in the 1990s seems to be dominated by men trying to be more like women – complaining about their oppression, their status as victims and how the world is conspiring against them.[1]

But these are only symptoms. The cause is an historic change in the relations between men and women: a shift in power and values that is unravelling many of the assumptions not only of 200 years of industrial society, but also of millennia of traditions and beliefs. Many of its features are most visible in the economy. Certainly the old work structures that are now unravelling were predominantly designed for men and their demise has brought new opportunities for women. In the last fifteen years, for example, two million men have disappeared from the UK workforce, while women's participation has risen from 53 per cent in 1973 to 65 per cent in 1991, and by the year 2000, it is expected that women will be taking as many as 90 per cent of newly created jobs.[2] The number of women earning more than their partners has also trebled from 1 in 15 in the early 1980s to 1 in 5 in 1995,[3] and women are rapidly advancing both in the professions (there are now more female solicitors under 30 than male and more female professionals under 35 than over)[4] and in new industries where employers increasingly want a more flexible, service-oriented and dexterous workforce.[5]

Economic shifts have been crucial drivers of change. But other social forces have also been influential. The contraceptive pill gave women much greater control over fertility, separating sex and motherhood. The legal changes which the women's liberation movement campaigned for have all had cumulative effects: everything from the passage of the 1967 Abortion Act, which has given women reproductive control, through to the outlawing of sexual discrimination and equal pay legislation. Advances in medical technology have also played a part and now enable women to exercise reproductive choice well beyond the 'choice' of abortion. Sperm banks, the option of artificial insemination and, in the years ahead, the vastly greater choice posed by genetics, are all enabling increasing numbers of women to control their own destiny and the terms on which they have children.

These shifts in power have been strikingly visible in popular culture. Through figures like Sigourney Weaver, Madonna, kd lang and Sharon Stone, popular culture has explored the blurred boundaries of male and female identity and the potency of female sexuality. Soap operas too have been as significant a medium as any in publicly working through changing roles.[6] And for a younger generation, cultural icons like Tank Girl capture the mood of a more assertive generation of young women who are attracted to the traditional male domains of power and violence.[7]

This combination of economic and cultural change has helped once marginal feminist ideas to seep almost subliminally into the mainstream,[8] as each new generation of women becomes more committed to equity between the sexes, more confident of their rights to equality and more inclined to feminist ideas.[9]

But the value shifts go much deeper than this. Feminism has also ushered in a more complex refashioning of women's values, involving a rising attachment to autonomy[10] which manifests itself in many ways, notably the view that motherhood is now but one option of many: in one survey only 13 per cent of women of childbearing age thought that children were necessary to feel fulfilled[11] and as many as 20 per cent of women born since the 1960s are expected to remain childless all their lives.[12]

Perhaps the most striking trend of all is the extent to which women are now taking on traditionally male values, such as commitment to success, risk-taking, hedonism and even violence.[13] Today's schoolgirls are also more ambitious, more likely to want to continue in education and less likely to want to start a family than their male peers[14] and, perhaps as a result, are increasingly outperforming boys at school and at university.[15]

Many older feminists have chosen to interpret the cup as half empty rather than half full. They have concentrated their energies on power shifts at the top – in Parliament and in the boardrooms of Britain – and have tended to play down the extent of these other changes. Their focus on politics is understandable. Much of the progress of this century towards gender equality has depended on legally enshrined political, social and economic rights that were won through bitter struggles from the feminist campaigns of the mid nineteenth century to the battles of the suffragettes in the early part of this century and the demands of the women's liberation movement of the 1960s and 1970s.

But in the 1990s it is striking how much change is taking place far away from the world of politics, in culture and the economy. Employers can often have more influence on women's lives than parliaments, not just because work plays more of a role in most women's lives but also because some employers have been far ahead of the politicians in developing family-friendly initiatives to accommodate the needs of working mothers, giving parallel rights to fathers through paternity and parental leave or providing creches for grandparents as well as children.

Certainly women seem strikingly disconnected from mainstream politics.[16] Less than 10 per cent of MPs in Parliament are female[17] and a MORI poll to accompany the seventy-fifth anniversary of women's rights found that 76 per cent of women of all ages were not involved in any form of party-political activity, while 4 out of 10 younger women said that they had absolutely no interest in politics.[18]

In other countries, parties have taken much more active steps than in the UK to keep up with change. For example, in Sweden women increased their presence as candidates through the use of voluntary targets, combined with the explicit threat that if these were not met mandatory quotas would be implemented. Norway's Labour Party decided in the early 1980s that at least 40 per cent of their candidates should be women. The other parties followed, and remarkably quickly the politicization of gender issues became less controversial (political styles also changed, with noticeably more informality). In Finland, the 1991 election gave 40 per cent of the seats to women, with an average age under 40.[19] In the USA women's organizations organized particularly effectively around abortion, and around the Anita Hill sexual harassment case, with big increases in the numbers of pro-choice and profeminist governors, senators and representatives (male and female) in the early 1990s.[20]

The lessons to be drawn from these experiences are complex. They seem to suggest that although enforced initiatives such as quotas generate resentment (and may alienate a younger generation of women who are resistant to 'special initiatives'),[21] they do have the potential, as transitional measures, to change the face of political parties.

Precisely the same pressure to reconnect with a younger generation of women has affected women's organizations. Across the Atlantic surveys consistently show that young women are more feminist in their values than any previous generation but they remain reluctant to identify with the leaders or the movement itself.[22] In Britain too, although young women have absorbed much of the feminist argument (and are more likely to call themselves feminists than older women), yet the vast majority still remain ambivalent about adopting the label.[23] Young women are certainly more individualistic, and more suspicious of organizations, ideology and parties. They see less need for organizations devoted solely to women's issues.[24] One result is that many of the older women's organizations have a declining and ageing membership and are finding it harder to attract a younger generation.[25] It is as if younger women have outgrown the movements whose values they have absorbed, with the majority emphasizing the need for women and men to work together for change.[26]

A variety of explanations have been offered to explain these trends. Some have blamed the rapid absorption of feminists within academia, which has brought with it a profusion of arcane jargon and theory, and diverted many of the brightest away from practical engagement and political persuasion.[27] The emphasis on ideology over pragmatism is a frequent complaint on both sides of the Atlantic.[28]

Others, like Susan Faludi and Marilyn French, blame a backlash which has worked systematically to undermine the gains that women have made, and which younger women have unwittingly colluded in.[29] Certainly their desire to distance themselves from association with the feminist label can be explained by the fact that the majority of young women are still strongly influenced by negative images of feminism and feminists and still tend to see the women's movement as extreme, manhating and separatist.[30] A male-dominated media has stereotyped and demonized feminists. Feminism is often caricatured as lesbian and aggressive. But the women's movement in the UK, as in the USA, must also bear some responsibility for failing to attract the next generation. Its antagonism to femininity has clearly alienated many, as has its strident tone, dogmatism and sectarianism.[31]

But the failure to connect to a new generation also has a more fundamental cause. Women born in the 1960s and beyond are the first to come of age since the great battles of the feminist movement in the 1970s and to have entered a labour market in which a framework of equal opportunities legislation and antidiscrimination legislation was in place. As the 'post-equality' generation, they feel less need to fight battles in a strident way. Moreover their increased confidence and assertiveness – in everything from attitudes to work and careers to sexuality – has created a new dimension to gender politics, which many women's organizations are only now beginning to grapple with. A more confident generation of women do not see themselves as victims, but rather identify with a 'power feminism' which emphasizes women's new sources of power.[32]

It is perhaps a sign of how disconnected feminist ideas, and many campaigning organizations, have become that the most incisive exploration of the new landscape of gender politics has occurred in antifeminist forums as well as 'postfeminist' ones. In America 'profeminist' men like Warren Farrell, the only man to have been elected three times onto the New York council of the National Organization for Women, have become turncoats and are now arguing that the equality agenda has become the 'inequality' agenda.[33] For them the gender issue has come full circle with men the new victims, discriminated against in a climate of political correctness which skews power too much in the direction of women, because of abuse of the sex discrimination legislation and an economic climate which needs women's skills. Recent events in the UK have often heightened these fears with evidence that men have been discriminated against when applying for jobs traditionally done by women.[34] Custody battles have also drawn attention to some of the cultural biases in our society against fathers. The Child Support Act has brought together an *ad hoc* coalition of embittered men.

Popular culture has been quick to capitalize on these shifts

– especially women's capacity to abuse power – with a spate of 'backlash' movies. Most visible perhaps was Michael Crichton's book *Disclosure* (and its translation onto celluloid in Hollywood) which centres on a powerful female executive who makes a pass at a male colleague and being rejected proceeds to accuse him of sexually harassing her.[35] In the UK authors like David Thomas and Neil Lyndon[36] have been active in publicizing sexual harassment of men by women, and pointing to the experience of men as victims of domestic violence.

Although there is nothing resembling parity in terms of abuse there is now no shortage of evidence of sexual abuse by women of children, of male victims of domestic violence and of a growing number of sexual harassment cases brought against female perpetrators.[37] Women are clearly able to abuse power when they have it and if anything the value shifts amongst a younger generation of women – their increasing attachment to values we have traditionally associated with masculinity or maleness – seem likely to translate into an enjoyment of power and a rise in phenomena such as sexual harassment of men.[38] These are disorientating shifts for many feminists whose essentialist view that women are naturally more 'civilized' directly conflicts with evidence of women's abuse of power.

In many ways responses from the women's movement to the signs of a political backlash have shown a lack of political maturity. Feminists have often dismissed out of hand male anxieties – over discrimination at work, or inadequate rights as fathers. They have tended to ignore issues such as sexual harassment by women so as to protect their superior claim to victimhood. Sometimes feminist organizations – like the men's groups – seem to be competing ever more fiercely to assert their suffering in a culture of complaint that fractures society into competing claimant groups jostling for a more privileged position in the hierarchy of misery. This reinforces the sense that feminism is not so much about equality as about the assertion of women's rights over men's.

But if victim feminism feels like a cul-de-sac, so too is its mirror, the shift to an almost triumphalist power feminism, which sometimes seems to relish men's new status as victims.[39] Far from solving problems, power feminism prevents people from making the connections between issues like sexual harassment by men or women, bullying and the abuse of power. For like 'victim feminism' it too perpetuates the view of gender politics as a war of winners and losers, escalating gender conflict, heightening backlash effects and polarizing men and women even further.

Even the most revisionist feminists still paint gender politics as a zero-sum game and although feminism has been reinventing itself, it has yet to advance to a higher level of maturity that would enable it to connect with the growing awareness in the men's movement that patriarchy has been as constraining for men as for women, disconnecting them from their families and communities and trapping them in the role of overstressed breadwinners.[40]

This is why gender politics in the 1990s is at a crossroads. It can either entrench itself even further in the language of victims and victors. Or it can choose to nurture a more inclusive approach, and build on the fact that most of the new issues in sexual politics – such as work-family balance, parenting time, long working hours, divorce law reform, and even reproductive control[41] – are no more about power than they are about victimhood.

Undoubtedly, the route of reconciliation, collaboration and common interest will be unsettling for an older generation of feminists and for a feminist movement whose identity has been predicated on the need for a separate agenda. For some, it may well prove a step too far, nothing less than sleeping with the enemy. But as 200 years of industrial society comes to an end we are having to think in fresh ways in almost every field. For younger men and women, amongst whom there are converging attitudes (even to feminism itself), a new approach makes obvious sense. They overwhelmingly welcome the advances made by women, and accept that there

4

The Postmodern Work Ethic

DAVID CANNON

Changing Perceptions of Time

In his landmark book *Beyond Culture,*[1] Edward T. Hall argues that understanding a culture's concept of time is essential to gaining an understanding of how a culture assigns meaning to events and how individuals assess whether their time is being valued. Hall gives the example of Americans and Northern Europeans being psychologically stressed in Latin American and Mediterranean contexts because they often perceive members of these cultures as responding slowly and hence not valuing their time.

There are other ways to think about culture besides those defined by geography and ethnic origin. For example, what if young people's sense of time differs from that of the prior generation who presently teach and employ them? If so, could differences in time perception result in differences in work habits and therefore be a source of misunderstanding and possible conflict between the generations? Findings from a twelve-year programme of research on the attitudes and behaviours of young people between the ages of 18 and 30, the so-called Generation X, suggest this subculture of society experience time in a way which is distinctive from the past. In common with their predecessors, young people's sense of time reflects their times.

By comparing opinions expressed by 1200 young people in group and individual interviews with those of employers, teachers and parents, three important trends in perception of time emerge. How widely one can generalize about these trends is debatable given that the sample is restricted to young people (mostly university educated) in the United Kingdom and North America. Clearly young men and women are not all the same; however, one message was consistently and strongly signalled by those who participated in the study – *How you value my time will be used as evidence in determining how you value me.*[2]

A Closer Horizon

The 'future' young people think about is a rather short period of time and there is evidence that it is becoming ever shorter. Although indicating they occasionally speculate about a more distant future, most said their concept of the future was limited to the next two to three years ahead. It can reasonably be argued that this 'short-term' view has always been the case with young people. What appears to have changed is the faith Generation X puts in the kind of long-term plans held by their forbears.

Long-term planning assumes an element of predictability in life, the sort of predictability which led young people's parents, tutors and employers to mortgage their lives, selling present time for potential future gain. Professions such as accounting, medicine and law are still perceived as offering such future promise; however, even these established success formulas are now losing credibility. Outside the professions, the concept of paying long-term dues in the hopes of a future senior management position or partnership is a belief held by a dwindling minority of young people. This loss of faith in the old psychological contract is not because Generation X think corporate employers are particularly deceptive, although some do. Instead it is the result of a perception that most organizations are simply incapable of delivering future promises with any certainty even when it is their intention to do so.

Prognosis: Employers' ability to convince employees, especially younger employees, to put up with present pain for long-term gain has been deeply diminished. Human resource strategies based on these motivational assumptions are flawed and demonstrate little understanding of the attitudes of today's young talent. The questions most often on the mind of the new generation of employees are: 'How am I feeling in the job right now' and 'What is going to happen in the next year or two?'

A Faster-Twenty-four-hour Clock

A shortened time horizon means a stronger focus on the present. Generation X is the first cohort to have grown up with high levels of exposure to communications technology and media – television, VCRs, computers, telephones, fax and e-mail communication. These technological influences have touched everyone's lives regardless of age; however, their impact on young people has been especially pervasive because they are the first generation to have experienced the high-tech world as children. Two new views of time have resulted – one concerns when things ought to be done, the other the rate at which things ought to be done.

Generation X clocks are set to what Stanley Davis calls 'anytime' in his book *Future Perfect.*[3] Davis argues that the business model of time is very much from the corporation's perspective, the focus being on internal reorientations and actions. Working '9 to 5', or more accurately '10 to 7' in the UK, is conceived of as a recurring event which includes a set of time-anchored routines that repeat themselves on a daily basis. The young people in this study saw their day as having twenty-four hours in which to eat, sleep, work and play, whenever it suits them. In this sense living in 'anytime' time means doing what you need to do when you want to do it. In many ways life at university gives young people the latitude to practise this.

The big shock for Generation X begins when they arrive

at the job and come face to face with the inflexibility of the work regime. They are surprised by employers who talk about working to results and then assign 'make-work', signalling to new recruits the requirement of putting in 'face-time' at the office. Willing to accept that their presence during certain 'core hours' is necessary, many young people in our study said they worked long hours at the office because 'it looked good' or because 'everyone else did', admitting much of this 'face-time' had more to do with positioning than productivity. As juniors in the world of employment young people typically comply. However, the deep cynicism about work found to be growing over the twelve-year period of the study is certain to have future ramifications.

Computers, cellular phones and faxes are seen by Generation X as technologies which allow the individual to work at different locations, freeing them to do their work at either 2 p.m. or 2 a.m. These technologies are said to be typically underutilized by most employers. Laptops and home modem connections are reported by young people to be often reserved for senior executives, some of whom still view 'typing' as not what they do. Although young people say their bosses talk a lot about using new technologies and flexible ways of working to enhance efficiency, their number one complaint about their seniors is that they waste time on needless politics and create situations in which doing the real work takes far longer than necessary.

An equally important perception of time is speed, where the rule of thumb is *slow = frustration*. This differs from the concept of wasting time because even in situations where time is felt to be effectively used, if the pace is slow, young people will become quickly bored. Generation X's need for speed is reflected in the media saturating their world. During the 1960s a one-minute television commercial in North America consisted on average of 8 to 12 images or camera shots. A recent soft drink commercial aimed at young people and aired on UK television presented 22 visual images in a 30-second period – close to an image a second. Music videos and fast-moving computer games are further examples of how information is increasingly delivered in decreasingly shorter time bites. An engaging and unanswered question is whether media and technology have acted to shorten young people's attention span through conditioning or whether manufacturers of these products are simply responding to market tastes for greater speed.

At work, Generation X frequently subdivide their time into short segments concentrating on a project or part of a project for 10 to 30 minutes then switching over to work on something else. Employer reports on the work patterns of younger employees characterize them as being more varied than their own. Young employees are described as flipping back and forth between different documents on their computer screen in order to work on several projects in the course of an hour, taking short breaks to check e-mail, play a quick computer game or visit a colleague down the hall. When forced to focus long and hard on one aspect of a job participants in the study said they typically became bored, reasserting their strong need for variety in their work. The complaint most frequently cited by employers of young people was not laziness but rather a perception that many recent recruits had difficulty concentrating and 'sticking to' a project. They openly wondered whether these bright young minds had sufficient 'commitment' and 'sustained motivation' to succeed long-term.

Prognosis: Employers who ignore already established work habits and patterns of stimulation can create work contexts that act to diminish productivity and creativity. Cases have been found in which young people fulfil their need for stimulation in inappropriate ways such as using company technology to work on private consulting projects, extensive e-mail correspondence or playing computer games with friends across the Internet. Although the research shows young people as 'unorthodox' users of time it also shows them as highly efficient users of time. Organizations whose aim is to overexercise control of young employees will reap fewer results and experience lower overall productivity than those which provide real flexibility and design work to maximize variety.

Blurred Lines between Worktime and Leisuretime

Generation X does not hold the belief that leisuretime is when one rests up from worktime. Almost all of the young people in our study were active in sport, social life or a personal interest such as music, computers, shopping, films and travelling, regardless of their socioeconomic background. Dull, boring people who 'need to get a life' were typically characterized as individuals who lack multiple interests. The ideal is to have a varied life. This is what Generation X mean when they talk about a 'balanced life'. They are not talking about a balance between work and rest – on the contrary, they want time off to work on other things.

A recent article by Alexandra Geiser entitled 'Japan's changing work ethic'[4] describes how young Japanese workers are no longer willing to make the self-sacrifice on which much of the past economic performance of their country has been based. Whether it is because Generation X is more prudent about their allocation of time or simply tempted by more available and immediate distractions is a debatable point – the message is clear, young people do 'want a life' and employers who choose to ignore this desire, do so at their peril.

Prognosis: Having a job, paying the mortgage and supporting a family still keep younger managers in their place. However, the study shows that employers are now perceived as having diminished capacity to deliver long-term financial security, upward mobility and an ever-increasing pay packet. In a very real sense employers have lost their most powerful cards in the bargaining game.

In knowledge-based businesses and the service sector where success depends on fully motivated employees, the big danger lies not in staff turnover. Although loss of tacit knowledge is worthy of close attention, employers need to be more concerned about those younger employees who decide to continue doing their jobs 'competently' while mentally 'clicking off'. Increasingly bored and cynical, they may not make the effort to come up with the two extra bullet points or new idea which lead to competitive advantage in a marketplace dependent on constant innovation. The cost of failing to engage fully young minds remains undetected by a company's control and accounting processes but it is there nonetheless.

Perceptions of Time as a Strategic Factor

Today's leaders will be faced with a choice of fewer men and women, whether American, European or Japanese, willing to bear the sacrifices borne by their predecessors – the rewards for doing so having lost their guarantee. However, designing work to be more stimulating and learning how to build flexible systems which accommodate a labour market with heterogeneous demands will help enterprises to maintain a pool of 'balanced' solid citizens from which to draw future leaders.

Some grey-haired directors may view this call for accommodation as mollycoddling and argue that there will always be a supply of people eager to do whatever is necessary, ambitious young people willing to sacrifice their time. This study confirms the existence of these seemingly compliant recruits but suggests that the supply is dwindling and not without risk. While temporarily adopting the organization's way of working, including its unwritten rules about time, highly ambitious young people privately report to having an agenda of their own. Typically, it is one that involves acquiring all the learning one can, in other words 'picking the company's brains', then moving on. 'High sacrificers' who do stay on are just as susceptible to the stresses of today's workplace as the less driven; however, because they tend to

5

How Are We to Live?

Ethics in an Age of Self-interest

PETER SINGER

In the 1980s we saw a remarkable boom and then a crash. High-flying entrepreneurs, who at one time were the folk heroes of culture, like Donald Trump in the United States and Alan Bond in Australia, fell from grace. Some went to prison; others lost their fortune but were able to stay out of prison. Their experience makes us re-evaluate the glittering heights of that decade and ask what it was all about and what it can teach us. Perhaps the neatest posing of that question in popular culture was in Oliver Stone's film *Wall Street*. There was a very wealthy stockbroker character called Gordon Gecko, played by Michael Douglas, probably drawn, at least in part, from Ivan Boesky, the self-styled king of arbitrage, who amassed a huge fortune of hundreds of millions of dollars through speculating on which companies were going to be taken over and buying up their shares in order to realize profits at a later stage when the shares rose in the light of the takeover. And there was a junior sharebroker, called Bud Fox, played by Charlie Sheen, who was trying to make it in the big-league world by working with Gordon Gecko, by giving him tips. But the story goes sour because one of the tips that he gives him is that the airline for which his father works is being taken over. And when Gecko in fact takes over the airline, he proceeds to strip it of its assets and sack all the workers, his father included. This makes Bud Fox reflect a little on what he's done and what the point of it is. 'Where does it all end?' he asks Gordon Gecko. 'How many yachts can you water-ski behind? How much is enough?'

If you look back through Western philosophy as far as Aristotle, you certainly don't get any idea of the accumulation of money as a good thing in itself. It's natural to want to acquire the things you need for the necessities and comforts of your life, to store up for unforeseen contingencies. But to accumulate money for its own sake, in Aristotle's view, is mistaking the means for the end, and is a sign of foolishness, not wisdom. And along with the Christian view of wealth goes the prohibition of usury, which didn't mean charging excessive or extortionate rates of interest on a loan. Rather, in the medieval conception, usury meant charging any interest on a loan, and that was not only a sin, but one of the central sins.

This lasted until the Reformation and then, perhaps for political reasons related to the need of the Protestant reformers to attract the support of the middle classes, fairly rapidly disappeared. Calvin said that to be wealthy is a sign of being part of the elect. In *The Wealth of Nations*, Adam Smith argued that in a market we each become wealthy by serving best the interests of others. In a famous sentence, he says: 'It's not from the benevolence of the butcher we expect our dinner but from his regard for his self-interest.' So the idea is that the market rewards those who meet the needs of others. A hidden hand sees that the pursuit of individual interests somehow works for the public interest, for the global interest. And the result of this, Smith thought, was not only to enrich the rich, but also to help the poor. He argued that this collective outcome is good for even the poorest person in a civilized country and added, 'the accommodation of a European prince does not always exceed that of an industrious and frugal peasant as the accommodation of the latter, that is the peasant, exceeds that of many an African king, the absolute master of the lives of ten thousand naked savages'. And this is a common theme among defenders of early capitalism, that despite the inequalities, it makes the labourers better off than kings somewhere. John Locke uses exactly the same point except that for him it's a king in America, who he says 'feeds lodges and is clad worse than a day labourer in England'. Some twenty years before Smith published *The Wealth of Nations,* he wrote a critique of a different work that was causing a sensation among intellectuals on the continent: Rousseau's 'Discourse on Inequality'. Rousseau took a very different view of modern civilization. He compared it unfavourably with the natural state of human beings, when the earth was left to its natural fertility and covered with immense forests, whose trees, Rousseau said, had never felt the blow of the axe and which therefore provided sustenance for humans and every species of animal. The noble savage could roam the forest plucking berries and satisfying his hunger and slaking his thirst at the first brook he crossed and then finding his bed in a pile of leaves at the foot of a tree, and with that all of his wants would be satisfied. Rousseau blamed private property for taking us out of this idyllic state of nature, for making us multiply our wants, leading, he says, to hatred, civil strife, slavery, crime, war, deceit and all the other evils of modern life. In contrast, Smith said that industry has let our ancestors develop the arts and sciences in ways which have turned the rude forests of nature into agreeable and fertile plains and made the trackless and barren oceans a new fund of subsistence.

It's interesting that Smith didn't defend the accumulation of possessions on the grounds that that was the way to happiness. On the contrary, he thought that it was a deception to believe that acquiring possessions is the way to happiness. Instead, he said, 'if we consider the real satisfaction which all these things are capable of affording, by itself and separated from the beauty of that arrangement which is fitted to promote it, it will always appear in the highest degree contemptible and trifling'. But although Smith thought we were deceived in believing that the accumulation of possessions is the way to happiness, he says that it is a fortunate deception, because it rouses and keeps in continual motion the industry of mankind.

I think we need to challenge this view of nature, and expose more fully the deception that he himself acknowledged. The reason is that we have been for a long period living on our inheritance, living on the inheritance of the accumulated resources of the planet, resources like fertile soils, forests, oil, coal, minerals, and, of course, the fact that our atmospheres and our oceans have been relatively clean and have been able to assimilate the wastes that we have put into them. On the basis of those resources we have built a huge global economy – one that has brought a great deal of prosperity and affluence for the middle- and upper-class citizens at least of developed nations. But the assumption that this expansion can go on without limit is a highly dubious one because we're using up so much of the Earth's accumulated resources: since the middle of the century we've doubled our per capita use of energy, and of steel, copper and wood. We've doubled our consumption of meat and quadrupled our car ownership and these are items that were already in large usage in the 1950s. There have been greater increases for new materials like aluminium, and of course we have greatly increased our output of our wastes to the atmosphere and the oceans. For those reasons, we really are living off capital. But if you look at the ratio, you find that the average American is responsible for the burning of between four and five tons of carbon per year. The average Indian or Chinese contributes roughly one tenth of that amount. How can we in the developed nations tell China or India that they should cut back their development or take steps that will be harmful or slow their development in order to achieve 1990 levels of carbon dioxide output when they were starting so far below us? It's no wonder that Indians and Chinese feel rather aggrieved. According to the Indian writer Anyul Agawul? 'India and China today account for more than one third of the world's population. The question is whether we are consuming one third of the world's resources and contributing one third of the muck and dirt in the atmosphere and the ocean.' And the answer of course is no, those countries are not. But if we were to share those entitlements out equally per capita, then we would regard every individual on the globe as having an entitlement to dump a certain amount of waste into the atmosphere or into the oceans – the kind of amount that is sustainable, that is not going to cause drastic climate change or a rise in sea levels which will inundate low-lying areas like Bangladesh or Egypt or island nations like Tuvalu.

Why does this refute Adam Smith? His argument was that the invisible hand works for the benefit of all, and he explicitly denied that the rich make the poor worse off. His argument was that, consume however much they might, what the rich consumed still left, to use Locke's expression, 'enough and as good for others to raise the level of the poorest beyond what it would have been'. But now we can see that by continuing to consume as much as we do, the rich are preventing the Third World countries from having their share of the good life, because if they were to reach our level the result would be catastrophe. Moreover, there is good evidence to support the point that Adam Smith already made about the deception I referred to earlier, that a high level of consumption is not associated with a happy life. There have been studies for example of the winners of major lotteries. They show that if you ask them to compare their lives, not immediately after they've won the lottery, but five years later, with their life before, very often they're prepared to admit they're not any happier. Similarly, studies of levels of happiness in different countries do not correlate with the gross national product of those countries – quite often poorer countries have populations who report higher levels of happiness. And looked at in a chronological way, there have been studies since the 1940s that have asked Americans how happy they are. Since the 1940s America has become much more affluent. Americans own five times more air-conditioners per head, four times as many clothes-dryers, seven times as many dishwashers, an almost infinite number of times more colour television sets, microwaves, video cassette recorders. And yet when the University of Chicago's National Opinion Research Center, which conducts these polls, asks people how happy they are, there has been very little change since the 1950s.

What is the alternative? I want to suggest that we can find an alternative in an ethical life. The view that has been put around for some time is that ethics is a goal that is incompatible with enjoying yourself, in other words a moralistic, perhaps a puritanical view of an ethical life, which sees it in terms of sacrifice, and sees it as a contrast to the private happiness we achieve through earning well and consuming successfully. I want to suggest that an ethical life should not be seen as a sacrifice, but as a chance to enjoy the fulfilment of feeling that you've been able to do something positive with your life, to have made a difference to the world. You can identify with a lot of writers, ancient and modern, who have taken this kind of view. I think part of the appeal of the pioneering feminist work *The Feminine Mystique* by Betty Friedan was that she was telling women to identify themselves with what she called a life plan, with lifetime interests and goals. She saw a job as a way of identifying with the larger society in contrast to the housewife role, which locks one in more to personal and private conceptions. Robert Bly's *Iron John*, which was in vogue some years back, may be a rather silly work, which suggests men can find their manliness by rushing off to the woods and twirling swords above their heads and watching them glint in the moonlight – 'rediscovering the warrior within them' was the phrase that Bly used. But Bly also noticed that the warrior needs a cause, as he put it. 'When a warrior is in service to a true king, that is to a transcendent cause, he does well and his body becomes a hard-working servant, which he requires to endure cold, heat, pain, wounds, scarring, . . . he can work long hours, ignore fatigue, do what is necessary to finish the PhD and all the footnotes, endure obnoxious departmental heads, live sparsely like Ralph Nader, write as T.S. Eliot did under a single dangling light bulb for years, clean shit and filth endlessly like St Francis of Assisi or Mother Teresa, endure contempt, disdain and exile as Sakharov did.' Causes do empower us, make us feel strong, and believe that we are doing something worthwhile. Causes are larger than the individual. A truly ethical approach is, in the words of the great, but unduly neglected English philosopher, Henry Sidgewick, the idea of putting yourself at the point of view of the universe and trying to see how things look from that perspective.

6

Animal Rights and Wrongs

ROGER SCRUTON

People have begun to ask themselves whether the differences between human beings and other animals are more significant, from the moral point of view, than the similarities. Animals suffer pain and fear; they have affections and attachments; their bodily needs and desires are as important to them as ours are to us. In other words, animals have interests, and ought to be included in the moral equation, if we are to deal with them as we ought.

Such, very briefly, is the burden of the argument put before us by Peter Singer, Richard Ryder and Tom Regan. And it is an argument that must be taken seriously. However, it is my contention that those who have so far proposed it have devoted insufficient attention to the differences between us and other animals, and focused too narrowly on the similarities. There are deep and difficult philosophical questions here, which people have been reluctant to explore partly, I believe, because they present an obstacle to easy and foregone conclusions.

I have no doubt that non-human animals have minds. But the mind should be seen as a system of capacities, hierarchically arranged. An animal may possess the lower capacities without the higher, but not vice versa. At the basic level, mind involves sentience – a capacity manifested by all forms of animal life. Perception and appetite occur at a higher level than sentience. But they are present in animals – such as insects – to whom we find it difficult to relate as individuals, and whom we are compelled to regard, as a rule, only as members of a species, replaceable without loss by any other of their kind.

We do not regard the higher mammals in that way, for the very good reason that their mental life *individualizes* them. They have risen to the *cognitive* level of the mind, which is to say that they exhibit beliefs, desires and learning. Such animals are distinguished from each other by their histories and attachments, by the things they have learned, and the desires they have acquired. They also have *intentionality*: that is, they respond to the world through their conception of it – a conception which may be true or false. We can enter into and influence their view of things, and so become part of their world. In the limiting case, we can exist for them as individuals, just as they do for us. This is the foundation of our relations with them, and the ground for our sympathy and concern.

That said, it is important to recognize that the mental life of humans exists at another level from that of most – if not all – of the other species with which we have daily dealings. Like dogs and cats, we are conscious. Like them, we feel sensations, emotions and desires. Like them we have beliefs and a changing store of information. But, unlike them, we have a consciousness of self and of the distinction between self and other. We have a conception of the past and the future as well as the present; of the possible and the impossible as well as the actual. We act and think in terms of a distinction between the world as it is, and the world as it seems, and in everything we distinguish our own interests and desires from those of other people and other animals.

These capacities are made possible by language, through which we represent the world and distinguish ourselves from it. An inevitable consequence of language is practical reason – the capacity to make choices, to justify and criticize our own and others' conduct, and to settle disputes by reasoning rather than force. This is the real foundation for the moral distinction that we make, and ought to make, between ourselves and other animals. To put the matter shortly, we, but not they, are moral beings. Moral beings have personality, self-consciousness, and a conception of interests other than their own. They settle disputes with others of their kind not by force, but by assigning rights and responsibilities, and by respecting the sovereignty and freedom of the other. Moral beings are potential members of a moral community, who attempt to live by negotiation and agreement with their fellows. As such, they are subject to the moral law, which confers rights and duties, and which commands our assent. Rights are interests which cannot be set aside without the consent of those who possess them. To acquire rights is to accede to the moral community: it is therefore to acquire duties and responsibilities, and a sovereign place in the moral order.

The idea of animal rights is, in my view, sophistical. Nobody who attributes rights to animals seems to attribute to them the responsibilities that are required as a payment. Nor is this surprising, for a creature with responsibilities must also have a conception of duty, and this is something that animals do not, and cannot, acquire. But the same goes for rights. To attribute rights to a creature that has no conception of rights, and no ability to recognize the rights of others, is to make an unsatisfiable moral demand. To do this, and to do it seriously, rather than as part of a sentimental charade, would be to relate to the creature not kindly but cruelly – since it would be to force it to conform to a way of life that is intrinsically alien to it, and which would impede the satisfaction of its most elementary desires. To assign rights to a cat you must oblige it to respect the rights of others: and this means drawing a line at every form of killing, and so depriving it of the activity which it most enjoys.

The fact that animals are not moral beings has important consequences. Not only does it mean that they have no rights; it also means that they have no duties, and therefore cannot be blamed or condemned for doing that which, in a person, would be wrong. You should not punish an animal, therefore, in order to exact justice for a crime: for this is to treat it in a way that it could not understand. The punishment of a human being is a part of moral dialogue, and is justified by its cause. The punishment of an animal is part of training, and can be justified only by its effect. You are inducing in the animal a conception of what is expected from it, and so imparting a guide to life in the human world. All domestic animals need this guide, since all of them depend on human beings for their needs and safety.

Although animals have no rights, it does not follow that we can treat them as we wish. Needless to say, the question of the grounds of moral judgement is one of the deepest and darkest in philosophy. But some progress can be made towards understanding it, I believe, if we look at the several sources of moral judgement, and recognize the impossibility of deriving a coherent moral code from one source alone. Many of those who have argued for the inclusion of animals in the moral equation have been utilitarians – that is to say, they have seen moral judgement as the outcome of a cost-benefit calculation, in which the happiness of the greatest number is the aim. In doing so they have seen the rights of human beings as negotiable interests, and their duties as provisional rules of thumb. Both of those results are inherently paradoxical, and lie at the heart of the devastating, and in my view unanswerable, objections that philosophers have made to the utilitarian conception of morality. Moral judgement should not be seen as a kind of economic reasoning, but as setting the *limit* to economic reasoning. Morality tells us where calculation stops. Those who demote human rights to negotiable interests have no difficulty in believing in animal rights, but only because what they call a right is no more than an interest.

The calculus of rights and duties stems from our nature as moral beings, and from the need to set the ground rules for a negotiated life among strangers. It tells us that rights are to be respected, and duties obeyed. It confers equality of moral status on all participants to the moral dialogue, and imposes on us an obligation to justify our conduct in the face of adverse criticism. It brings with it a battery of concepts which entirely transform the worldview and emotions of those who possess them: concepts like justice, desert, and punishment, which lie at the heart of our inter-personal responses. But, however important this calculus may be, as a source of moral feeling, it is not the only source, and would be impotent without the motives upon which it draws.

The first of these motives, and the largest source of our moral duties towards animals, is sympathy. While animals have 'sympathetic responses', in the sense of responses which are caused by the emotions of those in their nearest vicinity, they do not have sympathy. For this is based on a conception of self and other, and of the distinction between them. It is a disposition to take the feelings of another into account, and erupts in charitable gestures designed to alleviate the other's suffering and promote the other's joy. Without sympathy we should be less strongly motivated to obey the calculus of rights and duties. However, sympathy has favourites, and is bound to be in conflict with the impartiality required by the moral law. This is one of the principal tensions involved in the moral life, and it is a tension that we could not abolish without undermining the moral motive.

Our sympathies depend upon our conception of others as individuals, with interests of their own. With animals which hardly exist for us as individuals – animals like slugs and worms and insects which offer only a regimented caricature of our social feelings – we find it hard to sympathize, and it is no moral defect in us that we tend to think of them collectively, safeguarding the interest of the species, rather than that of any individual member of it. In the case of noxious species, like the locust and the tape-worm, it is hard to condemn an attitude of outright warfare – certainly wrong to think of this attitude as showing a corrupt or hardened heart. Indeed, we would rightly regard as perverse someone who entered the interests of tape-worms into the moral equation in such a way that they could cancel the interests of human beings.

There are two other sources of moral judgement, besides those already mentioned. The first is our attitude to virtue and vice. We are drawn to the traits of character which uphold the moral community, and repelled by those which undermine it. We have a vivid conception of the likeable, lovable or admirable person, and of the nasty or contemptible person whom we should rather avoid. These conceptions are by no means arbitrary, but grow from the very same social and rational responses which feed our judgements of human actions. Although our conceptions of virtue and vice are malleable, and change with changing social circumstances, they have an immovable core which derives from the experience of society itself. In all viable societies people are drawn to courage, prudence, charity and justice, and repelled by selfishness, cruelty, cowardice and greed. And it is easy to see why. We need to distinguish the people with whom we can live, and upon whom we can rely, from those whose presence is a threat to us. Moreover, we seek to emulate virtue, to inculcate it in our offspring, and to ensure that it is reproduced as a permanent feature of the human condition. We wish to live in a state of self-approval, and to know that others in their turn approve of us. This is the root of human happiness, which is impossible to achieve without the pursuit of virtue and the abhorrence of vice. Hence Aristotle's definition of happiness as 'an activity of the soul in accordance with virtue'. The philosophical arguments for this view are deep and complex; but its common-sensical nature goes without saying.

Finally there is the source of moral feeling which is most often neglected in the literature, but which in many ways bears most nearly on our relations with the natural world. I use the term 'piety' to refer to this fourth and final source, meaning not the adherence to this or that religious doctrine, but the underlying recognition of our fragility and dependence, and the attitude of respect towards the world and the creatures that live in it, upon which religions draw for much of their inspiration. This, I believe, is what the Romans meant by *pietas*, and it is the attitude which so many people – from environmental groups to landscape painters, from conservationists to animal welfare activists – are attempting to recapture, in a world where the results of human presumption are so horribly apparent. Even in an age which does not recognize it under its traditional name, piety is ever-present, a necessary motive in the living and a guarantee offered to those unborn. Putting it in that way has a slightly conservative resonance – recalling, as it does, certain famous words of Edmund Burke. But it is conservative with a small 'c' and, rightly understood, the account of morality that I offer is, I believe, a statement of what we should all accept, were we to look dispassionately on our condition as moral beings.

Having uncovered the roots of moral thinking, it remains to address the problem of animals and our dealings with them. If animals had rights then there would be absolute limits to the things that we could do to them. We could not, for example, kill them, breed them for our purposes, train them without their consent, or take them into captivity. We could not keep them as pets, nor could we use them in experiments – indeed, we should very rapidly fall out of relation with them altogether, and live side by side as distant competitors for resources which we alone would know how to monopolize.

But the moral problem arises precisely because animals do not have rights, so that the principles that impede our invasions of other people do not serve to protect them. How therefore should animals be treated? I believe that the answer depends first on the precise relation between us and the animals in question. The moral principles that govern our dealings with pets should differ from those which govern our dealings with farm animals, and with animals in the wild. In every case the answer to the moral question will draw on sympathy, virtue and piety – the three sources of moral feeling which remain, when the calculus of rights and duties is discounted.

The concept of cruelty is clearly crucial in defining our duties towards animals. It is a concept that derives its sense from sympathy and virtue. A cruel act is one that only a cruel person or a person of deficient sympathies would perform. The problem, of course, is that it is difficult to lay down hard and fast principles concerning what such a person *would* do, in what circumstances. (There are cruel and kind ways of extracting teeth, for example; cruel and kind ways of punishing; cruel and kind ways of inflicting pain. Melville even tries to distinguish, in *Moby Dick*, between cruel and kind ways of whaling.) For this reason, some people have tried to define cruelty without reference to human vice and virtue, by describing a cruel act as one that 'inflicts unnecessary suffering'. But this only compounds the difficulty. For what is 'unnecessary'? Our judgement of what is necessary depends upon our assessment of the purpose. Thus ritual slaughter inflicts suffering which is certainly unnecessary, if our purpose is to kill. But it is not unnecessary, if our purpose is to kill according to the precepts laid down by a given religious tradition.

We are on firmer ground, I believe, if we make a distinction between the motives for inflicting suffering (where suffering includes pain, fear and other forms of mental discomfort). There is clearly a radical distinction between the person who inflicts pain in order to achieve a certain purpose, and the one who inflicts it for its own sake, and in order to enjoy the sufferings of the victim. The second person is viciously motivated, and the capacity for this kind of enjoyment is one that human beings ought not to acquire.

But we should also pay attention to sufferings which arise not because they are intended, but because they are the known or likely by-product of some other activity. People train horses to race, without intending that they should suffer injury. Nevertheless, injury is a likely consequence. Here, it seems to me, we are up against a paradigm of the moral problem. Ought we to do this thing, despite the consequences for the animal? And my answer, in brief, is that it depends on the whole circumstances, including the nature of the relation between human and animal, the nature of the intentions of those who take part, and the sum benefit and cost to both the humans and the animals involved. In the case of horse-racing, I have no doubt that it represents a positive contribution to the sum of both human and equine well-being.

Here, then, is a brief summary of the conclusions. First, it seems to me that we must distinguish three quite different kinds of relation that we have to animals: as pets, as animals kept or reared for our uses, and as creatures in the wild. Towards pets we have an assumed duty of care, which to some extent parallels the duty that we have towards our closest human companions. In the limiting case, a pet is a kind of honorary member of the moral community. This means that his pleasures and pains cannot be regarded as a factor in some utilitarian calculation. Although a pet does not have rights, his owner has special duties towards him. Suppose that, taking compassion on a hungry lion, you feed your dog to it. You would be doing a great wrong, because you would be violating an assumed duty of care, and this is something that a virtuous person cannot do. If you drive a wild antelope in the lion's direction, it is not so clear that you are doing wrong: certainly not the same kind of wrong, or the same degree.

This does not mean that we cannot use utilitarian reasoning when it comes to justifying the *practice* of keeping pets. Although it is undeniable that this practice involves much suffering – especially for dogs pent up in city towers, or rabbits kept in cages – it also brings much joy and comfort into lives that would otherwise be joyless and comfortless. The practice is, on balance, a contribution to the good of all concerned.

In the case of animals bred, captured or kept for human uses, we must again recognize an assumed duty of care. But these animals are not honorary members of the moral community, and our duty towards them is exhausted, once we have done our best to confer on them a life that is as fulfilling as possible, given the use to which they are put, and to bring that life to an end, when this is required, as quickly and kindly as we can. But that is not the whole story. For we need also to justify the use to which the animals are put. While it seems to me that the use of animals for human food and clothing is in principle justifiable, more questions need to be asked about animals kept in zoos and those used in laboratory experiments. Here there must be a clear and substantial good to be achieved, before these practices can be embarked on. And even so, there are things that a virtuous person could not do. The principle that should guide us is this: that which can be done only by a callous person, ought not to be done.

We should also bear in mind that many animals exist only because we have a use for them. If they can be put to this use, while leading a life full of interest and satisfaction, shielded from the worst of fear and pain, then it is right to bring them into being, and also to train them so that they can perform the task that has been allotted to them. This argument, which applies to the cow, the pig and the horse, probably extends to the laboratory rat.

Wild animals do not benefit from a duty of care. Our dealings with them are therefore governed by other principles. We must strive to maintain the balance of nature, to protect our own interests where these are threatened, to consider the interests of all animals involved when interfering in the natural order, and to submit our conduct to the tribunals of sympathy, virtue and piety.

It is important to test such principles against controversial cases. The most obvious is angling. I dismiss the suggestion that fish feel neither pain nor fear. The capacity for pain and fear belong to the software, and not to the hardware of an organism. Nevertheless, anglers do not enjoy the pain and fear that they cause, and are (or ought to be) kind to their quarry whenever this is possible. At the same time pain and fear are necessary for the existence of the sport. Its existence is justified by taking into consideration all the interests involved – those of the anglers, those of the fish, whose environment is protected in order that they should be hunted, and those of other species who depend upon a lively human interest in clean and thriving waterways. One could imagine a sadistic sport in which fish are extracted from the water and tortured with hooks, to the delighted squeals of onlookers. Morally speaking, such a sport is at the opposite pole from angling, even though to the fish themselves there may be little discernible difference. Almost everything depends, in such a case, on our sense of the dividing line between innocent and vicious pleasures.

Similar considerations apply to fox-hunting, which has the interesting feature that the pleasure involved is not experienced by humans only but also – and to a far greater extent – by hounds and horses. This does not mean that foxes can be pursued anyhow. It only means that there are forms of the sport which can be engaged in by upright people, acting in morally permissible ways.

At the same time, for various reasons, angling and hunting will always be controversial, and the question arises whether there should be legislation to ease the conscience of those who have qualms about their continued existence. My view is that legislation must proceed from a basis of a complete understanding of the practice, and from a recognition that, where there is serious moral disagreement, and vital human interests are at stake, the law should not take sides. Minority pursuits engaged in without qualms by decent people should not be criminalized merely because a majority – not necessarily well-informed – disapprove of them. If we do not adopt such a principle, the law will cease to be an instrument for resolving human conflict, and become instead a means of provoking it.

7

Wellbeing and Time

GEOFF MULGAN and HELEN WILKINSON

Time is our most precious – and most wasted – resource. After decades when politics focused primarily on income, attention is turning to how we spend our time. In part this reflects prosperity. Richer societies tend to be more concerned about how to live, as well as having enough to live on. But concern also results from the tensions that are accompanying the transition from an industrial to a post-industrial order of time.

One sign of change is the fact that after a century of decline working hours are rising again (exacerbating fears that children are no longer getting enough attention from their parents who spend ever less time at home). A second is the growing gulf between those with too much work and those with too little. A third is the rise of a more individualistic and demanding culture in which people expect to have far greater freedom to decide when to shop, to have fun or use services.

At first glance the rise of new, more flexible approaches to time should be resolving these problems. Just-in-time production and multitasking computers, twenty-four hour shopping and video-on-demand, time-share holidays and flexitime working, late opening at schools and home banking, the shift from synchronous phone calls to asynchronous e-mail: all are innovations which should be ensuring that time is used less wastefully.

But so far remarkably few people are enjoying the benefits

of change. Although lifetime working hours have fallen by 42 per cent[1] over the last century, there is little sign that life has become much easier. Ironically, both the overworked and the unemployed share the sense that their position is involuntary. A large majority are suffering from stress because of the rising intensity of work and leisure (44 per cent of the workforce now report coming home exhausted).[2] More complex time patterns often mean more negotiation and more hanging around, problems which are exacerbated by persistent public policy failure in fields like transport and crime, which have led to increases in the time taken getting to work, transporting children, even shopping.

Moreover few people are entirely at ease with the speed of change. It is hard not to be disoriented by the pace at which crises spread across the world, by the rates of change of products, the extraordinary mobility and liquidity of money, or the rapid obsolescence of governmental programmes or fashions.

So how should we respond? By what principles should we make sense of these changes? We would suggest two starting points. The first is to distinguish good uses of time that give enjoyment, that develop our potential, that leave something useful behind, from bad ones that are inert, useless and mindless. The second is to distinguish chosen uses of time from ones that have been imposed.

These two sets of principles – quality on the one hand, and choice on the other – seem to us valid ones to take into the next century. By their standard, human history has not been a straightforward progress. The pre-agrarian hunter gatherers spent only fifteen hours each week engaged in work – work which was often more demanding of intelligence than most work today.[3] By contrast, backbreaking agriculture and repetitive factory jobs did little or nothing to use or develop the individual's potential, while the dominant model of industrial capitalism, whereby people sold their time to employers, without any ownership over work or its output, was biased against fulfilling uses of time.

Today we should be able to step beyond this heritage. The fall in working hours, at least until the 1980s, has provided people with the chance to cultivate broader interests in sports, the arts, or travel. Rising education levels have given people the opportunity to work in far more fulfilling ways. And automation is taking over the most repetitive tasks, albeit more slowly than expected.

But across the world policy regimes show few signs of having turned this opportunity into reality. No new model of time has yet come into view. Instead there is confusion. Some (such as Italy, the USA and Sweden) are raising retirement ages, while others (such as France) seek to encourage early retirement so as to create new jobs for the young. Some (like the UK) are deregulating shopping and opening up the evening economy, while simultaneously denying public institutions the resources to adapt their timetables to meet more complex needs. Some nations are radically rethinking their time uses – for example Japan recently announced the aim of cutting working hours to become the 'lifestyle superpower' of the world – while others (like the USA) are pursuing aggressive policies to get people to work harder. None has yet shown much success in ending the chronic waste of millions of hours of potentially active and fulfilling time.

To grasp the future we first need to understand the past. We have been brought up to see time as fixed; but this was never so. Instead, each era has made and remade time. Calendars have been repeatedly reformed (just as today debates continue about summer time). In the fifteenth and sixteenth centuries, some clocks even went anticlockwise.[4] In revolutionary France there were attempts to decimalize time. As late as the 1870s there were eighty different railway times in the USA and France still had fourteen regional times before the 1884 conference in Washington which introduced a World Standard Time and created twenty-four time zones.[5]

Looking back we can identify a series of distinct approaches to time. In pre-industrial societies, time was close to nature. Social life was ordered by the rhythms of the seasons, of day and night. People understood time cyclically, and in terms of key rites of passage through life, moments which were often experienced communally – birth, the transition from childhood to adulthood, from education to working life, from work to old age. Time was rarely measured; instead it was present subjectively rather than objectively. It was local, based on slow and steady rhythms. In this world time policies were generally concerned with regulating the festivals of saints' days, or seasonal celebrations. Even such early modern techniques as accounting take their forms from the agricultural year.

In the industrial era by contrast, as Lewis Mumford pointed out, time takes on the character of the clock.[6] It becomes mechanical, regular, removed from nature. Time comes to be seen as a resource to be managed: in E. P. Thompson's words it becomes a currency: 'not passed but spent'.[7] People 'clock in' to work, and society is conceived and organized around the machine-like regularities of the forty hour week and all those other institutions that adapt around this accordingly: the school timetable, regulated shopping hours and so on. In a remarkably short period these timetables came to be shared across whole nations, driven forward by railways and the telegraph, so that today it is routine for 20 or 200 million people to watch the same television programme simultaneously. Time became synthetic, uniform and continuous, systematized not habitual: captured in the production line of films like Charlie Chaplin's *Modern Times*. And with continuous production came the need to synchronize life and leisure to suit production, with shift working, and a host of measures from hire purchase to macromanagement to stabilize demand.

In the industrial era policies came to focus on quantities of time: regulations for working time were introduced in Britain in 1802, in Prussia in 1839, in France in 1841. Political struggles were mounted to cut the working day, guarantee holidays and sick leave, with celebrated successes like France's 1936 *congés payés*. Other policies established fixed age rights: rights to schooling, or pensions. For unions the key was to take control over time – and reduce it. For employers it was to get the most out of the time they had purchased.

Post-industrial time is different again. Like the programmable digital watch, it is even further removed from nature, endlessly flexible and malleable. Activities can be precisely synchronized (to the nanosecond on modern telecommunications networks) or through techniques like just-in-time and zero-carry-forward. In these as in other examples it is the interaction between technologies and human systems that is key. In Daniel Bell's phrase, if the industrial world is based around a game with nature, post-industrial society is a game between persons.[8] As organization is reshaped by the potential of digital technologies, so is time increasingly bound up with social life.

The other critical factor is information. As information comes to dominate the economy, time loses its materiality. Values become less solid than in the age when buildings or steel were at the heart of the economy. Obsolescence becomes the norm, and many of the most valuable things are shaped by their half-life (the time it takes for them to lose half their value) – things like chemical or genetic information, financial data or computer software. Moreover societies invest far more in time than in things: investment in the hours needed for knowledge and learning (most of it spent on schooling) is now greater than traditional capital investment in almost every industrialized society.

In place of the ordered shared rhythms of the industrial age, time also becomes personalised. Post-industrial society offers the promise that everyone can customize their time arrangements, working or shopping when they want, watching television asynchronously with the help of the video-on-demand or downloading information on a network. Domestic goods (like the freezer or the VCR) store up services, to be drawn down at will (rather as the book stored up information, so helping unleash the universities, science and culture). Post-industrialism brings with it, according to the philosophers, an extended present in place of the traditional distinctions between past, present and future.[9]

With personalization also comes another important feature: just as the mechanical time of the industrial era helped to speed work up, so does the programmed time of post-industrialism. With the help of technologies, it becomes possible to perform many different tasks simultaneously, whether in work or in leisure, and to distribute functions in time and space. More valuable time encourages 'time deepening' and intensification at leisure. As Staffan Linder put it 25 years ago in his classic *The Harried Leisure Class*, the modern citizen finds himself 'drinking Brazilian coffee, smoking a Dutch cigar, sipping a French cognac, reading the *New York Times*, listening to a Brandenburg Concerto and entertaining his Swedish wife – all at the same time with varying degrees of success'.[10] Today we could add to that talking on a mobile phone and checking the e-mail, while of course the Swedish wife would probably now be doing even more things simultaneously than her husband.

These three successive time cultures have never been uniform. Today only a minority experience post-industrial time in much of their life (perhaps the 0.5m customers of First Direct, or the 200,000 on the Internet in the UK), just as fifty years ago industrial, Fordist time had only penetrated some parts of life. Even today, a tiny minority of the very rich still enjoy the same stress-free existence as the aristocrats of the last century, while an equally small minority of New Age travellers and unemployed are deliberately trying to go back to a more 'natural' way of life.

As we shall argue, it is vital to acknowledge this lack of uniformity: many analysts have gone badly wrong by trying to generalize about the majority on the basis of minority experiences. But it is equally essential to understand that differences are functional. The industrial organization of time rested on pre-industrial norms for women who were prepared to work without contract or payment in the home. In the same way today the world of the post-industrial worker would not be viable if it did not rest on a vast array of work which is still essentially industrial: repetitive, mindless, regimented, and even pre-industrial in the form of domestic service.

Despite these differences the post-industrial model of time dominates the debate. It offers a clearly visible goal that seems to solve many of our current problems: a twenty-four-hour, 365-day working year, a world in which traditional time boundaries – with night as the time to sleep, and daylight as the time to wake – are no longer appropriate. It is a model rooted in the capacity of information and communication technologies to liberate people from the constraints of time and space.

But this post-industrial model of time doesn't just challenge physical or temporal boundaries. It also challenges social boundaries. So in place of fixed shopping hours, it points to twenty-four-hour shopping; instead of eight-hour days and shifts it points to a world of infinite flexitime; in place of a fixed period of school and university education, it suggests lifelong (even just-in-time) learning; instead of work as something to be done between education and retirement it suggests lifelong working; instead of a fixed period for having children, child-rearing is spread into the late forties, the fifties and even perhaps the sixties. Within work there is the spread of annualized working contracts (and at the other end, of zero-hour contracts).

The philosophical base of the twenty-four-hour society is the idea of autonomy – the promise of an escape from traditional norms of time use and into freedom. The common message of consumerism, of democracy, of an open media and a mobile society, is that people should be able to determine the shape of their own lives, free from coercion. In terms of time it means that people see their stock of time as something to be conserved: time spent in pursuing other people's interests or goals is more likely to feel wasted. Not only does this change how we think about such things as parenting, which cease to be duties and become instead choices shaped by the expectation that they will be fulfilling experiences. It also affects attitudes to life itself, as people come to believe that they can, and should, consciously shape their own destinies, making choices between different (and unknown) options so as to fulfill their underlying potential.

But the promise of autonomy is not being realized. Instead for most the post-industrial model of time has been experienced as an imposition. According to the latest research 57 per cent of British adults and a remarkable 86 per cent of women in full-time jobs feel they never have enough time to get things done.[11] More than half of all British workers suffer from stress. By almost every measure people are feeling more pressured, more stressed and more bothered about time than for many years.

Much of the stress – the sense of time being squeezed – reflects the pains of transition. Right across the West the old ways of managing time are disappearing. Fixed jobs, shared rhythms of shopping, travel and leisure, and common patterns of learning, marriage, work and retirement, are all on the way out. All of these are symptoms of a revolution, a transition from an industrial time culture based around fixed timetables and a clear division of labour between men who went to work and women who looked after the home, towards a new culture based around flexibility, customization and rapid flows of information.

This new post-industrial culture of First Direct, Internetters and teleworkers offers, perhaps for the first time in history, the promise of people using time for their own needs.

But far from ushering in a leisured utopia its most immediate effect has been a growing divide between those with too much work and those without any. In top jobs long hours have become if anything a mark of status and success. In the 1930s the phrase 'banking hours' referred to a leisurely working day that began at 10 a.m. and ended at 4 p.m., with a generous lunchhour in the middle. By contrast today's banker may be having to cope with twenty-four-hour capital markets. One in eight British managers works more than sixty hours a week and over half take work home during the week, partly to cope with the increased workloads that are left in the wake of 'delayering'. Part of the reason, too, is the insecurity that has swept through so many white-collar jobs, and encouraged the phenomenon of 'presenteeism' – staying in the office even when there isn't any work to do. But technology has also played a part in intensifying work. As Andrew Grove, Chief Executive of chipmakers Intel, put it, technology means that 'we'll be able to work ourselves to death – . . . ubiquitous computers mean that our work will always be with us and our competitors will always be working too.'[12]

These pressures aren't confined to top executives and professionals. While one in six households has no jobs at all, pressures to pay the bills and fear of redundancy mean that a quarter of all British male employees work more than forty-eight hours – which the European Union wants to set as a maximum – and nearly a fifth of unskilled and manual workers work more than fifty hours, in jobs like nursing, security or minicabs.

Indeed right across the world the long decline in working hours has stopped. In Britain weekly hours have gone up an hour since the mid 1980s (and women's free time has fallen by 10 per cent,[13] rather more in Sweden, while in America it was estimated by Harvard Professor Juliet Schor that the average worker now works the equivalent of a month more each year compared to the 1970s.[14]

But the changing patterns of time use aren't just about more work. The post-industrial model is also bringing a different texture to life. While work speeds up, becoming more global and more networked, with obsessive 're-engineering' to produce more efficient use of people and machines, leisure is changing too. Intensive sports like aerobics seem to be being substituted for slower ones like cricket or golf. Families are driving through zoos rather than walking around them. And teenagers 'multitask' their leisure, watching several TV channels at once while also fiddling with a personal computer.

Some of the costs of this transition to a post-industrial order are all around us. Not only unemployment and overwork, high stress and high anxiety, but also less obvious costs like the fatigue which has caused recent major accidents. But little has been done to address it head on, or to adapt institutions to a post-industrial way of life. Most institutions remain stuck in the industrial era. Within the family, even though most women now have jobs, women still do the bulk of domestic work – and consequently have fifteen hours less free time each week than men.[15] Within the public sector there has been remarkably little adaptation to the fact that two-thirds of households now have two adults in work. Few government offices are open after 6 p.m. Few public services have followed the lead of First Direct bank and made it possible – for example – to check on how a child is doing at school, or what's happened to a planning application, during the evening. Worse, the move to 'self-assessment' of tax, which seems to offer big savings for government, will only work by passing out a big new time burden onto everyone who will soon have to spend a few days each year preparing tax returns.

Nor has government been good at managing the larger systems which do so much to shape how we use our time. One example is rising fear of crime, which has loaded a massive new time burden onto hard-pressed parents. Because of anxieties over unsafe streets the proportion of ten-year-olds allowed to use buses by themselves fell from 79 per cent in 1971 to only 32 per cent in 1990. The result is that British adults are now estimated to spend 900 million hours every year driving their children to school.[16]

Yet for all the costs, the post-industrial model does have many attractions. Many parents – fathers as well as mothers – would like to be able to work from home. Recent work published by Demos and conducted by MORI Socioconsult shows large minorities wanting jobs with term-time working, chances for sabbaticals and four-day weeks, and growing resentment that existing jobs don't offer this.

Fortunately there are some signs of more imaginative thinking about time. Some of the new private pension arrangements could be used (as in Singapore) to finance far more flexible forms of leave. Many schools now stay open later, and many others could think more imaginatively about how to use the hours before parents come home. Some cities like Manchester have experimented with opening up the 'evening economy', with more relaxed licensing laws, which incidentally help to cut drunkenness and crime. Some Italian cities have gone further, deliberately opening up the evening economy, and employing an *Ufficio Tempo*[17] an office of time, responsible for such things as cutting waiting time at public offices, or coordinating later opening of shops and restaurants.

But taken as a whole time remains off the public agenda, treated as far less important than money or production. No party seems to have acknowledged just how much the landscape of time has changed. None is responding to the mood – universal amongst focus groups conducted by Demos around the country – that we need to find a better balance between work and life. And none has quite come to terms with the fact that the old industrial model is being rapidly left behind.

Yet around the world there are clear signs of a new mood. In Japan, which still has the longest hours in the industrialized world, what has been described as the 'grasshopper generation' (*kiri-girisu*) is rejecting the hard work culture of their parents, opting instead for the three v's: villas, visas and visits. This is an understandable reaction in a country where 10,000 die each year from overwork (*karoshi*) and where one survey found more than 120,000 Toyota employees suffering from chronic fatigue.[18]

But much the same signs are visible elsewhere. In America a recent poll found that a third of those questioned would be prepared to take a 20 per cent cut in pay in exchange for shorter working hours, and many leading firms are introducing more flexible working arrangements to make it easier for people to take time off for looking after children.[19] In Europe some unions have successfully negotiated deals with firms like Volkswagen and Fiat involving lower pay and reduced working hours so as to protect jobs.

None of this yet adds up to a wholesale rejection of overwork. But it does signal an important new search for a better balance between work and life, and a better balance between the demands of careers and the needs of children and families. And it does suggest that there is great untapped demand for more imaginative policies on time – changed opening hours for government offices and helplines; new financial instruments and employee rights to make it easier for people to pay for time out of work – time to look after children or ageing relatives, time for educational leave; and the kinds of policy that already exist in parts of Scandinavia and in Canada that make it possible to bank time.

Perhaps the decline in house prices will help. At the moment we have sophisticated financial instruments and government tax incentives for investing in houses: it would make far more sense to transfer these policies from bricks and mortar to the time which is the raw material of life, and, arguably, the most important tool for achieving a genuinely contented and highly skilled population (for example through additional tax incentives for saving schemes designed to finance time off).

For those seeking a better balance between work and life there is already a marvellous institution waiting to be used. Sabbaticals offer time off to recharge the batteries, to learn a new skill or just to travel the world. In the UK these are a rare treat for academics. France and Belgium by contrast already offer legal rights to sabbaticals at any age. With well-conceived funding arrangements it is not inconceivable that we could in the next century see every seventh year taken off as a matter of course.

A previous generation of writers thought the goal was to escape from work. But this misses the point. The most fulfilling activities for people are those entailing autonomy, demands on skills, and absorption. These have been described by the psychologist Mihaly Csikszentmihalyi as the characteristics of 'flow'.[20] Flow can be found in many kinds of work: sports, music, arts and crafts, indeed any kind of task with structured goals which places a demand on people's skills. It goes without saying that much work has been short of flow – a good deal of agricultural work, and most repetitive industrial jobs could almost have been designed to minimize fulfilment. It is this legacy of work as a burden which explains the attractions of many for greater free-time.

But why should we assume that leisure is inherently superior to work? And why should the release of time from work be considered a good in itself? Sociological analysis of time has long acknowledged that the quantitative measure of time is meaningless if it doesn't account for the quality of experience.[21] And the analysis of flow tells a very different story to that casually suggested by advocates of a liberation from work. It shows that many people – and not just professionals – find leisure less fulfilling and challenging than work (although most would still trade work for leisure because of the cultural assumption that work is a burden). The reason is simple: in general work is more likely to lead to flow, because of its structured tasks, feedback and challenge, whereas far too much leisure is passive, shapeless, unchallenging and literally unrewarding. This is surely one reason why surveys regularly report that large majorities would continue to work even if there was no financial need.

Free time by contrast is much harder to structure in fulfilling ways. So although greater leisure has led to some more imaginative uses of time, most still use it in low-intensity activities. On average Britons spend more than twenty-five hours each week watching television. In the 1980s only one in four men and one in ten women had taken part in an outdoor sport or activity in the previous four weeks. Few know how to achieve the inner discipline to shape time and use leisure for genuine 're-creation', and, as Csikszentmihalyi writes, we waste each year 'the equivalent of millions of years of human consciousness [as] the energy that could be used to focus on complex goals, to provide for enjoyable growth, is squandered'.[22]

The challenge of a post-industrial age is not to escape from work altogether but rather to achieve more autonomy, more ways for people to control the terms on which they work, its pace and texture. Soon, this will become a defining part of our politics. Indeed the political and commercial dividends for those who solve the conundrums of time will be immense – as they were a century ago for the firms and nations that first adapted to industrial time. Those who can capitalize on it, liberate it, improve it will not only make life easier for their fellow citizens and employees. They will also play a part in the next stage of human development, a further step away from necessity and towards freedom.

8

The Battle Over Britain

PHILLIP DODD

The present battle over Britain has lasted longer than the one staged during the Second World War. And in an obvious way it is more troubling. Then there was an identifiable external enemy; now the battle is joined by the British against themselves. At the heart of the fierce arguments over the monarchy or the European Union, over the decline of cricket or the BBC, lies a battle about who the British are, have been and might be: the question of national identity.

Some believe that once 'Great' Britain is now all decline and fall; others that those traditional ideas about Britishness are precisely the problem; yet others that we should try to revive the unifying spirit seen during the Second World War; and others still that the very political entity, the United Kingdom, needs to be broken up. The battle matters not simply because its outcome will shape particular political and cultural decisions. All of us need stories, national as well as any other, which can make sense of our lives to ourselves and others – and traditional stories about Britain and Britishness convince less and less.

This particular stage of the battle started, if dates are needed, when Mrs Thatcher early in her premiership set up her standard on the ground of Britishness, claimed that we 'have ceased to be a nation in retreat' and mobilized a British people and sense of Britishness that unnerved some and uplifted others.[1] The irony is that her rhetoric, far from bolstering British institutions and forging a settled national identity, helped to throw it all into what some believe to be terminal turmoil.

Nowhere is this more the case than with her own Party which seems more and more intent on tearing itself apart over what kind of Britain it wants[2] and whether further integration into the European Union threatens national sovereignty and thus the foundational identity of the British. In one corner there's Mr Major gallantly trying to hang on to his Baldwinite love of country and cricket and constitution, and at the same time negotiate his way into the heart of Europe; while in the other, John Redwood and Michael Portillo defend a kind of Britishness that we have learnt to call Thatcherite but which has actually deep historical roots within a national culture that has defined itself in the recent past in terms of its superiority to its 'untrustworthy neighbours'.[3] The battle over Britishness within the Labour Party may be much more contained but could easily become equally troublesome, particularly as the constitutional implications of its stance on Europe and its commitment to decentralization, including a Scottish Parliament, sink in. After all, ghosts of United Britishness past haunt the Labour Party just as much as the Tories – whether it is at the invocation of that great moment of 1945 or of a vision of a United Radical People, stretching back from the suffragettes through the Tolpuddle Martyrs and the Chartists, to the Levellers.[4] All these ghosts can be glimpsed as we run up to the election since British national identity is one of its key themes, most explicitly but not exclusively in relation to European integration and devolution and the possibility of the disintegration of the nation-state.

But the battle over Britain and Britishness has been staged in less obviously political places than Parliament. Indeed it may be the abiding limitation of the political class to believe that a new layer of government or even new constitutional arrangements is a sufficient response to the crisis over national identity. It isn't. After all, national identity matters at least as much in civil society as do political institutions.

It's been there in the schools and in the continuing arguments over the curriculum. Driving debates around the teaching of history are national, such as: Who are the British? Which History should be taught? Who are the British heroes?[5] It's equally tangible in rows over the shape of new buildings. When Prince Charles weighed in saying that developers were threatening to do to St Paul's what the Luftwaffe could never do, then no one could be in doubt that memories of national defence were being mobilized.[6] The battle is also going on in the streets, in a more literal fashion. It's there in the escalating number of racial attacks on the black British, fuelled by a conviction that those who complicate the simple equation white = British deserve all the hatred they get.[7] It's there, as a subtext, in the increasing anxiety over the 'swamping' of county cricket clubs by foreign players with the consequent damage to the English national side. It's also there in the agonized response to the 'decline of standards' and the sleaze that sticks to politicians, the royal family and sports personalities alike. It's been there in the debates about the BBC, that voice of Britain, and its continuing right to bring us together to share national events such as Wimbledon; it's even there in the claims that the British have lost their emotional moorings and a once patient and orderly people have become a disorderly rabble.

To recognize that Britain and its identity are in turmoil now is not to say that it has ever been simply a given. But the battle over national identities within these islands does arise most intensely, as now, at moments of change – whether it is the early sixteenth century and the emergence of an English polity, with English King Henry VIII's break with Rome; the late seventeenth- and early eighteenth-century Constitutional and Protestant settlement with William of Orange and the Union between Scotland and England; or the early 1800s, when patriotism became the cement to bind together an otherwise class-torn people in the face of the revolution in France. Or take a moment nearer our own: the years around 1900. This, too, was a period of massive social change for Britain, as new political institutions such as the Labour Party had to be accommodated within the national life; with military conflict from Ireland to South Africa; with the emergence of mass communications linking the nation together in new ways and with the economic battles with European countries; all were played out in the context of a self-conscious imperial Britain that had to make sense of its own identity in relation both to itself and its subjects.[8]

The issue is of course that the British identity stabilized in the late nineteenth century – with Queen Victoria crowned as Empress of India – is hardly suitable for the British in the twenty-first century. But nor is another, and more attractive identity; the one forged during the Second World War, of an uncowed people united by common adversity. (This is an identity which could still act as a touchstone for the Queen in her 1994 Christmas speech to the Commonwealth.) But it is no disrespect to those who suffered and fought in that war to say that the memory of such a united people, and let us for the moment not challenge the claim,[9] is simply not likely to mean anything to the generation coming to adulthood in 2000, who were born, like my own child, in 1981 and for whom the Falklands, let alone the Second World War, is not even a memory. But at least as important is the question of whether a single unifying identity – the British people – is ever possible outside of the conditions of war, when the enemy is identifiable and can be opposed with a call to arms. However much the Tories try, it seems unlikely they can make the European Union the equivalent of a wartime enemy – such an enormous threat that all internal strife must cease so that a united people can resist the invasion.

Import and Export

So if inherited stories aren't likely to be persuasive in the present, are there any alternatives that might be more successful in making political and cultural sense to the countries that make up the United Kingdom of Great Britain and Northern Ireland? Since all nations misrepresent their past,[10] I want to contribute to such a misrepresentation by introducing a glimpse of my own sense of what Britain and Britishness has been. Just for the moment, imagine a Britain that has been a multi-ethnic state for a long time, has had an appreciable appetite for change (as well as for power) and has been in the import-export business for longer than anyone can remember, trading goods, materials, ideas – and building its Greatness by trading people as commercial property, and appropriating land and resources. There are signs of this import-export business everywhere and not merely in Britain's history of overseas market trading that stretches from sugar in the seventeenth century to the financial services of the present. Signs of Britain's promiscuity can be seen all around us in the streets, whether in the city of Edinburgh where Tony Blair's old college, Fettes College, is designed as a French château; in Blackpool where the Tower is a clone of the Eiffel Tower; in Edward Lutyens's First World War memorials that stand in both Leicester and Delhi; and in the street names of West Belfast, just off the Falls Road – Lucknow Street, Kashmir Road and Cawnpore Street.

There are further signs of Britain's outward-going character in the traffic of ideas that it has engaged in, whether between Enlightenment Edinburgh and continental Europe in the late eighteenth century or between the USA and Britain in the postwar period. The British monarchy, at least as much as any aspect of British society, has been profoundly shaped by the nation-state's relationships with elsewhere: in the late nineteenth century it became a monarchy for the Empire; and more recently its unwillingness to shed some its late nineteenth-century spectacular trappings, and modernize in the way, say, the Netherlands royal family has, may in part be a consequence of its core role in the British tourist industry.

There are other signs of the centrality of the import-export business to Britain, if more are needed, in the various communities from Britain that have been exported elsewhere and in the communities within Britain that have been imported from other countries. Chinese sailors arrived here to settle in the eighteenth century, a time at which, according to one account, a quarter of the British navy was African.[11] During the same period, as the historian Linda Colley has recorded in her marvellous book *Britons*, the British of all classes travelled more than their European counterparts – something that seems to be a tradition since contemporary statistics suggest that the British are more emigrant minded than their western European neighbours.[12] Even the supposed scion of settledness, the people of the mining communities, moved from coalfield to coalfield, often pushed by economic necessity. It is an old Cornish joke that at the bottom of any mine in the world there will be a Cornish miner; and my own family moved from South Wales through Kent to Yorkshire within two generations. The British fascination with home is precisely an index of how often the British have left it, not how little.

If we were looking for an index of this place I have described, then the clothing (including fashion) industry might do. It is not merely that fashion and the clothing industry have been important elements of the national economic and cultural life for a long time, but that a casual glance at their history would show they have been part of the traffic between here and elsewhere, from the centrality of clothing industry to the slave trade as early as the seventeenth century through to the nineteenth century when Manchester and Indian workers locked horns over the provision of cotton to Marks & Spencer, a chain of shops set up by two men, one a member of the Russian Jewish community imported into Britain late last century.

If reference to fashion and clothing in this imagining of the British seems wrong-headed, why is this? Is it because fashion is trivial? But is it more so than football, which is pored over as an index of the state of the national psyche. Perhaps fashion and clothing are just not manly enough to represent a nation that has been taught to pride itself on its manliness, whether in the Sandhurst mess, on the rugby pitch at Cardiff Arms Park, the Manchester shopfloor or the Glasgow pub. Or is it the fact that fashion and clothing offer back to the nation a vision of itself as a curious outward looking place, fascinated by change and display?

Pure Lust

Of course this 'misrepresentation' of Britain as a promiscuous place hardly accords with the post-1945 Welfare State version of the British as a settled, decent, quiet and orderly people making slow but inevitable progress towards the green and pleasant Jerusalem of Blake's poem. But nor does it harmonize any more with the vision of Mrs Thatcher whose administrations so effortlessly pushed aside Butskellite Britain in the 1980s. To put it simply (and that was always her strength), Mrs Thatcher's Britishness depended on a sustained process of purification and exclusion. In her British story, enemies were here, there and everywhere – they were in the trade unions which thwarted British prosperity, within the Foreign Office which betrayed British interests, within the schools and universities which denied British achievements and rubbished our history, as much as in Argentina or Brussels. When she said 'There is no week, nor day, nor hour when tyranny may not enter this country, if the people lose supreme confidence in themselves, and lose their roughness and spirit of defiance', she acted as if she believed it.[13] At home the patriotism of her opponents was called into question; abroad, the enemies needed to be resisted and if necessary fought. There was only one way of being British and that was her way.

Of course, Mrs Thatcher hardly invented a strategy of insiders and outsiders since Britishness has for long worked on the principle of separating the (inside) sheep from the (outside) goats. Sometimes they have been Catholics, barred from public office (from the late seventeenth century until 1829), at another time they have been Jewish people, and more recently people from the Caribbean or Asia who have threatened to 'swamp' British culture.[14] While the groups may change, the principle does not – their presence threatens the historic identity of the British and they must therefore be stigmatized, deprived of power and influence and if possible excluded. It is not as if such rallying cries around purification have gone away entirely – look at any of the recent speeches by Michael Portillo for contrary evidence. But it does seem to be the case that they are no longer capable of providing an Island Story to which enough are willing to subscribe.

Mrs Thatcher was not the first to work in terms of insiders and outsiders, nor was she the first to look on the British (and before them the English) as a people with a special destiny. After all it was as long ago as 1500 that an Italian visitor said that 'they think that there are no other men than themselves and no other world than England'.[15] Explanations for the sense of superiority that the British, and particularly the English, have historically felt towards other nations and foreigners in general, has many sources. Linda Colley has been persuasive in demonstrating how important Protestantism was in the eighteenth century in helping to unify the various ethnic groups within Britain by marking them out from others, in Europe and elsewhere. At the core of this eighteenth-century Britishness was the sense of a destiny-driven militant (and where necessary military) Protestant people surrounded by a hostile Catholic Europe, and threatened by dangerous colonies from without and various enemies from within (whether Scottish nationalists or aristocratic renegade cosmopolitans). It might even be said that Thatcher was the last leader of that Protestant Britishness which saw itself as the guardian of light in the darkness – she was a Methodist and prone to speak of Britons. As she phrased it herself in 1984, during the Miners' Strike: 'We had to fight an enemy without in the Falklands. We always have to be aware of the enemy within, which is more difficult and more dangerous to liberty.'[16] For Mrs Thatcher, liberty, which was Britain's gift to the world, was the standard to which the British people were asked to rally in order to quell the enemy within – the miners – as much as the enemy without – General Galtieri. Thatcher's strength was the capacity not to appeal to some already constituted sense of Britishness – but to orchestrate elements of the national life and history, often contradictory ones, and help them make persuasive sense in her story.

Unsettling Britain

If Mrs Thatcher's regime tried to settle Britain and the British, the project of the day ought now to be to *unsettle* it – to keep open a range of meanings around Britishness. What it is to be British ought always to be plural, not singular as Mrs Thatcher contended: heterogeneous rather than pure; incomplete rather than monumentally finished. This is not simply ethically preferable to the 'Keep Britain Pure' position that was at the core of Mrs Thatcher's rhetoric; it also answers more adequately to the country's history as well as to Britain's present needs where a willingness to embrace heterogeneity as a resource rather than reject it as dilution, is likely to be a key to the country's political, economic and cultural success.

At one level the proposal to accept a heterogeneous Britain ought to be uncontentious since this place is made up of three countries (plus Ulster whose status in the United Kingdom is now as ever unclear), and so in the most obvious sense has lived with multiple affiliations and loyalties for a very long time. So settled is this settled country, in fact, that it doesn't even have a settled name. It's certainly arguable that its variety of names is simply a symptom of something else: that there isn't even agreement about what the nation-state is to be identified with: the monarch (United Kingdom), the people (Scottish, Welsh, etc.) or the systems of government? The passport may well say British – and of course Great Britain was effectively founded in 1707. But since 1801 it has been more accurate, if in practice unusual, to call the country the United Kingdom of Great Britain and Ireland

(and after 1921, this became Northern Ireland). But to do this leaves us with a country around the same age as the United States of America, an unsettling thought when the orthodox stories about Britain rattle on about how old this country is. And anyway, how many of the British say that they are from the UK?

Whatever the current fraught concern with national identity, not the least of the opportunities it offers is to flush out the English – for among the nations of this island it is they who have been most reluctant to come face to face. Of course for some this prospect is so unimaginable that they opt for the role of national elegist as was the case recently with academic historian and pundit David Starkey who wrote in the *Guardian*: 'England, like that other great empire of Rome, is dead. Like Rome, it survives as a legal system and a literature. It has become a place of the mind.'[17] Starkey's words suggest just how traumatic it may be for the English who have put others under the spotlight to find themselves the subject of examination.

Perhaps it is the intimate yet superior way in which the English have lived with so many other groups that has allowed them not to think of themselves. English slides so easily into British – whether in the case of the BBC where there is a BBC Scotland but no BBC England; or at crucial moments such as 1939 when a certain politician was invited to 'speak for England'. When daily newspapers recently demanded that Private Clegg as an Englishman accused of murder in Northern Ireland, should have access to British justice in the form of a jury trial, but did not go on to extend it to others tried in the Diplock courts in Northern Ireland, they were only doing what the English have often done: claim for themselves rights they don't feel the rest of the United Kingdom (never mind anywhere else) deserve. This has been going on for a long time, at least since the Welsh, in the words of the historian Gwyn Williams, were turned into 'unpersons without civil rights' during Glyn Dwr's rebellion by 'ferociously racist penal legislation'.[18]

Mongrel Britain

What is needed now, then, not only in relationship to England, but also with the whole of Britain, is a way of thinking about national identity that recognizes the extraordinary diversity, past and present, within the islands without making the mistake of thinking that Britain is made up of a series of archipelagoes. The danger of this 'archipelagoization' is most clear in 'racial' terms where the equation of Britishness and whiteness, enshrined not least in the British Nationality Act passed in 1981, has led certain black groups to adopt their own 'Keep Black Pure' line, whether the children of Nation of Islam or a strand of British Muslims.[19] Both sides of the 'fundamentalist' coin want to resist the import-export culture, which has been going on for centuries and retain fantasies of virginity. But dreams of purity also arise in more surprising quarters. In a review in the *Guardian* of a recent biography of Tony Blair, Michael Foot said Cherie Blair was 'pure English working-class' before he remembered she was partly Irish.[20] Against all such dreams of purity – whether of class, culture or nation or religion – we need to insist upon the historical experience of interpenetration. Caribbean Welshness or Asian Scottishness is no more a contradiction – despite what the recent Census would lead you to believe – than any of the many other combinations that are possible within Britain.

But given what is happening in the rest of Europe, the impulse towards a radical simplification and towards separation in Britain may be strong – along ethnic and national lines. Where such an impulse seems most strong at present is in Scotland, not surprisingly, given the gap between the political make-up of Scotland and Westminster.[21] It's possible to imagine someone weary of the continuing cultural, political and economic dominance by England of Britain saying, 'Let's start by simply shuffling off British identity' and going on to demand that the four countries are separated out: England, (Northern) Ireland, Scotland, Wales. The attractions of this are obvious and it would at least allow the possibility of recognizing the complexity that lies behind the term Britain. And there are certainly histories that can be called Scottish or Welsh histories that cannot be swallowed up in what has passed for British history and ought not to pass as footnotes to English history. And of course there are problems that are peculiar to each of the countries. If it is the Tory Party in England in the 1990s that has been subject to accusations of sleaze, the culprit in Scotland has been the Labour Party, at Monklands – something difficult to blame on the English.

It may be that the groundswell, say, in Scotland against London will demand more than devolution, will insist on independence – an independence which wants to see a Euro-federalist solution to the present battle over Britain. But even if this were the case, the issue of national identity in this island won't simply go away. First, the problem of definition isn't evaded by replacing Britishness with, say, Scottishness, if the belief is that the latter is transparent. As numerous commentators have said, there is at least as much heterogeneity within Scotland as there is between Scotland and England; and as Gwyn Williams has argued eloquently in *When Was Wales*? the North Wales Welsh have been historically reluctant to acknowledge the English-speaking people of the industrialized South as Welsh, and have been happier to talk of them as British or even, the worst insult, as English.[22]

It may well be that there are – as Settlerwatch who seem to wish to expel the English from Scotland claim – problems of the power of the English within Scotland, but what is important is that these problems are not formulated in terms of purity or impurity. It simply ought to be too late in history for that. This is a mongrel island and the people who make up its populations of the countries here have historically been mongrels. As Victor Kiernan, an historian, has said, the British are 'clearly among the most ethnically composite of the Europeans'.[23]

The second problem set up by the separatist position, which believes that smaller units are more clear-cut, is that it simply won't face up to how intimately the countries that make up Britain and the United Kingdom have been involved. While this could be shown by looking at the complex legal relationship among the countries, it is more visible and emotionally entangled in the field of sport. It isn't as if even on the sportsfield our loyalties are settled. For instance in football there are four countries including Northern Ireland, while in Rugby Union there are four 'home' countries (including the whole of Ireland) who play overseas as the British Lions; in Athletics there is a Great Britain team as there is in Rugby League even though the majority of players in the latter are drawn from a couple of counties in the north of England. Such is the complexity of the history, then, that if we are to move beyond the current version of Britishness – which is often a smokescreen for Englishness – it can only be done by going forward.

Of course part of the attraction of 'Europe' among some of the Scots and Welsh (as well as some of the English) is that it can apparently offer a way out from under a Great Britain dominated by the English. Through a hyphen the Welsh can become Welsh-Europeans, the Scots, Scots-Europeans and so on. But repentance is unlike innocence, as my Methodist teachers taught me, and there is no way *back* for any of the countries that make up the United Kingdom of Great Britain and Northern Ireland to some pristine and uncontaminated identity before the weddings – which in some cases were certainly shotgun.

It may be that Europe does offer great opportunities for the various nations that make up this nation-state, but joining Europe will resolve nothing if the British use it as another excuse for postponing having to come face to face with themselves. For coming face to face involves not only facing up to each of the historical identities of the countries that make up these islands in relationship with each other, and in relationship with Europe but also in relationship to the countries which once made up the Empire and whose histories and those of the British sometimes seem like that of Siamese twins. Sometimes the lust after Europe can seem just another excuse for amnesia about the historical connections of the British with other parts of the globe: from America to Hong Kong, from Jamaica to India. The question is: can Britain recognize this and reinvent itself and learn to live with its own diversity and that of others and slough off the profound habit of rule and superiority which has been part of its history?

Towards 2000

In the next century national identity will not exhaust the wider affiliations and loyalties that people will wish to commit themselves to within these islands. It does not exhaust them now. Some of these identities are familial, some local; some more expansive; some are built around gender and others around generation. But among the available identities are – and will remain for the foreseeable future – national ones. What is needed now are identities in Britain that do not have to be thought of primarily as a badge of either pride or shame. Too often at present national identity is talked of as if the whole of the British people were some rather large cricket team that either had or had not done its best. Being British (or for that matter being Scottish or Welsh or English) needs rather to be something you see is in your interest and something you want. Of course to propose a utilitarian version of national identity, one that is sufficiently flexible to allow numerous groups to have an interest and pleasure in subscribing to, may seem in poor taste. But it is precisely how Linda Colley speaks of the British national identity forged in the eighteenth century – it was something not inherited but learned, and something in the interest of the variety of ethnic groups to learn.[24] Is it now possible to make Britishness a sufficiently attractive and usable identity that people would wish to subscribe to? If it isn't, it does not deserve our attention. If it is, then a critical issue would have to be the forging of political and cultural institutions which can support and nurture these multiple affiliations and loyalties, rather than place them in a simple hierarchy. After all, such ranking was not always the case in the past. British national identity in the eighteenth century was an identity that did not demand the annulment of other loyalties. Professor Colley makes this clear throughout her book, nowhere more so than when she writes that Iolo Morganwg, the late eighteenth-century radical writer, could unhesitatingly say that Welsh was one of his two native tongues.[25]

It is that recognition of the possibilities and pleasures of multiple belonging that we need to engender – in order that we can see how foolish was Norman Tebbit's claim that a single decision, the team for which you cheer, of all things, is the litmus paper of your identity and loyalty. This seems to be a very difficult lesson to learn in Britain, although given the heterogeneous mix of peoples and histories that have nourished the history of the present British people, it ought not to be.

What we need now is a recognition that we can take the vexatious complexities of Britain's history and make of them an opportunity. This won't make for restful days and nights, even in that bolthole of the politician's mind, middle England. This is going to be more not less of a turbulent place, as Britain negotiates its life with itself and others, in an increasingly globalized world. What this Britain will need – among much else – are politicians who are willing to enter this turbulence and find ways of telling national stories that are inclusive and open-ended.

But these stories are going to be told in a world, as we all know, increasingly shaped by technologies that are effectively global, where the defining and most powerful images of national identity are likely to be on one form of screen or another. At this point a melancholic sigh about a new global homogenization and the death of national cultures is usually expected and often provided. Or there are jokes about the British lion tamed by a mouse. But what if this new technology is seen as an opportunity rather than a deadly virus –

and it is a simple fact that British homes are better provided with computers than their European neighbours. For whatever is put on the digital highway, it will undoubtedly include the contents of the old storehouses of national identity – libraries, galleries and even television stations – which will be able to be reconfigured in unimaginable ways. Perhaps this might presage a new campaign around literacy within Britain, not literacy in the usual sense but on *literacy about the nation*. For the importance of these new screens is not merely that they have the potential to disseminate and democratize knowledge about the nation. They remind us all of the provisionality of what appears on them, and of our power to act on them in ways that might aid us. This electronic world may provide us with an opportunity to imagine British national identity not as something immovable as a monument nor something that needs to be tended as a lawn but as something as provisional and capable of transformation as a wave; a wave that we might all ride.

LEARNING

Learning has gained a central position in modern societies. As life has become ever more shaped by information and knowledge – and by who has it and who lacks it – governments have understood just how important it is to foster effective institutions and cultures of learning.

Unfortunately, many of the dominant ideas about education are still stuck in the past – in the era of factory-based schooling, before the advent of the telephone and television, let alone the computer and CD-ROM. When it comes to policies, governments are far better at increasing the outputs of qualifications than they are at increasing levels of understanding. Moreover most writings about education assume that it all takes place within traditional educational institutions, schools and universities when in fact today learning takes place in all kinds of institutions, in factories and on television, in homes and clubs and in offices.

The essays in this section offer radical insights into how learning needs to change. Howard Gardner sets out his theories of multiple intelligence which widen the ambit of learning from the 'logical-analytical' to broader skills such as interpersonal and intrapersonal intelligence. He makes the case for a different structure of schooling and teaching, effectively seeing learning in terms of a learning ecology that includes parents and organizations external to educational institutions such as businesses.

David Hargreaves takes these ideas a step further with a far-reaching analysis of the future of teaching and schooling in which teaching would be redefined with a more complex division of labour between 'master' teachers and paraprofessionals, many of whom might be transferred from other professions in middle age. He also explains why we need far more specialist schools as well as general purpose, standard ones, in an argument that leapfrogs the often stale arguments about schools selection. Finally Douglas Hague highlights the importance of cultural change in enabling all types of organizations to learn – to think and adapt to their changing situation.

9

Opening Minds

HOWARD GARDNER

Over the last ten years the UK, like the USA, has been through two waves of concern about education. The first wave of reform focused on the need to raise standards and to make sure that all students had basic skills, like sight reading and elementary arithmetic. The second wave focused on the need to dismantle parts of the overblown bureaucracy and to return more of a school's decision-making to the site of the school itself.

What is striking is that both of these waves were silent about purpose. Dozens of articles appeared on educational reform without any discussion of the purposes of an education. It was easier to agree about the problems that existed – poorly performing students; bloated bureaucracy that pushed papers rather than taught students – than to agree about the kind of education they wanted.

In what follows I want to make four main points which arise out of the deficiencies of this debate. Firstly, I shall make the case that education should produce understanding. Secondly, I shall argue that education the world over fails to produce understanding. Thirdly, I shall show why even our best students in the best schools do not understand. And finally, I shall indicate what might be done about this unsettling state of affairs.

The principal purpose of education is, in my view, to produce understanding, both of various disciplines and of the world we live in. But how do we define understanding, and how do we know that we have achieved it? I shall define understanding simply as the capacity to apply knowledge, facts, concepts and skills in new situations where they are appropriate. Unless students can apply what they have learned in school to new situations, there is no evidence that they have understood.

For example, in its public rationale for its actions, the USA did not display much understanding during the Gulf War. If a person understands something about the Middle East, he or she will know that problems cannot be solved simply by turning a dictator into a monster or seeking to eliminate him, no matter how loathsome he might be. If a person understands something about physics, he or she will be able to aim a Patriot missile so that it will intersect a Scud. If people understand something about economics, they will appreciate that a country cannot suddenly spend billions of dollars on activities without some negative fallout resulting. Except for the smart computers, few policy-makers or policy-articulators have demonstrated much understanding in any of these areas.

Having defined the goal of understanding, we must face the bitter truth that most students in schools all over the world do not understand. In other words, given situations in which they must apply their 'school knowledge', they do not know what to do. They may have been able to regurgitate a learned response in the 'text-test' context, where one repeats the answer given in the textbook; they may be able to engage in a 'correct answer compromise', where teachers and students tacitly agree not to push one another, or simply to accept the response which the teacher has agreed to count as correct. But they fail to display sufficient understanding necessary to appreciate that the USA cannot eradicate Middle Eastern conflicts simply by eliminating Saddam Hussein or Muramar Qaddafi. Rather than revealing awareness of the complex amalgam of factors that interact in foreign policy, they readily adopt the same black-and-white solutions as would the young viewer of *Star Wars*.

A particularly telling example can be found in physics. Even students who excel in physics at the best universities do not understand the meaning of the basic principles of the discipline. The very students who receive distinctions answer very much like five-year-olds once they are tested outside the school context. They believe, much as a young child does, in mysterious forces. When asked about what happens when a coin is tossed, they speak of forces being transferred from the flipping finger to the coin, slowly petering out as the coin rises, and then, when the coin has lost the transferred energy, it collapses to the ground. In truth, once the coin is released the only force acting on it is the downward pull of gravity. But it takes years of physics thinking to understand this deeply. Thus the undergraduate and the five-year-old both readily revert to Aristotelian if not pre-Socratic thinking where objects move because of occult forces that seem to have a will and intentionality of their own.

But this lack of understanding is not limited to a difficult subject such as physics; it occurs across the curriculum. Even biology students who have taken two or three years of courses continue to regard evolution as an inexorable trend toward perfection, with each species being guided by an unseen hand to be more perfect than its predecessors. Mathematics students may master algorithms perfectly; they may know how to plug numbers into an equation when the numbers are given in a certain order. But that is not understanding. Once the problem is posed in an unfamiliar way, the students do not know what to do. They have mastered the syntax or the algorithm – the set of rules – but unless they understand what the formula refers to, they cannot use it in a generative way. Students are not alone in this respect. Many of us sense deep down that even when we give the desired answer, we do not really understand; if the question were phrased just a bit differently, we would fail. Those in history and the arts are not immune to this problem. A student will take a test about the causes of the First World War, brilliantly regurgitating the many factors that he or she has been taught. But asked about the causes of the troubles in the Middle East, however, this same student is likely to give the same stereotyping answer as a five-year-old – that bad guy called Saddam Hussein.

And those in the arts have known for seventy years how elusive is understanding. I. A. Richards asked Cambridge undergraduates to analyse poems and to judge their merit. He performed only one manipulation – he removed the authors' names. Under these conditions, England's 'best and brightest' spurned the great, time-honoured works and displayed the same aesthetic as a young school child. If it rhymed and the topic was pleasant, the poem was good; if not, it was cast upon the literary junk heap. It was as if sophisticated points about the use of language, the exploration of imagery, the presentation of metaphorical themes had either been forgotten or consciously rejected in favour of a simplistic aesthetic.

If we provisionally accept that even our best students rarely display understanding, can we explain why this is the case? Is it because our students are so stupid, or our schools so poor? Rather the answer is that we have far underestimated the strength of ideas that children develop when they are very young. In the first several years of life, without direct tutelage, young children develop very powerful theories about how the world works – the physical world, the world of living things, the mental and psychological worlds of oneself and others. In some ways these ideas are serviceable – the world does look flat, heavy objects do seem to fall more quickly than lighter ones, people who look the way you do are nicer than those who look different – but each of these ideas, and thousands like them, is wrong.

School is meant to teach us better, deeper ways of thinking about the world. And our curricula do contain the kernel of such ideas. However, schools and teachers have far underestimated the strength of children's theories, scripts, stereotypes and misconceptions. They have failed to engage these early misleading ideas. The result is that students – especially good students – learn to regurgitate what they have been taught but never actually change their underlying beliefs – ones arrived at in early childhood and inconsistent with the insights gained by scholars over the centuries. Once removed from school, they revert immediately to these older, more robust ideas.

In short, within all of us is the mind of the five-year-old struggling to get out. Early in life, a set of ideas is deeply etched onto the surface of the mind. The only way to replace these early patterns is to sand them off and painstakingly construct new ones. Instead, we ignore the early etchings and simply allow them to become coated with dust. As soon as the dust of school has settled, the etchings re-emerge. This seems a discouraging state of affairs: students – even good students – who do not understand, and a set of very powerful ideas, formed early in life, which prove virtually unremovable.

But some students do come to understand. Some individuals – we call them experts – are able to think about the world in new, more precise ways, and to explain new things that occur. What can we do to help our students become more expert, to enhance their understanding? The first clues come from two institutions, one very old and the other very new. In the first, apprenticeships, the young person works in the presence of an older expert, who exemplifies the useful deployment of knowledge every day. Under such conditions, the learner comes to see the meanings of the procedures in his or her field, and is far less likely simply to 'go through the motions'.

In the new institution, hands-on museums, youngsters have the chance to try out their skills in a variety of situations. They can conduct experiments and relate the formal terminology and equations of schools to the domains where these are applied. They are then much more likely to understand the concepts and principles to which they are introduced.

But though apprenticeships and children's museums may have their appeal, they would seem impractical and impracticable. We cannot return to the Middle Ages nor convert each school into a children's museum. However, it is possible to reflect the ideas about learning and understanding that these institutions embody in new educational practices.

We can fashion an education for understanding. To do so we must recognize the reasons for, and the power of, early forms of understanding. We must respect them. And we must work constantly to question them. In the sciences, we need challenging encounters, where students confront their early conceptions each day and see where these are adequate and where they are deficient. In maths, we must explore the domains to which the formulae apply and understand how they operate. In social sciences and the arts, we must learn to take multiple perspectives – to look at historical events or at works of art from a variety of perspectives.

People have multiple forms of intelligence. Our existing curricula heavily emphasize just two of these, what I call logical-mathematical intelligence, and linguistic intelligence. But there are also other forms: there is musical intelligence; there is the spatial intelligence which is displayed by sailors, engineers, surgeons and painters; the naturalist intelligence, valued in biologists, hunters and designers; and the bodily-kinaesthetic intelligence exhibited by dancers, athletes and craftspeople. There are also two other forms of personal intelligence: the interpersonal intelligence that recognizes how to understand other people, shown by politicians, teachers and salespeople, and the intrapersonal intelligence of self-understanding.

To foster these kinds of intelligence we need a far-reaching change in our understanding of learning and schooling. And we need, I believe, to develop the notion of an individual-centred school, one geared to optimal understanding and development of each student's cognitive profile, their mix of the different forms of intelligence.

The design of the ideal school of the future is based upon two assumptions. The first is that not all people have the same interests and abilities, and that not all of us learn in the same way. The second assumption is the one that hurts:

that nowadays no one person can learn everything there is to learn. We would all like, as we believe Renaissance men and women did, to know everything, or at least to believe in the potential of knowing everything, but that ideal clearly is not possible any more. Choice is therefore inevitable, and the choices that we make for ourselves, and for the people who are under our charge, might as well be informed choices. An individual-centred school would be rich in assessment of individual abilities and proclivities. I would seek to match individuals not only to curricular areas, but also to particular ways of teaching those subjects. And after the first few grades, the school would also seek to match individuals with the various kinds of life and work options that are available in their culture.

I want to propose a new set of roles for educators that might make this vision a reality. First of all, we might have what I will call 'assessment specialists'. The job of these people would be to try to understand as sensitively and comprehensively as possible the abilities and interests of the students in a school. It would be very important, however, that the assessment specialists use 'intelligence-fair' instruments. We want to be able to look specifically and directly at spatial abilities, at personal abilities, and the like, and not through the usual lenses of the linguistic and logical-mathematical intelligences. Up until now nearly all assessment has depended indirectly on measurement of those abilities; if students are not strong in those two areas, their abilities in other areas may be obscured.

Once we begin to try to assess other kinds of intelligences directly, I am confident that particular students will reveal strengths in quite different areas, and the notion of general brightness will disappear or become greatly attenuated.

In addition to the assessment specialist, the school of the future might have the 'student-curriculum broker'. It would be his or her job to help match students' profiles, goals and interests to particular curricula and to particular styles of learning. Incidentally, I think that the new interactive technologies offer considerable promise in this area: it will probably be much easier in the future for 'brokers' to match individual students to ways of learning that prove comfortable for them.

There should also be, I think, a 'school-community broker', who would match students to learning opportunities in the wider community. It would be this person's job to find situations in the community, particularly options not available in the school, for children who exhibit the usual cognitive profiles. I have in mind apprenticeships, mentorships, internships in organizations, 'big brothers', 'big sisters' – individuals and organizations with whom these students might work to secure a feeling for different kinds of vocational and avocational roles in the society. I am not worried about those occasional youngsters who are good in everything. They will succeed in any case. I am concerned about those who don't shine in the standardized tests, and who, therefore, tend to be written off as not having gifts of any kind. It seems to me that the school-community broker could spot these youngsters and find placements in the community that provide chances for them to shine.

There is ample room in this vision for teachers, as well, and also for master teachers. In my view, teachers would be freed to do what they are supposed to do, which is to teach their subject matter, in their preferred style of teaching. The job of master teacher would be very demanding. It would involve, first of all, supervising the novice teachers and guiding them; but the master teacher would also seek to ensure that the complex student-assessment-curriculum-community equation is balanced appropriately. If the equation is seriously unbalanced, master teachers would intervene and suggest ways to make things better.

Clearly, what I am describing is a tall order; it might even be called utopian. And there is a major risk to this programme, of which I am well aware. That is the risk of premature billeting. There is, however, nothing inherent in the approach that I have described that demands such early over-determination

– quite the contrary. It seems to me that early identification of strengths can be very helpful in indicating what kinds of experiences children might profit from; but early identification of weaknesses can be equally important. If a weakness is identified early, there is a chance to attend to it before it is too late, and to come up with alternative ways of teaching or of covering an important skill area.

We now have the technological and the human resources to implement such an individual-centred school. Achieving it is a question of will, including the will to withstand the current enormous pressures toward uniformity and one-dimensional assessments. There are strong pressures now, which you read about every day in the newspapers, to compare students, to compare teachers, states, even entire countries using one dimension or criterion, a kind of a crypto-IQ assessment. Clearly, everything I have described stands in direct opposition to that particular view of the world. Indeed that is my intent – to provide a ringing indictment of such one-track thinking.

I believe that in our society we suffer from three biases, which I have nicknamed 'Westist', 'Testist' and 'Bestist'. 'Westist' involves putting certain Western cultural values, which date back to Socrates, on a pedestal.

Logical thinking, for example, is important; rationality is important; but they are not the only virtues. And indeed, many societies rightly value an understanding of other people, a sensitivity to the arts, or the capacity to control one's own emotions.

'Testist' suggests a bias towards focusing upon those human abilities or approaches that are readily testable. If it can't be tested, it sometimes seems, it is not worth paying attention to. My feeling is that assessment can be much broader, much more humane than it is now, and that psychologists should spend less time ranking people and more time trying to help them.

'Bestist', the belief that all the answers to a given problem lie in one certain approach, such as logical-mathematical thinking, can be very dangerous. This is the fallacy to which computer scientists and others immersed in the latest technology may be particularly prone – 'If it doesn't compute, it doesn't count'. Current views of intellect need to be leavened with other more comprehensive points of view, including ones that are sensitive to contextual issues, ones that reflect values and priorities of other societies, and ones acknowledging that the questions asked are as vital as the answers put forth.

It is of the utmost importance that we recognize and nurture all of the varied human intelligences, and all of the combinations of intelligences. We are all so different largely because we all have different combinations of intelligences. If we recognize this, I think we will have at least a better chance of dealing appropriately with the many problems that we face in the world. If we can mobilize the spectrum of human abilities, not only will people feel better about themselves and more competent; it is even possible that they will also feel more engaged and better able to join the rest of the world community in working for the broader good. Perhaps if we can mobilize the full range of human intelligences and ally them to an ethical sense, we can even help to increase the likelihood of our survival on this planet.

10

Transforming the Dinosaurs

DOUGLAS HAGUE

> An artist must never be a prisoner of himself, prisoner of a style, prisoner of a reputation, prisoner of success ... Did not the Goncourt brothers write that Japanese artists of the great period changed their names several times during their lives? ... They wanted to protect their freedom.
>
> MATISSE

The lesson of the dinosaurs is that creatures which cannot adapt to external change do not survive. The same is true of organizations, especially in the private sector. If there are exceptions to this Darwinian rule, they are in the public sector where bodies created to support one phase of a country's development may not suit what is required later and yet are not allowed to fail. For example, a country like Britain cannot operate without a foreign policy or a monetary policy; thus the Foreign Office and the Bank of England cannot simply be closed down, even though discussion with opinion formers reveals great unhappiness about the performance of both.

The role of this essay is twofold. Its emphasis is on organizations which no longer keep up with a changing world. Either they fail to meet what external attitudes and developments require of them, as has happened with top executive pay in Britain's privatized companies. Or they may fail to keep up with best practice in internal policies or administration. I examine ways in which such organizations can be improved, even transformed.

The subsidiary theme is that, however unpalatable it may be, the final resort may be closure, especially if the organization which cannot be rescued is one of many with a similar role, as with hospitals or schools.

Any analysis of the success or failure of organizations in renewing themselves, has to concentrate on organizational culture. Sociologists define this as reflecting the way those in the organization think and act as they carry out their tasks, but an organization's culture is not independent. To work, it must flow directly from the organization's values and ethos. Values and ethos take precedence over culture because they represent the guiding beliefs which define the character, identity – personality even – of an organization. They define for the body and those who work in it 'what we stand for' or 'the kind of people we are'.

Beginning from ethos and values, those who work in an organization will define its culture as reflecting how they think and act. It shows 'how we do things here',[1] and will in time become a reflex response to demands made on it. It follows that established cultures become a problem when the environment and circumstances of the organization change so much that the inherited 'reflex response' will no longer do.

This means in turn that if culture and values are not compatible, those who work in an organization may find it difficult to take their work seriously. The culture will not fit with the ethos/values which the organization pretends to espouse and sooner or later, employees will become disillusioned and resentful.

In short, the values and culture of any organization, public or private, should be compatible. As time moves on and the world changes, values will change and the culture will need to change too. The whole thrust of this paper is that such change is not easy. But organizational cultures can be changed and there are four ways of doing so.

The first is *coercion*, for example, the pressure exerted by competition or recession, which forces cultural change on businesses. Businesses are also coerced by threatened or actual takeover bids, or by strikes. All organizations are coerced by direct government interference in their affairs, and even more so by war, occupation by an enemy, or revolution.

The second mechanism is *contagion* which occurs when individuals or groups move in, or are brought in, to enable an organization to absorb the culture of the organizations from which they come. This is by no means easy because individuals cannot achieve change on their own. Nor indeed can a group of newcomers if they come from different organizations, and do not share a common culture. Change depends on there being a coherent critical mass of contagion.[2] Takeovers are one way of providing this, so long as they bring a team which is sufficiently big, coherent or clever to reinforce its numbers and get its way.

The third approach is *coaching*. When a sufficient number of an organization's management team decides that the culture must be changed they may seek outside help. The organization brings in experts to identify what changes in culture are needed and to find ways of achieving them. There is broad agreement among experts on organizational change about how this can be done although there is disagreement about the detail, as individual consultancies seek to promote their own approaches.

The fourth, and most desirable way of changing a culture is for the organization to set about doing so for itself. It is desirable because an organization which learns how to define and establish a new culture will be able to change it further if there are continuing internal or external shifts. It is, in today's vogue phrase, a *learning* organisation.[3] Few bodies in Britain have yet moved far in this direction, but it is what the future requires. There are three reasons. First, we are moving into a world where knowledge is the basis for producing many goods and services – aeroplanes or telecommunications systems, for example – and where knowledge itself is traded, in the form of research and development, market information, consultancy, training, etc.

The second reason derives from the fact that, to enable people to operate well in the knowledge age, the educational system will have to devote more time to helping them to learn how to learn. Having done so, they will need to continue to learn as individuals, which most people enjoy provided that the educational system has not destroyed their ability to do so. Third, the issue goes beyond individuals. Organizations are increasingly seeing the need for employees to learn within their own teams. Most of us have had the enjoyable experience of working at some time in a successful team, with people working well together and so producing good results. What we actually enjoyed was being part of a learning organization. Many larger organizations have now reached the stage where learning teams can be set up, their members encouraged by their experiences in earlier days or other fields. Where that does not happen, and perhaps even if it does, coercion, contagion and coaching will be needed too.

Cultures in the Private Sector

The enormous range of organizations in the private sector, from large companies to one-man businesses, results in a similar range of cultures. In terms of numbers, small businesses dominate the economy; but by employment and turnover the position is substantially reversed. Out of some 3.5 million businesses in the UK only 3000 employ more than 500 people and they account for half of business employment and two-thirds of turnover.

Some large companies work hard to maintain their cultures – or to change them when competitive success or survival requires that. The great majority of small businesses rarely consider their cultures and certainly do not devote time or energy to consciously altering them. But those cultures exist and many are very strong.

Inevitably, business cultures lag behind the ideal. Large,

well-established companies become overbureaucratic as times passes so that, at intervals, substantial cultural change is attempted, but not always successfully. Many multinational corporations go to great lengths to maintain the same company culture in all countries where they operate, seeing this as so important for business success that they will tolerate the occasional conflicts with local governments and communities which result. Japanese companies moving into the UK bring their culture with them, and so on. Most small, entrepreneurial companies inherit a culture from their founder, often a rather authoritarian one, that can inhibit later growth.

In recent years, media and public debate has concentrated on the culture at board level in large companies – on 'corporate governance'. In the early 1990s, the worry was whether there was sufficient oversight and engagement by major investors or whether their weakness allowed some firms to act irresponsibly, even illegally. A committee chaired by Sir Adrian Cadbury recommended changes, especially a greater role for nonexecutive directors through audit and remuneration committees.

More recently, concern has focused on the pay and perks of company directors, especially in the privatized utility companies, for example, gas, electricity and water. Another committee of enquiry, this time chaired by Sir Richard Greenbury, recommended full disclosure of payments, including pension contributions, to all directors in quoted companies.

There was also concern in the early 1990s over the length of time which about a dozen chairmen or chief executives of very big companies had been in office – seven of the twelve had been there for more than twenty years. These figures may be misleading for the future. Most of the twelve have now retired and, on average, the holders of their posts have been there for about five years. Nevertheless, if one looks simply at company directorships – executive or nonexecutive – a surprising number of people have served on the board of a particular company for more than twenty years. I will return to this issue later.

The Public Sector

By comparison with the private sector, the public sector appears stable, even sedate. It is certainly more homogeneous, but in some respects it is more complex. Running a private business can be rather easy compared with operating in the public sector.

The first reason may appear paradoxical. A modern business deals with great complexity, arising from its technology, products, processes and people. A large company will have thousands of employees, each with their personal skills, attitudes to work, private lives, etc. It will sell hundreds of products, all with their own customers, production problems, marketing programmes, and so on. It will operate in many localities, each with its local circumstances. And this list is only a beginning.

Nor is it static. The elements in it and the relationships between them, will steadily change. In all organizations – even small ones – there will be great complexity, which will be increased by the external influence of competition, legislation, the rules and procedures of the stock exchange, and so on. Complexity drives those who manage businesses to make the process of management tolerable by heroic simplification.

They reduce the huge complexity of the business to a relatively small number of figures – often financial – in its management accounts and other documents. To be sure, the documents may themselves be complex but they are nevertheless simple compared with the complexity they are reflecting. A management will often simplify its task by concentrating on equating changes in performance with changes in profit. This attitude is supported by reports in the media which frequently reduce the huge variety of a multinational business to a single profit figure – the ultimate variety reduction.[4] They do not reflect complex systems; they avoid admitting that they *are* complex. The more private businesses 'manage by numbers', the more the moral dilemmas and intellectual conundrums which management could – perhaps should – face are concealed or avoided.

The second simplicity open to a private business is that it can define its purpose and objectives for itself in the light of its values. If part of the company becomes too unimportant or too burdensome for nonfinancial reasons, it can be closed down or sold. More frequently, a unit or subsidiary will be closed because it is losing money and because, were losses to continue, the future of the whole business would be threatened. The media and the public may agonize about jobs lost and markets sacrificed: there may well be agonizing within the business. But the company can insist that its decision is acceptable because, in the end, it is compatible with its values.

The three big differences between the public and private sectors are therefore these. First, the role of a public sector organization is defined for it, however generally, from outside. Its objectives will almost always be broader than those of a profit-oriented private sector entity. Among other things, this means that it is harder to 'bend the rules', and that more people must be involved in, and told about, decisions. There is a consequent slowness or reluctance to change, sometimes even to act.

The second big difference is that it is almost always more difficult for a public sector organization to abandon activities than it is for a private business. Schools cannot decide to stop educating five-year-olds. The health service cannot refuse to treat patients in Sussex. Yet a private company can easily withdraw from some markets, or reduce its product range.

The third difference is that, by comparison with the private sector, top civil servants are moved between jobs more frequently and deliberately. This is one clear benefit which derives from the fact that the civil service is monolithic. Movement can be planned centrally – and enforced. So, Sir Robert (now Lord) Armstrong was Secretary to the Cabinet for eight years; Sir Peter Middleton was Head of the Treasury for eight years and Sir Douglas Wass for nine. The four predecessors of the present Permanent Secretary of the Department for Education served for an average of less than five years.

There are, however, worries about the fact that so few of the leading mandarins move outside the public sector during their careers. Many do so after they retire. We return to this issue later.

The Cultures of the Civil Service and Education

Unlike the private sector, the public sector outside the civil service is dominated by large groupings of related organizations dealing with functional fields like health, education or policing. From these we shall consider the core civil service, which has its individual culture, and education – schools and universities – where several cultures interact.

The civil service is chosen because it plays a dominant role in national policy making. Education is considered because, apart from the clashes of culture which it demonstrates, its performance in the next decade will considerably influence the success which Britain has in moving into the knowledge age and in developing 'learning organizations'.

The Civil Service

The civil service is at its best when establishing procedures, setting rules and applying these, on the whole rigorously, to high-volume and rather routine activities, like the payment of social security benefits. Such routine processing activities – for example, the issuing of driving and vehicle licences – have been hived off to more than a hundred relatively independent organizations. These 'Next Steps' agencies are still part of the civil service and therefore part of government but some of them will probably soon be privatized. The Stationery Office may well be one of the first.

With these functions devolved, the core civil service is concentrating on policy work and the supervision of the agencies. To do that well will call for a substantial change in the way civil servants think and operate.[5] Many of them will deny this. But they will do so mainly because they under-rate their own deficiencies in tackling issues of strategy and policy. In my view there are three major weaknesses.

First, the traditional qualities instilled into civil servants by their training and reinforced by the civil service culture are inappropriate for policy work. This requires vision, imagination and innovation, not obedience to rules established by others and careful attention to detail.

Second, the civil service culture is predominantly literary. The best civil servants write well, but even the best writing is not always sufficient. To make sense of the complex socio-technical systems of the modern world requires theory and analysis to match. Mathematics, statistics and diagrams are essential.[6]

This leads to the third failing. Such modes of thought give much the best results if used by groups, not individuals. Groups can best argue over equations, and even more diagrams, if they use such things as flipcharts and whiteboards. Indeed, some argue that the test today of how far someone is a leading-edge thinker is how long it takes him or her to jump to the whiteboard to show an equation or a diagram to others in the group.

Civil service thinking and policy making is too often a solitary process. Given the complexity of the world one person's brain, however outstanding, can no longer hope to analyse it well. To do so would require so large an investment of time in learning a range of academic and other disciplines that it is no longer practicable. In that sense, Renaissance Man is dead.

The analytical and policy work on which the central civil service will now concentrate requires not individuals but multidisciplinary teams, whose members between them have good scientific, technological, economic, social and managerial knowledge, together with down-to-earth intellectual and practical experience. The apparent failure of the civil service even to comprehend the issues which this raises, let alone to construct and use this kind of team, represents its most serious failing.[7]

When challenged, any mandarin will assure you that strenuous efforts are being made to improve civil service management. My own experience, for example with the financial management initiative, is that the Whitehall culture is too often unable to do little more than convert interesting managerial ideas into arid essays or boring check lists.

Some perceptive civil servants would argue that there is an even bigger gap. Sir Peter Kemp, a former permanent secretary for the civil service, believes that it lies between the policy makers and those responsible for implementation. The civil service lacks what he calls project managers who, told what a new policy is, will say, 'this is how to implement it', or even, 'this cannot be done'.

Education

I have already argued that, in the knowledge age, education is important because most people at work will need to know how to learn and how to pass knowledge on. The education system should therefore be working hard to wean students away from reliance on teachers and towards books, electronic data bases and interactive computer programmes. That this is not yet happening in the UK is indicated by the fact that staffing per student is higher in secondary schools than in the earlier stages of education. Chalk and talk also still play too big a part: schools are too concerned with the top left-hand corner of Figure 1.

Figure 1 provides a useful tool for studying educational institutions, which should have the initial responsibility for promoting a learning culture. The vertical side shows the components of education, the horizontal axis the means of learning. It draws on important and refreshing work by Howard Gardner, Professor of Education at the Harvard Graduate School, not least his book *Frames of Mind*.[8]

As in the USA, we in this country are instilled with the

FIGURE 1 *How to Analyze Educational Institution*

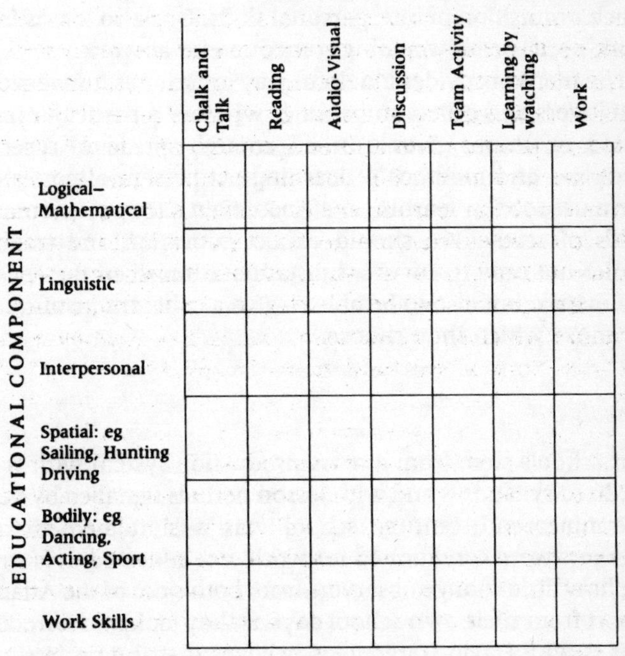

belief that the prime aim of education is to give us what Gardner calls logical-mathematical skills. Linguistic understanding is also given, but all too often without the ability actually to speak a foreign language at all well. The acquisition of interpersonal skills is largely ignored. So are spatial skills – like sailing or hunting – which are important in primitive societies, and whose modern equivalents can be found in construction, manufacturing and driving today. Finally, bodily skills may be acquired, such as dancing, acting and sports.

Along the top are shown the ways in which education is carried out. These begin with 'chalk and talk', the reading of books and the use of information and communications technology. All are largely concerned with logical mathematical learning. Only with discussion and teamwork is there much acquisition of interpersonal skills. One also learns from work itself, or by watching someone else at work.

The matrix provides a helpful way for schools, universities, employers and others to consider whether a particular institution or course gives a broad enough spread of types of discipline and methods of learning. At present almost all of them use too few learning methods, even if they offer enough fields of study. We should expect education and training bodies not only to cover a substantial number of the cells in the matrix, but also to be able to give a coherent justification for those which they choose.

Schools

Our schools stem from a mass-production system with standardized syllabuses and with lesson periods signalled by bells. The nineteenth-century school was a simulated factory. Workers were conditioned for work, not educated. It is striking how little change observers from both sides of the Atlantic report from their own school days as they look at classrooms. This is why David Hargreaves believes that the professional culture which teachers have created around the structure of the school and classroom may be the biggest barrier to educational change.[9]

Among the worst consequences of this is that politicians and many teachers believe that education takes place at school, when most learning is actually from family, friends, television and computers; even most parents agree that teaching calls for specialized teachers, whereas most children arrive at school having learned their own language with their mother the main teacher. Most school education remains hampered from the very beginning by this inhibiting parental/educational culture. Sensible movement towards more flexible classrooms, timetables and teaching methods is hampered. What happens at school is too artificial and contrived.

A related point has been well made by Howard Gardner. His book, *The Unschooled Mind*, points to the alarming transition faced by children when they start school. 'Somehow the natural or intuitive learning that takes place in one's home or immediate surroundings during the first years of life seems of an entirely different order from the school learning that is now required throughout the literate world.' He goes on: 'those of us in education have not appreciated the strength of the initial conceptions [and] stereotypes that students bring to their learning nor the difficulty of refashioning or eradicating them. We have failed to appreciate that in nearly every student there is a five-year-old "unschooled" mind struggling to get out and express itself.'[10]

Educators therefore need to exploit the innate powers of the infant mind, to recognize the difficulties which schoolchildren have in learning particular disciplines – not least mathematics – and, on this basis, to restructure the whole school system. Gardner argues that reform depends on working equally on four different issues: assessment, curriculum, teacher education and community support. British educational policy is homing in on some of these but in far too uninformed a way. Our educational culture has not caught up with the modern world.

How to 'deschool' one aspect of the classroom is shown by powerful research by (mainly American) cognitive scientists, which is splendidly summarized by John Bruer in *Schools for Thought*.[11] This shows that each child's education should as far as possible be tailored to his or her personal characteristics, skills and interests.

The research also emphasizes that few children 'learn to learn' as distinct from remembering what they have read or been told. This may fit the preconceptions of politicians dreaming of children 'sitting in rows' but does not meet the needs of the evolving knowledge age, where businesses 'want people who know how to learn'.[12] Employees must have higher order (especially learning) skills that were expected from only the best students a generation ago. Schools must move as quickly as is reasonable towards Bruer's key precept: 'Knowledge is constructed by learners, not transmitted by teachers. Learning is active, not passive.'[13]

To do this will require widespread experimentation and that means pluralism – much local experimentation. Unless there is dramatic change, this will conflict with one of the most inexplicable failings of the British educational culture at the political level. Despite – perhaps because of – the fact that politicians understand education so little, they too often engage in what David Hargreaves, in an outspoken critique, calls 'Utopian social engineering'. An ideal is defined – comprehensive schooling, or the National Curriculum, for example – and very large sums of money are found with no apparent difficulty to spend on this ideal. Yet, instead of being subject to local trials in a number of schools and disseminated only when difficulties have become clear and been resolved, these Utopian policies are 'generated with enormous confidence and then subjected to instant implementation'. For example, despite the predictions of problems, the National Curriculum was implemented in this way, with Sir Ron Dearing later brought in 'to sort it out'.[14]

With the National Curriculum, of course, the culture of the civil service came into play at the implementation stage. As a result, the size of the curriculum was itself too big and the amount of outside direction and form filling on a scale which only a civil servant could have thought appropriate.

English schools – Scotland, especially, organizes education much more successfully – are a battleground for conflicting cultures. There is the educational culture, but also a public-sector one, largely mediated through the teachers' trade unions which strongly influence schools. Opinion research shows that most fourteen-year-olds think that schools should prepare them usefully for work but because school is their day-to-day culture, too many teachers are cut off from the world in which their students will work. Most see how the everyday world outside the school operates as they live their own lives, but few teachers really understand how businesses operate. David Hargreaves claims that, because teaching has been their only job, 'most teachers are occupationally sanitized' and that if they are to give real help to young people moving into jobs, they 'must have more direct experience of other occupations'.[15] Teachers' views of future real-world skills demanded by businesses are based on second- or third-hand interpretations of what work currently requires of school leavers, rather than the skills which will be demanded in the early twenty-first century.

And all the time the tensions and conflicts between the five cultures – political, parental, civil service, school and trade union – hamper the process of educational improvement.

Universities

As with schools, the mixture of cultures influencing universities is complex. Within universities themselves there is, first, an *academic* culture concentrating on producing future teachers and researchers. Closely linked to this is a *discipline* culture, seeking to enable students to acquire knowledge for its own sake across the whole range of subjects, but in the hope that both specialist knowledge and the general skills of thinking and learning acquired from a university education will help in later careers.

The academic and discipline cultures are very similar and both derive from the culture of prewar universities which largely catered for an elite and provided little explicit training for a career. The *professional* culture associated with such training, for example in engineering, business studies or law, was distinctly frowned on by the first two cultures, which dominated most of the fifty-three universities in the UK before 1993.[16] The number of universities in the UK has now roughly doubled, with the addition of the former polytechnics and colleges. This has given the 'professional' culture a bigger overall weight, because it was important in polytechnics. Yet all three cultures are dominated by the vision of an idealized, archetypal university where everyone is a scholar, engaged equally in both teaching and research. The academic community is reluctant to allow even outstanding individuals or universities to specialize in research, leaving others to specialize in what are seen as less prestigious activities, like teaching.

From the mid 1980s the central funding authorities, in which civil servants play a significant role, began to attempt to assess the performance of universities, but took over the 'elitist' view that university staff should be judged on their ability as both teachers *and* researchers, so that specialization in one or other was still resisted. More recently, the Higher Education Funding Council for England, which now deals with seventy-three English universities, has been switching funds towards about ten universities with the 'best' research performance. But the assessment process still gives too much incentive to individual academics in all universities to try to perform well in both teaching and research. There is too little specialization.

The result of the civil service accepting the elite academic culture is that too little effort is devoted to ensuring that students learn how to learn and too little research which is up to scratch. To civil servants it seems obvious that the 'measurement' of performance must be centralized. That is neo-Stalinism, with the failings of Soviet economic planning. The quality of teaching is measured by the presentational performance of teachers, not its long-run impact on students. In research, more publications are better than few, provided that they are in 'refereed' journals, even if the referees belong to inward-looking peer groups. As Simon Jenkins has put it, since this audit of performance 'demanded quantity, quantity it would get, even of the inherently unquantifiable'.[17]

Worse still, while the evolution of the knowledge age means that opportunities and threats to universities are developing rapidly the civil service, with its non-innovatory culture, does not know how to manage the diffusion of innovation, even if it recognizes the need to do so. Innovation would require experimentation by a critical mass of universities, but that would mean pluralism, which centralized bureaucracies cannot orchestrate.

Within universities, the legacy of the elite culture means that, more than schools, universities do not try hard enough to ensure that graduates learn how to learn. The model of a community of scholars and students, 'inspired but not directed by the teachers . . . is now essentially a minority provision'.[18] Diana Laurillard argues that academics who are being trained in management and marketing methods 'might be better served if they went on courses on how to teach better'.[19]

Universities will also have to abandon the notion that knowledge for a lifetime can be acquired in three years around the age of twenty. Courses may need to be longer, and will certainly need to be spread over, say, a decade rather than three years, even though this will lead to logistical problems. Such problems will also accompany the need for 'lifelong learning' in the knowledge age. As more new knowledge is generated, old knowledge atrophies faster and frequent reskilling will be *de rigueur*.

This will expose one of the universities' worst failings. They too readily ignore their alumni who work in business and the professions. Of course, it is difficult to keep in touch with growing numbers of graduates, but this is a tremendous opportunity. Follow-on and refresher programmes represent a big potential source both of income and interest. But there is a big challenge too. Graduates returning for more professional education will not be satisfied with the lack of contact of too many academics with leading-edge thinking and practice in the real world and with their sloppy presentation.

Nor will this be helped by the lack of infrastructures for information and communications technology and the material to use with them. Universities will have to develop educational programmes using television (including teleconferencing), video, CD-ROM and, before long, virtual reality. The number of universities pursuing these developments enthusiastically is barely into single figures, though the Open University is a splendid exception. Thames Valley University is also determined to use technology well to aid learning. In many other universities, relatively small groups are working on leading-edge technological developments, but are largely ignored by their colleagues.

One oddity of the university culture is that the high prestige given to research is too often not matched by an enthusiasm for sharing its findings with anyone outside a specialist peer group. Even when of great interest to non-academics, research findings are too rarely presented in a form and in publications which ensure that the 'real world' will read them. To a degree which no one has measured research findings are 'wasted'. This is not so true in science and medicine though even there it probably happens more often than its practitioners would accept. Certainly in the social sciences, whose role should be to reflect the realities of society back to us, too much university research is too theoretical and too remote. And too much is made available too slowly.

In this respect, in their reluctance to welcome alumni as students and indeed as teachers, advisers, etc. and in the difficulty they find in striking up useful relationships with business, the universities remain too cut off from the outside world. The institutions which have joined the university system since 1993 are more in touch with alumni, business and local communities than the others, but not always enough.

Applying the Model for Culture Change

In the first section of this paper I identified four ways of changing the culture of an organization: through coercion; contagion; coaching and learning. I now apply this simple model of the forces which make cultures change to the whole private sector and, within the public sector, to the civil service and education. This will show how effective the four influences are in bringing about cultural change in key areas.

Changing Cultures in the Private Sector

COERCION

While coercion is often painful and resented by those who suffer it, it is a major source of culture change in the private sector. Private organizations have no choice but to respond to changes in their environment, especially their markets, by changing products, processes, policies and, if necessary, cultures. Shareholders and financial experts in the City and the media will exert pressure for change on the organization if they judge its performance to be inadequate. Beyond this, there is the ultimate example of coercion – takeover – and that keeps potential victims on their toes.

In practice, of course, the pressures of coercion are very much concentrated into periods like the recession of the early 1990s, when the ultimate penalty for not performing well enough is failure. Failure is a tough discipline, and not all victims of recession 'deserve' to fail. But an economy with no failures would be less successful than ours, even though some of the 'wrong' businesses fail alongside the 'right' ones. Even if a business does fail, some at least of those who work for it will later find new jobs, painful though the transition may be. Similarly, the more successful divisions in a firm which fails may be taken over or reconstructed and will continue to operate.

There are also institutional organs of coercion. For example, an active government competition policy helps to keep competition strong. In the UK this means relying on the Office of Fair Trading to identify potential problem areas, and on using the Monopolies and Mergers Commission to investigate them imaginatively and the Department of Trade and Industry to act wisely on its recommendations.

For as far ahead as one can see the strength of global competition, linked to relatively free international trade and rapid technological change, will act as a powerful coercive force. But it will still need reinforcement through an effective competition policy. The present arrangements give great power to the President of the Board of Trade who can, if he wishes, reject recommendations from the Monopolies and Mergers Commission without giving reasons. There is similar concern that only the Office of Fair Trading can ask for an investigation by the Commission. Some therefore argue that, as in Germany, competition policy should be sanctioned by giving members of the public the right to call for investigations.

There are similar worries that recommendations like those of Cadbury and Greenbury may not be implemented stringently enough. For example, how helpful is it to suggest a stronger role for independent nonexecutive directors? Their attitudes and culture may not prevail if these are at odds with the remainder of the Board.

We should note, however, that there is also coercion for major investors. For example, Alistair Ross Gooby of Postel Investment Management Limited has taken a high public profile, especially in seeking shorter contracts for top executives.[20] Perhaps there should now be similar coercion on companies to ensure that top executives do not remain in any one job for too long.

CONTAGION

In the private sector, the distinction between contagion and coercion is blurred. Contagion means bringing outsiders into key positions in the hope that they will 'infect' the organization with the culture from which they come, which is usually the objective of the acquiring company in a takeover. But contagion is then forced on the organization by a form of coercion.

Even where the top management or board decides to bring outsiders into key positions, hoping that they will bring contagion from their previous cultures with them, there will often be some coercion from big investors, for fear of unsatisfactory performance.

The movement of key individuals within a business may achieve some contagion. Unilever, for example, takes pride in having an enlightened policy for moving its promising managers between quite different posts within the company. So, a production manager may become a transport manager; a finance manager a factory manager; and so on. But such moves will not expose them to radically different cultures because, like many large businesses, a Unilever seeks to make its culture all-pervasive. Even a manager moved to a different country within the same business will often find the same culture. To 'infect' cultures requires new questioning, even iconoclasm. It will be most effective if there is movement between organizations, not within them, and that calls for long-term career moves.

COACHING

A great deal of coaching goes on in the private sector, often when outside trainers/educators organize programmes to improve managerial knowledge and performance, which often means changing culture too. Objectives are usually worked out carefully between the organization and the coaches, and success carefully evaluated later. The fact that so much coaching does go on implies that much of the private sector feels that it is beneficial.

It is, however, doubtful whether enough individual directors or complete boards, especially in smaller businesses, are ready enough to seek coaching. Too few individual directors think it necessary to continue to learn; even fewer boards do so to improve their collective performance.

LEARNING

Efforts to create 'learning organizations' are very recent so that only time will show how far they are succeeding. What is undoubtedly new is the way that individual managers are accepting increased responsibility both for their own continuing learning and for that of their immediate teams. Lifelong learning through development programmes in universities and elsewhere will reinforce this.

To sum up, the cultures of private sector organizations change through all four influences, but especially through coercion. Obviously, change would be faster if private sector organizations were quicker, without coercion, to see the need for their cultures to evolve. Yet – even for those which are very slow to change – in the end competition, takeover or outright failure bring it about. The mills of God (or is it Mammon?) may grind slowly, but they grind effectively in the end.

Changing Cultures in the Public Sector

CIVIL SERVICE

COERCION

There is little interest in changing the culture of the core civil service for the reasons given earlier, but the creation of nearly one hundred agencies to administer relatively straightforward processing activities was deliberately designed to coerce these agencies to change. Each employs its own staff, has clearly defined responsibilities and concentrates on improving the delivery of its own service, while also improving the efficiency with which it is delivered. The civil service did recognize that for the new agencies to work well each would have to create its own distinctive culture so it was always stressed that it would be necessary to provide appropriate training, secondment to other organizations, and also with early promotion. These intentions were admirable, representing coercion at its best. It remains to be seen how things work out.

CONTAGION

Since coercion has little to offer in changing the culture of those who remain in the core civil service, contagion should be strongly encouraged. We have seen that most top civil servants do not stay in their jobs for long but they do stay in the public sector for most of their lives. There is still a gulf between the cultures of the private sector and the civil service and it needs to be bridged. There will always be some differences between these cultures, but they should be reduced.

It would be impractical to move large numbers of people between business and the civil service. The best hope is to encourage movement into and out of carefully chosen top civil service posts, with the gains likely to be greatest from movement *into* the civil service rather than out of it.

It should, however, be remembered that the civil service folk memory already contains antidotes to this kind of contagion, ready phrases implying that action will be taken to contain or neutralize newcomers. Thus, there is talk of 'repelling boarders'. Or newcomers may be welcomed hoping that they will 'go native' and accept the civil service culture.

When I joined the Advisory Board for Research Councils (ABRC) my background meant that I looked at it against the culture of a business school and found it concerned with management questions yet not seeing them as such. I explained this in a lecture. Soon after, a distinguished scientist on the ABRC took me aside and told me: 'It's a pity you gave that lecture so soon after joining. After another couple of years you will see that the way that the ABRC operates is absolutely right.'[21] He clearly thought I would 'go native' in the end: but I did not.

I must immediately point out that many of those at the top of the civil service now agree that 'contagion' is important. Indeed, exchanges of people between business and the civil service have taken place for many years but with limited effect. One reason is that while the exchanges did not last long – say, two years – it was long enough to make really promising people (and their superiors) feel that a move would disrupt their career path. Those exchanged were rarely the best people and they were therefore not taken very seriously. They were seen as boarders to be ignored, if not repelled. And few incomers worked at a high enough level to bring about real change.

Perhaps the most important exceptions were businessmen like John Hoskyns, Derek Rayner, David Young and Robin Ibbs whom Mrs Thatcher brought in to work in top jobs and who did have a significant impact. Even so, that impact was less permanent than it might have been because they were not succeeded by outsiders of similar experience and drive.

Cultural contagion in the civil service demands the movement of more and more able people from outside the service, for longer periods (five years or so) and into really senior posts. This will not be easy but the idea must not be given up. Above all, the civil service needs people with an ability to act as effective, persuasive change agents and not simply as conventional administrators.[22]

COACHING

There is much coaching in the civil service. As in the private sector, internal and external consultants and management trainers help in this, though their impact is greater in 'Next Steps' agencies than in the core civil service.

There is, however, a significant problem. While those running training programmes seek to change the civil service culture, this is far from easy since many of those being 'coached' work in the same culture: there are few change agents among them. The Top Management Programme for the civil service which does mix senior public sector people with senior managers from other organizations – not all businesses – is a welcome exception.

LEARNING

Given its traditional role of following established rules to perform routine activities, one would not expect the civil service to be as willing as the private sector to develop learning organizations, though there are now some action learning programmes in the hived-off agencies. The core civil service, which needs to work out ways of enabling itself to analyse and handle complex systems effectively, still resists the challenge. Most civil servants see the notion that it can do this by developing learning organizations as eccentric, or worse. For example, in the report which established government agencies, written by 'core' civil servants, the intention of 'changing . . . cultural attitudes' is explicitly stated but the world 'learning' never appears.

SCHOOLS AND UNIVERSITIES

We have seen that both schools and universities are subject to a range of influences and pressures whose character is determined by the cultures of those who initiated the pressures.

With schools, politicians have imposed dramatic 'social engineering' initiatives – like comprehensive schooling and the National Curriculum – which imposed massive change on schools but without adequate experimentation and testing. Implementation was then managed, in excessive detail, by the civil service which had later to tackle the resulting turmoil in schools. Part of that turmoil resulted from the imposition by civil servants of overdirective and overbureaucratic rules and procedures which derived directly from the civil service culture.

Politicians have been more reluctant to interfere in the broad policies of universities, perhaps in the hope that, if ignored, problems would go away. They have, however, been less reluctant to raise detailed issues, for example, over job tenure and student loans.

The civil service has therefore been given a clear run in holding down public expenditure on higher education and in seeking to 'raise standards'. As with schools, the 'assessment process' used has been too bureaucratic, too unimaginative and has totally failed to match the nature and complexity of innovation needed in universities.

In both schools and universities there has been substantial coercion from above, but of the wrong kind. In schools, conflicts between the different cultures of politicians, parents, civil servants, teachers and trade unions has held back progress towards schools where children both learn how to learn and are prepared for twenty-first-century jobs.

Universities have thus far been more successful in holding outside cultures at bay. Civil service-dominated assessment procedures may be infuriating, but the civil service has largely swallowed the 'elite' view that academics are both teachers and researchers and has not so far imposed specialization in teaching *or* research on individual universities, which is what higher education in the twenty-first century will require. To the extent that universities have allowed in outsiders – alumni, businessmen, local communities, etc. – they have essentially done so on their own terms. Most universities remain teenage ghettos with intruding adults largely kept at bay.

If schools and universities are to meet challenges of the twenty-first century, they need either less coercion and contagion from above, or coercion and contagion which recognize the needs and nature of innovation in education, though this seems too much to hope.

Any policy to change the cultures of schools and universities has to begin from two facts. First, too few academics, and even fewer school teachers, have a real understanding of the thinking and skills which will be needed in the twenty-first century. Nor do they understand how businesses operate and, in particular, the importance and role of team work.

In an ideal world, teachers would move between jobs in education and elsewhere several times during a career. As a minimum, one would like to see every teacher working in one or two nonschool, preferably private sector, jobs before the age of forty. And the period outside should be not less than two years. Nor is there any reason why those who teach in further education colleges should be treated differently. David Hargreaves makes more detailed suggestions along similar lines.[23]

In universities, there is also a strong case for more movement of individuals between universities and the rest of the economy, but movement should be inward as much as outward. The need for 'lifelong learning' is bound to increase what I have defined as discipline and professional programmes run for adults. Perhaps more important, though, universities should deliberately organize themselves to bring in well-qualified people as lecturers, researchers or tutors because people outside universities are now working in similar ways and have similar education and talents. There is a new opportunity here because those who come in from outside will do so more innovatively and with greater vigour because they will be untrammelled by academic traditions and preconceptions. This will be a powerful force for contagion and may in the end move even farther and force universities into abandoning the pretence that only a university faculty is capable of running a university.

What I have elsewhere called 'the new republic of the intellect' will have arrived.[24] And it will have done so partly because developments in information and communications technology will make the educational market worldwide. Universities, which are reluctant to recognize national as distinct from institutional boundaries will have to meet the challenges of operating in an international context.

How Long in a Job?

Since we are concerned with changing organizational culture, the main concern must be with the top, where the tone is set. We have seen that whether individuals stay in the same job too long is mainly one for the private sector, but must continue to be taken seriously in the public sector too. Those who lead organizations need to be fresh and imaginative. Nothing can guarantee this but what will almost guarantee the opposite is for those in the top two or three levels of an organization to remain there for long periods. They become habituated to the way the organization operates, lose their acuteness in observing what is going on both within the body and outside, and perhaps their judgments of people and decisions become less acute.

There is therefore a strong case for saying that no one in a top job should remain there for longer than five years. Well before the end of his or her first year, the newcomer will have had time to work out what changes are needed. A further year will normally be enough to make them. Two more years will give time for the changes to be absorbed and the organization to return to operating on an even keel. At the end of five years, the incumbent should be ready to move on.

Even in entrepreneurial businesses, people need to move on, devastating though this may seem to the typical entrepreneur. There is a barrier through which the entrepreneurial firm must pass if it is to grow. Some say this is when the entrepreneur no longer interacts with all employees and I myself would put it at a turnover of £3 to 4 million per annum. To move beyond this the founding entrepreneur, or entrepreneurial team, will have to surrender some control. When a full takeover happens, the acquiring firm should presume that the existing management team will have to be replaced. The common practice of inducing management teams to remain, through the offer of 'earn-outs' offering them substantial payments if predetermined results are achieved in the next few years, is almost always a mistake.

A nearly universal response to my proposal for more job changes is that it will destroy the accumulated experience and memory which an organization needs. The reply, of course, is that most organizations have *too much* experience which is precisely why cultures become moribund. If anything, I am not going far enough. To move a limited number of outsiders into carefully chosen senior posts and to move others within the organization more frequently to give them new challenges, will still leave the organization with a great deal of experience, if not too much.

The Birth and Death of Organizations

The most radical way of changing cultures is through the birth or death of whole organizations. The idea of organizational death is seen as so traumatic that it is widely resisted, even by people unconnected with the organization under threat. Birth is easier.

By far the biggest proportion of new organizations being created in the UK are businesses and, by definition, they establish distinctive cultures deriving from the founding individual or team. Despite the difficulties mentioned in the previous paragraph, large-scale creation of new businesses keeps economies flexible. The enterprise society of the 1980s was not a political gimmick. It was brought into being by underlying forces, partly technical, for example, computer systems which made greater automation in manufacturing possible. It was also partly the result of the potential for the development of knowledge businesses now that knowledge was becoming an important commodity. Such firms are engaged in design, marketing, financial and other advice, consultancy and training. In an era when they are an engine of economic growth, the main role of policy-makers in government must be to put as few obstacles as possible in the way of the birth and growth of new businesses.

We have seen that the public sector contains the main obstacles to the changing of cultures by the death – and indeed the birth – of organizations. Birth will be difficult because public expenditure in the UK is bound to be constrained for the rest of the century at a time when we know that transfer payments such as social security and pensions are bound to increase. The scope for establishing new public sector bodies is bound to be limited.

This makes it important for the public sector to do what it can to generate movement within it by closing organizations down. One sentence in Donald Schon's 1970 Reith Lectures has remained with me over the years: 'In government, as in most other established institutions,' he said, 'the organizational equivalent of biological death is missing.'[25]

It is important that we should take what opportunities there are to kill off parts of the public sector that are no longer useful. In the USA, for example, the disbanding of an agency is 'an event frequently discussed, but almost never undertaken'.[26] Yet there are many ways in which organizational death could be arranged.

PRIVATIZATION

Privatization does not mean closure, but it does mean shaking off the civil service culture.

So long as an industry is in the public sector its sponsoring government department is extremely reluctant to stop monitoring it, and interfering with it in differing degrees. As everyone knew, and as privatization has shown, it was unnecessary to have large numbers of officials in a sponsoring department monitoring an industry, while a similar number of people within the industry were employed to monitor the monitors.

PROJECT ORGANIZATIONS

Whenever a new public sector body is established – and indeed for ones which already exist – those responsible for its establishment should, if possible, plan to disband it once its task has been completed. The strength of the desire to do the opposite is shown by the fact that, even in the rather rare cases where a body is set up to perform a time-limited task, it will look for ways to continue once the task is completed.

An outstanding example is the National Aeronautics and Space Agency (NASA) which was set up in the USA to carry out the space programme and to put men on the moon. Once it was clear that the scale of the space programme was to be substantially reduced, NASA exerted strong pressure on politicians and sought public support for it to be given a major new task, for example, to revitalize American cities. NASA's employees did not want the personal and professional upheaval which they would otherwise face. In the event, no alternative to the space programme was established.

In this country, we should have begun much sooner to explore the use of project organizations. Having failed to do so, we should now establish the principle that wherever possible, public bodies should be given a clearly defined task to carry out. Once it is completed they should be closed.

TIME-LIMITED ORGANIZATIONS

Indeed, we should go further and establish the principle that, after a specified period of time, all public sector bodies will be examined on the assumption that they will be closed unless they can show good reason for continuing. This does happen with parts of some public bodies, but it is not a regular practice with complete organizations.

BRANCHES

Where a large organization like the National Health Service or the state school system has many relatively small units, there will often be pressure to close some of them. For example, a local population may have declined relative to other areas. There will always be strong resistance to such changes. The recent furore over the London teaching hospitals is just one example. Whatever the merits of the case, it is fairly easy to orchestrate a media campaign against change.

The obvious answer is an enquiry into a closure proposal – with evidence from all concerned. The problem is that any enquiry will probably be conducted by peers. They will find a genuinely independent judgement difficult. They will either not want to damage a friendly institution, if only because they may fear weakening their own positions if their institutions come under similar pressure in future. Alternatively, if they are enemies, they may welcome an opportunity to undermine it.

Even so, given that change in the public sector culture is so difficult, it is important that none of the few genuine opportunities for change through closure should be missed.

Technology will provide some of these. For example, given that universities need to be far more innovative in their use of information and communications technology, there is a case for closing some of the lowest ranking ones now and replacing them with a second (and even a third) open university.

FOSSILIZATION

The most difficult choices arise where an organization's culture no longer leaves it fully fit. Unfortunately, no organization will itself admit that it has ceased to fulfil its purpose adequately while outsiders, lacking information, will find it difficult to prove. The argument for toughness must be that the organization is so inappropriate to the present era that even if it is still needed, it should start afresh. Beginning with an entirely new set of people may be the only way out.

In the private sector, most of us have candidates for closure, perhaps followed by later rebirth, but there are already pressures enough on private businesses. Some would nominate fringe bodies like the MCC for closure but only traditional cricket enthusiasts would really care.

The public sector is different. I have noted that conversations with opinion-formers show strong antagonism to the Foreign Office and the Bank of England. But closure is impossible. These are monolithic entities. The position is different where a number of bodies make up a part of the public sector, as with education.

Given that it may be difficult to judge from the outside whether a body is outmoded there is a case in some fields for adopting a rota system for closure. This would be especially appropriate with universities. No one who has visited a university or department where most of the staff have been in the same place for twenty years or more could be happy with the weary cynicism and lethargy which now infect it.

On the same basis, I have at intervals suggested that one or two Oxford or Cambridge colleges should be closed each year, at least over the next two decades. Each could be allowed to restart after three years, on the understanding that no one who had ever taught in either university could join the resurrected college. Just imagine the media campaign which would follow that!

A concluding message must be about organizations being open and porous. Coercion, contagion and coaching are impossible in a closed organization, and only an open one can learn how to learn.

One may well ask whether, if changing organizational cultures is so painful, change is really necessary. What are the risks if the dinosaurs are *not* transformed? The most general answer is that the Thatcher years did transform the private sector. Even if imperfectly, market pressures and new legislation forced substantial change, which is continuing. The public sector has changed less and that this *does* matter is shown by the examples chosen. The top of the civil service needs to develop a culture appropriate to analysing and solving the problems of a complicated modern country, not least in the complex sociotechnical systems of inner cities, housing, transport and health care. Until it does this, the dissatisfaction of the public with the performance of government departments – and therefore governments themselves – will be dangerous.

Education has been highlighted because, in a competitive global economy dominated by information and knowledge, our educational system must be good enough to enable Britain to play a significant part. At present – certainly in England – there is much to be done.

The list of fields where culture change is needed is long. This paper has offered a blueprint for providing such change.

I end as I began. The quotation from Matisse takes an extreme view of an artist prepared continually to alter his approach, even his identity. Few individuals are so radical; organizational radicalism is even harder. Yet there has to be a compromise between total inertia and total revolution in the degree to which styles, cultures and identities change. As with Matisse, the antennae of organizations should continually gauge the need for change and respond sooner rather than later.

Matisse's other theme is wholly appropriate. Organizations must never become trapped by reputation and success. It is precisely when all seems to go well that new plans have to be made and old attitudes and identities altered so that values and cultures, and through them the organization itself, can thrive. Only by changing themselves before style, reputation and success take them prisoner can organizations gain the freedom to create their own futures.

11

Education

DAVID H. HARGREAVES

Almost everywhere in the English-speaking world, schools have in recent years been restructured and reformed. Politicians of both left and right have become convinced that schools are not good enough: educational standards, the yardsticks by which student performance is judged, are too low or are falling, and too many students leave school with inadequate knowledge and skill for the changed world of work in a 'knowledge society' seeking to flourish in rapidly changing and increasingly competitive international market. The reforms, both here and abroad, have strengthened the role of central government in education as well as of parents and the local community: it is the middle tier – the local education authorities (LEAs) in this country – which has lost out.

In England and Wales, the main changes over the last decade have been the National Curriculum and new modes of testing; the delegation of budgets from LEAs to schools; the enhanced responsibilities of governing bodies; open enrolment and greater parental choice of school; the introduction of City Technology Colleges (CTCs) and grant-maintained (GM) schools free of LEA control; regular inspection of schools; teacher appraisal; making the initial training of teachers more school-based. Schools have been made more accountable and compete against one another for students. Though there is growing evidence that the overall impact of these reforms has been beneficial, it is questionable whether they have gone far enough to meet the original aim of generating a major improvement in the quality of education. In the most recent Annual Report of HM Chief Inspector of Schools (1994–5) it is said that the overall standard of pupil achievement needs to be raised in about half our primary schools and two-fifths of secondary schools. It is for this reason that, six years after the Education Reform Act of 1988, more attention is being paid to teachers and how they teach.

Teachers feel overwhelmed by these manifold changes, some of which, though desirable in principle, were implemented in a fashion that needlessly wasted millions of pounds and much teacher time and energy. They naturally would like a quieter period of consolidation. They will not get it. In this essay I describe some of the further reforms that should be on a governmental agenda for education.

Secondary education continues to be a source of concern. In rural areas, where there is a single comprehensive secondary school, little can be done to extend choice and competition. In larger towns and cities, parents are divided on the quality of what is on offer. The 'standard' comprehensive school – the common secondary school designed to meet the needs of all the students from its local catchment area – is probably in decline. Parents have been given choice, and want a richer variety of schools from which to choose than a list of look-alike or interchangeable comprehensives that differ only in their position in an examination 'league table'. In short, choice is serving as a pressure to increased diversity of secondary schools.

Many on the political right would see diversity as an occasion for the reintroduction of selective, or grammar, schools. From an incoming government of the left, there is unlikely to a return to the *status quo ante*. The retention of the comprehensive principle – no selection on the basis of an intelligence test for eleven-year-olds – should not stand in the way of a vigorous programme of increasing the degree and forms of variety of provision. The minority of GM schools are to keep their independence, but the handful of CTCs have done little to change the secondary school landscape.

The more extensive diversification I have in mind can take several forms. The first is curriculum specialization – specialized schools, in urban areas, in science and technology, languages (both modern and classical), the arts, and sports. To some, such an idea is too close to the 'magnet' schools developed in the United States in the early 1980s, or even the later 'charter' schools. The fear is that they threaten the principle of comprehensive education, selecting by ability rather than aptitude, interest and preference. The magnet schools themselves are popular with parents and also students, who truant less frequently and achieve more, and so are rarely criticized directly. The argument is that they leave a remnant of 'sink schools' attended by the most deprived; this is said to offend the comprehensive principle. But there are already 'sink schools' within the comprehensive system, so the argument is not convincing. Moreover, it is perfectly possible to have specialized schools where admission is not based on some general ability: there is no need to return to some kind of eleven-plus. Many adolescents are less enthusiastic about school than about education: if more schools developed a curriculum specialization attractive to students, their motivation and achievement might rise sharply. And since the National Curriculum now requires schools to offer breadth and balance in the curriculum, specialized schools would not sacrifice breadth to depth.

These specialized schools would, of course, have more staff in the subject of curriculum specialization. They would be better resourced in their field, and be the site of innovations in curriculum and teaching method. They should, therefore, be schools which serve as teachers' centres, offering professional development and in-service training to all teachers of that subject in other schools in the area. In addition, since such schools would attract high calibre staff, they could play a central role in the initial training of teachers in the specialism.

The other form of diversification is specialization along

philosophical, ideological or religious lines. That is, state-supported schools should offer choice to parents, not so much in terms of rank in league tables of exam results or truancy rates, but in terms of distinctive educational and religious values – as has been the case in the independent sector for many years. This means the acceptance of Islamic schools as well as Roman Catholic, Anglican and Jewish schools. It means many smaller schools, especially before the age of sixteen, i.e. more eleven-to-sixteen rather than eleven-to-eighteen schools, to provide the necessary range of choice for parents.

Teacher choice of school is as essential as parental choice, since unless a school is staffed by teachers who are committed to the school's philosophy, educational and/or religious, the notion of a distinctive ethos is largely rhetorical. As Peter Drucker puts it, 'Only a clear, focused and common mission can hold the organization together and enable it to produce results.'[1] Too many schools are prevented from developing a clear and distinctive philosophy, and then living by it, simply because some staff decline to commit themselves to it or strive to subvert it. Such people would not be allowed to survive in a business: why should they in a school?

The drive to improve the efficiency and effectiveness of schools has been impeded by a reluctance among educators to question their assumptions about school organization as well as the kind of people who should staff schools and undertake teaching functions. Compare the management and organization of a teaching hospital with that of a comprehensive school. The main difference is that in schools qualified graduate teachers comprise most of the staff and undertake most of the work, whereas in hospitals doctors are a minority of the staff and do only selected and specialized aspects of the total work. Schools should in some ways become more like hospitals. First, schools should develop non-teacher chief executives to administer and manage the school, leaving the teaching staff to spend far more of their time and energy teaching. We should abandon the pretence that gifted teachers necessarily make good headteacher-managers; and advancement should no longer entail less teaching. The present system takes many of the best teachers out of classrooms, and leaves the less effective there for life. Promotion of teachers should not normally be into management but instead to the consultant-like status of the 'master teacher'. The headteacher would be just that: the leading educational professional working in partnership with the professional manager. Indeed, much of the so-called senior management in secondary schools could be reduced. The division of teachers into 'management' and 'teachers' has not served schools or teachers' relationships well. Any management tasks, pleasant and unpleasant, that are indeed better undertaken by teachers rather than administrators should be shared or rotated and all teachers should see themselves contributing to the formulation of school policies as well as to their implementation. A much flatter professional hierarchy and a more collaborative style are appropriate for high quality teams of professionals – in this regard the teachers could set a pattern for doctors to emulate.

Secondly, schools should acquire the equivalent of nurses, i.e. assistant teachers who work under the supervision of teachers, are less qualified but carry out essential support to students, leaving the design of the curriculum and the overall organization of teaching and learning to specialized and demonstrably competent teachers. At present teachers spend far too much of their time in the supervision, management and control of children in classrooms and around the school: such tasks do not require a person of graduate status. Assistant teachers need not be graduates and could be prepared for the job with a relatively short training. They would be paid less than teachers. As qualified highly skilled teachers become fewer, they should be paid more. Young people of eighteen years of age or more might become assistant teachers to test whether they liked the idea of being a teacher. Assistant teachers of any age could, after a few years, proceed on a full, or part-time basis to a university degree and more formal training for full professional status. A hospital run entirely by doctors without the support of nurses would be grossly wasteful. Why do we not see schools without assistants to teachers as similarly prodigal with scarce resources?

Thirdly, the problem of the ineffective head and the ineffective classroom teacher has to be openly addressed. For many years the issue of how to make schools more effective has been discussed and debated, but one fundamental aspect, how to get rid of a small but significant minority of incompetent teachers, is constantly side-stepped.[2] All teachers should be on five-year renewable contracts and performance-related pay. The majority would have their contract renewed regularly and many would be more effectively rewarded for their dedication and achievement. Those who for whatever reason contribute less should with reason forfeit some pay and those who become seriously deficient cannot expect to have their appointments renewed. The departure of incompetent heads, who sell their teachers short, and incompetent classroom teachers, who sell students short, would probably make the single most important contribution to raising standards and performance of both teaching and learning. It would be for the school's governing body to renew contracts, in association with an LEA where appropriate. In the absence of LEAs, the decision on the renewal of a headteacher's contract would lie entirely with the governors, and heads considered to be inadequate would simply not have their contract renewed; the contracts of teachers would be renewed by governors, on the advice of the headteacher. Without radical action here, it is unlikely that the worst schools can be levered up to the levels of effectiveness that their students and parents deserve. And it is such schools that constitute the drag on national standards.

Radical as all this might seem, it is not enough. It has been shown that virtually every fourteen-year-old thinks school should teach things that are useful for jobs. But most teachers are in a weak position to do this, simply because teaching has been their only job. I do not know any figure on this and doubt whether any national records are kept. However, there is no doubt that most teachers enter the profession immediately on graduating or shortly thereafter. In recent years 'mature' (i.e. aged over twenty-seven) entrants to the profession have been rising in number, but they remain a minority. Most teachers are occupationally sanitized, though one (just one) of the functions of schooling is to prepare the young for the world of work. If teachers are to make their teaching genuinely and usefully more relevant to the world of work, they must have more direct experience of other occupations. This is not best achieved by occasional short secondments to business and industry, beneficial as these might be to the minority who have the opportunity. The best starting point is the lack of satisfaction many teachers experience in teaching. If one were to ask those who have been teachers for, say, fifteen or more years since graduation if they would like an opportunity (a) to work full-time in another occupation or (b) to work part of the week in another job, which is then shared with teaching, I suspect a majority of teachers would be interested. To provide them with such opportunities would be good for them as people and good for their teaching.

Such a possibility is on the horizon. We are entering an age of multiple careers, when people do not want a single job for life, but rather a succession of jobs, serial occupations (with or without serial monogamy). A change of job at regular points serves as a renewal and reinvigoration, as many find. The alternative is the portfolio occupational pattern, so attractively described by Charles Handy. In this version, one's occupation is 'a collection of bits and pieces of work for different clients'.[3] Why should there not be teachers one of whose 'bits' is part-time work in schools combined with a range of other 'pieces' in business and industry, in consultancy, in working from home as a telecommuter? In my experience, part-time teachers of this kind make refreshing and invigorating contributions to school life. Their alternative occupational life outside schools provides antibodies to the debilitating occupational diseases to which the full-time teacher is prone.

The traffic between schools and business and industry ought to be two-way. There are many people in industry who might wish to spend some time teaching in school. At present they are put off by employers who do not see the potential advantages, by the problem of different salary and pension arrangements, and most of all by the requirement of lengthy training to become a qualified teacher in school. Ironically some of these people are engaged in educational activities in business and industry, where they are not required to take a teaching qualification. The system needs a radical overhaul so that those with relevant experience from outside teaching can enter school teaching with a minimum of fuss and with maximum support through on-site training, allowing them to adjust to the different world of schools.

Once the principle of 'portfolio teachers' is accepted, the new sources of teacher supply are readily found. Recently Handy has reflected on the Third Age, which follows the period of full-time employment but which comes too early for full-time retirement.[4] People want, and increasingly may need, to supplement their reduced income; they want something useful and constructive to do. If the existing barrier of the requirement for extensive and expensive initial teacher training could be removed, a new generation of teachers, from a rich variety of backgrounds, might be discovered.

But it is not just the teachers, in their many new varieties, who will move between sites. Students also should be on the move. There is no good reason why students spend so much time in schools: it has simply become accepted that this is where they belong. Business and industry already do much of the further education and training of their employees. Why should not schools contract some of their teaching out to business and industry, allowing students to spend some of their time off-site? This would be enormously attractive to many students, who usually find the now common short work experience placements interesting, partly because at their best they confer a sense of maturity and seriousness about relevant learning. Business and industry will, over coming decades, have to spend more time and money upgrading employee knowledge and skills: constant retraining is becoming part of all jobs except the lowliest. This means that those in the later years of schooling and the first years into the job are likely to be pursuing education and training with older and more experienced colleagues. What a virtue this would be, for it would mix people of different ages and end the absurdly rigid age-grading that characterizes schools.

Ten years ago, it would have been unthinkable for state schools to 'contract out' any of their activities; it is now commonplace. It simply remains for them to contract out more of the *teaching*, not just the school dinners: it could be cost-effective for business and industry to take on some of the work. Teachers should be on both sides of the school–industry divide, regularly moving between sites. The very nature of what it means to be a 'teacher' must change – and so should how they are prepared for and supported in their teaching activities, now to be partially embedded in other occupational activities.

Schools are, under the Education Reform Act (1988), required to help to prepare pupils 'for the opportunities, responsibilities and experiences of adult life'.

The problem of Britain as a pluralistic society is how to find some social cement to ensure that people with different moral, religious, and ethical values as well as social, cultural and linguistic traditions can live together with a degree of harmony; and to discover the contribution that the education system should play in generating social cohesion. Jonathan Sacks has rightly pointed out that the more pluralistic a society we become, the more we need to reflect on what holds us together. Part of the solution is:

> . . . to think of a plural society not as one in which there is a Babel of conflicting languages, but rather as one in which we each have to be bilingual. There

> is a first and public language of citizenship which we have to learn if we are to live together. And there is a variety of second languages which connect us to our local framework of relationships: to family and group and the traditions that underlie them.[5]

Schools are in a state of confusion over religious, moral and civic education. Recent government reforms have created chaos. Far more clauses of the 1988 Education Reform Act are devoted to religious education and worship than to the rest of the National Curriculum and in 1994 the Department for Education issued a sixty-page circular on the theme in a desperate (and unsuccessful) attempt to clarify matters. Many parents who support the provision of religious education are not themselves active members of a religious community; over two-thirds want their children to be taught that there is a God, yet more of them think the main purpose of RE is to learn a moral code rather than to understand and perhaps acquire religious belief.[6] Evidently they want RE as a kind of social antiseptic, to endow young people with moral and ethical values to protect them from the ubiquitous dangers of drugs, sex and crime and guide them into being upright and happy. This is natural enough, since the dangers are real and immediate, whereas the concept of social cohesion is abstract and remote. And they are following a line established by government in 1944, when religious education became compulsory – at that time the only such subject – with a right for parents to withdraw their child from RE lessons. The aim has been not so much to make children practising Christians, for the teaching is nondenominational; rather it is to provide the religious (and implicitly Christian) basis for morality and teaching the difference between right and wrong. It is, perhaps, part of British culture to assume that the Christian religion forms the best, or even the only, basis for morality.

This conflation of moral and religious education persists. To be sure, the emergence of ethnic minorities with other religious affiliations, especially the Muslims, added complications. At school level RE was transmuted, in the interests of meeting the needs of all students and of increasing understanding of different religions, into a multifaith study of religion; and the corporate act of worship, where practised, lost many of its Christian trappings in order to avoid causing offence to other religious and nonreligious groups. This challenged the dominant position of Christianity in the curriculum and thus its distinctive basis for a shared morality. In 1988 there was a determination to restore the position of Christianity. This irritated other religious groups, especially those who, like the Muslims, aspired to have their own state-funded religious schools, partly to maintain their own religious, cultural and linguistic identities and partly to transmit to students a morality grounded in their culture and faith.

Many parents, in their natural concern for the moral development and welfare of their children, will continue to support religious education, perhaps in any form, because they see few alternatives. Yet there are times when government should beware of responding directly to parental wishes, and instead look beyond them to the more deep-seated needs of the young within a rapidly changing society. In this case it means acknowledging that the attempts to bolster and rationalize RE since 1988 have failed; that morality is not as closely linked to religion, especially the Christian religion, as in the past; that moral education will in the future need to be more closely linked to civic education if it is to provide a common core of values shared across communities in a pluralistic society.

The notion of a nondenominational core RE to be offered in all schools as a buttress to moral education is becoming less and less viable and should now be abandoned. The multifaith pick 'n mix tour of religions easily trivializes each faith's claims to truth. As an academic discipline, it has little appeal to most children and comes before they are mature enough to engage in the necessary historical and philosophical analysis. But what could and should replace RE? Several changes are needed.

First of all, there should be more religious schools, of Christian and other faiths, and a requirement that all schools, religious or secular, should provide a common core of civic education. The increasing differentiation between schools is a growth point and an opportunity for religious schools, for all the main religious groups in contemporary Britain and for all the denominations or subgroups within these religions. Within this more differentiated system religious schools should nourish a distinctive ethos, thus increasing the choice available to parents. More importantly, such schools could confidently and without apology assert the fundamental link between morality and religious faith which is so prized by religious groups. This is achieved by religious schools, especially when home and school are jointly committed to the transmission and living experience of a shared moral and religious culture, but not when schools are expected to transmit and practise what is ignored or denied in the home. Such schools would, then, sustain the very communities, including the family, on which moral and religious convictions ultimately depend for their sustenance and development.

This proposal is vulnerable to a double argument; on the one hand that religious schools are socially divisive and on the other that the creation of secular schools (though they exist in many European countries) undermines the moral education that parents and politicians wish to strengthen. The existence of religious schools is not inherently divisive any more than the existence of different cultural, linguistic or ethnic groups is inherently injurious to social harmony. Indeed, the resistance at local and national levels to state support for Islamic schools is inconsistent (since such schools would undoubtedly buttress the strong moral basis of the Muslim community), hypocritical (as long as voluntary aided Christian schools are supported) and racist (white British religious minorities rarely meet such opposition). The existence of such schools does, however, entail that members of society respect the differences between subcommunities, teach their young to do so, and introduce penalties for those who will not abide by that minimal respect, the tolerance of difference. Indeed, a central feature of a harmonious pluralistic society is an acceptance by all that the right of their own community to practise its way of life depends upon the granting of similar rights to others.

Secular schools do not have to abandon moral education because they no longer teach religious education. On the contrary, they have to show that whilst many people see a close link between the moral and the religious, even seeing the former as deriving from the latter, there are many others who believe that moral conduct does not require a religious basis and that a moral code without religious belief is tenable. Of course such a moral education could not entirely ignore religion. Religion, and in Britain the Christian religion especially, has exerted a deep influence on so much of our culture – our social institutions as well as literature, art and music. This is sometimes used as a justification for RE. But the importance of religion in these regards could be as well taught through the curriculum in English and the arts. If religious schools do have an advantage over secular schools in these matters, that is a factor which parents will take into account in making their choice of school.

Religious and secular schools will approach the fields of religious and moral education in different but complementary ways. Religious schools have a duty to teach their students that morality without religion is an intellectually defensible and socially respectable position; in the same way, secular schools have a duty to explain to their students why a morality grounded in religious belief takes a certain form. Both kinds of school can remain committed to some notion of a common curriculum with regard to religious, moral and civic education, and especially in regard to the last of these.

To help to create social cohesion, to develop a moral cement that will withstand the strains of being pluralistic, schools should take the lead in teaching what Sacks called 'the first and public language of citizenship': here is the shared or common core of a civic, moral and religious education. The government mistakenly took religion to be this first language. It is not. As Sacks rightly noted:

> . . . our second languages are cultivated in the context of families and communities, our intermediaries between the individual and the state. They are where we learn who we are; where we develop sentiments of belonging and obligation; where our lives acquire substantive depth.

Secular schools cannot teach these second languages; only specialized and religious schools can do that. But all schools can and should teach the first language.

Civic education is about the civic virtues and decent social behaviour that adults wish to see in young people. Citizenship is also more than this. Since Aristotle it has been accepted as an inherently political concept that raises questions about the sort of society we live in, how it has come to take its present form, the strengths and weaknesses of current political structures, and how improvements might be made. In the popular mind political education has sometimes come to mean party-political education, and the propagation by teachers of their own political beliefs. In practice, the majority of teachers are wary of disclosing to students their political convictions and are able to promote political literacy among the young through a balanced presentation of positions and arguments. It should be a matter of deep concern that so many young people are politically illiterate: they have little understanding about quite basic political concepts, such as democracy, and frequently display boredom, indifference or cynicism in relation to political issues and participation. But how can there be any form of community participation that is not in some sense political? Community participation stripped of its political content is no more than self-serving neighbourliness. Active citizens are as political as they are moral; moral sensibility derives in part from political understanding; political apathy spawns moral apathy.

In secular schools, a basic civil and moral education should normally precede any systematic RE. In part this is because it is essential to demonstrate to the young, from the beginning, that whilst a moral stance may be, and frequently is, grounded in religious belief, moral and civic values are just as important and tenable in the absence of religious belief. In part it is because understanding a religious faith from the outside requires a degree of maturity; much school RE comes too soon and leaves a residue of religious faith as a mixture of superstition and fairy stories. A sound, core civic and moral education should inculcate a respect for beliefs, values and ways of life that one does not immediately understand.

The British have produced some outstanding contributors to political theory and philosophy – Thomas Hobbes, John Locke, Adam Smith, David Hume, Edmund Burke, Thomas Paine, Jeremy Bentham, William Godwin, John Stuart Mill. We should be proud of them and be ready to discuss their universal contributions to an understanding of modern societies and citizenship. Yet their names are hardly known to the vast majority of British school-leavers. We should be deeply embarrassed at this neglect. Of course some students will find political and moral philosophy, even in elementary forms, difficult to grasp. This is not of grave consequence, since civic education should be taught by example as much as by study. Civic education, like any moral or religious education, requires immersion into a shared culture and is best practised before it can be intelligently discussed. Students should learn how to value and sustain a wide range of communities in a pluralistic society that has means of avoiding or resolving intercommunity conflicts. This would entail the school becoming a more central and therefore permeable institution in the community and one in which parents were evidently in a more extensive partnership with teachers.

In the age of the computer, the educational potential of the new information technologies, especially in interactive forms, is considerable, but has yet to be realized. This potential lies particularly in its capacity to motivate young people, to make learning more enjoyable and less judgemental. Teachers make poor entertainers of bored and reluctant students. There are severe limits to the capacity of classroom teachers to motivate that substantial minority of young people with little commitment to conventional schooling, who develop a sense of failure and resentment, whose achievement levels are worryingly low and who are destined to be an unemployable and alienated underclass. The challenge they pose should be a general force for change; but recent reforms, such as the National Curriculum, do little for this group. If a fraction of the time and money of the multimillion pound computer games industry were devoted to education rather than leisure, we might, under certain conditions, retain these young people's commitment and esteem. Computer games motivate and challenge; they do not lower their expectations because of the perceived background of the player. If the game is hard, the machine frustrates, but is far less likely than a teacher to humiliate. Information Technology (IT), like teaching assistants, potentially permits teachers to spend less time on what Oakeshott calls the communication of information and more on the heart of education, the communication of judgement.[7] Moreover, IT allows schooling to overcome the geographical limits of the school, by providing students with opportunities to work more at home and become telecommuters working from home but in touch with teachers and fellow learners via the technology (alongside parents who could take a more active role in formal education than they do). IT opens up new forms of interactive communication between home and school, and between students and distant peers and mentors. Here are the seeds of a major challenge to teachers' monopoly over teaching; they should respond to the challenge by contracting out pedagogic activities and functions to a whole range of new agencies, some community-based and others based in the world of work.

Technology, then, could support Gardner's notions of 'assessment specialists' to understand the abilities and interests of students, 'student-curriculum brokers' to match student abilities and interests to particular curricula and styles of learning, and 'school-community brokers'[8] to match students to learning opportunities in the wider community – all of which are a contemporary reassertion of Ivan Illich's (1971) conceptions of educational networks and learning webs. But look what happened to Illich's prescient 'deschooling' ideas: they crashed on educational conservatism and the popular assumption that schools are custodial institutions for young people and the best place to learn.[9] Exciting ideas may be a necessary condition for reform, but they are never a sufficient one. The IT enthusiasts are still a small minority: the majority of teachers remain indifferent. Though most schools now have computer rooms the impact is relatively limited and many teachers and heads are now rather sceptical about the educational value, not least in the light of high recurrent costs, which always make a solicitous nurse of an infant doubt. As Larry Cuban has pointed out, certain deep-seated cultural beliefs,

> . . . such as that teaching is telling, learning is listening, knowledge is subject matter taught by teachers and books, and the teacher-student relationship is crucial to any learning, dominate popular and practitioner thinking. Most taxpayers expect their schools to reflect these centuries old beliefs. School organizations shape classroom practice with its self-contained classrooms separating teachers from one another, a curriculum divided into segments of knowledge distributed grade by grade to students, and a schedule that brings students and teachers together to work for brief periods of time. These structures, profoundly influencing how teachers teach, how students learn, and the relationships between adults and children in each classroom, are especially difficult to alter after a century of popular and practitioner acceptance and they are alien to

> the impact that the new technologies would make on schools.[10]

Schools are still modelled on a curious mix of the factory, the asylum and the prison. New technology will not change this. Schools must be constructed on the basis of a new institutional model before the technologies will be admitted and allowed to develop to their full potential. Factories are disappearing: modern businesses look very unlike the nineteenth-century, heavy-industry factory. Changing the character of the teaching force, moving students between education and business premises, letting students spend more time working from or at home – all these should lead to a restructuring of the school day and the school year. But it will also be necessary to build on experiments conducted by a few pioneering schools – those restricting conventional lessons to the morning, and using the afternoons for project work and independent study; abandoning the conventional school day or week for integrated, complex and real-life problem-solving projects with students working in supervised teams in a variety of settings; flexitime arrangements that give teachers and students more control and reduce the sense of oppressive routine and predictability; restructured days giving teachers space to devote more time to planning and preparation; parents abandoning their conventional prejudices about what 'schooling' must mean when they see new structures enhancing the commitment, motivation and achievement of their children. In schools engaged in rethinking their organization, such as the Brit Performing Arts and Technology School in Croydon, the visitor is instantly struck by the fact that the school feels less like a school – a sensation that is profoundly refreshing. This is the shape of things to come, as schools come once again to resemble contemporary institutions. We are glad to see the end of the traditional factory; why should we expect the school modelled on it to be welcome to children?

WORK, TIME AND LIFE

It used to be common to forecast that the end of the twentieth century would bring the dawning of a leisure society. Instead, if anything, work has become more important than ever. For those who have it, work defines their identity, and motivates them to devote ever longer hours to it. For those without a job, its absence cuts them off from the normal life of friends and neighbourhoods, citizenship and sociability.

Huge new imbalances have arisen, partly because technological change has destroyed old jobs and created new ones, partly because of new gender patterns that have brought millions more women into the labour market, and partly because of shifts in the global division of labour.

The result is a set of new challenges which governments have proven remarkably feeble at tackling. One of them is the chronic and apparently permanent unemployment for a large minority, which is described, along with the range of viable solutions, in the essay on 'The end of unemployment'. But there is also a widening gulf between those with too little work and those with too much: those we describe here as the 'time-squeezed', who include not just managers and professionals but also many on relatively low pay. As 'Wellbeing and Time' shows, for women in particular time is becoming a critical issue – how to take control of it, how to manage more varied rhythms of living – yet most of our institutions still try to stick time into the old boxes, the linear progression from schooling through work to retirement, the standardized working week, the fixed age of retirement.

In the near future our guess is that this will all change. We may reappraise the sabbatical – seeing it as something for everyone to enjoy, not just a minority of academics. We may come to rethink the balance between parenting responsibilities and work, not just for women but also for men, as Amitai Etzioni argues. And more fundamentally we may reappraise how our uses of time contribute to our wellbeing and happiness.

12

The Convivial City

LIZ GREENHALGH and KEN WORPOLE

'Too many broken eggs and not enough omelettes', was J. B. Priestley's gloomy verdict on the planning blight he witnessed on his *English Journey* in the 1930s. He was appalled at the spread of suburbia and new patterns of ribbon development, blending what were once self-contained towns and cities into great conurbations of placelessness and this horror of formlessness framed much of postwar policy. It led to the green belts, formalizing the boundaries between town and country – and in the closing years of the century one of its legacies is a powerful public desire to live closer to a rural idyll.

In his influential book, *English Culture and the Decline of the Industrial Spirit,* the historian Martin Weiner described how frequently the industrial masters moved to join the rural aristocracy once they had made their pile.[1] Today the urge to leave Albert Square or Coronation Street to live in Ambridge still seems a pervasive ingredient of the English dream. While more than 80 per cent of British people actually live in cities, over two-thirds would choose to live in a small town or a country village if they could, and where people can leave cities, they do. In eleven cities or metropolitan boroughs – Bristol, Bromley, Cardiff, Greenwich, Hounslow, Leicester, Merton, Middlesbrough, Sheffield, Southwark and Sutton – studied in 1994–5 for the Comedia/Demos *Park Life* report on urban parks and open spaces, all suffered depopulation between 1981 and 1991. In just one decade, Bristol dropped from 438,038 to 370,300 and Southwark from

313,413 to 196,500, although both now claim to have halted the exodus.[2]

Many people today prefer to use out-of-town shopping malls easily accessible by car, multifacility 'leisure boxes' built on green-field sites, country parks with car parks and interpretation centres, and modern schools to which their children can walk in safety. The Demos/Comedia *Park Life* study showed that city dwellers with cars prefer to visit a country park or an out-of-town garden centre at the weekend rather than walk to their local park, and the CPRE report, *Leisure Landscapes*, published in 1994, detailed the scale of the urban invasion of the countryside as a place for sport and recreation, noting that 45 per cent of all car journeys are now made for leisure purposes.[3]

This desire to escape the city suggests that we have lost a model of urban living that can inspire and sustain people. The benefits have been masked by the costs, above all by a concern about security. Anxieties about crime now dominate people's thoughts and fears, even more than the prospect of illness, unemployment or accidental injury.[4] These are highlighted by the occasional political scare-mongering about fear on the streets, the threat posed to city car drivers by 'squeegee merchants', the need for 'walking with a purpose'. Social policy is currently being defined by the security industry, a burgeoning sector of the urban economy, in which the control of space and the security of people is largely regarded as a technological problem, amenable only to expensive surveillance systems. Forms of private security – car alarms, burglar alarms, electronic fencing, gated residential estates, mobile phones – are now important consumer goods.[5]

At the same time traditional public spaces have become places of fear. Only half the population now dares go out after dark, fewer than a third of children are allowed to walk to school, and public fear of strangers regularly erupts after such public murders as those of Jamie Bulger and Rachel Nickell.

So far the main response has been surveillance. A recent

survey found that: 'Seventy-five towns, including Blackpool, Swansea, Glasgow, Edinburgh, Hull, Torquay, Wolverhampton, Chester, Bath and Brighton have installed sophisticated surveillance systems to watch public areas, and more cities go on-line every week . . . They are concealed above doorways, inside vending machines, and behind two-way mirrors. They are being installed in bank cash machines, inside buses and on rooftops.'[6]

This equation between safety and surveillance has been one of the factors behind the popular support for a move towards the out-of-town shopping centre, an American-style mix of cars and commerce, leaving behind the old Victorian public spaces as unloved, unsafe and dingy. New shopping centres such as Lakeside in Thurrock, Meadowhall in Sheffield and the Newcastle Metro Centre provide controlled and attractive shopping environments, with strictly controlled security. They offer a pure antithesis to the countryside, wholly protected from the vagaries of the weather and the organic, natural world. And they provide an umbrella around which many other functions can cluster – other businesses, leisure centres and public buildings such as colleges, in the form of a new micro-city.

But this new model of the city, based around the car and shopping, has not been as successful as might have been expected. Its failures give us some important clues as to how thinking on cities will develop in the next century, and as to why many people now talk of the monolithic shopping centre as likely to become the 'tower block problem' of the next generation, a dangerous anachronism without public affection or loyalty.

An Air-conditioned Nightmare?

One reason is that the commercial spaces have strikingly failed to become a natural part of everyday life. Many are well-managed and enjoyable places in which to spend an afternoon but most remain lifeless, homogenous, too controlled to mesh in with the memories, the dreams and ghosts which fill more traditional public spaces. They have not succeeded in becoming the places where people live their rites of passage. Unlike the malls, parks remain the place where lasting childhood memories are formed, where teenagers get their first experience of love and sex, where young parents take their children to play, and where the old commemorate their absent partners with memorial trees and benches. Nor can malls compete with the less predictable roles which parks are taking on: social services departments, for example, now use parks as the neutral space for estranged couples to meet, and some doctors even prescribe walks in parks to help their patients recuperate.

The second reason is anxiety about the exclusion that is built into many shopping centres that have used design as a way of distancing them from social problems: for example, by minimizing seats to deliberately exclude the old or unemployed who don't spend enough money, or using closed circuit TV to keep out the homeless. US cities – and US politics – serve as warnings of how entrenched division and mutual resentment can become. In some big cities the dominant concern of the planning brief is to find ways of excluding unwanted groups. The new planning language includes such terms as enhancement districts (where federal antidrug penalties are raised) and exclusion zones (where there is anticamping legislation to keep out the homeless). In Los Angeles the police department now has an effective veto over planning decisions which it used recently to block provision of public toilets in parks and subway stations. In Houston exclusion has gone a step further with a whole network of streets built underground for the white office workers to keep them insulated from the rest of the city.

In Britain by contrast people still favour more inclusive spaces. More than half the population has a public library card, nearly half regularly use parks, and most enjoy the unpredictability and the social mixing these facilities involve. If anything there has been a renewal of interest in the social and bonding role that public facilities such as libraries and parks can play in creating a neutral space where all sections of the community can freely mix – a modern commons, if you wish.

The third reason is the link between public spaces and employment. A generation ago, the great majority of public spaces were full of public officials, tending the parks, guarding stations, selling tickets or patrolling the streets. Several decades of rationalization and cutbacks have dramatically reduced these numbers. More than sixty British Rail stations in London for example now have no staff, and more than a hundred have staff only for a few hours each day. Many parks are policed by security guards in vehicles who come for a few minutes at a time and then speed off, just as the 'bobbies' on the beat have been replaced by cars, or estate caretakers by mobile patrols and CCTV.

In other parts of the world the job of caring for and overseeing public spaces provides employment for millions of older people who often lack the skills to go into the new jobs in services or technology. The concierge and the warden are part of the fabric of life. Here too we may increasingly see the benefits of combining two problems – high unemployment for the middle-aged and the elderly, and intense public insecurity about open spaces – to create a new solution. Much the same lesson was learnt in New York, where the Parks Commissioner commented after a drive to replace park attendants with mobile crews that 'the worker who appeared to be idle much of the day had in fact been lending a presence to the park that moderated disorder and gave a touch of humanity to a neighbourhood lacking in social services'. Here in Britain we have found that a sense of security depends far more on the presence of people (both employees and members of the public) 'crowding out crime', than it does on cameras and mobile security patrols.

A fourth reason is that the new model has not automatically won the support of ethnic minorities. Britain's Black and Asian communities overwhelmingly live in cities (and within them in quite specific concentrations or districts), and are likely to be the last groups to venture into the rural hinterland – even for a day, let alone to live.[7] They have tended to recreate some of the feel of cities in their countries of origin: close-knit, dense and based on walking rather than driving. Cities continue to be laboratories for the ideal that different cultures, religions, belief-systems and lifestyles can coexist in close proximity. When interviewed by one of the authors, the Guyana-born London-based novelist Mike Phillips was effusive about the magnetism of the city: 'You must understand,' he said, 'we never had the myth of a rural paradise. We embraced the city because it meant progress, material progress, intellectual progress, educational progress.'

The final reason has to do with culture. Recent decades have seen a steady industrialization of public space. Everywhere has to have a defined purpose. More and more spaces are consciously programmed as to their atmosphere, their music, and who can use them for what. In work precisely the same pressures to intensify the use of time and spaces are increasing levels of stress as well as productivity. As this happens we come to value all the more those spaces which have no overt purpose, where time stands still, the places like libraries, parks, street corners or cafés which are best simply for idling, chatting or meditating.[8]

Unfortunately, despite the flaws of the Los Angeles model, policy-makers have not projected a credible alternative. Assessments of recent policy have had to conclude that urban regeneration policies of the last two decades have been fragmented and ineffective, too concerned with property and not enough with people.[9] Few policy-makers have been clear about whether urban problems should be understood as problems fundamentally *of* cities or problems *in* cities.

In our view we need to take much more seriously the extent to which urban unease cannot simply be understood in terms of problems that are concentrated in urban areas.

Instead we need a new approach that builds on the central virtues of the city – its role as a place of conviviality, a place where people meet, trade, exchange, share ideas, and that avoids the error of seeking to replace the vitality of the city with the sterile atmosphere of the shopping centre or of replacing it with an ersatz rural design.

The first starting point would be a better balance between the parts and the whole. Without some responsibility for the system as a whole cities fall apart. British cities in particular lack the capacity to act strategically. But equally there are important new ways to devolve some power downwards: neighbourhood councils, advisory groups, citizens' juries, 'planning for real' exercises are all providing new means for people to connect to decisions about their locality. Of course self-defining and self-elected community groups or informal networks can be as sectarian or as exclusive as any formal bodies. One community's neighbourhood patrol is another community's vigilante group. Public spaces such as streets, parks and town centres (particularly at night) are often battlegrounds of conflicting interests and desires: car-drivers versus pedestrians, homeless people versus tourists, parents of young children versus dog-owners, those seeking peace and quiet versus those who want to party, women being harassed by men, racial tensions and so on. But in some cases it may be better to hand over parts of the city – such as a park – to a local trust, than to leave it as the direct responsibility of an overstretched municipal department.

A second element would be a return to high density. One of the stereotypes of urban life has been overcrowding and, as a result, lowering urban population densities has been one of the long-term goals of the planning profession. It is only now that the idea of increasing density is again being discussed, as the growth of one-person households in cities casts a new light on the debate. Recent studies have indicated that it is the sense of privacy and control over one's immediate living conditions that are important. Lower density housing may not reduce 'urban problems', as many edge of city estates can now testify. Instead reductions in pollution, crime and noise may help to engender a sense of increased personal control over life in the city.

Thirdly, we will need to think about a new pattern of time organization, to assist the rise of the twenty-four-hour city. Changing patterns of employment and leisure are producing a multiplicity of lifestyles, many of which are increasingly enacted at night rather than during the day. For young people, for example, dance culture is an all-night affair, and the 'evening economy' generally is now a standard programme item of many local authority economic development strategies.[10] In some areas of cities the evening economy is now more dynamic than the day-time economy.

Fourthly, there needs to be an encouragement of a public culture. The traditional assumption that a vibrant street life and public culture was only possible in warmer, more Latinate cultures, is now disputed. In fact it was the English who invented the promenade (or the 'monkey parade' as it was more popularly called), as well as the culture of the coffee house (which for the German philosopher and historian, Jürgen Habermas, was the founding institution of the European tradition of public life). Scandinavian cities such as Stockholm, Helsinki and Copenhagen, have been very successful over the past two decades in creating a café culture and public cultural life where none existed before.[11] Festivals, happenings, fireworks displays and concerts that use public spaces in new ways – all are means for reinforcing the sense of the city as a convivial melting pot.

The fifth element is a move away from the hegemony of 'the design solution'. The dominant discourses of urban renewal in Britain are still those of urban design and landscape architecture ('designing out crime'), allied to the leading role assumed by architects, planners and street furniture manufacturers rather than sociologists, representatives of social movements or community groups, as well as the city inhabitants and users themselves. Design is prioritized over desire, planning over people. The priority in the future will be to combine physical thinking and social thinking in new ways.

Sixth, there is the increasingly pressing issue of sustainability. Sustainability is a new buzzword, loudly signalled at the beginning of every mission statement, corporate policy, or environmental manifesto. It has encouraged some valuable moves to rethink the ecology of cities – how they manage waste, energy, transport and water – and programmes for the 'greening of the city' which have turned derelict sites into attractive and heavily used recreation areas. What have been less well understood are the links between ecological sustainability and social sustainability. People who do not trust each other will not become involved in programmes of mutual aid, land reclamation, waste sifting, or indeed in moral arguments about reduced consumption.

Seventh is education, now a much more dynamic part of the urban scene. The dramatic impact of the rapid growth of higher education in many towns and cities is already a major factor in urban renewal, while the revolt against the car is now becoming part of a new planning orthodoxy. Ten years ago neither of these factors was anticipated. The combination of new economies of knowledge and information, high capacity communications networks, and greater understanding of the role of creativity in urban life is giving a new slant on cosmopolitanism, the role of the city as a melting pot of ideas and innovation. It is also generating new roles for the library (which can become an access point to a range of information services as well as a meeting place or study centre).

Eighth and finally, we need to think far more seriously about transport. The new tram systems in Manchester and Sheffield have done more to present a sense of quick, clean, efficient and above all modern change in these cities than any number of passing regeneration policies. Future transport policies will determine whether cities come to be seen as anachronistic polluting gridlocked structures or as places that make the most of individual mobility and therefore enhance the opportunities to get about and make the most of the convivial city.

Some years ago Raymond Williams, in his book *The Country and the City,* asked the following question: if the countryside represents the past, and the city the future, where does this leave the present? The answer may be that today, just as the public has lost confidence in the city's models of the future, so too the countryside no longer seems able to fulfil the promise of a peaceful idyll. While in rural areas battles are fought over the aesthetics of wind farms (and as Raymond Williams pointed out, 'landscape' was always the enemy of a working rural economy), in cities people are trying to find a new balance between greening and the messy cosmopolitanism that gives many British cities their energy. As they do so they are beginning to understand the future of the city in terms that redefine its attractions and reinforce the continuity with the past: the continuity of the idea of the city as a place of conviviality and social interaction, of creativity and experimentation, tolerance and dissent, which cannot be reduced to the instrumentalities of a communications network, a proliferation of shopping and other leisure opportunities, or architecture as a heritage experience.

13

The End of Unemployment

Bringing work to life

CHARLES LEADBEATER and GEOFF MULGAN

For the last twenty years unemployment has been steadily rising across the industrialized world. At first it caused great consternation. But more recently in many countries it has quietly come to be accepted as a fact of life. It is common to pay lipservice to the need to address unemployment, but genuine political energy is missing.

Much the same was true of inflation in the mid 1970s. Many came to believe that inflation was an unavoidable feature of the times, a product of deep-seated conflicts over distribution and the public's apparently insatiable demand for ever higher public spending. Instead, once the costs grew too high, politicians of both left and right found that they did in fact have the political will to deal with inflation. Today inflation is a relatively marginal problem for most of the OECD countries.

Could we now be in a similar position with regard to unemployment? Could the costs at last be prompting a more serious reappraisal? As yet the signs are unclear. But despite the policy inertia there is growing awareness that the costs are not only high but also cumulative. Moreover there is a broader perception that persistent unemployment does not only waste talent, undermine public finances, cause unhappiness and ill health and unravel social cohesion, but that it also has a subtler effect through the insecurity of those in work.

Even those in the very best jobs realize that something is badly awry in a labour market that leaves a widening divide between those forced into the idleness of unemployment and those stressed by high-paid, high-pressure jobs; between work-rich families, which bring home several incomes, and families without work which survive on a mixture of welfare benefits, and in many cases, on undeclared cash in hand payments for odd jobs and petty crime. Charles Handy puts it well in his book *The Empty Raincoat*: 'If work were so great,' quipped Mark Twain, 'the rich would have hogged it long ago.' They have, Mr Twain, they have.'[1]

So far Western governments have offered little but palliatives. Economic solutions are repeatedly proposed, implemented and then discarded as ineffective. Across the spectrum, from the free market right to the green left a depressing conventional wisdom has taken hold – that high unemployment is inevitable and irreversible. It is blamed on impersonal, global economic forces which are beyond our control or on the moral failings of individuals who are not prepared to look hard enough for work. We rarely recognize it for what it is: the failure of much of the culture of work and many of its institutions to adapt to sweeping change.

This cultural and institutional dimension helps to explain why economic diagnoses and cures have proved so disappointing. Our first task, then, is to understand why existing approaches to unemployment have failed.

First, training: although skills training is a necessary part of any programme for making people employable it is not sufficient. Training in specific skills may be less important than learning more general competences. Training for adults may come too late if they leave school inadequately prepared. It will be worthless unless jobs are created. Any programme that depends too much on training provision without tackling other dimensions of work is doomed to failure. Even Sweden, often cited as a model of active training-based labour market measures, kept unemployment low primarily by high public sector employment.

Second, macroeconomic intervention. Misconceived macroeconomic policies can harm employment, particularly if they lead to unnecessarily heavy shake-outs and the loss of accumulated experience and organizational capital. Once jobs are lost in a recession it is very hard to get them back again. But macro policies on their own can do little to create jobs in the long run. Over the past four decades there has been no simple correlation between growth and unemployment, and no guarantee that demand expansion creates sustainable jobs.

Third, deregulation. In the USA, policies to deregulate the labour market have helped to generate jobs. But the costs have included growing wage inequality, strong incentives for young men to go into crime (since the rewards of crime relative to legitimate unskilled work have risen so much) and a huge increase in the prison population.[2] Deregulation in Britain has encouraged firms to employ more women in part-time jobs (partly by allowing relative wages to fall), but it has done little to reduce male unskilled unemployment. The unskilled in Britain are competing directly with low-wage economies such as southern China. The wage reductions needed to compete are so great that they are virtually inconceivable, not for economic reasons but for social and cultural ones.

Fourth, regulation. The prevailing social democratic approaches to employment have lost credibility. Over-regulated labour markets have preserved wages and security for some only at the cost of high unemployment for others. Nonwage labour costs, such as social security contributions, have reached levels which seem to be unsustainable for developed economies facing mounting competition from the rising economies of East Asia.

Fifth, alternatives to work. The imaginative approaches of the greens and advocates of the post-industrial leisure society welcome a shift away from work and call for a basic income to be provided for all. These approaches pose a vital question – can we find alternatives to work as a source of status and income? Many simply assume that work will inevitably become less central to our lives. But much of the evidence points in the opposite direction, which is why some fear that basic income schemes might simply entrench social division and exclusion by removing any responsibility for government to find work for people. There is also another good reason for doubting the potential of simplistic schemes to reduce working time or years in work. Already the movement of many under twenty-five and over fifty out of the workforce is exacerbating fiscal strains and, paradoxically, making it harder for governments to act on unemployment.

Sixth, demographics. Some now hope that falling numbers of young people entering the labour market will take unemployment off the policy agenda. But although demographic trends will make it easier to cut unemployment (and possibly crime) in the years ahead, there is no evidence that they will in any way be adequate to a problem which has far deeper roots.

Why then is unemployment so high? The key facts are these: since 1950 five million jobs in the UK have gone from the goods-producing industries. About eight million new jobs have been created in services, both public and private.[3] But this has not been enough to prevent unemployment rising, partly because the new jobs have not been taken up by unemployed men and partly because many more women have taken up work.

Meanwhile, the structures of work have been transformed. Many jobs at the bottom and top of the scale remain relatively unchanged: the manual services of cleaning, cooking and caring on the one hand and the jobs of top civil servants, lawyers and even business people on the other. But in the middle a revolution has taken place: old, semi-skilled repetitive industrial jobs have gone; repetitive, white-collar jobs, filing and form-filling, have been replaced by computer systems; jobs demanding very specialized skills, particularly knowledge jobs such as consultancy and law, have become more common. Jobs which could be easily done by anyone, and jobs dependent on physical strength, have disappeared in their millions.

The long-run patterns are striking. While in manufacturing a third of all jobs disappeared after 1979, jobs in finance, insurance and property rose over 700,000. Since 1950 jobs in community, social and personal services increased by 3.5 million, including a million in health and 1.2 million in education. Perhaps surprisingly, 1.25 million of these new public service jobs were created after Margaret Thatcher came to power in 1979.

These patterns are set to continue. During the 1990s it is forecast that employment will fall by 24 per cent in primary activities (like mining) and utilities, 12 per cent in manufacturing and 3 per cent in construction. By contrast, according to the Department of Employment, there will be 16 per cent more jobs in business and other services, and 8 per cent in public services.[4] Part-time work will also continue expanding, partly because it suits employers, and partly because it suits many people: across the EU three times as many full-timers want to go part-time as vice-versa.

The brunt of the collapse of industrial employment has fallen upon the shoulders of the less skilled. About a third of unskilled men are without a job, because in addition to those unemployed and seeking work, an even larger group has withdrawn from the labour force altogether.[5] Not only are unskilled men more likely to be unemployed, they are likely to remain unemployed longer. The inflow into unemployment in Britain is lower than in the United States: fewer people become unemployed. Yet once unemployed, people in Britain remain jobless for much longer.

By contrast women's employment, particularly part-time employment in the service sector, has risen sharply in the past two decades, for two main reasons. The combination of rising aspirations and employers' demand for workers with higher skills has brought many qualified women back into the labour market and women have been prepared to take up part-time, low-wage jobs that men have spurned.

But women have not entirely escaped the concentration of long-term unemployment upon the unskilled. Employment is increasingly unequally divided between households. Women are much more likely to work if they live with a man who works.

About 60 per cent of women with working husbands are also in jobs, compared with only 24 per cent of women with unemployed husbands.

Although the burden of unemployment is concentrated on the least skilled, the threat of unemployment is spreading to virtually all jobs and classes. As technological change accelerates and widens in scope, and as international competition penetrates more areas of the economy, so more jobs – white-collar administrative jobs, managerial jobs, skilled software jobs – will be vulnerable.

Virtually everyone in the modern economy now faces the risk of some period of enforced underwork, whether through involuntary part-time work, early retirement or bouts of unemployment.[6] This may be why workers in most countries now value security even more than income, particularly British workers who, according to a recent survey of twelve OECD countries, feel the least secure in their jobs.[7]

Behind the shifts in technology and industry and the rising tide of economic insecurity, there is another cause of the unemployment crisis: a deep-seated imbalance between work and consumption.

The past two decades have exposed an alarming gap between the speed at which different markets, cultures and institutions respond to change. Financial capital moves vast distances in seconds. Its productivity is measured in minutes. The microelectronics revolution has radically reduced the useful life of physical capital, machines and computers. Consumer goods markets are in constant flux, subject to rapid shifts in demand, from product proliferation in periods of boom to basic value-for-money products in recession. The rapidity of these shifts in the finance, capital and consumer goods markets has penetrated deep into everyone's economic life and they have brought with them equally rapid shifts in the competitive standing of countries, regions and companies.

The dislocation between these markets is not purely economic. It reflects a cultural and political imbalance. The financial markets are awash with information and analysis, measuring minute movements in financial assets. Consumers have a plethora of information and advice on what to buy, ranging from high impact advertisements to more objective advice from bodies like the Consumers Association and consumer magazines. In contrast the labour market is malnourished. There are far more television programmes and magazines devoted to food and drink than there are to work and jobs. For most people there is little easily available information about the quality of employers, about training and education or likely career opportunities in five or ten years' time. We are well abreast of the latest developments in the currency markets, fashions for clothes and cars, but often quite clueless about technologies which will soon revolutionize – and perhaps abolish – our jobs.

Although the customer may be king at the supermarket, today's citizens are often still treated as disposable commodities at the workplace, where they are caught up in repeated waves of technological and organizational change. The costs are both psychological and economic. Job stress is thought to cost the UK up to 10 per cent of GDP annually, through sickness, poor productivity, staff turnover and premature death.[8]

These figures should serve as a warning. For the vast majority of people work remains a far more central part of their lives than consumption, occupying half of all waking hours on a typical day. Compared to consumption, work is a more important source of satisfaction,[9] learning and socialization and a better creator of meaning and purpose.[10] But more in Britain do mindless, repetitive work than in comparable countries, and fewer workers in Britain feel that their job is of value to society than in other societies.[11] Much socially vital work is undervalued, in terms of both money and status.

And far too few people have made the transition from simply doing jobs to developing their talents in a career.

The implication is that although chronic unemployment is particularly acute for groups made vulnerable by their lack of flexible transferable skills, this is only the bleakest manifestation of a wider problem: work is becoming ever more insecure, demanding and pressurized for anyone exposed to competitive markets shaped by technological change.

The full employment policies of the 1940s were part of a much larger programme of reform which embraced education and the welfare state, for those in and out of work. Policy today must be equally ambitious. It must pull in tax and benefits, as well as education and families, the needs of the employed and the unemployed. It will only succeed as part of a raft of measures to ease the central tension in our society: that despite – or because of – work's increasing insecurity, it is ever more central to our lives. It is to these measures that we now turn, setting out the seven main areas where change is needed.

1. Serious Learning

The economic base of our society is ever less embodied in buildings and machines and ever more in people: in what the Japanese call the 'gold in people's heads'. A profound change is underway in the asset base for our economies. Alongside financial capital, the most important assets in the modern economy are knowledge and skills, underpinned by culture and values.

This change in the nature of economies has been underway for a long time. It has been estimated that the amount of labour (and raw material) needed for each additional unit of output in manufacturing has been declining at a compound rate of 1 per cent per year since 1900. By contrast, the incremental amount of knowledge and information needed for each incremental unit of GNP has been going up at a rate of 1 per cent per year compound.[12]

Those societies which invest effectively in knowledge and information will be better placed to secure high-skilled, high-income jobs in the international economy. They will also be more secure in a world where security depends more on brainpower than on weapons; this is one reason why the UK should worry that it has the highest ratio of military spending to spending on education of any OECD nation. And brainpower is only partly a matter of qualifications. People's confidence and capacity to shape change are just as important.

Investment in the 'hard' infrastructure of transport and telecommunications links will generate some jobs, but probably fewer than investment in less tangible, 'softer' assets like organizational innovations or education. All the institutions involved in generating those soft assets – families and schools, companies and the state, the tax system and the training system – will have to adapt and to learn new priorities.

First is finance, a necessary though far from sufficient condition. In the 1980s many nations believed that stable and independent control over money would provide the key to prosperity. Today, skills and knowledge have become the currency of the modern economy. The value of this currency needs constant care and long-term dedication. Such commitment has a corollary: that we need to reassess the role and purpose of schools and other institutions that spend public money. Education standards need to be raised, especially for the vast majority of middle-achieving children under sixteen. To do this we need to rethink the purpose of schools. In tandem with stressing standards and league tables, schools need to develop as more flexible and porous institutions. The key skill the modern economy demands is the ability to understand and shape change. Schools should become more individualized to promote excellence in different forms of intelligence, whether mathematical, linguistic, musical or interpersonal. The enhancement of those forms of intelligence needs to be linked to different types of work experience, with much more systematic links between schools, employers and the outside community.

Next we must radically rethink the task of the teachers whose role as imparters of knowledge is losing its centrality when facts (and learning tools) can be more easily accessed by computers. Instead they need to become ever more like tutors or brokers matching children's competences to courses, and helping them prepare for a rapidly changing labour market.

We also need to create much better screening and selection mechanisms to match the diverse array of intelligences and competences to the different types of useful work in the private, public and voluntary sectors. A careers or jobs advisory service should be one of the highest status institutions in the land. Instead, the careers service is poorly run. We should develop a mentor system, so that children spend time with a mentor (who will coach/tutor them) throughout their schooling. In parallel we should develop a system of careers brokers who would be professionals charged with careers advice and pastoral care, and who would help young people deal with employment and further education institutions outside the school.

We need to rethink the sources of social equity. Equitable outcomes depend on more equitable investment. The UK spends less than half as much on an unemployed trainee as on an undergraduate. Sweden by contrast spends the same. This is one reason why its income distribution – like the East Asian societies and Germany – is much more equal than the UK. We must shift spending away from tertiary education (which currently spends 75 per cent more per capita than primary and secondary education, and much of which could be financed through loans repaid from future incomes) to universal pre-sixteen schooling, probably starting at the age of three.[13]

Britain's problem is not that its private education sector is too large but that it is too small. Like Japan, Singapore or Korea, we need to create a much more active, broadly spread education market outside school, with private tutors and small companies providing local education services, especially in the hours between the end of the school day and the end of the working day for many parents. Private investment in education should become the norm, not the exception. The state could provide collateral for career development and education loans, which families or individuals could take out to spend on private tuition outside school or work, as already happens on a modest scale in many countries.

New technology – interactive, multimedia technologies linking computers and televisions – can deliver huge improvements in learning to the school, the workplace and the home. As a result the organization of, and provision of access to these multimedia networks is becoming a central public policy issue.

These are just a few of the prerequisites for developing the economic base for the twenty-first century. We might have added the radical transformation of the universities and support for all those institutions that have taken over much of their role in developing and disseminating knowledge and ideas.[14] We might have stressed school's evolving role as a community hub, not only for parents but also for the unemployed, single parents and the elderly. These too will be essential to securing our economic base in the future. For if the old, Keynesian way to tackle unemployment was to dig holes, the modern way is to fill brains and release potential.

2. Wise Taxes

Most of the responsibility for improving education falls upon national or local government, or their agents. But much will also depend upon employers, individuals and families taking more responsibility for their own learning. Encouraging this will mean tax changes.

In the 1950s and 1960s, the role of fiscal policy was to deliver enough demand to ensure full employment. In the 1980s the focus was on tax cuts to create incentives for the well-paid. Apart from periodic proposals for subsidizing the wages of unskilled workers there has been little debate about using the tax system as a tool to make the labour market more responsive. Something far much more radical is now required.

The tax system should be overhauled, shifting its bias towards human capital creation. Tax concessions currently applied to property should be given instead to brain power – providing clear incentives for those taking time out of work to gain new qualifications in accredited institutions. Incentives currently targeted at physical machinery should be redirected to companies which are certified as good trainers and educators. Public purchasing could be skewed towards companies which meet basic standards of employee development.

Over the medium term, government should reduce payroll taxes such as national insurance that increase the cost to firms of creating jobs. Accounting and tax rules should be changed to allow training expenditure to be written off over the average length of employment at the company rather than when the money is spent. Institutional shareholders, too, should be pushing for much better reporting of the true long-term sources of future value – the brain power of employees. Tax increases on consumption, property and environmentally damaging activities should allow sustained tax cuts on jobs without a deterioration in the public finances. In the 1980s taxes were cut to promote consumption, undermining public finances. In the 1990s we must cut taxes to promote employment growth while protecting the public finances through raising other taxes.

3. Mass Enterprise

Sweeping reforms in learning will provide the base for a strong economy. But this alone will not create new jobs. That will require new means to match workers' abilities to the wants and needs of consumers.

The OECD estimates that one in ten jobs disappears each year. Even standing still requires massive job creation. The past record suggests that this will not be easy, particularly in Europe. The two great generators of jobs after the Second World War – the expanding public sector and large companies – will not provide job growth in the future. The public sector's expansion is constrained by political limits on public spending and taxation. At the same time most large companies are shrinking their workforces.

Our economic culture is moving towards more flexible, smaller-scale forms of employment. This is only partly due to the decline in employment in large plants and large firms. There is also a cultural change underway. Nearly half of young people want to be self-employed. Much of the hostility to wealth creation which used to characterize Britain's elite has diminished.

In this environment, job creation doesn't come from big firms branching out but from small firms reaching up. Maximizing this entrepreneurial capacity is a top priority. For without a fertile enterprise culture it will simply not be possible either to create anything like enough jobs to replace those disappearing elsewhere or to meet the aspirations of millions more, whether women or the semi-retired, who want to have some paid work.

One important element of such a culture is a fairly loose framework of regulations, making it easy to create firms and to take on staff. Any moves to devise new regulations for the economy should be viewed with great caution. Another such element is a well-functioning finance market for small firms, run by people able to judge competences and with good understanding of the nature of business and technology; overcentralized systems of appraisal, of the kind that have become the norm in many banks, do not work well in this respect.

Those out of work should also be trained more effectively to create jobs for themselves. This can be particularly helpful for ethnic minorities and women, who are already at the forefront of new firm creation as they try to escape the discriminatory hierarchies of larger firms. Entrepreneurship has become a skill vital to everyone. The image of the entrepreneur as a young, well-dressed male, with slicked-back hair and a mobile phone, is deeply misleading. All of us at some point in our lives may be dependent on a small company that we set up or work for and increasingly self-employment is becoming an option for the old and retired as well as the young. They too will increasingly need access to specialized venture capital, community development banks and loan funds.

4. Secure Flexibility

Few expect the work environment of the next century to be anything other than insecure, fast-moving and unpredictable. In the future the main source of security will be an individual's employability rather than their employment by a large, hierarchical employer or protection by a trade union.

At the workplace this will require a major shift in attitudes. Rosabeth Moss Kanter argues that employers should now be offering a new social contract based on the concept of employability. This will mean recruiting people with potential, not just the narrow skills to fill existing slots; providing abundant learning opportunities at work from lunchtime seminars to formal training; rotating jobs and work experiences; measuring performance in ways beyond numbers, and sharing data to allow learning by doing; recognizing team and individual achievements, to build external reputations and tangible indicators of value; setting up educational sabbaticals and external internships; finding job opportunities in the firm's network of suppliers, customers and venture partners; and, crucially, ensuring full pension portability.[15] For trade unions it implies a much greater commitment to helping people become employable, rather than protecting them in existing jobs.

But security will also depend on a larger, public-sponsored

framework of insurance to provide income and training during periods without work, one which is likely to be turned to by a far larger proportion of the population in the future than in the decades after Beveridge. To balance a much faster moving and more flexible economy we must have greater certainty and diversity in the structures of public support.

5. Ways to Share

The measures already discussed would do much to cut unemployment well below current levels, as well as improving the quality of work. But they would still leave a gap, a significant pool of people who would like to work but cannot.

Recent history suggests that the only societies that have achieved anything like full employment for long periods have deliberately fostered a sector of job creation and absorption. Typically, the first part of the economy has been outward-looking, competitive and efficient, based on world-class firms. The second part has been less efficient, effectively subsidized by the first, and able to absorb labour when necessary.

The best examples are Scandinavia and Japan. In countries like Sweden, government acted as the second economy, rapidly expanding employment in the 1960s and 1970s to absorb jobs displaced from manufacturing. In Japan, the second economy has been in agriculture and services, both of which are protected, highly labour-intensive and relatively inefficient.

Each system had a sharing mechanism: a means for those in the first economy working for successful firms like Ericsson and Mitsubishi, Toyota and Volvo, to pay for those in the second economy. In Sweden they paid through taxes and in Japan they pay through higher prices for food and services. In other countries other mechanisms achieve the same effects: for example, in Korea the big industrial *chaebols*, not government, take responsibility for retraining and redeploying their employees.

These examples show that the level of employment is

largely a consequence of how a society is organized: whether the open competitive sector of the economy is large enough, and whether those working in it are willing to make sacrifices to support those in the more protected areas of work.

The conventional wisdom that governments cannot create jobs misses the point: given the resources any government can create useful jobs. The huge increases in public employment in fields like community care confirm that a long-term trend is continuing. The barrier to public job creation is the level of taxation required to pay for it.

Tax in one form or another is likely to be the way to transfer resources in the absence of the kinds of very powerful conglomerates or regulatory frameworks that do it elsewhere. But given the strong resistance to tax increases it seems likely that new transfer mechanisms will be required to provide for the education or employment of those that otherwise would not be employed. The existing pooled tax system is too monolithic, too opaque and too at odds with the rest of our culture to make clear our choices and to make good the connections we need to transfer resources efficiently.[16]

6. Twin Economies

In the 1990s and beyond, government's role should no longer be conceived in the model of the 1930s, as an orchestrator of great armies of the unemployed. Instead it should play a more subtle role – managing the ecology of different types of work and economy to help create work for people excluded from the formal economy.[17] Society is already responding to unemployment in this way, by promoting work in the cash-in-hand, localized service economy. The development of this sub-sector should now become an explicit aim of government policy.

The reason is that the economy has lost its capacity to absorb labour. In past eras labour displaced by productivity rises in one sector was taken up in others. Improvements in agricultural productivity led to jobs moving to manufacturing. Productivity in private manufacturing in the twentieth century saw workers being displaced into services, partly through the growth of the public sector. At other times the armed forces and the construction industry have played a vital role in soaking up labour. Gender inequality has been another traditional means of enforcing sacrifices on one part of the population to benefit another. Women have often been excluded or removed from the labour market to curtail unemployment. In Japan, one reason why employment looks relatively stable is that women bear the brunt of downturns. This is no longer an option in developed Western societies, in part because women will not accept such a role and in part because many employers are now deeply dependent on women's part-time work.

The economy's lack of a sector which can perform this task of absorbing labour displaced from the internationally competitive sectors highlights a new purpose for public policy: to synthesize a new absorptive sector. Such a sector is being created de facto by displaced workers falling into long term unemployment, inactivity and the unregulated, cash-in-hand economy. We argue that public policy should aim to go further, fostering a range of different types of economic sphere to take on the role which in other societies is performed by the state, the family and the service sector.

We envisage a policy which would develop several overlapping sectors which would be relatively labour intensive, with slower technical change than the internationally competitive sectors, and made up of a string of very localized markets. They would also require novel approaches to the exchange of labour for services, measures of the value of those services and methods of paying for them. In addition these new areas of activity would need to be connected with the lives of those in the formal economy to avoid them becoming simply a ghetto of special schemes for the unemployed.

How could such a sector be synthesized? We propose three very different approaches.

One is the deliberate creation of a parallel, protected

economy which would be separate from the fully monetized normal market economy. This would involve the provision and exchange of services – particularly domestic services – with payment in kind or through special vouchers which could be converted into hard currency or used to pay for other services. These would be offered as an alternative to cash to the unemployed and other benefits recipients, and to public institutions like schools and hospitals. They would be used to purchase informal services and underused public assets such as off-peak travel. The goal would be to create a parallel or 'twin' economy protected from the uncertainties generated by the international market, building on the many experiences of parallel economies worldwide. These include the economies organized within large companies, the money systems devised in places as diverse as the towns of eighteenth-century northern England and interwar Austria, and the many thousands of LETS (local exchange trading systems) currently functioning around the world, whereby people in a town or village exchange services.

Two, a range of more imaginative policies to promote the cash-in-hand economy as a distinct and vital sector of the economy. Some parts of this economy are criminal and exploitative: the growth of drugs and prostitution for example. But in general the development of the cash-in-hand economy is a sign of how society and the market is coping with change. Rather than attempt to restrict or curtail it, the government should be attempting to manage its development. Virtually no household in the economy is entirely insulated from the cash-in-hand economy, whether through small acts of tax avoidance or payment in cash for services. Its scale is substantial, particularly domestic services, spending on which rose five times in the last decade to more than £3 billion.

While unemployment remains high, the cash-in-hand economy needs to be promoted as an alternative to theft and burglary. Several simple ideas are worth considering such as raising further the thresholds for VAT payments, relaxing corporate registration requirements for small businesses and allowing people to register as cash-in-hand workers. In return they would get a much higher tax allowance for cash-in hand earnings, but they would lose all entitlement for benefits and face a much higher marginal tax rate if they were found to be earning more than the limit.

Three, a sphere of community service, organized not as a sink for the long-term unemployed but as an activity in which all would participate at various times in their lives. Instead of the existing system whereby unemployment benefit keeps people inactive (and penalizes them if they take up voluntary activities) we would recommend a new category of 'activity benefit' to be paid to people engaged in socially useful activities ranging from community projects to full-time parenting.

7. *Working Ethics*

Attitudes to work have gone through enormous changes. Tilgher described them in his classic book *Work: what it has meant to man through the ages*:

> to the Greeks work was a curse and nothing else. Their name for it has the same root as the Latin sorrow ... coloured with the sense of a heavy burdensome task which we feel in the words fatigue, travail ... [By contrast] it is in work that the man of capitalist civilization finds his nobility and worth.[18]

This, the importance of work to human development, used to be well understood by the economists. Adam Smith wrote that the 'understandings of the greater part of men are necessarily formed by their ordinary employments' and that the person engaged in repetitive industrial work 'becomes ... stupid and ignorant'.[19] Alfred Marshall too wrote that people's characters are formed by how they use their faculties at work. But their modern counterparts have lost interest.

The result has been a failure to understand the importance of the cultures of work.

For just as the once dominant forms of work are declining so are the cultures and values which went with them. There are still work ethics but they are weaker than they were. The public sector's ethic of dutiful service is embattled, as is the voluntary sector's ethic of care. The values of traditional skilled manual work, which were embedded in craft unions and apprenticeship schemes, are dwindling. Even the professional ethics of doctors, accountants and lawyers are less confident than they were, more a defence of privileges than a code of behaviour and a sense of social responsibility.

The decline of these work ethics has had a tremendously destabilizing effect. They helped to define who someone was both at work and in society. They defined a sense of responsibility for work, loyalty to colleagues and obligation to others, expressed through guilds, unions and apprenticeship schemes.

But those settled cultures are no longer tenable. As a result of their decline much of our cultures seems rootless and individualized. Our cultures of work are feeble and ephemeral – the high-achieving ethic of the well-paid, the job-skipping cultures of computer programmers, the money culture of the financial markets. None of these individualized achievement cultures matches the comprehensive old work cultures which embraced obligation and responsibility to others as well as personal achievement.

That is why we now need to cultivate new working ethics which bring together personal advancement and social responsibility, autonomy and security.

There are two keys: revitalizing and strengthening the notion of sovereignty as self-reliance; developing more flexible, diverse and malleable contributions to and forms of communal support to insure against the periods of insecurity which are now inevitable parts of everyone's lives.

The ideal of individual sovereignty and autonomy is deeply embedded within our culture. Yet it is increasingly confined to consumption and leisure. The idea that work is a vital domain for individual action and self-expression has been virtually written off. Neither of the dominant political traditions has much to say on the subject. The right talks of the authority of management, the sovereignty of the consumer and the ultimate power of shareholders. The labour movement mirrors this, its approach to work is determined by the trade unions' defensive concern to prevent abuses and exploitation at work.

What we need now is a more rounded sense of sovereignty based on self-reliance at work. There will be no single work ethic in future. But it is likely that the emerging cultures of work will have to combine four key elements.

First, work, especially for the unskilled, will have to borrow increasingly from consumption and leisure as its model, in part because of dwindling respect for hierarchy and authority. People are spending more time at work; they want it to be challenging and interesting, enlivening and motivating.

Second, self-employment and small company employment will form the environment. Even in large organizations people will be working in smaller, less hierarchical groups, where they will take more responsibility for the outcome of their work as well as being judged more directly on their performance. Those brought up to expect and respect protective hierarchies will struggle; those who are able to move laterally and work with others will prosper.

Third, where the old work cultures promise a predictable progress up an occupational ladder, the new work cultures must equip people to embrace uncertainty, switching careers and jobs, companies and locations. If the twentieth-century model has been employment in the large enterprise or government department, the twenty-first-century model may be closer to self-employment for all: self-development through a range of different jobs and organizations.

Fourth, all economic activities are being modelled ever more on services rather than manufacturing, software rather than hardware. Increasingly people will not see the expression of their work in a physical product but in intangibles, such as consumer satisfaction. As a result the most useful models of work will change; the caring ethic, still associated with women's work at home and in services will be more relevant to the future than the physical strength and engineering skills traditionally associated with men.

Above all, what we need in the world of work is a new balance. On the one hand self-reliance – and the understanding that security depends on our own skills and competences more than the benevolence of a paternal state or employer. On the other, a reinvigorated sense of responsibility and interconnection with others. Because it is in work, perhaps more than ever, that people find their connection to the wider society, that they find a sense of purpose and self-respect. For millions that connection has been broken. We now have to make it anew.

14

The Parenting Deficit

AMITAI ETZIONI

Consider parenting as an industry. As farming declined in industrial countries since the beginning of industrialization, most fathers left to work away from home. Over the past twenty years millions of mothers have sharply curtailed their work in the 'parenting industry' by moving to work outside the home. In the USA by 1991 two-thirds (66.7 per cent) of all mothers with children under eighteen were in the labour force[1] and more than half (55.4 per cent) of women with children under the age of three. At the same time a much smaller number of child-care personnel moved into the parenting industry.

If this were any other business, say, shoemaking, and more than half of the labour force had been lost and replaced with fewer, less-qualified hands and we still asked the shoemakers to produce the same number of shoes of the same quality (with basically no changes in technology), we would be considered crazy. But this is what happened to parenting. When men and then women left to work outside the home, they were replaced by some child-care services, a relatively small increase in baby-sitters and nannies, and some additional service by grandparents – leaving parenting woefully short-handed. The millions of latchkey children,[2] who are left alone for long stretches of time, are but the most visible result of the parenting deficit.

Is this the 'fault' of the women's movement, feminism, or mothers *per se*? Obviously not. All women did was demand for themselves what men had long possessed, working outside the home not only for their own personal satisfaction, but because of what they often perceived as economic necessity. Whatever the cause, the result is an empty nest. Only it isn't the fledglings who grew up and took off: it is the parents who flew the coop. Those who did not leave altogether increased their investment of time, energy, involvement and commitment outside the home.

Although parenting is the responsibility of both parents – and may well be discharged most effectively in two-parent families immersed in a community context of kin and neighbours – *most important is the scope of commitment.* Single parents may do better than two-career absentee parents. Children require a commitment of time, energy, and, above all, of self.

The prevalent situation is well captured by a public service advertisement in which a mother calls her child and reassures him that she has left money for him next to the phone. 'Honey, have some dinner,' she mutters as the child takes the twenty dollar bill she left behind, rolls it up, and snorts cocaine. One might add that the father didn't even call.

The fact is that parenting cannot be carried out over the phone, however well-meaning and loving the calls may be. It requires physical presence. The notion of 'quality time' (not to mention 'quality phone calls') is a lame excuse for parental absence: it presupposes that bonding and education can take place in brief time bursts, on the run. Quality time occurs within quantity time. As you spend time with your children – fishing, gardening, camping, or just eating a meal – there are unpredictable moments when an opening occurs and education takes hold.

The Institutionalization of Children

Is the answer to the parenting deficit building more child-care centres? After all, other societies have delegated the upbringing of their children, from black nannies in the American South before the Civil War to Greek slaves in ancient Rome.

But in these historical situations the person who attended to the children was an adjunct to the parents rather than a replacement for them and an accessory reserved mostly for upper-class families with leisure. A care-giver remained with the family throughout the children's formative years and often beyond: she was, to varying degrees, integrated into the family. The care-giver, in turn, reflected, at least in part, the family's values and educational posture. Some children may have been isolated from their parents, but as a rule there was a warm, committed figure dedicated to them, one who bonded and stayed with them.

Today most child-care centres are woefully understaffed with poorly paid and underqualified personnel. Child-care workers are in the lowest tenth of all wage earners.[3] They frequently receive no health insurance or other benefits, which makes child-care an even less attractive job. The personnel come and go, at a rate of 41 per cent per year at an average US day-care centre.

Bonding between children and care-givers under these circumstances is very difficult to achieve. Moreover, children suffer a loss every time their surrogate parents leave. It would be far from inaccurate to call the worst of these facilities 'kennels for kids'. There are a few fine, high-quality care centres, but they are as rare and almost as expensive as the nannies that some truly affluent families can command. These exceptions should not distract us from the basically dismal picture: substandard care and all too frequent warehousing of children, with overworked parents trying frantically to make up the deficit in their spare time.

Government or social supervision of the numerous small institutions and home facilities in which child-care takes place to ensure proper sanitation and care, even to screen out child abusers, is difficult and often completely neglected or only nominally carried out. We should not be surprised to encounter abuses such as the case of the child-care home in which fifty-four children were left in the care of a sixteen-year-old and were found strapped into child car-seats for the entire day.[4]

Certainly many low-income couples and single parents have little or no choice except to use the minimum that such centres provide. All we can offer here is to urge that before parents put their children into such institutions, they should check them out as extensively as possible (including surprise visits in the middle of the day). Moreover we should all support these parents' quest for additional support from employers and government if they cannot themselves spend more on child-care.

Particularly effective are cooperative arrangements that require each parent to contribute some time – perhaps four hours each week – to serve at his or her child's centre. Not only do such arrangements reduce the centre costs, they also allow parents to see first-hand what actually goes on, ensuring some measure of built in accountability. It provides for continuity – while staff come and go, parents stay. (Even if they divorce, they may still participate in their child-care centre.) And as parents get to know other parents of children in the same stages of development, they form social bonds, which can be drawn upon to work together to make these centres more responsive to children's needs.

Above all, age matters. Infants under two years old are particularly vulnerable to separation anxiety. Several bodies of data strongly indicate that infants who are institutionalized at a young age will not mature into well-adjusted adults.[5] A study of eight-year-olds by two University of Texas researchers compared children who returned home after school to their mothers with children who remained in day-care centres:

> Children who stayed at the day care centre after school were having problems. They received more negative peer nominations, and their negative nominations outweighed their positive nominations. In addition, the day care third graders made lower academic grades on their report card and

> scored lower on standardized tests. There was some evidence of poor conduct grades.[6]

Unless the parents are absent or abusive, infants are better off at home. Older children, between two and four, may be able to handle some measures of institutionalization in child-care centres, but their personalities often seem too unformed to be able to cope well with a nine-to-five separation from a parent.

There is no sense looking back and beating our breasts over how we got ourselves into the present situation. But we must acknowledge that as a matter of social policy (as distinct from some individual situations) we have made a mistake in assuming that strangers can be entrusted with the effective personality formation of infants and toddlers. Over the last twenty-five years we have seen the future, and it is not a wholesome one. If we fervently wish them to grow up in a civilized society, and if we seek to live in one, we need to face facts: it will not happen unless we dedicate more of ourselves to our children and their care and education.

Equality Within the Family

Who needs to bond with children? Both parents. It is no accident that in a wide variety of human societies (from the Zulus to the Inuits, from ancient Greece and ancient China to the present), there has never been a society that did not have two-parent families. Societies have varied a great deal in the roles they assigned to other members of the family (aunts, uncles, grandparents) and in the educational roles of other members of the tribe. They have also varied a great deal in the specifics of the relationship between the parents and the child. But in the hundreds of known societies throughout recorded history, two-parent families have been the norm.

To argue that the two-parent family is 'better' than the single-parent family is in no way to denigrate single parents.

It's akin to saying that for most purposes a two-bedroom home is better than a one-bedroom home. Moreover, just because most people prefer a two-bedroom home does not mean that those who have a home with only one bedroom are in it only or firstly by their choice.

There are several compelling reasons why two-parent families are the most suitable form for children. First, child-care and education are labour-intensive, demanding tasks. Young children are a very needy bunch. They can soak up huge amounts of care, attention and love. Second, parenting works best when there is a division of educational labour. One parent may be more supportive, the source of emotional security that all children require if they are to grow up in a threatening world. The other parent may be more achievement oriented, pushing children to extend themselves beyond the comfortable cradle of love.[7]

In many countries mothers have historically often fulfilled the former role, while fathers have typically adopted the latter. But the two-piston engine of effective education can work the other way around. Indeed, in some contemporary families children are cuddled by their fathers and disciplined by their mothers. What matters most is the two-parent mode. True, some single parents can shift back and forth between the supportive and achievement-oriented modes of parenting quite successfully. But this is difficult to accomplish on top of other difficulties faced by a single parent, who is often the sole breadwinner as well.

Another essential feature for a family effectively to carry out its parenting mission is a mutually supportive educational coalition. The parents as educational agents, must be mutually supportive because their specific educational goals are in part contradictory. Goading children to achieve generates stress ('Did you prepare for your maths test yet'), while reassuring them generates a relaxation response ('Don't overdo it – Rome wasn't built in a day'). Hence, only if the parents are basically in agreement can they make education work and avoid being unwittingly played off one against the other by their children, to the detriment of education. (This is, of course, a major reason divorced parents have such a hard time working together to bring up their children, even when they have joint custody.)

The sequence of divorce followed by a succession of partners, a second marriage, and frequently another divorce and another turnover of partners often means a repeatedly disrupted educational coalition. Each change in participants involves a change in the educational agenda for the child. Each new partner cannot be expected to pick up the previous one's educational role and programme. The educational input that each adult provides is deeply affected by his or her total personality and upbringing. As a result, changes in parenting partners means, at best, a deep disruption in a child's education, though of course several disruptions cut deeper into the effectiveness of the educational coalition than just one. (The discussion presumes, somewhat optimistically, that new partners are willing to get involved in the first place.)

When I testified on these matters before a US Senate committee, I was asked whether I was implying that single parents cannot bring up children properly. I answered:

> As I read the social science findings, it would be preferable to have three parents per child, or to draw upon grandparents and child care staff to supplement, but not replace, their two parents. Parenting is a heavy duty load for single parents to carry entirely on their own, especially if they are employed full-time outside the household.

I should have added that the sad fact is that most divorced fathers quickly fade away as parents, and that fathers who were never married to their children's mothers infrequently play a paternal role.

The Valuation of Children

When discussing parental responsibilities many ask how it is possible to have more time for children if the parents need to work full-time to make ends meet. Our response requires an examination of the value of children as compared to other 'priorities'.

Nobody likes to admit it, but between 1960 and 1990 American and British society allowed children to be devalued, while the golden call of 'making it' was put on a high pedestal. Recently, first-year undergraduates in the USA listed 'being well off financially' as more important than 'raising a family'.[8]

Some blame this development on the women's rights movement, others on the elevation of materialism and greed to new historical heights. These and other factors may have all combined to devalue children. However, women are obviously entitled to all the same rights men are, including the pursuit of greed.

But few people who advocated equal rights for women favoured a society in which sexual equality would mean a society in which all adults would act like men, who in the past were relatively inattentive to children. The new gender-equalized world was supposed to be a combination of all that was sound and ennobling in the traditional roles of women and men. Women were to be free to work any place they wanted, and men would be free to show emotion, care, and domestic commitment. For children this was not supposed to mean, as it often has, that they would be bereft of dedicated parenting. Now that we have seen the result of decades of widespread neglect of children, the time has come for both parents to revalue children and for the community to support and recognize their efforts. Parents should be entitled not just to equal pay for equal work, equal credit and housing opportunities, and the right to choose a last name: they also must bear equal responsibilities – above all, for their children.

One major way that commitment may be assessed is by the number of hours that are dedicated to a task over the span of a day. According to a 1985 study by a University of Maryland sociologist, parents in the United States spent an average of only seventeen hours per week with their children, compared with thirty in 1965.[9] Even this paltry amount of time is almost certainly an overstatement of the case because it is based on self-reporting.

And we all need to chip in. Many parents point to the great difficulty they have in teaching their children right from wrong. They remind us that they are fighting a culture that bombards their children with unwholesome messages: that it is supremely important to keep up with the Joneses; that you can discharge your human duties and express your feelings by buying something; that violence and raw sex are as pervasive and corrosive as shown on TV and in music tapes, discs, and records. A community that is more respectful of children would *make parenting a less taxing and more fulfilling experience*.

This revaluation of the importance of children has two major ramifications. First, potential parents must consider what is important to them: more income or better relationships with their children. Most people cannot 'have it all'. They must face the possibility that they will have to curtail their gainful employment in order to invest more time and energy into their offspring. This may hurt their chances of making money directly (by working fewer hours) or indirectly (by advancing more slowly in their careers).

Many parents, especially those on lower incomes, argue that they both desire gainful employment not because they enjoy it or seek self-expression, as many radical individualists would have it, but because they 'cannot make ends meet' otherwise. They feel that both parents have no choice but to work full time outside the home if they are to pay for the rent, food, clothing, and other basics. A 1990 Gallup poll found that one half of those households with working mothers would want the mother to stay home if 'money were not an issue'.[10] (The same question should have been asked about fathers.)

This sense of economic pressure certainly has a strong element of reality. Many couples in the 1990s need two pay cheques to buy little more than what a couple in the early 1970s could acquire with a single income. There are millions of people these days, especially the poor and the near poor, who are barely surviving, even when both parents do work long and hard outside the home. If they have several children and work for low wages, they may need to draw on the support of others just to stay afloat. A growing number of working-class families and some of those in the lower reaches of the middle class have also fallen on hard economic times. And surely many single women must work to support themselves and their children. But at some level of income, which is lower than the conventional wisdom would have us believe, parents do begin to have a choice between enhanced earnings and attending to their children.

There is considerable disagreement as to what that level might be. Several social scientists have shown that most of what many wealthier people consider 'essentials' are actually purchases that their cultures and communities tell them are 'essential', rather than what is objectively required. They point out that objectively people need rather little: shelter, liquids, a certain amount of calories and vitamins a day, and a few other such things that can be bought quite cheaply. Most of what people *feel* that they 'must have' – from VCRs to shoes that match their handbags to Nike sneakers to designer frames for their sunglasses – is socially conditioned. This is further documented by the fact that what is considered 'necessary' varies a great deal within the society and over time. Some people cannot live without fancy jeans. Others 'need' garden gnomes on their front lawns (and the lawns themselves!). A colleague who lives in a suburb of New York City was miffed by my implied criticism of people who are so preoccupied with consumer goods that they do not attend adequately to their children. In his letter to me, he observed that because he and his wife had worked long hours outside the household, they were able to buy cars for their children.

Well, the children might just have been better off if they'd had to walk or bike but had more time with their parents. In short, although there may be conflicting notions regarding how high an income level is sufficient for people to satisfy their basic needs, there is clearly a level at which they are able to make choices.

Take a couple of successful young professionals – lawyers, perhaps – who are planning to have a child. They need to decide whether they will continue to invest themselves entirely in their work – putting in long hours at the office, taking briefcases full of work home at night, seeing and entertaining clients on the weekends – or whether they will lighten up on their workload once the child is born. (Lightening up, or course, will reduce their billable hours, and hence their income, and may even delay the time it takes for them to make partner.) They must further decide how much parental leave they are going to take, whether they will try to work different schedules so that at least one of them can be at home at most times, and whether one or both of them will try to work more at home than in the office. (These choices will, in turn, be deeply affected by what their law firms will welcome or at least tolerate; but the firms, too, are likely to be influenced by changing societal values.) All these decisions reflect more than the tension between commitment to a child and to a career and money; they also show that even if both parents choose to remain gainfully employed full time, they still have several options in terms of the relative intensity of their commitment to their children versus other values.

Inner Joy

Ethical theorists have a device that helps people sort out their priorities. They ask you to consider what you would like to have written on your tombstone, how you would like to summarize your life's work. Would you prefer to have it written that you had made more money than you ever believed possible, more than your schoolmates or neighbours? Or would you rather be remembered for helping to bring up some lovely human beings, your children? Having actively participated in bringing up five lovely children, I would conclude that children are not pieces of property that you add to your acquisitions and then turn over to a staff. As the great ethicist Immanuel Kant would have put it, children are ends in themselves, persons full of value – like you and me.

The community – that is, all of us – suffers the ill effects of *absentee* parenting. For example, according to a study by social scientist Jean Richardson and her colleagues, thirteen-year-old students who took care of themselves for eleven or more hours a week were twice as likely to be abusers of controlled substances (that is, smoke marijuana or tobacco and drink alcohol) as those who were actively cared for by adults. 'The increased risk appeared no matter what the sex, race, or socioeconomic status of the children,' Richardson and associates noted. The study found that 31 per cent of latchkey children had two or more drinks at a time, compared with 17 per cent for supervised children; 27 per cent of the latchkey children expected to get drunk in the future, compared with only 15 per cent of the others. And students who took care of themselves for eleven or more hours a week were one and a half to two times more likely 'to score high on risk taking, anger, family conflict, and stress' than those who did not care for themselves, a later study by Jean Richardson and her colleagues found.[11]

Gang warfare in the streets, massive drug abuse, a poorly committed workforce, and a strong sense of entitlement and weak sense of responsibility are, to a large extent, the product of poor parenting. True, economic and social factors also play a role. But a lack of effective parenting is a major cause, and the other factors could be handled more readily if we remained committed to the importance of the upbringing of the young. The fact is, given the same economic and social conditions, *in poor neighbourhoods one finds decent and hard-working youngsters right next to antisocial ones. Likewise, in affluent suburbs one finds antisocial youngsters right next to decent, hard-working ones.* The difference is often a reflection of the homes they come from.

What Can We Do?

What we need now, first of all, is to return more hands and, above all, more voices to the 'parenting industry'. This can be accomplished in several ways, all of which are quite familiar but are not being dealt with nearly often enough.

Given the forbearance of trade unions and employers, it is possible for millions of parents *to work at home*. Computers, modems, up- and down-links, satellites, and other modern means of communication can allow you to trade commodities worldwide without ever leaving your den, to provide answers on a medical hot line from a corner of the living room, or to process insurance claims and edit books from a desk placed anywhere in the house.

If both parents must work outside the household, it is preferable if they can arrange to *work different shifts*, to increase the all-important parental presence. Some couples manage with *only one working full-time and the other part-time*. In some instances two parents can share one job and the parenting duties (for example, the post of Washington deputy bureau chief for the *St Louis Post-Dispatch* is shared by a couple). Some find *flexitime* work that allows them to come in late or leave late (or make some other adjustments in their schedule) if the other parent is detained at work, a child is sick, and so on.

These are not pie-in-the-sky, futuristic ideas. Several of the largest firms already provide one or more of these family-friendly features.

Given increased governmental support and corporate flexibility, each couple must work out its own division of labour. In one family I know, the mother is a nurse and the father a day labourer. She is earning much more, and he found it attractive to work occasionally outside the home while making the care of their two young daughters his prime responsibility. He responds to calls from people who need a tow truck; if the calls come while his wife is not at home, he takes his daughters with him. I met them when he towed my car. They seemed a happy lot, but he was a bit defensive about the fact that he was the home parent; he giggled when he spoke about the way his domestic life was structured. The community's moral voice should fully approve of this arrangement rather than expect that the woman be the parent who stays at home. At the same time there should be no social stigma attached to women who prefer to make their choices; stigmatizing any of them is hardly a way to encourage parenting. Re-elevating the value of children will help bring about the needed change of heart.

15

Freedom's Children and the Rise of Generational Politics

HELEN WILKINSON and GEOFF MULGAN

For most of this century class has been the main cause of political division in the Western world. Parties based themselves on the interests of different classes, and the big battles over redistribution essentially concerned how much was to be taken from the rich and given to the poor.

As the century draws to a close a new division is coming into view. The combination of ageing populations, fiscally stretched welfare states and rising distrust of government, is turning attention to a potential new divide, the conflict of culture, power and economics between the generations.

In some respects this is nothing new. Generational tensions have been in the air ever since the 1950s, and the birth of a modern mass youth culture. It is thirty years since Roger Daltrey of The Who sang 'I hope I die before I get old', and ever since then musicians, filmmakers and writers of popular culture have painted a picture of mutual incomprehension between the generations, whether from the standpoint of idealistic optimism (like the hippies or the rave culture of the 1990s) or of pessimism (like punk's nihilist assertion that there was 'no future').

But two factors have given a new spin to this now familiar story. The first is technology. The sheer pace of change in the forms of communication now means that each new generation is being shaped in very different ways by the technologies with which it is brought up. The mindsets of a generation brought up on television and the VCR are different from those brought up on print and radio, just as the mindsets of the generation being reared on computer games and the interactive CD-ROM are different again. The distinct cognitive structures implied by each new medium, and the distinctive perspectives they implicitly bring to bear on such things as truth and simulation, structures of argument and the place of emotion, create a frightening scope for mutual misunderstanding. Perhaps even more important in the long run is the fact that for the first time in history the young, and often the very young, are more competent than the old in the leading technologies of the age. For the first time ever the old have to learn from the young, bosses from their juniors, and even schoolchildren of ten can develop highly marketable computer software far beyond the capability of their teachers.

The second new factor is demography, the slow but cumulative pressure that mounts as societies age, and as the burden on those in work of supporting those no longer in work grows too. In the EU there are 4.5 workers to every pensioner. By 2020 this will have shrunk to 4 in the UK; 3.5 in France; and 3 in Germany.[1] A third of the EU population will be aged over sixty. In Britain the numbers aged over seventy-five are set to double during the next fifty years and the numbers aged over ninety to rise fivefold.[2]

The economic implications of this shift in the balance of the population are stark. It costs roughly thirteen times as much to pay for the health care of someone over eighty-five as it does to pay for the average adult under sixty-five.[3] Add these to the costs of pensions and long-term care and it is not surprising that across the world there has been a fairly consistent correlation between the age of populations and the proportion of national wealth devoted to public spending.

Over the last decade the political implications of demography have begun to attract notice. The OECD recently warned of 'a heavy and increasing burden on the working population in coming decades. Such a financial strain may put intergenerational solidarity, a concept on which all public retirement pensions are based, at risk.'[4]

In individual countries, the signs of impending conflict are rapidly becoming visible.

The first symptom has been the rise of grey power which has become not only an important factor in consumer markets, but also part of the political landscape. In the US the American Association of Retired People (AARP) is one of the most powerful lobbies of all and in the Netherlands and Germany grey parties have even begun to make an impact in elections.

For those leading them, their demands for generous pensions provision seem eminently reasonable. But like all new movements grey power has sparked off a both a political reaction and an intellectual one. A recent poll found that only 9 per cent of Americans aged between eighteen and thirty-four believe that the social security system will have adequate funds to provide their retirement benefits (as Newt Gingrich pointed out this is fewer than the proportion who believe they will meet an extraterrestrial in their lifetime)[5] and many organizations claiming to represent the interests of young people have emerged in response to the rising power of the grey lobby.

Third Millennium is one, a 'post-partisan' organization set up to 'represent and express the generational concerns of Americans born between 1961 and 1981', and advancing generational politics on issues ranging from social security spending to protecting the environment.[6] Another is 'Lead ... or Leave' which has organized demonstrations against pensioners' groups and encouraged young people to burn their social security cards, asking why they should pay for the profligacy of previous generations.[7]

These various groups are beginning to foment resentment not only between the young and the old, but also between the young and the middle-aged. Rob Nelson and Jon Cowan, leaders of Lead or Leave and authors of *Revolution X: A Survival Guide for our Generation*, argue that '... as the baby boomers [Americans born in the post World War Two boom between 1946 and 1960] age, their economic interests will directly clash with those of our generation and the generation behind us – their kids and grandkids'. Increasingly they are telling young people not to vote for politicians unless they can credibly promise to eliminate the still-vast budget deficit which future generations will have to pay off.

There are real grievances behind their apocalyptic rhetoric. Recent figures from the Committee for a Responsible Federal Budget show that entitlements for the elderly already represent 35 per cent of the total federal budget, and that current budget plans would increase the share of the budget going to the elderly to 43 per cent by the year 2002.[8] Perhaps the best picture of this intergenerational shift was suggested by the social philosopher Daniel Callaghan. The typical small town in middle-America, he suggests, now has a shiny hospital and a dilapidated school, a symptom of the way in which future generations are being bled dry to finance the old.[9] Similar arguments have been made in other countries. In New Zealand, for example, analysts have convincingly argued that the generation that was young when the welfare state was designed has steadily steered welfare towards old people as they have aged.[10]

The demographic and political basis for a breakdown of the social contract is less evident in Britain than in countries such as Germany, Japan or France, or indeed than some of the East Asian tigers which face extremely rapid ageing.[11] There is also still a fairly strong commitment to intergenerational solidarity. A recent survey for example found that 45.9 per cent of people strongly agree that people in employment have a duty to ensure through contributions or taxes that older people have a decent standard of living.[12]

But it would be wrong to underestimate the scope for problems. The Henley Centre have shown that the twenty-something generation are worse off than preceding generations,[13] and that for the first time in living memory this generation expects to be worse off (56 per cent of sixteen to twenty-four-year-olds do not expect their living standards to exceed those of their parents compared to 31 per cent of forty-five to fifty-nine-year-olds).[14] Our own analysis of the British Household Panel Study found nearly four times as many eighteen to thirty-four-year-olds in negative equity as any other age group, many more in debt, partly because of the costs of going through higher education, and many more suffering from the sharp end of job insecurity. The Henley Centre conclude that 'if the plight of the new generation, relative to that of its parents, becomes more widely understood . . . pressure on the older generation to make its share of sacrifices . . . will intensify'.[15]

At the same time the balance of welfare provision has also shifted. One attempt at generational auditing in the UK by Paul Johnson and Jane Falkingham at the LSE in the late 1980s found that the proportion of the retired population receiving incomes below the official poverty line was falling rapidly just as the numbers of families with dependent children were increasing.[16]

Many eighteen to thirty-four-year-olds are rightly worried that if benefits such as pensions fail to keep up with earnings, they will get the worst of all worlds – higher taxes to pay for the old, but no guarantees that there will be adequate pensions or long-term care for them.[17] Far from wealth cascading down the generations, as John Major promised, the flow may be going in the reverse direction.

Some still believe that the welfare state can contain these tensions; that growth will continue to fund generous provisions for old age and that people will be willing to pay higher taxes. Technically, the shifting demographics should be manageable. Britain has coped with a huge demographic shift over the last thirty years without the welfare state falling apart and there is certainly still a strong public commitment to income redistribution between different age-groups. If economic growth and productivity growth can be maintained, there is no intrinsic reason why productivity gains cannot be shared between those in work and the retired.

The problem, however, is that these economic issues are intimately bound up with less tangible questions of trust and mutual commitment. In the eyes of many young people, older generations seem to be showing remarkably little commitment to their needs. Whereas previous generations might have hoped for a job for life in a large firm or public service, today's employers seem to be offering far less commitment. Not surprisingly, young people are responding in kind, with a far more instrumental, less committed approach to work.[18]

But it is in politics that the disconnection and loss of trust is most stark. We found that people under twenty-five are four times less likely to be registered than any other age group, less likely to vote for or join a political party, and less likely to be politically active, even on issues like the environment.[19] Nor is this just an effect of the peculiarities of the British parliamentary system, or of having one party in power for so long. Similar trends have become apparent in almost every Western country.[20] In itself this loss of interest in politics might not matter; it might even be a sign that young people had found better things to do with their lives. But disconnection from politics seems to correlate fairly closely with other forms of disconnection: with unwillingness to obey the law, to play by the rules, or to pay for the needs of others. In our survey we found that just 49 per cent of thirty-four-year-olds are willing to sacrifice some individual freedom in the public interest compared to 61.5 per cent of people aged between thirty-five and fifty-four and 64.5 per cent of people aged over fifty-five.[21]

Clearly if intergenerational conflict is to be contained, the terms of a new intergenerational contract will need to be defined. Politicians will need to be able to justify the changing balance of spending between pensioners (both poor and rich), lone parents, school-leavers and the unemployed. They will need to acknowledge that today's twenty-somethings may not retire until well into their seventies, and that some form of compulsory saving may be necessary if the costs of long-term care and pensions are to be adequately covered.

Around the world many governments are stumbling towards a new deal, through piecemeal policies to raise retirement ages (as in the USA, Italy and Sweden), to increase the value of pensions contributions and reduce entitlements, and to encourage self-funding.[22] Some are experimenting with new ways of interweaving the lives of the old and young, by involving old people more in the work of schools, by getting schoolchildren to teach pensioners how to use computers, by planning towns and cities to avoid generational segregation, by easing the transitions both into and out of the workforce and even by developing contracts between parents and children to specify their mutual responsibilities.

At the same time, in some countries intergenerational solidarity has become an issue of high politics. France, for example, witnessed fierce conflicts in the early 1990s when millions of young people took issue with the government over minimum wage and educational policies. One response was President Chirac's appointment of a Minister of Solidarity Between Generations, and his warning that 'the debts we contract today will have to be paid by our children in ten or fifteen years. It is our responsibility not to burden their future with taxes they are not responsible for.' Germany too has a Ministry of Family, Senior Citizens, Women and Youth which tries to take into account conflicting priorities, as for example in the recent requirement for employees to contribute to insurance against long-term care.

Intergenerational issues have also become an issue in setting budgets. In the USA, new techniques are being developed for analysing how much each generation contributes to public spending and how much they get back. Laurence Kotlikoff, in his book *Generational Accounting,* called for a 'switch from an outdated, misleading and fundamentally non-economic measure of fiscal policy, namely the budget deficit, to generational accounting – the direct description of the government's treatment of current and prospective generations over their lifetimes',[23] and a good deal of work is now underway to give greater precision to the nature of the deal between the generations.

But just as important as new policies and new techniques is the reintegration of the young into politics. As we have seen, in many countries the old are far more likely to vote and to organize than the young. In the UK pensioners already comprise 24 per cent of the electorate[24] (and as much as 40 per cent in some constituencies)[25] and by 2031 a third of the electorate will be pensioners.[26] Already many young people say that it is not worth voting because no one takes any notice: in the near future the temptation to opt out altogether is bound to rise.

The only way of solving this disconnection is to build new bridges: bridges not only between the more focused single-issue organizations that young people feel more at home in and the traditional political parties, but also bridges to make it easier for the young to engage. One important strand of reform will be to make it easier for young people to register to vote (as the US is doing with schemes like the Motor Voter laws which register people automatically when they get driving licences and which has added as many as 20 million people to the electoral rolls).[27] Within a few years it should be possible to spread elections over a week and to enable voting through smart card technology, alongside more open electronic fora for finding out about policies and commenting on them directly. And if none of these matches up to the scale of disconnection there may be a strong case, too, for introducing Australian-style compulsory voting, which extends the principles of the jury and compulsory registration to ensure that young people do indeed exercise their rights.[28]

Our political culture has yet to come to terms with the new politics of intergenerational equity, which is set to affect everything from the environment to pensions, from welfare reform to education. But if slower growth exacerbates the already powerful pressures on welfare budgets, the intergenerational issue could soon be the most important, and most difficult, challenge that modern politics has to face. It should not be impossible to cope. After all, young people do in time become old people. But recreating a sense of intergenerational solidarity, and beyond that a sense, in Edmund Burke's resonant phrase, of society as a contract between the dead, the living and the as yet unborn, will require a far higher calibre of political leadership to convince people, both young and old, that they are part of a larger whole, rather than just competitors grabbing for a slice of a finite cake.

DEMOCRACY AND GOVERNANCE

It is no longer controversial to admit that there is something badly wrong with how we organize power. Democracy seems like a feeble version of empowerment if all it means is a choice every few years between two or three highly packaged alternatives.

In this section we therefore set out some of the ways of rethinking how governance can work in societies where citizens are no longer less informed than their governors, and certainly are not prepared to be dictated to.

'Back to Greece' explains some of the new tools for democracy and in 'Lean Democracy' we show how leadership has become confused and weakened in recent years, as it has lost its moral direction and failed to deliver its promises. We argue instead for a model of governance that draws on thinking in other fields, in particular learning from 'lean' organizations with a more direct relationship between the government and citizen.

'Reconnecting Taxation' analyses the heart of the modern relationship between states and their citizens, the tax relationship. Throughout history tax has been the cause of revolts and revolutions and today it remains probably the most sensitive political issue, ferociously argued about at general elections. The essay argues that part of the problem is that tax has become disconnected from its uses, disappearing into the black hole of national treasuries. More efficient and legitimate uses of taxes require a fundamental re-engineering of how tax is raised and spent.

Perri 6 argues that the next phase of the 'reinvention of government' will require governments to go beyond the application of financial incentives and competition to influence cultures of behaviour – from civil servants themselves, to teachers and parents, police and public.

In 'The Audit Explosion' Michael Power examines another side of how governance has changed as accountability has been redefined less in terms of democracy and more in terms of the spread of audits.

Robert Cooper shows how the world is moving towards a quite new model of governance which breaks decisively with the traditions of national interest and sovereignty over territory. Instead, he argues, Europe in particular is moving towards a postmodern structure fitted perhaps for a post-industrial economy based on information.

Finally John Gray sets out how in the wake of the exhaustion both of social democracy and of neoliberalism we need to think about the basic principles of politics, focusing in particular on the relevance of 'complex fairness' to fostering more inclusive societies in the next century.

16

Back to Greece

The Scope for Direct Democracy

ANDREW ADONIS and GEOFF MULGAN

Immature Democracy

Democracy has been around for more than 2000 years. But despite the rhetoric of their leaders, no Western state has a government by, for and of the people. Nor has there been much innovation in the forms of democracy this century. Genuinely imaginative measures to engage the public in decisions have been rare.

Instead, rather than being democracies in the full sense of the word, Western governments can most meaningfully be described as oligarchies of political professionals, constrained to a greater or lesser extent by five forces: the media; party activists; intermittent elections; Bills of Rights; and institutional divisions between different groups of politicians, such as political parties, second chambers, constitutional courts, and federal divisions of power.

This is the starting point for any discussion of the deficiencies of democracy, a basic fact that overshadows any discussion of constitutional reform. But the particular concerns of British debate arise because in the UK only the first three constraints apply – the media, party activists and elections held about once every four years. Most of the commonly suggested palliatives for the ills of British government, which go under the label constitutional reform, concern the introduction of the fourth and the fifth constraints above – namely a Bill of Rights, and institutions (regional assemblies and a reformed House of Lords) and voting systems (PR) to increase the number of political professionals, erect more barriers between them, and change somewhat the relative balance between the political parties which they dominate.

These additional constraints might improve the quality of governance in Britain. But their limitation is that they would do little to answer the basic deficiency of modern democracy.

They would, in short, do nothing to reduce the dominance of politicians. Instead they would simply shuffle power from one group of politicians to another, with the addition of a few judges.

This judgement may seem harsh. But the truth is that not only decision-making, but also political debate more broadly, is dominated by political professionals to a far greater extent than they would ever admit. Politicians develop the themes, the language, the policies, project them through the national media and test them through polls with the public present as a largely passive observer of a closed system. When public concerns burst through, demanding that politicians respond, this is usually experienced as a crisis. Normally, the popular opinion upon which democratic parties and governments draw – both directly through elections, and indirectly through polls – is to a large extent an echo of their own voices. And to the extent that it is not, it is prone to the weakness of nonprofessional opinion in any field, namely that it is liable to be inconsistent, underinformed, ill-considered and unreflective.

James Fishkin puts his finger on two of the weaknesses of today's 'poll-driven, sound-bite version of televised democracy' – namely the rational ignorance of ordinary citizens, and the tendency of polls to report nonattitudes or pseudo-opinions.[1] The explanation for the rational ignorance of the ordinary voter is easy to find. As Anthony Downs noted as long ago as the 1950s, it is rational for voters not to find out about issues when their opinion is never going to be called upon. Extending the argument, it is easy to see why increased levels of educational attainment will not necessarily produce – and in fact probably have not produced – a more politically animated electorate in Britain.

There is, however, an intriguing – and significant – qualification to be made. On Downs's approach, it is usually irrational for a citizen even to vote in elections. Since the prospect of an individual vote affecting the outcome of a particular election is infinitesimally small, while the effort required to vote is appreciable, the rational course is not to bother making the effort. Yet typically more than 80 per cent of the registered and resident electorate do vote in national elections, and around 40 per cent vote in local elections. Although the turnout is generally a little higher in marginal seats (where it would be more rational to vote), the difference is not great.

Indeed, voting is only the thin end of the wedge of contemporary political activism. The British Election Study for the 1987 election found that 26 per cent of the panel claimed to have contacted their MP. Two-thirds said they had signed a petition; 7 per cent had been on a demonstration; and 6 per cent had joined a protest group.[2] The mid 1960s Widdicombe enquiry into local democracy unearthed a similarly surprising level of local activism and awareness. Nearly a third of those surveyed could name correctly at least one of their local councillors, while 20 per cent had had some contact with their councillor.[3]

Explanations as to why so many bother to vote are varied. But most of them come down to the argument that individuals see voting as a responsibility of citizenship, or at least as a matter of custom (which may amount to the same thing). As James Q. Wilson argues, voting is at least in part an expression of an underlying moral sense and a sense of belonging, senses which can either be cultivated or allowed to atrophy.[4]

If voters do indeed regard voting in these ways, it is difficult in principle to see why they should treat further modest duties of political participation in a different light. If they take the trouble to inform themselves, there is little reason in principle why individuals, at large or randomly chosen, should not be able to offer judgements on public policy issues more valuable – in terms of democratic worth – than those taken by politicians claiming to act on their behalf. Indeed one might argue that across a broad range of issues ordinary voters unencumbered with the personal and ideological baggage of the typical politician could be expected to reach a more reasonable decision than today's decision-makers.

The standard response to this is that complexity makes wider involvement impossible. But of all the arguments against deeper democracy, the complexity of the decisions facing decision-makers is the least convincing. In most public policy spheres politicians have to choose between competing, but fairly clearly defined, alternatives. In complex fields such as economics and law, few of the politicians involved understand the complexities; they make a choice between worked-up policies on the basis of prejudice tempered by some attempt to master the issues involved.

Why are voters never called upon to make such choices on their own account? Tradition and the self-interest of the political class are the overriding reasons. Assuming, as we do, the self-interest of the politicians to be an insufficient justification for the modern oligarchy, we need to appreciate the traditions supporting the status quo in order to understand the scope for change in the future.

Tradition and Democracy

Until the nineteenth century, the term democracy was generally held to denote a society without a class enjoying an entrenched legal supremacy – a society, in other words, in which all citizens enjoyed legal equality, and therefore a large measure of social equality. Implicit in the concept, historically, was the notion of social and economic power moving from an aristocracy to a mass, whose aim was to promote its own social status thereby. Aristotle deliberately classed democracy as a deviant form of government, in which the poor (i.e. the mass) ruled in their own interest.[5] In the nineteenth century, Mill and de Tocqueville saw democracy as, in effect, rule by the middle class (i.e. the new social and economic leaders); Marx as rule by the proletariat (ditto).

The term held obvious connotations for the exercise of power, but almost invariably it was assumed that the democratic rights of the mass extended no further than the right to consent, or to withhold consent from, representatives – representatives motivated (depending on the theorist) by elevated notions of the general good or by the interests of the dominant class in society. For the first group, it was essential that the mass did not play any direct part in government; for the second, it was superfluous for them to do so – particularly if they were suffering from that Marxist affliction, false consciousness.

In many states another force was at work, the legacy of aristocracy. In Britain constitutional advance in the nineteenth and early twentieth centuries was predicated on an aristocratic system of government, in which 'public affairs' were naturally conducted by aristocratic 'public men', and democratization took the form of progressively extending rights to, and broadening the basis of consent from, a 'mass' still generally held to be incapable of self-government. Gladstone, the great Liberal prime minister to whose genius Britain's smooth progress to representative government can largely be attributed, doubted in the 1890s whether even a Wolverhampton solicitor was fit to sit in the Cabinet. The mass franchise for men dates back to the Reform Acts of 1867 and 1884, yet for those with the vote the scope for popular participation in government is no greater today than at Gladstone's retirement in 1894, a century ago.

It ought perhaps to come as no surprise that nineteenth-century European liberal theorists, who saw themselves at a democratic crossroads, wrote far more seriously about the possibilities of a democratic state than their twentieth-century successors, who have generally accepted the form of the democratic state as given. None wrote more eloquently or incisively than Alexis de Tocqueville, whose *Democracy in America* highlights the fundamental predicament facing modern democracies – how to generate a democratic political culture in a socially democratic society.[6]

De Tocqueville described the collapse of traditional aristocratic society across Europe in the decades after the French Revolution as 'a great democratic revolution'. By that he meant that it heralded the gradual, progressive development of social equality. His greatest insight, however, was to recognize that 'social' democracy, however far-reaching, did not necessarily lead to political democracy in the sense of self-government. On the contrary, without careful crafting of institutions, and the inculcation of a democratic culture through them, predemocratic norms and social tensions could just as easily result in tyranny, or in government by remote bureaucracies paying lip service to the democratic good.

So concerned has the twentieth century been with the first of those threats – tyranny – that it has paid little attention to the second – democratic bureaucracy, or in plain English the rule of politicians and bureaucrats. Fighting for their collective lives on the military, ideological and economic battlefields, until the collapse of the Berlin Wall, further democratization was on almost no one's agenda in the avowed liberal democracies. Instead the concern was (a) survival, and (b) the replication of the Anglo-American regimes in states won from tyranny, albeit (notably in the postwar German, Japanese and Fifth Republic French constitutions) with reforms designed to improve the effectiveness of politico-bureaucratic government.

Even if de Tocqueville's democratic social revolution had not proved so fragile in its first century, the progress of political democracy would inevitably have been painful and problematic. For until recent decades ideas of popular rule – as opposed to popular consent to rulers – have been held not just to be undesirable, but also impractical in three particular respects: in that the typical voter is insufficiently educated, interested or accessible to play a direct part in decision-making or to make informed judgements if he or she were able to participate.

By any objective standard, the third argument (accessibility), and to a lesser extent the first (education), have become progressively less convincing, given modern mobility, technology and levels of educational attainment. The question, then, is this: can we take up the other half of de Tocqueville's democratic challenge, and transform our regimes from social and bureaucratic democracies to political and open democracies? Put differently, can new democratic institutions be wedded to processes which tap the informed judgement of the electorate? The next sections look at possible ways forward, developed from contemporary US and UK initiatives.

Referendums

The referendum is hardly new. It has been around in one guise or another since the classical democracies, and has a fairly continuous modern history since the French Revolution. In Britain it has a long – but now forgotten – history in local government; ratepayers' polls were a frequent occurrence in the Victorian period, and continued into this century. A. V. Dicey, the Victorian theorist of parliamentary sovereignty, was also a strong proponent of the referendum, which he dubbed the 'People's Veto' – 'a democratic check on democratic evils'. When the powers of the House of Lords were curbed in 1911, serious parliamentary debate took place on the introduction of the referendum as a check on the unfettered power of the House of Commons. The Conservative party, then in opposition, committed itself to introducing the referendum and but for the First World War it might easily have become a central feature of Britain's constitution.[7] Instead, it was seriously discredited in the interwar years by its manifestations in fascist Germany.

The referendum has nonetheless secured a place in British constitutional practice. In the past twenty years Parliament has called one national referendum (on European Community membership) and three regional referendums (on devolution for Scotland and Wales and the Northern Ireland border). Local referendums have been held on issues ranging from local taxation (Coventry and Tower Hamlets) to refuse collection (Hertfordshire); the most visible recent example was Strathclyde's referendum on water privatization which achieved a turnout of 78 per cent, roughly double the norm for local council elections. In the early 1980s Mrs Thatcher's government seriously considered forcing local councils to hold referendums before imposing 'excessive' rates increases, and it only dropped the idea in response to opposition from Tory councillors and backbenchers.[8] Mrs Thatcher revived the idea at the height of the poll tax crisis in 1990. Referendums appear to be popular. Not only have turnouts ranged from the respectable to the high, but in 1991 MORI asked, as part of its 'state of the nation' poll, whether there ought to be provision for a referendum to be held on a specific question when a million voters requested one, and 77 per cent thought this a good idea. A similar proportion told pollsters they wanted a referendum on the Maastricht Treaty, a demand the main parties united in resisting.

For all the vocal warnings of political leaders that representative democracy is in danger of death by repeated referendums, the device is still remarkably little used. At national level, more than 1000 have been held across the world since the rise of modern constitutional politics.[9] However, nearly half of them have been held in just one country – Switzerland, where both the referendum and the initiative (a referendum called by demand of a set number of citizens) have held sway since the nineteenth century. Switzerland apart, only in a number of US states are referendums conducted with any regularity. Indeed, of the 600 non-Swiss referendums, fewer than half have been held in Western liberal democracies. As Butler and Ranney note laconically: 'politicians usually dislike referendums. They take decisions out of established hands, and elected leaders can never control – or be responsible for – their outcomes.'

The case for referendums before major constitutional change is hard to refute, if one believes that in a democracy power ultimately flows from the people. There is also a strong argument for referendums to produce long-debated constitutional reform, as witnessed recently in Italy and New Zealand. However, when it comes to referendums on specific policy issues, the key test for those concerned that decisions follow deliberation is whether a referendum is ever likely to reflect an informed popular judgement. There are also legitimate concerns about the coherence of government if voters are free to pick and choose measures to promote or reject. In the case of an initiative called by a set number of citizens on any issue of their choosing, there are particularly good reasons for supposing that the result will not reflect informed judgement. For one reason above all: that by its nature the device lends itself to minority issues little debated by the public at large.

However, in the case of referendums on major legislation passed by Parliament – or decisions of local councils – the argument is less convincing. In the first place, cranky issues would only go to a referendum if Parliament itself, or a local council, was in the hands of the cranks. As to debate, post-legislative referendums would, in all likelihood, take place only on matters the subject of hot media and parliamentary debate – or, of debate at local level, in the local press and councils. Moreover, the limitation to postdecision but preimplementation issues is itself a guarantee of a relatively focused public debate, since it clearly limits the number of referendums which could be held at any one time, and ensures they will be on issues of public moment. In Switzerland, it should be noted, fewer than ten of the hundred and fifty-odd postlegislative refendums held since 1848 have gone against the earlier parliamentary decision.

In the longer run there may be a strong case for opening

up a genuine initiative politics which would allow citizens to frame referendum questions themselves, subject to receiving a given level of support – such as 2.5 per cent of the electorate, or roughly one million voters. In present circumstances, however, it is unlikely that such initiatives would meet the 'consideration' requirement. As a first step we believe Parliament should codify existing practice and make statutory provision for local councils to call referendums and for referendums to accompany major constitutional change, and, at the same time allow postlegislative – or, at local level level, postcouncil-decision – referendums to be held where at least 2.5 per cent of the relevant electorate requested one by petition. These 'voter vetos' would be advisory, not mandatory.

Juries and Magistrates

Moving to distinctly new democratic media, the application of the jury system to the political process may be one of the most fruitful avenues of democratic reform for this and succeeding generations. When de Tocqueville visited America for democratic inspiration in 1830, he highlighted the jury not just as a judicial institution, but, significantly, as one of America's foremost democratic institutions, with a unique capacity to shape democratic habits and responsibility. 'The jury serves incredibly to form the judgement and increase the natural intelligence of a people,' he wrote in *Democracy in America*. 'That . . . is its greatest advantage. One must consider it as a free and open school, where every juror comes to learn about his rights . . . where laws are taught to him in a practical fashion.'

Juries, of course, play a significant role in Britain's judicial system. But their scale and development are ill appreciated. In all, 200,000 members of the public serve on juries each year. They make themselves available for at least a fortnight, and are eligible to serve again after a two-year period. But juries are only the final extension of lay involvement in the criminal justice system; more than 95 per cent of criminal cases are dealt with by 29,000 lay magistrates, few of whom are legally trained, and whose commitment is to sit for a minimum of just twenty-six days a year. Only a minority of serious criminal cases go before lay juries.

It is quite wrong to think that either the current scale of lay involvement in the administration of justice, or the current working of the jury system, has a long history. In fact, the jury system as we know it is of fairly recent origin. Until twenty years ago only ratepayers – mostly middle-class men – could sit on juries. Until the eighteenth century – i.e. just before the beginning of the movement towards modern-style representative government – the operation of the jury system was largely foreign to modern practice. It was common for only one jury of twelve, chosen from among the richer tax-payers, to hear all the cases in a sessions. A court would typically deal with twelve to twenty cases in a day with few barristers and most of the questioning done by the judge. The jury would deliberate on cases in batches; often they did not retire to consider verdicts, and when they did, they had little if any balanced guidance from the judge as to issues at stake and engaged in little if any of the rigorous deliberation expected of a modern jury. It was not until 1670 that it was even established that a jury was free to bring in a verdict contrary to a judge's instruction.[10]

So the jury as we know it is largely the creation of our modern criminal justice system. It has survived because it was there to start with, and because, however imperfect, it has always been regarded as bastion of individual liberty. Even now, however, there is no uniform jury system within the UK. Scotland has a very different system from England and Wales; its juries are fifteen-strong, and majority verdicts of eight are permissible, as against ten out of twelve south of the border.

We know surprisingly little about what goes on in British jury rooms, but the research done on shadow juries in the 1970s suggests that juries are both conscientious and not unduly swayed by strong personalities.[11] Conversations with jurors tend to confirm that, if only anecdotally. The 1970s research found little evidence of perversity in the final decisions although in assault cases juries were found to be strongly influenced by the social background of defendants. There was, moreover, found to be considerable use of pooled experience, and impatience with legal definitions and professional prescriptions.

For our purposes the issue of serious fraud trials is of particular interest, since no decision put to a 'political' jury is likely to be as complex, or require as long to resolve, as a complex fraud case. In the 1980s the Roskill Committee recommended that complex fraud trials be removed from juries, citing all the evidence (complexity, length of trials, strain on jurors, etc.) that comes naturally to mind. Yet the evidence taken by the committee gave little or no support to the recommendation and the government did not act on it. Instead, Roskill's recommendation that in technical cases more care be taken over presentation to juries – with schedules of evidence, glossaries of technical terms, improved visual aids, etc. – has been taken up. Two courts in the Old Bailey are specially fitted with overhead projectors and other devices to enhance the presentation of cases to juries.

How might the experience of juries be applied to politics? One notable experiment has been conducted by the Jefferson Center for New Democratic Processes, a Minneapolis-based foundation promoting new forms of democratic participation. The Jefferson Center has held fourteen juries on major policy issues since 1974 – each directed to one of 'America's Tough Choices' facing the political class. Its most recent jury, in October 1993, was on the Clinton administration's health-care plans.

The health-care jury consisted of twenty-four citizens, half men, chosen from a randomly selected group by the Center. Fourteen of the participants were educated to high school level or less (i.e. without higher education). The jury met for five days in Washington, with members' expenses, plus a stipend, paid by the Center for the duration. Its charge was to answer the dual question: 'What is it we want from health care in America and is the Clinton plan the way to get it?' The jury deliberated for more than sixty hours, taking evidence from twenty-three witnesses including health experts, administration officials, and politicians. The process attracted extensive local and national media coverage. The proceedings were guided by three moderators and two advocates. At the end, nineteen jurors voted for moderate health-care reform, four for major reform and one for minor reform, with the Clinton plan rejected 19:5.

Leaving aside the conclusions, three features of the process are particularly striking:

* the proportion of jurors saying that they understood most of the major points in the health care reform plan rose from 33 per cent to 88 per cent over the five days.
* the appreciation of the trade-offs involved in any reform grew markedly over the five days. For instance, the proportion believing the Clinton plan would help control health costs rose from 50 per cent to 75 per cent; the proportion believing it would need new taxes rose to 100 per cent; while the proportion believing it would force many small businesses to close fell from 88 per cent to 67 per cent.
* the twenty-four members of the jury, apparently without exception, found the experience challenging but enjoyable, and claimed not to have been overawed by it once it had started.

This example is one of many. Across North America there is now a substantial body of experience in innovative forms of voter participation, usually through selected samples. These range from the Oregon benchmarks to the Alaskan Television Town Meeting, from the highly structured use of particular techniques such as the Charette and Syncon to the New

Zealand Televote. In both Spain and Germany juries have been used to advise on local planning issues.

All of these experiences confirm that there is a willingness to participate, particularly if people are selected in relatively small groups, presented with a specific question and given a clear sense that their opinion matters. They also confirm that in many cases politicians benefit from involving the public in decisions on difficult priorities where politicians alone may lack the legitimacy to act.

Electronic Democracy

Most of these experiments were carried out with little more than meetings and telephones. But there is one other crucial driver of change: the advance of communications technology. For several decades many writers and thinkers have viewed technology as a means for encouraging members of the public to become more engaged in political decisions. They have pointed to the anachronism of much political decision-making. Certainly at first glance our current system seems peculiarly archaic and peculiarly resistant to rich and modulated communication from voters to politicians. On election days, modern citizens come home from offices and factories crammed full of computers, faxes and digital phone systems, to homes almost equally cluttered with telephones and videos, and on the way vote by scribbling a cross on pieces of paper which are then put into tin boxes, to be counted by volunteers in a method that has scarcely changed since the introduction of the secret ballot in 1872. Parliament is equally locked into not only pre-electronic but even pre-industrial forms. More than a hundred years after the invention of the telephone, and a decade after most of the population became familiar with ATMs and PIN numbers, representatives still troop through the lobbies where tellers record their vote. Typically, it was only after decades of attrition that the British Parliament accepted the intrusion of television cameras, more than thirty years after television had covered the coronation.

The more utopian advocates of a push-button democracy have argued that widespread access to high capacity telecommunications and databases will enable citizens not only to be much better informed but also to participate directly in decisions. Technology would permit the bypassing not only of parties and parliaments but also of the mass press and broadcasting, the manufacturers of consent in Walter Lippman's words. Optimists hope that active engagement, or ease of engagement, will directly translate into knowledge and responsibility.

Today much of the technology that could support more direct communication has become widely available: cable systems with some interactivity, cheap fibre optic connections and widespread use of computer and videoconferencing. But as technologies spread it has become harder to be a 'blue skies' optimist. It is simply not clear yet whether new technologies of information and decision-making necessarily aid genuine understanding. It is just as easy to use them to reduce issues to soundbites and instinctive judgements and to further the divide between the information-rich and the information-poor, those connected to decision-making and those cut off.

These questions are not resolvable theoretically. Instead it is likely to take many years of experiment and learning to discover which methods of using technology entail which effects.[12] As in many fields the USA is the most obvious cauldron of argument and experiment, and the main source of tentative answers. Change is being driven forward by two main forces. The first is presidential politics which has long led in the political uses of television, the soundbite and the photo-opportunity. The link was taken a step forward in 1992 when Ross Perot expounded his theories of the electronic town hall to a receptive audience. If elected, he promised to foster on-line debates and direct electronic votes on major issues. The corrupt and distant Congress would be bypassed by a direct link between government and citizens. After the election Bill Clinton picked up the theme. His campaign had already made much use of the new media, with their ability to target audiences more precisely, whether rock fans watching MTV or over-sixties on an afternoon chat show. Immediately after the election he went further, first with the 'economic summit' held in Little Rock, and then with the satellite links used on the night of the inauguration to put on display a new vision of a multiethnic pluralist America. 1993 then saw a series of electronic town hall events designed to create a closer link between the president and the electorate (and to bypass a less sympathetic press corps). More recently the president has widely publicized his e-mail address, and ensured public provision of White House information on-line and on CD-ROM, while the 1996 election is the first to use deliberative polling techniques in its television coverage.

The second driver in the USA has been local activism. With cable systems licensed by city and local governments, cable companies often went out of their way to promise new forms of democratic participation. Since the mid 1970s several small-scale experiments have drawn on these commitments to test the potential of electronic democracy. The biggest experiment has been the 'QUBE' cable system in Columbus, Ohio, on which local leaders debated issues while viewers periodically registered agreement or disagreement. Others have used mixtures of different technologies. In the Televote Project in Hawaii, packets of information and argument were sent out prior to telephone votes which were in turn publicized in existing media, while the Honolulu Electronic Town Meetings combined television discussions with viewers calling in or casting votes. In Massachusetts, Representative Edward Markey used the Compuserve network to create an 'Electure', setting off discussions on the computer network of his position papers on the nuclear freeze in such a way that participants could interact with each other's contributions. California's assembly and senate allow citizens to access a database about current debates and register comments or questions.

These are still early days, and there are very real barriers in the way of a rapid move to new technologies. People still find it hard to master complex technologies; the millions of half-understood VCRs (the houses where the time is always 0.00 hrs) are visible proof of this. Unless technologies are used very regularly (like phones, ATMs or microwaves) there is considerable resistance to learning how to use them. There is also a fundamental barrier of legitimacy. Until cable and other technologies reach close to 100 per cent penetration they will not be legitimate as voting mechanisms.

But even before electronic democracy becomes more than an interesting idea, three other sets of developments are creating the conditions in which modest versions of it could thrive. One is the growing use of telephone polls in the press and television, and the spread of formal or informal referenda in local government. These already have an advisory rather than constitutional role and can be a useful adjunct to parliamentary debate. The second is the proliferation of media, whether using cable or digital terrestrial transmission, which is already fostering a very different kind of television. Instead of a world of mass channels, we are moving into an era where alongside dominant channels like the BBC or satellite film channels, there are much more specialized ones: diverse channels for health, education, for professional groups or corporations. The idea of microtelevision is already here, and it may not be long before groups like the BMA or the accountancy profession (both of which have had dedicated television services) attempt electronic referendums of their membership. These too will provide an infrastructure for a richer and more involved democracy. Television can also help with overseeing representatives. In the USA channels like C-SPAN and Cal-SPAN (in California) are taking politics directly to voters' homes while the cable channel in West Hartford in Connecticut has been particularly successful at using good editing to make local meetings exciting and watchable.

The third trend is the spread of technologies within the public sector. The best example is smart cards, which are acclimatizing the population to the use of PIN numbers, and other electronic equivalents of voter registration. New York, for example, has used smart cards for food stamps (as well as other innovative technological applications such as automatic vehicle identification for tolls), while France has taken the lead in using them for health records. Canada's government is considering turning much of its social security over to smart cards (with the hope that this will release paper-pushing civil servants to become trainers and counsellors).

Together these various experiments are changing people's sense of how they can talk to government and politicians. They are cultivating a more interrogative culture in which it is more normal to ask questions and be asked for opinions. They are also cultivating a more open access to public information which now ranges all the way from dedicated channels and bulletin boards (like Pasadena's PARIS or the various services on France's Minitel), to touch-screen kiosks (like Hawaii Access or the IBM-backed twenty-four-hour City Hall project introduced after the LA City riots).

One of the most interesting experiments in the USA is Santa Monica's Public Electronic Network (PEN), an attempt to bring together two distinct goals – improving the quality of democratic decision-making on the one hand, and on the other using technology as an adjunct of efficient public-service delivery. Its initial role was to ease access to public information. Via home computers or terminals in public locations, citizens could access information, complete transactions, send e-mail to officials or representatives and participate in computer conferences on issues of concern. Usage has been substantial though not massive (about 10 per cent of households are registered), and most observers agree that there is a genuine levelling effect as people from different levels communicate on equal terms in ways that are easier than face-to-face communication.[13]

The various experiments like the now-discontinued QUBE and PEN remain only small-scale simulations of democracy. For the foreseeable future their role will remain an advisory one: giving a more in-depth sense of public concerns and priorities to elected decision-makers and officials. But inevitably they are already raising deeper issues of principle.

One of the consistent themes of political argument during recent decades has been that elected members and governments have too much power and too little responsibility. Public-choice theorists argued (despite considerable contrary evidence) that this inevitably fuels excessive spending and bureaucratic growth. Any downwards passage of power to electorates will be bound to raise the same issues in a new form. For example, will citizens continue to show signs of citizen infantilism – wanting better services and lower taxes – or will greater responsibility foster deeper awareness of the real trade-offs? Will minority spending priorities be more at risk than under representative structures?

Experience on these questions is mixed. But the overall story of democracy is clear. Every extension of popular power has disproven the prophets of doom and shown, instead, that electorates generally turn out to be remarkably sophisticated, and fairly (small c) conservative, and unlikely to vote for outlandish options however attractive on paper.

In the next century we anticipate that democracy will again begin evolving. The forms of representation that became stuck in this century will be complemented with new forms, such as referendums, juries and electronic deliberation. As this happens the role of the politician will increasingly have to change. The era of the professional representative monopolizing power may be coming to an end, and in its place we may be seeing the rise of a model of democracy in which power is shared.

17

Lean Democracy and the Leadership Vacuum

CHARLES LEADBEATER and
GEOFF MULGAN

Across the Western world leadership is in crisis. Electorates are at best uninterested and at worst sullenly hostile to those in power, and there is a sense that today's leaders are diminished figures compared to their predecessors.

Some have explained this crisis in terms of the short-run effects of recession or the end of the Cold War. But these explanations are inadequate. They miss the extent to which a deeper change is underway as politics itself loses the capacity to lead and as it comes to be seen as a realm of promises that aren't carried out, of systematic untruths, a world which no longer deserves deference and respect.

In many countries there is now abundant evidence of disconnection from politics – of what the Germans call *Verdrossenheit.* Where thirty years ago political leaders worried that the public was becoming too politicized, today they worry about apathy. In most countries, faith and interest in politics seems to be becoming a minority attachment, and today a political activist is more likely to be rich than poor, a man than a woman, highly educated rather than less educated – almost the opposite of the old assumption that politics was a tool for the relatively powerless.

Why has this happened? Why has democratic politics appeared to lose its way? In this essay we seek to understand the causes of the leadership vacuum and to explain some of the means by which politics might be brought back to life.

First we need to understand the causes of the current crisis. At its heart, we believe, is a clash between the culture of democracy and its forms. Although we elect our leaders any of the models of government were transposed to democracy from monarchy. Centralized bureaucracies, general taxation, rational management principles can all be traced back to absolutism and monarchical rule (as can most of the buildings and even titles used by governments today). All of these models are based on a premise of public passivity, an asymmetry between the knowledge and judgement of the governors and the governed. In a sense democracy has not yet learned how to remake government in its own image. But in an era of far greater access to education and information this means that there is a clash between the culture of democracy – of self-government – and the institutions which rule over people (a clash which also becomes particularly apparent in debates over European integration).

The second, related, problem is low involvement. Today's citizens are rarely directly engaged in the political process. They vote in elections only occasionally. They have little direct contact with politicians, and governments have not been good at managing their interface with citizens, thinking of themselves as service industries rather than as bureaucracies. By contrast our involvement in civic organizations, religions, clubs tends to be much more active, more regular, more engaged and our involvement with commercial services has been revolutionized beyond recognition.

The third is limited choice. Electors can choose between a handful of party programmes but these are often vague and confusing, and in any event are often abandoned once in power. Moreover, we are offered only one package of taxes and policies, with little scope for choice. With greater convergence between the main parties it sometimes seems as if Henry Ford is alive and well – any colour you like so long as it's black (or a mix of red and blue or red and yellow). As consumers, by contrast, we enjoy a widening array of choice and more sophisticated product marketing.

The fourth is poor delivery. Politics is widely seen as ineffective, good at promises, worse at carrying them out. It is inherently slow moving, even powerless, in the face of sweeping changes in technology, economy and foreign policy. And government bureaucracies seem to be facing a law of diminishing returns as their great earlier successes in establishing grand systems of education and law, infrastructures of roads and health, have been followed by ever fewer new success stories.

A fifth is time. Many activities depend on substantial investments of time. Good relationships and happy families are obvious examples. Democracy too depends on people being prepared to invest the time to find out about issues, to attend meetings, to sit on committees. But today we have a sense of unprecedented pressure on time. In part this is because working hours have just started rising again in most Western societies after a century of decline. In part it is because most families now have two earners not one, so far more people are juggling child care and jobs. In part it is because the value of our time has risen – twenty-five times since the mid nineteenth century, and so we are far more impatient of time-consuming activities – we want soundbites not the three-hour speeches of a Lincoln or Gladstone and lengthy committee meetings. Many sectors have adapted to this new pattern of time. Fast food, fast leisure on television, sports that replace golf with aerobics. But politics remains relatively unmodernized, and so this squeeze on time draws energy out of it, leaves it only as a place for the old and the young, or for people with careers in mind. Most of its mechanisms remain inefficient in their use of time, and there has still been far too little use of modern technologies – like committees meeting by e-mail, parliaments voting from afar, virtual parties – and far too little thinking about how to use time more effectively, despite some exceptions like Texas which has moved to weeklong voting, or Oregon (which doubled turnout by holding an election by post).

We can perhaps crystallize some of these failings, some of these sources of antipolitics, if we compare how politics is organized with the way the leading contemporary organizations manage themselves. The lean organizations in manufacturing (and increasingly in service industries) provide a useful benchmark, a model of effectiveness, even though their activities are so different. These are their characteristics:

1. *Inward Focus*. Lean organizations focus clearly upon their core tasks. They concentrate on their core technologies and those products critical to their competitive position. They home in on what they do most profitably and most productively, with clear goals and responsibility.
2. *Outward focus*. Lean organizations also have a clear outward focus. They base themselves on networks of relationships to suppliers and researchers, collaborators and customers. Open and porous, they take their lead from their customers. They recognize their dependence upon others – subcontractors, suppliers, partners – for services and ideas outside areas they concentrate on. Particularly in high technology fields, lean companies recognize that only by entering into cooperative alliances with other companies they can master increasingly complex technologies.
3. *Culture*. Lean organizations are direct. They respond swiftly by removing as many unnecessary layers of white-collar bureaucracy – which stand between customers, the production line and suppliers – as possible. They also take a direct approach to pay and performance. If they can assign responsibility for measurable tasks, then they can also measure employee performance. They link reward and promotion to performance, rather than to time serving: people have to earn their way.
4. *Lateral organization*. The best organizations have fairly flat hierarchies and are good at managing teams which draw together people from a wide variety of disciplines.
5. *Skills*. Lean organizations are highly skilled. While the organization itself focuses upon core skills, the people within

it need to have multiple skills. The company constantly tests, develops and renews its skills base.

Although politics is so different from business it is instructive to compare these with the political system. The political system perpetually shifts its focus; it frequently has blurred vision, and jumps to short-term priorities rather than long-term ones. It attempts to deal with anything and everything – from regulating family life to framing the world trading system. And because the political system does so, it is often unclear where responsibility for its work lies – somewhere between several ministerial levels and the civil service (there is an interesting contrast here with the single-issue pressure groups, whose appeal is precisely their focus on direct and usually achievable goals).

Democratic politics also tends to have a fundamentally indirect culture. Many layers of political and civil service bureaucracy separate the customers (citizens) from the producers (power-holders). Whereas lean factories work to just-in-time production schedules – producing only when an order comes in and in just the right quantities – the political system works to a just-get-by schedule, producing decisions only when forced to do so with procedures and practices inherited from the nineteenth century, generally hierarchical and adversarial rather than flat and team based. Behind all of this is a relatively unskilled profession, with little formal training and appraisal (in Britain the newly elected MP receives no training at all, and a newly appointed minister is expected to make decisions immediately).

But perhaps the most crucial difference concerns scale. Most organizations – a Shell, Siemens or Greenpeace – can adjust their shape and scale to their market or function. But politics remains trapped in the national scale, the scale at which historically it grew up. So although in practice governance works by sharing tools in ever more complex structures – especially in Europe – politicians have to behave as if issues are resolvable at a national scale. This is becoming acutely problematic – Lyndon Johnson once said that all politics is local but in a sense today the opposite is the case and all politics is becoming global.

It should not be surprising then that the output of the political system is often of low quality with high levels of waste, of disappointment and disillusion. And all of these problems become most apparent in the case of our leaders, who sometimes seem condemned to come to power on waves of excitement and anticipation that then crash into sullen hostility, a half life of enthusiasm that now seems to last only about six months. In part that's because we're losing faith in leaders' and governments' efficacy – their ability to get the job done, to cut unemployment or crime. But it's also because we're losing faith in some of their other roles.

One is a moral role. Throughout the West people are slipping and sliding on the moral screes. We want moral clarity and direction, on everything from abortion to Bosnia, obligations to future generations or to the homeless. We want politicians to speak a moral language (not least because of the declining authority of other moral leaders in the church) but their image as cynical and self-serving makes this far harder.

In Italy and throughout Eastern Europe moral malaise was one force which impelled political revolution, the replacement of large swathes of the political system and the class which prospered from it. It was no accident that people turned to outsiders to wipe the slate clean. Novelists, playwrights and musical instrument makers led the East European revolution; independent prosecutors, former central bankers and business leaders the Italian one.

But these are only the extreme cases. All Western societies are experiencing a sense of moral drift which neither the church nor political leaders can effectively address. In part this is a problem of narratives. The American psychologist, Howard Gardner, has argued that one of the most important roles of political leaders is to weave compelling narratives: stories that make sense of how politics can protect people or advance their interests and values. They help define an us and a them; they set challenges and goals; and they embody in their own lives the missions they set for their people.

But politicians may be losing the ability to do this. In part this is because overprofessionalization means some enter professional politics almost straight after university, which means that they lack experience of many different walks of life, ways of talking, an almost intuitive understanding of what makes people tick that the greatest leaders have. And in part the problem may be that a more diverse society made up of many cultures, professions and lifestyles means that they are much less likely to share a common store of images and metaphors – like the biblical images that were so potent a source of political rhetoric in the past. As a consequence political rhetoric (at least within the mainstream) has to be blander, more an inoffensive lowest common denominator than an inspiration.

There is also a problem of ideas. For most of this century politicians could draw on fixed and reliable ideological systems. Social and Christian democracy, liberalism, communism – delivered sets of principles from which leaders could read off policy implications. They could generate solutions internally.

But today this is no longer the case. The main traditions grew up amidst a particular era of industrial society, a class and industrial structure which no longer exists. As a result they have become rather bankrupt, bad at generating good solutions for the most pressing problems of our times, and ill suited for the era of derivatives trading and satellite TV.

This era demands a very different type of leadership. In the old model, the leader set a clear ideological and political agenda, and others (such as party research departments, or junior spokespeople) filled in the gaps. Today with a far greater pluralism of ideas the best leaders are open ones: able to draw on a global marketplace of ideas.

The best ones do not assert the certainty that they have all the answers, but rather present themselves as having sufficient capacity to absorb complex ideas and weave them into a whole. In the era of fuzzy logic and fuzzy knowledge perhaps we need leaders who no longer feel the need to have an answer to everything. For them it might be better to be able to demonstrate a willingness to ask questions well and then communicate the best answers to the electorate.

So what do these problems add up to? Certainly not a simple account of political failure, of betrayal or corruption. We expect our politicians to play a dizzying mix of roles, one moment to offer convictions, principle and moral guidance, the next to be fleet-footed, pragmatic, deal-makers. We decry their poor quality, their lack of skills and yet we endorse and enjoy the relentless media scrutiny of their lives and performance which drives most people away from politics towards jobs elsewhere.

We are now in a period of considerable flux in response to this situation which has made the public so antipolitical. And one of its features is that our politics is being defined by new lines of division between competing leaders which don't so easily fit into the old divides of left and right.

The most basic new divide in politics is emerging from the widespread discrediting of the established political class: it is the divide between outsiders and incumbents, those who make their claim to power based on their nonpolitical credentials and those who climb to power as professional insiders. Reformist political leaders seek popular support by appearing to come from outside the discredited world of politics, to come from the regions rather than the capital, to have their roots in the nonpolitical worlds of culture, community or commerce, rather than politics. This trend for political reform to be carried by leaders who come from outside the political establishment or at least to have broken with it, has been the dominant single development in democratic politics in the last five years across a very wide range of societies.

Silvio Berlusconi's Forza Italia and Ross Perot's presidential campaigns are only the most obvious examples of the rise of antipolitical outsiders. Both countered technocracy with populism – Perot's great pitch was to 'get under the hood' in

Washington, while the name for Berlusconi's political alliance was created in the football terraces. The roles of both Colin Powell and Steve Forbes have been similar. Elsewhere the 'outsider' groups range from Zhirinovsky's 'Liberal Democrats' to East Germany's PDS (a fascinating example of an insider party remaking itself as an outsider party, a channel for anger against the system).

The political realignment in Japan was created by a break with the ruling Liberal Democratic Party and carried initially by Morihiro Hosokawa, a former regional governor who launched his own party. Yet the Japanese case also highlights the ambiguity of this polarity between outsiders and incumbents. The original split with the LDP was partly opportunistic and the real power behind the reformist coalition was Ichiro Ozawa, a renowned political fixer. President Bill Clinton (like Ronald Reagan) also straddles both worlds. He was an outsider to Washington, rising to power from the governorship of one of the poorest, smallest and least fashionable states in the USA. Yet he is a lifelong professional politician, dedicated to winning power and mastering the details of public policy. The best political insiders will also attempt to present themselves as fresh outsiders.

Electorates are unlikely to settle at one end of this pole. They are likely to swing more or less violently between the poles. The outsiders' chief attractions, that they are fresh, nonpolitical, and cut through the political grunge, are also the sources of their weakness. The way they bypass traditional political mechanisms may mean they tend towards authoritarianism. What they see as gridlock in the political system, others see as democratic clash of interests. They may be fresh, but they are also unworldly and inexperienced. These weaknesses mean that it is likely that outsiders will be called upon only at times of greatest political disillusion. At other times electorates are likely to swing back towards pragmatic, experienced, insiders, even if they are partly stained by a history of political corruption.

Eastern Europe is the clearest example of this cycle. The

initial anticommunist revolutions were carried forward by outcasts, dissidents whose moral qualities were founded upon their backgrounds as musicians, playwrights and philosophers. But in almost every East European state the old political leadership has regrouped, often by allying with conservative nationalist or religious forces, given itself a face lift and replaced the early reformers.

The second great dividing line is that around identity, which is well described by Vincent Cable in his contribution. The most bitter battles of our times aren't between left and right but between groups committed to a sense of exclusive identity and those committed to a more inclusive, open one. In America the battles over NAFTA are a prime example, with the lines of division passing through the main parties. Pat Buchanan is a good instance of identity politics, with his call for 'America First'. In France the arguments over Maastricht and GATT fitted into this pattern too (as well as uniting the 'insider' social groups, the educated city dwellers against the 'outsiders', in rural areas and unemployment). The same is true of the British arguments over Europe which are tearing apart the Conservative Party between its open, freetrading instincts and its nationalist ones. But similar patterns can be seen elsewhere. In Eastern Europe there is a clear divide between the cosmopolitan urban parties and the conservatives ones, which are often also anti-Semitic. In the Islamic world there is a divide between the fundamentalists and the modernizers, in India between the BJP and Congress. In part this shift away from the left–right axis is a consequence of 1989, and the convergence of left and right politics. But it is also a result of economic and social insecurity that seems to push people back to older certainties of identity.

If these are some of the problems of democracy what then might be the solutions? How could we modernize our politics to better fit the best of modern societies, to ensure better performance and more legitimacy?

The first key is that we need to continue to innovate new forms of government. We have already described the limits of the absolutist legacy which survives in the norms of how government is done. The great hierarchical models of government are no longer sufficiently effective or legitimate. Instead we need to think about government in fresh ways, asking how it can be a broker and energizer rather than a provider or direct regulator, how it can think of itself as servant as much as master, how it can learn to unblock itself, to stop doing things as often as it starts doing things, with less fixity and permanence (and thus reducing its dependence on organized interest groups, like the farmers or the military industries), and crucially how it can forge means for citizens to hold a dialogue with government. And in tax, we will need to see a remodelling based on choice and transparency with far greater earmarking of taxes to particular ends.

The second concerns representation, a concept which is at the heart of democracy. To renew politics it may not be enough to have a more balanced membership of professional politicians. Instead the demise of faith in the efficacy of representative democracy may take us back to an older model of democracy whereby decisions are left to bodies deliberately designed to reflect the public, as in ancient Athens where bodies were chosen by lot. The same principle is at the heart of our legal system in the right to trial by jury, and similar ideas are spreading into democracy: the citizen jury; the user jury for overseeing services, the deliberative poll; the use of opinion polls as a guide to policy. Around the world there is a great ferment of experiment taking place (see pp. 239–42) – from Oregon's initiatives in health-care consultation and in setting overall policy benchmarks for the state, the televote experiments in Hawaii, teleconferences in Alaska, the Electronic Town Meeting held in Calgary – in each case creating genuinely representative, randomly chosen assemblies in parallel with the assemblies of elected professionals organized in parties.

Third, we need to add direct mechanisms to representative democracy. All over the West referendums have spread, particularly to resolve problems where parliaments lack legitimacy. Switzerland, Italy, Ireland and many US states use referendums on issues ranging from changes to constitutions, to issues of public morality. All told there have been 1000 referendums at national level around the world, although fewer than half of those held outside Switzerland have been in nondemocratic countries. There are legitimate fears of the manipulative uses of direct democracy, and referendums bring their own problems (although no one in countries like Switzerland seriously proposes doing away with them). But in an era when citizens expect to be consulted more, when they may have as much information as their representatives, and when technologies of communication have superseded the need for parliaments, there is a strong case for them, at least where we can be sure that they will be accompanied by a full public debate.

Fourth, we need a much tougher commitment to truth and honesty. At the moment we regulate advertisers but not politicians. There are few if any limits to what they can promise and what they can say, and many countries have seen a downward spiral of political campaigning with the negative driving out the positive. Perhaps we need not only the media but others too to specify charges and claims made in their electioneering material, including party political broadcasts which are at present outside any requirements to be honest. Truth and integrity have become rare qualities in politics, not because politicians are evil but because the system rewards dishonesty. We need counterpressures.

Finally we need to understand complexity. It is the nature of a more complex, interconnected world that there are more variables, more uncertainties. Governments and politicians can no longer monopolize power as they once did. Greater complexity makes it harder for government to know everything. It makes it necessary for it to work with networks, to collaborate with others. And it also makes it more vital that it concentrates on overall missions and cultures, rather than trying to do everything at once and ending up doing nothing satisfactorily.

All of these changes might do something to change our relationship to government and politics. But perhaps the biggest change we may need is a more cultural one. Many of the most pressing problems of today are either macrocosmic in nature – like global warming or the spread of AIDS, or microcosmic like the relationships between men and women. Both sets of issues, the macrocosmic and the microcosmic, are soluble less through the passing of laws and decrees than through changes of culture and behaviour, a different balance between government responsibility and individual responsibility, and often governments may be more effective if they can help to promote a different culture rather than simply using the traditional tools of spending programmes and laws.

There is of course also a more positive way of viewing much of what has happened. It's easy to understand why some people see antipolitics as growing up. If in the past we expected kings to solve all problems, seeing democratically elected leaders as their successors, today we are wiser. No one can wave magic wands. We cannot delegate our lives to others. We cannot carry on like children, seeing political power holders as father figures, not least because they do not have the means to fulfil our expectations. And so the optimists conclude that the crisis of politics and leadership is on balance a good thing.

Yet it is ironic that the political philosopher who most readily sums up the age is not an optimistic theorist of liberal democracy such as Mill, nor a postmodernist such as Baudrillard, but one of the earliest. Modern society in the wake of the Cold War most resembles the world of Hobbes, a war of all against all, in which the state is required at the end of the day simply to impose order, to ensure social survival, to maintain discipline and the conditions for civil association but to do little else. It is Hobbes writing from a world of civil and religious wars who seems most in tune both with ethnic and religious wars in Eastern Europe and the flux of modern life: an endless attempt to satisfy our shifting desires, people forever in motion, without tranquillity, finality or repose, passing from one desire to the next, in each trying to secure the grounds for the next, but without ever fully escaping uncertainty or insecurity.

Politics is, as then, in part an answer to chaos and disorder. Today too the alternatives to politics, at least within a Western tradition, are likely to be worse. A quicker descent into chaos and anarchy, a faster route to mutual indifference and hostility. Politics shares with business and the media an ability to reach across cultures, communities and interests. Yet politics is the only force which can draw the strands together, potentially making societies more than the sum of their parts by articulating a common purpose.

At present politicians are marooned within their political castles, while their subjects are torn between deriding them and imploring them to lead. In this piece we have tried to set out some of the conditions for revitalizing the links between governed and governors, politics and nonpolitics. We have shown that the good leaders need much greater clarity about what they can and cannot do. That they will need a sense of history and identity, of narrative and meaning as well as a command of policy priorities.

These are all new tasks. The Western societies confront their problems simultaneously. This is why today no Western societies are taken to be models by the rest of the world. None displays the confidence that comes from knowing your place in the world, and knowing how to act in it. Instead, all are fumbling. Yet all can teach and all can learn. And the best leaders will be those that can do both.

18

Governing by Cultures

PERRI 6

> Economics is the method, but the aim is to change the soul.
>
> MARGARET THATCHER

Solving problems is generally a matter of changing how people do things, or how they see the world. However much we say we would like government to leave us alone, when we are faced with large social problems, we expect government to make every effort to change the behaviour or beliefs of those people involved either in creating or in solving those problems. Put simply, we usually expect government to try to change people's culture.[1]

Those who think that government ought to leave us alone – still variously called neoliberals or neoconservatives or 'new right' – have powerful arguments against this. Some of them suggest that government cannot solve social problems: its tools are all too blunt.[2] Others argue that it is wrong in principle that government should be granted the power, let alone the authority, to interfere with our cultures.[3] In political and intellectual circles, these thinkers have had a great deal of influence in recent years.

In this chapter, I argue that their position faces a fundamental difficulty, which has already had large practical consequences for the character of modern government, and that the future will probably belong to those who are prepared to talk about how we can decently change people's cultures in a liberal democracy, not to those who dispute whether we may or whether we can.

The first central difficulty of those who think that government ought simply to get off our backs and shrink as far as possible, is that they too want to change people's cultures, but in one particular way. When they are candid, they acknowledge that creating the cultures of *complete* self-reliance they want to foster will involve huge wrenches in the expectations of many people, in their ideas about fairness and their sense of their relationships with one another.[4]

The second difficulty is that people's expectations that the state will seek to buttress particular cultures of aspiration, responsibility and behaviour are resilient.[5] Many – perhaps most – people naturally think that fostering certain cultures is one of the moral tasks we want the state to carry out. In practice, no administration – despite the rhetoric of many new right theorists of recent years – has ever promoted *only* the cultures that would be needed for living with the minimal possible government.

Instead of shrinking the state and promoting only the cultures of abstaining from its services, what the administrations that used this rhetoric have done, is to 'reinvent' government.[6] Even as their intellectuals proclaimed the impotence of its toolkit, these administrations – Thatcher, Reagan, Bush, Mulroney, Lange – have redesigned the tools of government. While libertarians denounced as little better than totalitarian, the idea that government should 'brainwash' its citizens by aspiring to change their cultures, 'actually existing' government has sought to bring about vast cultural change.[7] The project of the Thatcher, Lange and Reagan administrations was not merely to end 'the dependency culture' among the poor and unemployed. Rather it encompassed efforts to instil 'family values', to restigmatize recreational drug use, to introduce entrepreneurial aspirations and behaviours among those providing public services, to eradicate cultural prejudices against the idea of a role for for-profit firms in welfare services, to change workers' aspirations toward the idea of 'employability', and so on.[8]

In this chapter, I argue that the important policy lessons to learn from the experiments of the centre-right administrations are the following. Firstly, government is inevitably in the business of changing the cultures of its own staff, the organizations that cluster around it, the users of its services and the wide public. Secondly, the culture change of living with the minimal state probably cannot be achieved legitimately in a democracy, because citizens' expectations will always expect government to attempt to solve problems that require it to take more powers than the 'new right' would like. Thirdly, therefore, we need to understand the full range of tools with which governments can influence cultures.

The chapter proceeds by reviewing the real achievements of the period of the 'reinvention' of government and examining the problems that it has bequeathed to us. I then consider the arguments over the legitimacy and feasibility of government influencing cultures in a liberal democracy that places clear ethical limits on the lawful exercise of state power over individuals. I set out a classification of the tools available in order to argue that not all of them are as blunt as the new right argued. Finally, I offer a few examples of how this understanding might inform practical policy-making. However, I begin by going back to first principles, and asking what we expect government to do for us.

Most people still think of the role of government as being that of managing the economy – of the control of exchange rates, interest rates, government borrowing, maintaining the standard of living, and setting levels of taxation.[9] The big debates about government in the twentieth century – how big should government be, as a proportion of national wealth? by how much should it abridge liberty? and so on – have all been conducted under the assumption that the goals were the increase of national economic wealth and welfare.[10]

By contrast, until the nineteenth century at the earliest, the tools of government that fascinated politicians, commentators and many citizens were those that enhanced the capacity of the nation-state in war and imperial aggrandizement. Then as now, the big debates – the national siege economy and later the imperial preference versus free trade, the costs of maintaining a global naval and military capacity – were about alternative means of achieving national power. From the perspective of the twenty-first century, the economistic view of government's powers in the twentieth century may come to seem as obsolete as the military and imperial view of earlier centuries. We may come to see the role of government in far broader ways, and we may come to recognize the narrowness of the current conventional economistic wisdom, according to which the global integration of markets has drastically diminished the power of governments and blunted tools at its disposal.

Yet, for more than a century, the debate about government that has fired the greatest passion has been the one about how big it should be as a proportion of all economic activity.[11] Directly related have been the questions about how many services it should provide and which should be left for private action. For example, by the 1990s the British public sector spent more than 40 per cent of GDP (more than four times as much as it did a century ago) and employed the equivalent of more than four million full-time staff, again vastly more than a century ago.[12] This vast engine presides over many areas of life, from policing to families, money to water quality. These questions are still at the heart of the concerns of libertarian right politicians like Newt Gingrich in the USA[13] and Alan Duncan in Britain,[14] and of thinkers on the traditional social democratic left like J. Kenneth Galbraith in the USA[15] or even moderate centre-left politicians like Frank Field in Britain.[16] These competing visions and claims for radical resizing will remain part of political debate.

Yet it has become clear in the wake of the collapse of communism, the meltdown of the 'Swedish model' and the collapse of the 1981–3 Mitterrand experiment on the one hand, and the chronic failures of the USA to sustain both an effective and affordable system of either state education or private health care or even law and order, that size isn't everything. Clearly, a state that is too big or too small overall doesn't work, but there is a range of sizes across countries as diverse as Japan and the Netherlands that are perfectly viable. The prospects for Republican radicalism in drastically reducing the size of the federal state in the USA look bleak, and here, a divided Conservative Party and an increasingly centrist Labour Party suggest that large-scale shifts in either direction in the crude volume of state activity may be off the agenda for some years.

Although a minority on the left continue to imagine that government can achieve anything if it has the will and the popular support, and a minority on the intellectual right still believe that all the tools available to government are blunt, the debate has been dominated by more pragmatic attempts to improve the tools and scale up the capacities of government to use them. The 'new public management' has attracted governments from the left and the right across the world.[17] The advocates of these ideas stressed that they were borrowing 're-engineering' and 'quality management' from business and trying to adapt them for public-sector contexts. Following American public management gurus, David Osborne and Ted Gaebler,[18] let us call this the 'Reinvention Programme' and its proponents, 'the Reinventers'.

In almost every OECD country, the Reinventers have brought about enormous upheavals in the services that government either provides or oversees.[19] The programme involved the following main elements (the examples are all from the British case, but there are analogous initiatives now in most developed countries).[20]

First, policy-making and purchasing have been separated from implementation and service provision. For example, in British health care, the 'internal market' has created a formal split,[21] and in local government, compulsory competitive tendering has produced a similar effect.[22] In central government, market testing is only one initiative intended to achieve the same end.[23]

Second, Reinventers have redesigned regulation of service providers in many public services.[24] To do so, they have made greater use of dedicated regulatory agencies. In education, the Office for Standards in Education, and in personal social services, the Social Services Inspectorate are both the product of major overhauls in regulation. The Housing Corporation has become a more active regulator of housing associations,[25] and a swathe of new regulatory bodies have been created to oversee financial services and utilities.

Responsibility for delivery has been decentralized, and in many cases, hived off to dedicated agencies. The Next Steps Agencies system now covers everything from child protection and benefits administration, through government statistics to water regulation and forestry management.[26] A similar process can be observed in the creation of NHS Trust hospitals by offering incentives for voluntary hiving-off of hospitals and other units.

Formal contractual relationships within the public sector and between the state and private suppliers have replaced both direct management and informal grant aid or implicit contracts, with all the attendant costs of drawing up, monitoring, enforcing and renewing external contracts.[27] In community care, these usually take the form of legally binding private law contracts, but in health care, they are public law arrangements not enforceable in courts.[28]

All this has involved greater authority for managerial, purchasing and monitoring functions. It has also led to the emergence of new powerful professions such as auditing.[29] District auditors have been followed by the creation of powerful new internal audit functions within local authorities and health authorities, in turn subject to the Audit Commission, while central government departments and agencies are subject to scrutiny by the National Audit Office and, in a different way, to the Efficiency Scrutiny Unit of the Cabinet Office. Performance measurement has gradually extended into the development, not merely of efficiency and outcome measures, but measures of specific standards of service to consumers such as the Citizens' Charters.

The use of incentives linked to performance measurement became the main instruments for changing behaviour; I shall call this 'the incentives paradigm'. For example, tax incentives have been used in the effort to stimulate saving (TESSAs, PEPs, etc.)[30] and charitable giving (GiftAid), although with limited success.[31] Within the public sector, performance related pay is a widely used incentive. Incentives are offered to the users of public services such as the discounts for local authority tenants to buy their own homes or the incentives for unemployed people to become self-employed through the Enterprise Allowance Scheme. Provider agencies are often subject to incentives, as in the case of job-training providers contracting with Training and Enterprise Councils on systems of outcome-related funding.[32]

The 'Reinvention' programme was adopted with equal vigour in the 1980s by both the centre-left (most notably by Al Gore and Bill Clinton's Democrats,[33] and in the leadership of Australian and New Zealand Labour Parties[34]) and the centre-right (as in the case of the UK). Although the centre – left 'Reinventers' stressed partnerships with the private sector and citizens and deregulating to enable public action at the lowest level,[35] and the centre-right laid their emphasis on hiving-off and contracting-out subject to greater central state surveillance, the scope of agreement was substantial. The slogan of both centre-left and centre-right was that governments of all levels should be 'enabling authorities' that 'empowered' citizens, producers and consumers alike.[36] At first, the results looked dramatic. There were major improvements in efficiency and effectiveness. But the time is now ripe for a more sober appraisal of what was achieved.

The Reinventers were partly right and partly wrong. They succeeded in improving how government does whatever it does. Health care probably is better managed than ever before: driving licences are issued more efficiently, as is the administration of benefits. Yet this was never going to be enough. Both the libertarian right and the social democratic left justly criticized the Reinventers for failing to understand that reforming government is not just a matter of improving the machinery, but of more basic questions of political goals and purposes. Equally fundamentally the Reinvention Programme, by focusing on the internal workings of government, ignored the wider cultural consequences of what government does, and, when it did address culture, did so solely in terms of financial incentives.

The incentives paradigm tends to assume that people will respond in certain ways to changes in the financial costs and benefits attached to certain choices because they value monetary gain and loss above all other factors. However, what we know of the ways in which many cultures work, is that they attach much more importance to other things. Table 1 summarizes some of the range of motivations that the incentives paradigm ignored, but with the grain of which government must work.

As I shall argue, this cultural deficiency is crucial to understanding how governments can evolve in the future. But first, what has been the legacy of the Reinventers?

Five sets of problems have been left behind by the various different programmes of institutional reform.

The first is *distrust*, which appears in the evidence of falling public confidence in the integrity of public services.[37] There is now ample evidence of falling trust in local and national government, in the judiciary and police, even though trust levels for some groups, such as GPs, has remained high.[38] Survey data from MORI, the Henley Centre and other sources shows that the public is more doubtful now about the trustworthiness of most governmental institutions than at any time since the Reinvention programme began.

The second related problem is one of *ethos*. Part of the problem is concern that public agencies may have lost valuable ethos. People fear that the incentives, the managerialism and the competitive arrangements that now characterize

TABLE 1 *Motivations other than financial gain for stake-holders in public services*

Type of motivation	*Public bureaucracies*	*Private organizations*	*Service users*	*General public*
Resources	Maximize budget	Maximize turnover, market share	Maximize consumption for a fixed budget	Secure trust in appropriateness of overall resource allocation system
Power	Maximize legal and regulatory authority: maximize authority of chief executive or board or divisional satraps; maximize professional autonomy	Maximize authority of chief executive or board or divisional satraps	Increase representation on boards: secure proxies, eg ombudspeople	Limit power of special interests, including those of producers and service users
Choices	Shaping agencies to concentrate on policy making and shedding implementation or service provision tasks to others	Maximize autonomy	Increase range of services, but not to the point of congested choice	Control the costs arising from greater autonomy for producers and choice for consumers

public service may have come to replace older attitudes of public service, accountability and commitment to redistribution that were the traditional motives for people working in these fields.[39]

Certainly this is one of the factors behind public distrust. But equally important is inertia: the ethos of many government bureaucracies has survived almost unchanged. Indeed, some Reinvention measures have reinforced the caution and rigid hierarchy classically associated with government

is almost the reverse of modern business thinking.

In most countries, the promises of bonfires of government manuals, books of regulations and granting real discretion to managers to innovate and find the best way of achieving policy goals, have amounted to rather little. Performance-related pay may have spurred some to greater effort, but by concentrating on individual achievement, has also tended to undermine the team spirit on which effective organizational culture depends.

The third problem is one of *expectations*. Citizens probably expect more from government now than ever they did before.[41] Indeed, it was popular dissatisfaction with the quality of many public services in the 1970s that led to Reinvention. The charters are one recent response to the continuing trend. The welcome that has greeted experiments such as televoting, citizens' juries and electronic town halls reflects a desire for more opportunities to influence government decisions.[42] Yet high levels of dissatisfaction are still reported by most surveys. Reinvention policies (like the citizens' charters) may have done more to fuel expectations than to satisfy them.

The fourth problem is difficulties in *steerage*.[43] The new models have brought more complex problems of steerage, and not only amongst the flotilla of executive agencies, quangos and regulators. Fragmentation in government has probably improved the quality of local feedback between consumers and providers, and enabled better management focus in many service providers. However, for policy-makers, it is now more difficult to obtain information from services directly, and more difficult to give direction or influence the culture and priorities of a large variety of organizations.[44]

The fifth problem is that of rising 'transaction costs'. The Reinvention Programme has made some aspects of government much costlier to carry out. All the writing of contracts, monitoring and surveillance of contractors, the audit, regulation and performance measurement is expensive.[45] True, in some cases, these losses may be offset by gains in productive efficiency and the costs of delivering services. However, transaction costs are visible to the public and to politicians as a new form of bloated bureaucracy of purchasers, auditors and lawyers.[46]

Few of the reformers have very convincing ideas about how to tackle these problems. But the difficulties of managing governance are also being exacerbated by a rapidly changing environment.

The first set of challenges come from the new information and communications technology. The smart card, the Internet, the fibre-optic cable, the integrated cable television, telephone, and electric power service, present new tools to help governments but also new problems.[47] They have created opportunities for individuals and organizations far to outstrip the competence of public agencies to control or survey them, and not just futures traders. Many systems permit matching of personal data which can threaten the rights of citizens to privacy and confidentiality of personal information.[48] The power of the 'delete' key over the waste paper bin for the fraudster looking to cover his tracks and the reach of the modem for the hacker are of as much importance as the anonymity of the white supremacist or pornographer on the Internet escaping the short and technologically arthritic arm of the law.

Secondly, the globalization of economic activity, of governance problems, of information flows and of organizations that provide public services creates some new problems even as it solves old ones.[49] New kinds of information and greater efficiency savings from global competition may enhance the performance of government, but national governments face grave difficulties in controlling or regulating activity that transcends their borders. They face this particularly acutely when they purchase goods and services from far larger providers who may possess almost global monopoly power over expertise.[50]

A third dimension is concerned with values. Governments now have to operate amidst a rather more fragmented, individualistic, demanding and undeferential public than in the past.[51] The public has become used to much more choice in private sector retail services, and is growing frustrated at the one-size-fits-all culture of many public ones.[52] Moreover, mistakes made in publicly purchased services are immediately amplified by the media and legitimacy for the Reinvention has to be won rather than assumed.

Where, then, should governments go next? One option is simply to go further along the current paths, with the more determined introduction of 're-engineering' methods into government.[53] But in my view this will do nothing to address the problems and the challenges of the new environment. Instead governments in the late 1990s and the next century must start where Reinvention left off. They must be 'change agents' – that is, forces that either use the authoritative tools available to them to directly bring about change or else act as catalysts and persuaders for change – in four cultures, namely, those of the nexus of agencies that now make up the public sector itself; the network of organizations that governments steer, regulate, purchase from, influence, make grants to, award tax concessions to, etc.; the users of public services; and the wider public.

Culture is now the centre of the agenda for government reform, because we now know from the findings of a wide range of recent research that culture is perhaps the most important determinant of a combination of long-run economic success and social cohesion.[54] The mistake of both statist left and *laissez-faire* right was to ignore this fact.

In the long run, the societies that show the greatest economic dynamism and viable social cohesion are the ones where a culture of high trust enables individuals to create organizations readily, to take personal responsibility but also to sustain long-term cooperative relations in trading with and employing people who are strangers to them. The libertarian right failed to understand this because much of their intellectual paradigm was drawn from neoclassical and Austrian economics. It is to economic sociology, business studies, and political science[55] that we need to look for this crucial insight.

Creating and sustaining the cultural resources necessary to make privately based economic dynamism and social viability possible is the central task for a society. In other words the most important task of government is to make it possible for a society to organize itself.

In traditional thinking about public administration, culture was something marginal, soft, lacking in rigour, intangible, hardly worth analysing. Government dealt in hard facts, with clear rules, using hard intellectual disciplines like economics and money accounting. The dominant organizational element was the Treasury and the institutional configuration for which it stood was the paradigm of sound government. If the word 'culture' was uttered in the same breath as 'policy', it usually meant opera houses, galleries, and state patronage of the arts. A government policy for the wider culture was either denounced as so ambitious that only a totalitarian regime would attempt it, or else doomed to failure because government has neither the tools nor the capacities to influence culture.

In the 1990s, this understanding is being turned on its head. It is precisely the 'hard', 'objective' tasks of macroeconomic management, of maintaining low unemployment and a stable international political order based upon the balance of power, that governments have performed so poorly. We have begun to recognize that government is, willy-nilly, always a powerful influence on the wider culture. Taking up two-fifths of the economy, being the largest employer, government is necessarily a key player in the culture. For example, policies toward local government such as capping can affect local cultures of civic pride and responsibility, for example by undermining willingness to stand for election as a councillor, which is a problem widely perceived in local government circles. Policies toward the benefit system such as removing income support from sixteen- and seventeen-year-olds might have had the positive cultural effect of reinforcing families by throwing teenagers back on their parents for support, but they may also have contributed to family breakdown and to subcultures of teenage disaffection. Certainly, the apparently rising levels of youth homelessness reported in most major cities,[56] and the apparently endemic use of drugs by young people[57] are symptoms that family policy has not been a success in the UK, the USA and other countries.

Some have argued that for government to have an explicit cultural policy is illegitimate.[58] Yet government cannot help but think of its policies in cultural terms, because attending to culture is a central part of understanding the consequences, intended or otherwise, of public policy. Indeed, a government with no vision of what impact it would like to bring about on the cultures of its own bureaucracy, the networks of organizations around it, the users of its services, or the wider public, is almost certain to be an ineffective one. We have seen in many countries during the 1980s and 1990s that, without a clear understanding of how cultures can be influenced, governments fail. Three examples suffice to make the point. The 1988 Housing Act failed to stimulate private renting to the degree that the government hoped, because the legislation did too little to build relations of trust between potential landlords and tenants;[59] government exhortation campaigns to young people to abjure hard drugs failed because they spoke the language of officialdom and parental authority to a youth culture that had no respect for such things;[60] the tax advantages provided on TESSAs and PEPs have done little to stimulate new savings, but merely induced those already saving to move their accumulated wealth from less tax efficient forms to more tax efficient forms.[61]

The challenge of using government to bring about cultural change requires more than the simple withdrawal of the state combined with a few incentives for firms and individuals. Cultural change is a much more long-term and complex task than was understood by those who speak blithely of ending the 'dependency culture' with cuts in welfare combined with in-work benefits, or creating an 'enterprise culture' simply through privatization, contracting-out and a little cash support for unemployed people to go into self-employment.

It is inescapable in almost every major policy area today. There is little prospect of increasing educational performance without a shift in the mentalities of parents and children towards valuing education and investing time and energy into it. Policies in law and order can only be effective if they can mobilize the commitment and change the cultures of people living in high crime neighbourhoods. Environmental policies depend not only on taxes and regulations but also on mobilizing willingness to cut energy usage or separate rubbish into different bags. And policies against unemployment have to address not only the economic barriers to jobs for the long-term unemployed, but also their own cultural and attitudinal handicaps.

The heart of the problem, however, is that Britain is still essentially a low-trust society,[62] and most of these policies depend in some ways on trust. Consider, for example, the small firm sector. The family firm remained for too long the most common organizational form, because people remained unable to trust professional managers and unwilling to lose individual or family control. Because British small business entrepreneurs are rarely willing to share equity with people other than their kin, they continue to rely heavily on such inefficient and costly forms of financing as overdrafts. Consider also the vicious circles of low trust between labour and management which brought British business into crisis in the 1970s,[63] and how little has been done in the 1980s and 1990s to foster the 'social capital' that sustains trust.[64]

Pointing out the need for a culture of high trust and social capital is not an argument for *more* government,[65] or for emulating Germany and Japan. Rather, it is an argument about how best to enable a viable capitalist social order to organize and sustain itself.[66]

Adapting and expanding some widely used classifications from recent research,[67] we may divide the tools of government into *effectors*, instruments that bring about change in society, economy or polity; *collectors*, instruments that collect financial resources from the wider economy; *detectors*, instruments that take information from the society according as it is desired by government; and *selectors*, or instruments that select, present, organize, manage and manipulate that information. Table 2 reviews the toolkit available to government; table 3 gives more detail on the eljectors – the tools that give more direct leverage in cultural change.

TABLE 2 *The tool kit of government*

Effectors	*Collectors*	*Detectors*	*Seclectors*
Information delivery (propaganda, persuasion, example, demonstration projects, training, etc.)	Direct taxation	Requisition	Performance indicators
Direct government	Indirect taxation	Inspection	Cost measurement
Government owned corporations	Service fees and charges	Purchasing information	Cost-benefit analysis; resource budgeting
Regulation: mandation: prohibition: permission	Levies	Appeals (incl. bounties)	Audit
Contract purchasing	Appeals	Barter	Management review
Grants-in-aid; matching grants			New communications technology
Loan guarantees			Scenario planning
Tax expenditures			Formal modelling
Systems of redress			

TABLE 3 *Ejectors in more detail: Power tools open to government for changing behaviour*

Power tool/ target	*Command*	*Incentive*	*Persuasion*	*Example*	*Interaction*	*Redress*
Bureaucracy	instruction	performance pay	training: codes of ethics	leader role models	competition cooperation transparency	complaints systems
Field	regulation	output-related funding	publicity	demonstration projects	competition cooperation transparency	courts
Clients	legal duties	tapers, conditional entitlements	moral praise and blame	leader role models	competition cooperation transparency	courts
Public	legal duties	equal opportunity laws	exhortation	leader role models	competition co-operation transparency	courts

In effect, the Reinventers tried to shift the main effectors away from direct government and toward regulation, purchasing and the use of incentives.[68] Regulators now form a large industry, and on both the left and the right there are great and probably unrealistic expectations of what regulation can deliver.[69] But the biggest change was the great expansion in the number and sophistication of the selectors – the various performance measurement techniques to help government to be effective.[70] For example, systems of resource-based accounting, requisition of information by regulatory and audit agencies, and performance league tables were all central innovations of the Reinvention Programme. Yet governments are still very poor at measuring the cultures, the social capital and the extent of social trust among their populations of individuals or of organizations.[71] The vast majority of government measurement and organization of information is geared still to monitoring financial flows, the activities of services, and in very crude terms, outcomes that are at best poorly related to the outputs of services.

We can now see the case for a rather different focus on tools in the period ahead. One is redress which is centrally important in securing social trust. If one has no other reason to trust someone as a trading partner or as an employee, then the possibility of recourse to law must remain the only basis. Of course, a culture of too-ready redress rapidly becomes distrusting and people have every incentive to exploit the system of redress by using litigation to evade personal responsibility. The ever increasing litigiousness of the USA is but one symptom of that country's trust problems. Britain has suffered some of the same trends, but Britons have not found redress correspondingly easier. Indeed, Britain seems to have the worst of both worlds.

A second is the power of government to persuade, which was often ridiculed by Reinventers as 'idle moralizing'. It was assumed that without incentives, persuasion was ineffective or even counterproductive and with them, unnecessary. Of course, persuasion alone is likely to be as feeble as the use of any other single tool. Yet it is becoming increasingly important for governments to persuade their citizens not merely to behave in particular ways but to invest in social capital and social trust.

We need to think more carefully about how to use all these tools of government for much bigger and longer-term purposes of cultural change. If communitarian thought has a useful message for those thinking about government, it is not to celebrate nonprofit organizations as a solution to problems, but to set government the challenge of creating the trust necessary for a self-organizing society and economic dynamism.[72]

Cultures cannot be built – only destroyed – very quickly. This is because cultures are systems of beliefs, expectations, aspirations.[73] It usually takes time to institutionalize expectations, to change people's aspirations and to refocus their energies.[74] Our cultures are close to the centre of our sense of own identities and the reasons why we work in a certain field, such as the civil service or local government or a voluntary organization. In a liberal democracy, therefore, where electors can insist on their own political culture, policy recommendations for cultural change must be long-term, slow-burning, microlevel interventions. This makes them rather less exciting than, say, short-term proposals about interest rates, trade treaties, privatizations, or Next Steps agencies. But the search for drama in public policy is not particularly healthy. Dramatic policy changes are not always the most radical or even the most effective, however much they satisfy the need to show that 'something is being done'. Indeed, they can induce instability that, over long periods of time, can erode social capital and trust in government. Therefore, I make no particular apology for offering microlevel, cumulative, slow-burn policy suggestions.

For government to play its part in creating a culture of trust and trustworthiness, it must start with improving its own trustworthiness. Organizations tend to be trusted when their purposes are clear and acceptable, when they are not only treating their customers well but are believed to be doing so not merely to exploit them later (think of the high reputation of IBM), offer restitution in the event that they might fail (think of Marks and Spencer's 'no quibble' return policy), conduct their business according to basic principles of probity and fair dealing (although few experts in broadcasting and health policy accept the popular view, most of the British public considers the waiting list system of rationing in the NHS to be fair, and considers the BBC to be scrupulously impartial). Agencies of government too often fail these straightforward tests.

Sir Douglas Hague has distinguished four strategies by which cultures can be deliberately changed: *coercion, contagion, coaching* and *learning*.[75] In the case of *coercion,* circumstances such as the defection of consumers or the exercise of government command leaves a culture with no option but to change. In the second case, individuals are introduced as catalysts or change agents to import an alien culture: bringing new management and staging takeovers are both examples of *contagion*. Where outside assistance is called in to provide *coaching*, the need for change is usually recognized within the culture. Finally, organizations can, of their own volition, *learn* as the primary route for cultural change. In practice, change is usually the result of a combination of these processes.

The Reinventers tended to rely, despite their rhetoric of pluralism in management style and despite the large-scale use of private consultants in government, more heavily on coercion and contagion in reforming government itself than on coaching or learning. The Financial Management Initiative, which at once reinforced Treasury control and imposed new agents of financial control in many agencies, provides a paradigm example of both.[76] Allowing coaching and learning requires slow-burn thinking about culture and greater trust in staff and other associated agencies which is not always common among the political elites bent on projects of rapid transformation. Indeed, the focus of many of the Reinventers on process re-engineering, total quality management and delivery in those parts of government that provide services[77] may partially have undermined the capacity of organizations to learn more imaginatively. Too often they rushed to achieving service goals by buttressing traditionally hierarchical systems of management and Taylorist ideas of supervision, which can sap motivation and morale and reduce the flow of information. New models for managing cultural change that will promote learning from within and greater use of coaching will now have to involve taking longer time horizons for change. Systems of financial management that are geared to controlling expenditure – *economy* and *efficiency* – are very poor at creating cultures of risk-taking and entrepreneurialism that bring about *effectiveness*. As Pollitt has remarked, the three e's do not always march in step.[78]

Reluctant to use pilot projects either from impatience or a belief that pilots are always poor guides because of the Hawthorne effect (people perform much better in pilot schemes than they would if the system in use were the norm, simply because they are being paid so much attention[79]), British Reinventers often tried to bring about cultural change through across-the-board reforms, such as the National Curriculum in education, or the internal market in the NHS. Even where health and educations systems were changed by allowing individual units such as schools and hospitals to 'opt out' or GP practices to choose to become 'fundholders', early opt outs were not treated as experiments to be evaluated and learned from before proceeding with an innovation, but simply as vanguards who would be followed by sluggards.

The obvious *effector* instrument of long-term cultural engineering that policy makers reach for, when wanting to change hearts and minds, is schooling. However, it is important that education for cultural change is not simply another item on the curriculum or yet another goal for a school system that already has a surfeit of them, but the integrating and overarching concept in curriculum development. In the Anglo-American tradition, schooling is centred on the measurement of individual performance. For example, 'copying' is penalized, and 'conferring' on homework sharply discouraged. Even project or investigation-based work is often still expected to be a solitary effort. The consequence of this is that many pupils and students emerge from full-time education with none of the skills of cooperation and teamwork that are required in the world of work generally, and especially important in the creation and sustaining of new organizational capacity. By contrast, in many Pacific Asian countries, the educational culture is very different, and consequences for economic performance are clear to all.[80]

However, *persuasion* in its many forms will be important. Exhortation can also be valuable. For example, the high levels of private savings in Germany and Japan over recent decades do genuinely seem to have been partly a response to government propaganda about the importance and value of saving.[81] Again, programmes of training can – in the context of the full use of other tools – be an effective way of using exhortation to change behaviour. Some governments have experimented with training in the inculcation of ethical codes of conduct into the behaviour of their own staff, and have found some success.[82]

Howard Gardner has stressed recently the importance of *example* in the activities of leaders and this is also important for government.[83] The more that government can invest in its own trustworthiness, can show its leaders engaging in volunteering, and the more that government can show in its own conduct of its affairs that it eschews both profligacy and dishonesty, the more likely it is to be able to convince its own citizens to behave in these high-trust styles. Simple things such as prompt payment by governments of invoices, or provision of complaints systems have been important in setting an example to the private sector.

It is a difficult but important task to improve the system of civil law *redress* without simply encouraging people to evade personal responsibility through ever more litigation. However, some things could be done. Building on the relatively successful and low-cost, lawyer-free experience of the small claims court, more could be done to enforce payment of bills. Late payment, not least by government, is a major problem creating distrust, especially for smaller enterprises. A cheaper and quicker enforcement system could be devised, and all government agencies could be under clear duties to pay against invoices within twenty-eight days of receiving the bill.[84]

There is a role for government in stimulating a healthy ecology of private organizations, by facilitating both the birth of new agencies and the death of moribund ones.[85] Programmes of *purchasing, contracting, franchising, loan guarantees and grant-making* should be reviewed regularly to ensure that they are not simply privileging incumbents. More radically, there is a strong case for imposing sunset clauses on many public agencies: the near-immortality of government agencies is legendary and must have damaging cultural consequences for organizing capacity.[86] This would also be an important element in government setting an example.

The *detectors* and *selectors* of government are also important. In order to design policies that more effectively change cultures governments must first learn to measure the cultures of their own agencies, the networks of organizations with which they work, their users and the wider public. They might draw much more on recent research that has attempted to define, classify and develop instruments and questions to measure such cultures.[87] There has yet to be any comprehensive and rigorous survey of the different organizational cultures within the civil service or to map the ways in which hiving-off, contracting-out, decentralization, splitting policy formulation from policy implementation, and strengthening the dominance of financial management have changed these cultures. Indeed, it was in the face of strong opposition from the Head of the Home Civil Service, Sir Robin Butler, and the then Public Services Minister, William Waldegrave to a proposal from the Treasury and Civil Service Select Committee that the civil service conduct its own survey on the limited cultural indicator of current morale, that the First Division Association commissioned their own, the results of which were never accepted by government.

From the pessimism of the high intellectual right that all the tools of government are intrinsically blunt, and from the intellectual hyperoptimism of the centre-right and centre-left Reinventers that the restricted toolkit of the new public management would suffice to transform government, there is emerging a welcome recognition that government can effect real change, but subject to strict limits.

It is in this context that governments need a richer understanding of why culture matters. A credible political project for government in the next decade can no longer be about managing government services better or about getting government down to some correct proportion of GDP – 'right-sizing' – or even about defining all and only the tasks that government should do – 'right-tasking'. It must be about nothing less than changing the whole culture.

In some respects this is nothing new. The Conservatives in Britain certainly believed themselves to be engaged in changing culture, as the quotation at the beginning of this chapter, makes clear. But what is striking about the Conservative programmes for cultural change is that – despite the rhetoric – they do not show the coherence of a grand cultural project. The enterprise culture and individualistic culture was lauded to the skies, except in the public sector and within the family, where cultures of hierarchy and authority were to be reinforced. Consumer rights were promoted in some public services, but half-heartedly for fear of stirring up expectations about change in the systems of rationing services.

The new right of the Conservative Party wanted and still want a more radical and more coherent programme of cultural change, under which much of civil government can be closed down.[88] Yet that movement has yet to articulate a clear conception of how the cultural dimension of their programme is feasible. The problem for the nightwatchman state is that public loyalty, legitimacy and support for government comes from its willingness to solve the problems that citizens present to it, visibly to offer them something in return. By contrast the attempts to combine commitment to the nation-state and governmental minimalism are incoherent, as every serious nationalist in Europe has realized since the nineteenth century.

If the left wanted the security state and the right the nightwatchman state, the challenge today is to construct a new settlement in which civil government acts as a catalyst for self-organization wherever possible, without imagining that it can ever completely put itself out of a job.

Who will be the agents of this new settlement? Are politicians up to the challenge? Some will no doubt argue that the short-term, election timetable oriented nature of British politics prohibits slow-burn policy-making for long-term cultural change: the electoral demand for the quick fix will override everything. Others will add that the apparent tendencies of the two main parties to converge in many areas of policy-making is another obstacle. In fact, the present political configuration presents an excellent opportunity for politicians to engage in long-term policy thinking about culture, because they are not – as they have been in more polarized times – always fearful that their every innovation will be overturned when their rivals come to power. This is an historic opportunity to remake government on the better understanding of the simple fact that the most successful societies are those that can manage themselves.

19

The Audit Explosion

MICHAEL POWER

The word 'audit' is being used in the UK and around the world with growing frequency. In addition to financial audits, there are now environmental audits, value-for-money audits, management audits, forensic audits, data audits, intellectual property audits, medical audits, teaching audits, technology audits, stress audits, democracy audits and many others besides.[1] More generally, the spread of audits and other quality assurance initiatives means that many individuals and organizations now find themselves subject to audit for the first time and, notwithstanding protest and complaint, have come to think of themselves as auditees. There is a real sense in which 1990s Britain has become an 'audit society'.[2]

What are we to make of this explosion of 'audits'? What changes in the style of government does it characterize? Is this a distinctive phase in the life of advanced industrial societies?

The extent of the audit explosion is difficult to quantify but there are a number of indicators. The establishment of the National Audit Office and the Audit Commission in the early 1980s consolidated the audit resources of central and local government respectively, and provided an institutional focus for addressing the economy, efficiency and effectiveness of publicly funded activities. Both these organizations have expanded their work, particularly in value for money audit, bringing intensive scrutiny to many new areas such as the various elements of the criminal justice system – police, forensic science, crown prosecution and probation services.[3]

Medical and teaching institutions are also set to become subject to extensive auditing regimes. Medical audits have acquired prominence in response to a recent government white paper[4] and the newly established Higher Education Quality Council (HEQC) and its auditing activities will become increasingly influential.[5] In the field of quality assurance more generally, the British Standards Institute has successfully promoted BS5750, its standard for quality assurance, and has used it to develop the BS7750 standard for environmental management systems. The European Commission has issued a regulation for a voluntary Eco-Management and Audit scheme which closely resembles BS7750. The likely take-up of these initiatives is still unclear but it has been estimated that there is a $200 billion market to be covered by environmental consulting[6] and the number of consulting organizations in this area has risen dramatically in the last ten years.[7] The recent development of accreditation schemes for environmental auditors has provided a further stimulus.[8]

Another indicator is the size of the major accounting firms, which grew very quickly during the 1980s. The proportion of university graduates entering traineeships with accountancy firms peaked at more than 10 per cent in 1987 and is currently running at about 8 per cent.[9] Of this number, a majority receive their primary training in financial audit work although relatively few remain in this field. Thus one important dimension of the UK audit explosion is that unprecedentedly large numbers of young people are being trained and socialized in the context of auditing.

In traditional financial audit the trends are less conspicuous. While the number of statutory entities requiring audit has grown steadily, it is the more intensive role of audit which is more notable. The statutory financial audit of companies has become more highly regulated and codified over the last twenty years. The Auditing Practices Committee, replaced by the Auditing Practices Board in 1991, was formed in 1976 and has produced technical guidance on a wide range of issues. Developments have been evident in two particular fields: financial regulation and charities. In the case of both fields, particular statutory initiatives have extended the role of audit. The Financial Services Act 1986 and the Banking Act 1987 have given auditors newly explicit responsibilities for assessing internal controls and for communicating with regulators. Many have complained that the costs of these arrangements are out of proportion to their benefits.[10] Charities have also come under renewed regulatory scrutiny. Supplementary provisions to the Charities Act 1992, and accounting guidance specifically tailored to the sector, reflect a determination to subject these organizations to increased financial discipline via audit.[11]

In other areas, the audit explosion has taken different forms. Safety and hazard audits in industry have grown naturally from health and safety legislation. Data audits (which analyse the integrity of research data), which originated in the United States and are less prominent in the UK, have arisen from concerns about scientific fraud.[12] UK public science will soon find itself subject to value for money, intellectual property and technology audits as government seeks both to make science accountable to its funding publics and to exploit its intellectual property base.[13]

Despite these developments, the audit explosion is only in part a quantitative story of human and financial resources committed to audit and its extension into new fields. It also concerns the spread of a distinct mentality of administrative control, a pervasive logic which has a life over and above specific practices, as ever more individuals and organizations come to think of themselves as subjects of audit.

What can we say about this explosion and how should we respond?

First, despite differences in context and meaning, there is a common thread to the new uses of the word 'audit'. Sceptics may doubt whether the proliferating usage of a single word really signifies any systematic relationship between the diverse contexts within which it is invoked. After all, audit is hardly an unambiguous concept and it could be argued that the practices to which the label is attached are in fact diverse and that they are constituted by very different bodies of knowledge. For example, it is possible to distinguish audits on the basis of their relation to the auditee. Many audits, for example in medicine, are conceived primarily as internal reviews to improve decision-making. Some of the growth of audits has been of this kind, intended to support rather than to discipline, and very different from ex post verifications which have much more the character of a policing role and for which the independence of the auditor is crucial. The extent to which audits are oriented towards verification is therefore variable and many commentators would wish to argue that value-for-money auditing plays an entirely different role.

But there are important linkages between the different contexts of audit. Even forms of 'self-audit' rely upon bureaucratic procedures which can in principle be used for independent verification purposes, even in contexts such as medical audit.[14] Indeed, checklists and protocols for apparently internal purposes often derive their authority from their potential use for external verification. Formal documents can be used outside their original context and in ways unanticipated by those who may have designed them. In addition, the experience of other management areas suggests that even predecision reviews may have an ex post justificatory function.[15]

Second, audit is not just a series of (rather uninteresting) technical practices. It must also be understood as an *idea*. It is usual, particularly in official documents and textbooks, to conceive of audit only in terms of its technical and operational qualities, a routine activity to make activities transparent. While this image reinforces its reputation as a boring and parasitic practice, it disguises the importance of auditing as an idea. Audit has become central to ways of talking about administrative control. The extension of auditing into different settings, such as hospitals, schools, water companies, laboratories, and industrial processes, is more than a natural and self-evidently technical response to problems of governance and accountability. It also involves rationalizing and reinforcing public images of control. The audit explosion is the explosion of an idea that is internal to the ways in which practitioners and policy makers make sense of what they are doing.[16]

Third, the spread of audits and audit talk corresponds to a fundamental shift in patterns of governance in advanced industrial societies. The explosion of audit practices in new areas (from the environment to schools) is, at least in the UK, not simply a quantitative intensification. It arises out of changing conceptions of administration and governance.[17] Accordingly, to understand this explosion we must dig deeper and look wider than preoccupations with technical and institutional issues, and recognize that audit has emerged at the boundary between the older traditional control structures of industrial society and the demands of a society which is increasingly conscious of its production of risks, in fields ranging from the environment and foodstuffs, to medicine and finance.[18] It is one of many features of a far-reaching transition in the dominant forms of administration and control, both in government and in business.

As such, audit is a way of reconciling contradictory forces: on the one hand the need to extend a traditional hierarchical command conception of control in order to maintain existing structures of authority; on the other the need to cope with the failure of this style of control, as it generates risks that are increasingly hard to specify and control (examples include everything from the BSE 'mad cow disease' scare to unreliable pensions).

Fourth, the pervasive feature of the new wave of audits is that they work not on primary activities but rather on other systems of control. For example, in higher education the trend has been towards ever more audits of the quality assurance systems of universities and colleges.[19] This gives the audit a more remote assurance role than is often understood by the publics which they are intended to serve. Audits are often not directly concerned with the quality of performance, whether environmental, educational or financial, but rather with the systems in place to govern quality. This 'policing of policing' distinguishes the audit explosion from an older tradition of engineering-based quality control and its statistically grounded methods.

Fifth, audits do not contribute automatically to organizational transparency. Despite the fact that audit talk is driven by demands for greater transparency of organizational and individual action, the capacity of audit to deliver this is problematic. Often the extension of audits can make organizations more obscured, and the audit process itself remains publicly invisible despite the commitment to making organizations transparent. It may be that the audit explosion signifies a displacement of trust from one part of the economic system to another; from operatives to auditors.

Sixth, audits have the remarkable capacity of being invulnerable to their own failure. In recent years the primary concern of public debate has been with financial audit. Often regarded as a model for other forms of audit, it has been the subject of extensive critical commentary, set off in large part by the recent demise of the Bank of Credit and Commerce International (BCCI) and the Maxwell empire. Rightly or wrongly, corporate collapse is always accompanied by scrutiny of the role of the auditors and, in some cases, litigation on the grounds that they have performed their task negligently.[20]

One of the surprising features of these experiences is that they tend not to call into question the role of audit itself. Instead, where audit has failed, the common (and understandable) response has been to call for more of it (rather as most failures of policing lead to calls for more policing, rather than a questioning of why the techniques are not working). Indeed, the great puzzle of financial audit is that it has never been a more powerful and influential model of administrative control than now, when many commentators talk of an auditing crisis.[21]

Seventh, audit is not passive but active. Not only does it shape the activities which it controls in critical ways but it represents a very particular conception of accountability. Far from being passive, audit actively constructs the contexts in which it operates. The most influential dimension of the audit explosion is the process by which environments are made auditable, structured to conform to the need to be monitored ex post. Audits do not passively monitor auditee performance but shape the standards of this performance in crucial ways, and public conceptions of the very problems for which it is the solution.

Eighth, notwithstanding the dominance of audits there are other ways of achieving accountability. Any society or organization can use very different models of control and accountability, which can be summarized in the following lists:

STYLE A	STYLE B
Quantitative	Qualitative
Single Measure	Multiple Measures
External Agencies	Internal Agencies
Long Distance Methods	Local Methods
Low Trust	High Trust
Discipline	Autonomy
Ex Post Control	Real Time Control
Private Experts	Public Dialogue

The audit explosion has involved an overwhelming priority for style A as the solution to any problem (although value-for-money auditing could be regarded as embodying both).[22] Quantified, simplified, ex post forms of control by outsiders have increasingly displaced other types of control. As a result of its institutional power, and its power as an idea, proponents of alternative styles have found it hard to gain an audience.

This shift has brought a 'complex bundle of gains and losses'.[23] It is not my intention to suggest that there have been no gains at all from the growth of audit. However, these gains are likely to be most visible when used in conjunction with, rather than in opposition to, elements of control style B. One example of this is when medical audits help practitioners reflect on clinical methods and management as well as offering a mechanism for external evaluation. A more balanced use of audit methods may also do far more to underpin public trust than today's dominant methods.

In the end, looking beyond audit requires that we also rethink what it is that makes organizations work. So far Western fascination for Japanese organizational structures seems to have been unable to affect the audit mentality,[24] even though Japanese structures depend much more on 'style B' types of control: horizontal rather than vertical, trust-creating, qualitative rather than quantitative. Like them, we would benefit from having less respect for abstract forms of portable knowledge and more respect for non standard and tacit kinds of knowledge which are complex and close to their products.

Although this would undoubtedly challenge existing structures of professional status, we would not be sending the nation's brightest and best to work in an abstract 'economy of compliance'. Instead we would be placing them closer to productive processes – in services, manufacturing and the public sector – in all their diversity. In this way we will surely be in a better position to create quality rather than merely to police it.

20

Reconnecting Taxation

GEOFF MULGAN and ROBIN MURRAY

> Public finances are one of the best starting points for an investigation of a society. The spirit of a people, its cultural level, its social structure, the deeds its policy may prepare – all this and more is written in its fiscal history, stripped of all phrases. He who knows how to listen to the message here discerns the thunder of world history more clearly than anywhere else.
>
> JOSEPH SCHUMPETER, 1954

Modern Western politics is obsessed with taxation. Over the last two decades, the irresistible upward pressure of public spending has set off a succession of tax revolts, from California's Proposition 13 (a citizens' initiative which sharply cut taxes in the 1970s) and the Progress Parties of Norway and Denmark, to rebellions against VAT in Japan and the poll tax in Britain. Tax-raising governments have lost elections and oppositions that promise new taxes have failed to win them.

Some expected that the backlash against tax would give governments a clear mandate to break the inherited welfare consensus and to cut taxes and spending. The Thatcher and Reagan governments interpreted their election victories in this way. But in spite of the cuts, the closures and the privatizations – measures which became common in the West, irrespective of party – tax continued to go up. In Britain it rose from 34.1 per cent of GDP in 1980 to 35.6 per cent in 1990. The great majority of OECD countries shared in this relentless historical trend.

Today it is as if the argument about tax has become becalmed. Although some politicians continue to promise dramatic new tax cuts they find it hard to explain how. Many of the marketable public assets have already been sold. Charges for some public services are approaching market prices. Social security benefits have been squeezed, and eligibility narrowed. Public-sector pay curbs have already critically undermined the quality of staff and thus of services. And large groups of voters, particularly the old, react vociferously against any attempt to reduce their entitlements.

For politicians the effect is a near permanent sense of crisis since the demands on government show no signs of decreasing. In Britain the NHS needs an annual real growth of 2 per cent to survive even at current levels, personal social services require 2.5 per cent, and education will need an extra 0.5–1.0 per cent of GDP to bring post-school education up to European standards.[1] Everywhere there has been a steady increase in the number of people dependent on those in work – those staying on longer at school, living longer as pensioners, and above all those who are unemployed.

Governments find themselves at an impasse. On the one hand there is the resistance to tax, on the other a continuing demand for expenditure. Electorates say they want better public services, particularly health and education,[2] yet they consistently vote against the means of delivering it.

Much of the political debate has focused on the problems of spending: which services should be provided for whom and in what way. But there has been less advance on the other side of the equation, that of tax and revenue raising. The argument remains locked between parties favouring low taxes for low spending, and those favouring high taxes for high spending. The former have proved incapable of cutting taxes, while the latter have proved incapable of winning elections. Both are trapped in an irresolvable debate. This essay is about changing the nature of the debate. It seeks to shift the axis of discussion away from the levels of tax, to the nature of the tax relationship itself.

The key point about this relationship is that it is always coercive. Our contemporary view of tax is inevitably influenced by the fact that tax was at the economic heart of earlier despotic and feudal regimes, and of all colonialisms. All acted as predators on their populations and their histories are full of tax revolts which gave us such folk heroes as Lady Godiva, John Ball and William Tell.

The modern era began with a wave of rebellions against tax, sparked off when the rising cost of warfare drove taxes up right across Europe. Some were unsuccessful, as in Austria and Ireland. Others became historical turning points. The American War of Independence was sparked by the battle over customs and contraband. In France it was tax that brought to a head the great class conflicts of the 1789 revolution, with the popular sacking of customs posts, the burning of tax registers and the declaration by the third estate that all existing taxes were null and void.

But the development of capitalism and liberal democracy did not mean the end of tax. Early capitalist states found that they too needed taxes, but their forced character was at odds with the culture of free exchange. Ever since, tax has been a channel for wider discontents. The Poujadist movement of the 1950s in France, for instance, started in a village in the Lot region, as a protest against the visit of a tax administrator. It represented a refusal by small farmers and shopkeepers to accept the impositions of a bureaucratic state, which they saw as allied with the forces of impersonalization – large trusts, big shops, and high finance. And it focused on tax because it is such a pure expression of the state's absolute power.

Even in the most benign democracies there have always been tensions around the legitimacy of taxes. These tensions, revolts and compromises, provide the spine of tax history. They mark its eras and points of transformation.[3]

In modern times, there have been two historic moments of transition. The first in the late eighteenth and early nineteenth centuries replaced an absolutist tax regime with a capitalist one. Under absolutism, taxes had been mainly paid by traders and the poor. The nobles, clergy and the wealthier urban class were largely exempt except in times of war. The political economists and Enlightenment thinkers campaigned against such privileges, arguing that all should pay their share. Internal tariffs should be dropped, and revenue raised from rents and wealth. This was the programme of financial ministers and enlightened despots, but it took the French Revolution – and the fear of its spread abroad – to deliver it in Europe.

The new order was marked by five features: an end to privileges and feudal dues; the growth of indirect taxes on foreign trade and domestic consumption, with a lightening of the burden on necessities (like salt) and an increased dependence on drink and tobacco duties; a readiness to tax rents and wealth, with the help of improved land surveys; the growing centralization of finance and spending decisions in national treasuries, and the establishment of direct tax administrations; and the subordination of public finance and expenditure to parliamentary control through the medium of the budget. These took effect at different times according to national and political circumstance. But together they constituted a new fiscal order, a new settlement, which filled out and developed as the nineteenth century progressed.

The second turning point came in the 1890s, in response to a sudden expansion of public spending and the growth of the labour movement. It involved a shift from tax neutrality to tax progression, and centred on a new role for income tax. In Britain indirect taxes accounted for the great bulk of tax revenue during the eighteenth and nineteenth centuries. The first income tax had been raised by Pitt in 1799, and became permanent from 1842. But its yield was modest. It was seen primarily as a convenient tool of revenue raising, and was never intended to be progressive. Gladstone said that the principle of graduated income tax tended to communism and fought the 1874 election on a platform of abolishing income tax altogether.[4]

But by the turn of the century the yield from direct tax surpassed that from indirect tax, and in 1909 Lloyd George's 'war budget against poverty' not only endorsed progressivity but included a supertax and a form of capital gains tax on land values. In paying tax, he said, people ought to contribute in proportion to their means. For his prime minister, Asquith, progressive tax became 'a mark of the democratic neo-liberalism of the twentieth century [which] had little in common with Gladstonian liberalism'.

There was a parallel timetable elsewhere. Income tax was introduced into Sweden in 1861, Italy in 1864, Japan in 1867, and in many of the German states in the last decade of the century. The principle of progressivity was adopted in conservative Prussia in 1891, in liberal Belgium in 1893 and in democratic America in 1894. By the time of the First World War, progressive direct taxes had become the norm.

What marks their development in the twentieth century is the steady growth in the number of direct tax payers and the rise in yield. In Britain in 1909 only one million paid income tax. By the Second World War the number had risen to 4 million, by 1948 to 14.5 million, and by 1990 to 25 million. Deducted at source by the large employers after the Second World War, income tax became a mass tax to fund universal services. It fitted well with the new forms of mass production. It contributed not only to public revenue raising but also to redistribution and, from the 1930s, to the regulation of the macroeconomy. It depended on a dominant formal sector, a distinct national economy, households supported by a male earner[5] and the social consensus of the welfare state.

By the 1970s income tax and social security contributions made up the majority of tax revenue in all major OECD countries. In many it contributed two-thirds of all tax. Those countries where industrialization occurred later – Ireland,

Spain, Portugal and Greece – rapidly caught up both in terms of the significance of income tax and the overall size of tax revenue. The spread of mass production appeared to bring with it a complementary set of public institutions to finance and service the elements of a social wage.

If there are clear contrasts between nineteenth- and twentieth-century taxation, there are also continuities. There is a pattern of movement away from feudal regressiveness to liberal and social-democratic progressiveness. There is the importance of the nation-state as the boundary for both fiscal rights and obligations, and the justification for them. There is also the continuing drive for the centralization of revenue-raising and expenditure approval, and the growth of representative government as the key channel for democratic control over tax. Representation and taxation are the twin pillars of the new form of government which emerged in the late eighteenth century, grew in scale and scope, and is still the dominant democratic model today.

During previous periods of transition, the need to finance higher government spending exposed the limitations of the inherited tax regime. In the late eighteenth century the growth of spending was the result of the external costs of war. In the late nineteenth century it was due to the internal costs of peace. Today it is caused by the rising relative costs of maintaining labour-intensive public services and the growing number of people dependent on the state.

The first major characteristic of current tax regimes we term disconnection: the separation of the tax bill from the benefits it finances. Traditionally, taxes were largely raised for specific ends: above all, warfare. In the eighteenth century war and the costs of war debts accounted for 85 per cent of state spending in Britain. The connection between tax and spending was evident to all. But with the growth in the size and complexity of the state this link has been lost, principally because of the centralization of tax collection and disbursement.

The vast multiple service system of the modern state is still organized largely on the models established in the nineteenth century. In the UK tax money is pooled into the central treasury and distributed to spending departments, according to a budget and subject to approval by Parliament. Local government has adopted a similar model. Where once local services were financed through separate rates, by the 1930s these had been combined into a single rate to cover all services.

When there was a consensus on state spending, such as in wartime or in the postwar period of rebuilding and funding the welfare state, central pooling was not problematic. The shared sense of purpose helped to legitimize higher taxes: the end justified the means. In the early years of this century central pooling also fitted well with prevailing administrative wisdoms: it enabled government to plan and prioritize.

But as the welfare consensus started to break down in the 1970s, the political foundations of pooling began to crack. Cuts provoked a widespread, and often divisive, debate about priorities. A more confident consumerism demanded greater transparency and accountability in the use of state finances, particularly as the sheer complexity of modern government was making it far harder for the average citizen to understand. And a generation more sensitive to choice and identity was becoming less deferential towards government and more suspicious of handing over blank cheques.

The administrative centralization that once seemed so eminently sensible has lost much of its authority. The separation of tax collection from service provision has left the links to be made through cost budgeting by senior civil servants and politicians in invisible procedures, according to scarcely visible criteria. Levels of finance are shaped by departmental and ministerial rivalries rather than by popular support. No attempt is made to consult with electors. Public debate about tax is diverted onto the spectacle of the annual budget, which springs new taxes on a passive population (after a secrecy far in excess of what can be justified by the need to restrict price-sensitive information). Nor has electoral politics done much to assist public understanding, for recent election campaigns, both in the UK and elsewhere, have tended to obscure far more than they have clarified.[6] To the outsider government appears to be a black hole into which resources disappear.

The ways in which taxes are raised and spent make it peculiarly difficult for electorates to support them. Each tax is merely one of many tributaries to the centralized pool.[7] There is no clear link between taxes and services, no consultation beyond occasional elections, and little if any reference to public views. The budget process is preceded by little debate and involves no test-marketing. Instead the predominant forms of tax still carry the trace of an era when tax was the prerogative of sovereigns who set taxes at whatever level they could get away with and for whom the legitimacy and ethics of taxes mattered little.[8]

Political debate over the last fifteen years has been dominated by the new right's response to Western electorates' renewed hostility to tax. Theorists such as Samuel Brittan, Walter Eltis and Milton Friedman made two important arguments. The first was that the state was soaking up too much wealth and crowding out private investment, and thus in the long run undermining its own sources of income. High tax was threatening economic growth and the wellbeing even of those who were supposed to benefit from fiscal redistribution. The priority was a sharp reduction in the quantity of tax being raised from all sources, to be achieved by encouraging people to take greater financial responsibility for their own education, health, housing and transport.

In parallel, there was a second, microeconomic argument that high marginal rates of tax on income and profits damaged incentives to work and invest. From this it followed that there should be lower top marginal rates, greater rights to inheritance and capital gains, and a shift to nonprogressive expenditure taxes.

For a period this seemed to be the basis of a new consensus, as the weakening of labour movements reduced the pressure that led to the introduction of European welfare states in the first place. It seemed as if the conservative governments of the 1980s were going to turn back the course of twentieth-century tax development with their renewed emphasis on indirect taxes, the strong move against tax progression, and the radical deconstruction of the welfare state. The next steps in this historical retracing would be further to simplify the tax system, to cut pensions and benefits, and to raise VAT on necessities, and charges for the health service. Such is the outline of a possible tax regime for the twenty-first century.

But in the countries which first implemented the new right model its flaws soon became evident. As we have seen, the most obvious was that the promise of lower taxes and public spending did not materialize. In the 1980s, in the words of Sir Douglas Hague, a former adviser to Mrs Thatcher, 'her government was mainly engaged not in reducing public expenditure but in containing it . . . a case of running fast to stay in the same place . . .' Revenues exceeded 40 per cent during only three years in the 1970s, but in the 1980s 'despite the rhetoric of tax cuts, general government revenue never fell below 40 per cent,'[9] and by the mid 1990s the share of public spending in GDP was back over 44 per cent, a higher proportion than in 1979.

There has been a similar story in the USA and Germany. In each country the conservative government discovered that there was no stable consensus around lower taxes and lower spending, no political eldorado waiting to be found. In each case politicians succumbed to temptation and postponed their problems through mushrooming debt.

Despite incentives to opt out, overwhelming majorities continue to be dependent on state provision of health and education. Shifts in demography and employment are increasing the numbers who are dependent on benefits, reducing the electoral rewards for parties which argue too fiercely for the rights of the working taxpayer relative to those who receive benefits and depend on services.[10]

At the same time fears of higher crime and riots hold back

middle-class support for truly far-reaching welfare cuts. And while high unemployment tempts many governments to cut back on benefits, most fear that this will simply lead to higher costs of policing and security as the system loses legitimacy for a significant swathe of the population. It has not been lost on other countries that in the UK the two fastest growing areas of expenditure in the 1980s were social security and law and order.

The economics of the new right's tax programme has also lost conviction. Despite some evidence that cuts in marginal tax rates do improve productivity[11] the story does not end there. Competition between different areas wanting to attract footloose capital (such as a German or Japanese company wanting to set up a microelectronics plant) depends not only on low wages and taxes, but also on the balance between costs and the quality of the economic environment: the provision of education, infrastructures and social stability. Excessively low tax rates can frighten off investors as effectively as high marginal rates if they result in disorder and underproduction of public goods. The key point is that today's economy is increasingly systemic: the whole depends on the effective functioning of each of its parts. Transport, good schooling, and healthcare, cities without bombs, neighbourhoods without fear – all these are part of modern production and all require effective public provision.

In what follows we set out an alternative. It is designed not only to solve immediate policy problems but also to establish the framework for a new relationship between governors and governed and a new structure of accountability. Its central argument is that the system's crisis of legitimacy can only be resolved by remaking connections in new ways.

It should be clear right from the start that this is a project which involves nothing less than a change in the very conception of the state. For at the moment our tax system is shaped by the inheritance of despotism. The political model is that of Hobbes, with governments having the right to collect whatever level of tax they deem necessary, and to use whatever powers they regard as appropriate to the task. It is a top-down model, which begins with the needs and interests of the government rather than with the directly expressed needs and interests of the citizens.[12]

But there is another tradition which has always been suspicious of the state, tracing its roots to a fiercely anti-monarchical democracy. It can be found in Jeffersonian liberalism, in Catholic social thinking[13] and in more recent years in feminist and green approaches to government. This tradition works from the ground up. It sees sovereignty shared between elected representatives and citizens, and emphasizes the richness of the channels of communication between governors and governed.

It is in the light of this tradition that we now need to find the elements of a new alternative of reconnection. Its starting point is a set of three general principles.

– the first is the principle of hypothecation, that is to say wherever possible directing earmarked taxes towards specific ends, and reversing the trend towards pooling and consolidation.

– the second is the principle of democracy, wherever possible making the tax authorities and service providers directly accountable to the constituencies they serve.

– the third is the principle of subsidiarity, bringing tax-raising more closely into line with the appropriate levels of service provision, and reversing the trend towards national tax collection for local service delivery.

All three build on the premise that in sophisticated modern societies legitimacy needs to be built from the ground up, through a multiplicity of relationships between payers and providers rather than through a single line of accountability passing through parliament and cabinet. Legitimacy, in other words, comes from connections.

Some elements of this agenda are not unknown. Many US states require voters to approve increases in local property tax rates, known as the millage, and new bonds. In some states, such as California, voters themselves put issues on the ballot. In Switzerland, too, there is a long tradition of direct democratic control over taxes at a cantonal and communal level. But these practices have scarcely begun to renew the tax relationship. The time is ripe for a much bolder and more imaginative period of experimentation and it is to this that we now turn.

There have been a number of examples of hypothecation, the transfer of taxes from a specific source to a related purpose, during the course of British tax history.[14] One is the TV licence fee, which is levied on sets and goes directly to the BBC. Another was the Eady levy on cinema seats introduced by Harold Wilson in the late 1940s to fund the British film industry. These types of earmarking are most common in the early stages of tax development. In developing countries it is common to find airport and hotel bed taxes used to finance tourist development. Petrol tax is often used to finance road building. Just as winding country roads reflect strong local property rights and a weak state, so hypothecated taxes reflect the need for emerging states to win popular consent. And just as winding roads are replaced by the motorways of strong states, so hypothecated taxes are replaced by pooled collection and the assertion of treasury control over administration.[15]

We are suggesting a return to hypothecation, as a way of restoring people's sense of connection. There are three approaches to be considered.

The first is functional hypothecation, where a tax is used to finance another part of the same functional system. Transport is a good example of how this could work. There is a widely acknowledged imbalance between road and rail transport, and a lack of integration between different transport modes which has been exacerbated by misconceived models of funding and accountability. Hypothecation could put things right by imposing more appropriate incentives and signals.

The simplest approach would simply be to pay a proportion of the road fund licence, or of the revenue derived from urban road pricing, into rail. But a more promising approach, which demonstrates the wider potential of hypothecation, would be to introduce an annual public transport fee, similar in principle but not in form to the BBC licence fee.[16] This would fund a public transport agency which would in turn finance railways, buses, cycle hire groups, franchised taxis and other transport providers. It could be financed out of a range of sources, the most appropriate of which might be taxes on fuel: the important issue is that its level should be clearly visible to the public so that, as with the BBC, the level of finance would become a matter of public debate, dependent less on the decisions of cabinet committees and more on transport operators' ability to generate popular support through the quality and extent of services. Each would therefore have an incentive to maximize usage within the overall budget constraint, just as the BBC has an incentive to keep its ratings high. The key indicator for the railways, for example, would not be the financial deficit but rather the cost of each passenger mile.

Hypothecated funding, dependent on public support, and directed to an agency responsible for the overall system of transport, would then lead to a very different approach to transport provision. By giving a new incentive to maximize usage it could encourage transport integration, the reopening of stations, the return of free carriage for bicycles on trains, the adoption of the French system of cheap bicycle hire at stations, and the use of railway property for transport intensive activities like supermarket shopping or leisure. It could encourage more systemic thinking, such as improved containerization and luggage handling to encourage the integration of driving and long-distance rail travel. And it could foster integrated ticketing and an expansion of information systems, such as electronic bus availability data at stations and bus stops.

Forced to justify a transport fee, the transport agency, and those seeking its funds, would have to consider the interests of all potential users. Financial efficiency would still count, because a higher fee would reduce public support. But finance would no longer be the sole criterion.

This is just one example of functional hypothecation. There are many others: pollution taxes to fund environmental programmes, taxes on graduates' income to fund universities, taxes on child benefits to fund creches, taxes on cigarettes to help finance the health service, and taxes on air travel to fund urban infrastructure and open air arts. Tourism is particularly open to functional hypothecation since effective management of tourism relies heavily on urban and rural facilities which cannot adequately be charged for (thus the Swiss have maintained subsidies to small farmers as a means of sustaining their tourist industry).[17] The point in each of these cases is not merely that there is an explicit spotlight thrown on systems of provision and how well they interconnect, but that the recipients of funds are required to justify themselves publicly rather than just to ministers.

A second example is temporal hypothecation: the transfer of earmarked taxes to different stages of the life cycle. Insurance of this kind has been one of the central principles of twentieth-century welfare and underpins the British system of national insurance and social security contributions. Although the contributions and payments flow not through insurance funds but through the central Treasury pool, many people still prefer to think that their contributions are directly related to benefits.

Recent debate has tended to see links of this kind as a thing of the past. But there are many new areas where these may turn out to be better solutions than the available alternatives. One example is the shift from reactive to proactive insurance. The twentieth-century tradition of insurance was restricted to temporary or low-risk dangers. But with the growth of sustained high unemployment, work-related health problems, and regular demands for reskilling the workforce, there is a strong case for shifting the balance of social security provision towards tackling the roots of the problems rather than compensating for the consequences. It is often wiser to invest in reskilling rather than unemployment benefit, in preventative health care rather than curing, in pre-school education rather than heavy policing of teenagers.

Free markets do not usually encourage this kind of pro-active investment.[18] But collective insurance systems could be extended to protect against potential common threats. Their managers could be given incentives to invest in ways that reduce future payouts. Training and continuing adult education is an obvious example which could be funded by a distinct charge (part employer and part employee) and treated as an insurance against future unemployment. As with the French training levy, funds could be jointly controlled by employees and employers, rather than passing to the state. Another example would be prevention of work-related illnesses (both old ones and new ones like repetitive strain injury). In each case the effect would be to foster new mutual interests in prevention rather than cure. Instead of seeing social security as a social wage which is bound up with a wider distributional struggle between employees and employers, the insurance system would instead become a means of funding common benefits.

Another example of the new forms of temporal hypothecation is the use of insurance to support flexibility in working time. Rather than insuring against the risk of brief and occasional periods of unemployment, the insurance system could instead help employees plan working lives with more flexibility, both short-term (part-time work, flexitime, length and timing of holidays) and long-term (maternity and paternity leave, sabbaticals, and time for reskilling). It could help remove the traditional sharp distinction between full-time employment, unemployment and retirement and replace it with a more variegated system where national insurance payments provide rights for all classes of employees to take time off. This would not only help people manage the more 'lumpy' working lives which are becoming increasingly common, but could also help dampen the business cycle. Higher national insurance contributions during booms could be matched by incentives to encourage employees to take their time off during recessions, for example, seeing them as an opportunity to reskill. Between full-time work and complete dependence there would be a continuum of packages mixing work and funded time off in varying degrees.[19]

These are just two indicative examples. But they show how the concept of insurance, the earmarking of payments to future uses, could become more important in the twenty-first century, whether or not it is the state, or more likely trusts of one kind or another, which are charged with managing payments and provision.

The last category is distributive hypothecation: the earmarking of tax payments from one group to finance benefits for others. One of the tenets of twentieth-century taxation was that it allowed a redistribution from rich to poor. Subsequently most of the debate about redistribution has focused on this type of subsidy, and whether it still has public support. This debate has often been somewhat misleading, since the opacity of the budget hides many different types of redistribution, not least the huge subsidies for mortgage-holding homeowners, car users and the university-educated.

The virtue of hypothecation is that it could help to make these transfers more explicit. The annual budget could be required to show the tax source of each area of spending: revealing for example how much of the income tax bill pays for mortgage tax relief and how much for pensions. The virtues of providing free university education could more clearly be weighed against the virtues of training single parents. The aim would be to place a stronger pressure on recipients to justify their subsidies to a wider public.[20] Greater budgetary transparency about who benefits from public spending, would create the conditions for a more informed debate about priorities.[21] Information of this kind would have precisely the same value as sound accounts for a shareholder: it would show the public what their assets are doing.

But hypothecation could also have a profound effect on attitudes. At the moment those who vote for tax cuts can be among the first to contribute to charities. They do so because in the latter case there is a clear link between action and effect, and because they trust the body concerned. Tax pooling prevents these connections; hypothecation would remake them. For example, a government committed to greater redistribution might earmark a tranche of top-rate income tax for action against poverty by not-for-profit organizations. It is one thing to evade tax when the only loser is the Treasury, another when the losers are the homeless in the town centre or a disabled neighbour.[22]

These three forms of hypothecation, functional, temporal and distributive, are about the making of connections. They render services more independent of central budgetary processes. They encourage providers to look outwards – to the publics they have to convince, and to the funding sources on which they depend. This is why the Treasury and many senior politicians are so hostile to hypothecation. It weakens central control by making lateral connections. These are not the only examples of hypothecation: the model has obvious application at the local level (for example through special levies to finance job creation in a town or city) and at the neighbourhood level (for example through special payments for a school).

But the key point is that any sophisticated system of hypothecation points the way to a very different kind of state which no longer monopolizes choice and decision. For the modern nation-state, like the dynasties and empires that preceded it, rests on a system of tax. Unlike them, its governments have to cope with a world where money has become almost infinitely flexible, and where there is the constant need to be seen as legitimate by the citizens who pay the bills.

Over the last two decades governments have found themselves perpetually buffeted by their failure to solve either problem. They have placed a rising tax burden on an ever more resentful group of relatively immobile citizens whose patience has worn thin. And they have failed to devise a more international system of tax to fit the age of instantaneous transactions and global markets.

The new right reforms of the 1980s were a radical attempt to solve the problem by going backwards to the taxing and spending regimes of the nineteenth century. For the reasons we have outlined they failed, and left governments less confident and less legitimate. If governments are not simply to stumble from crisis to crisis, a new period of reform is now needed which more clearly addresses the prime sources of the crisis, above all the problem of legitimacy.

21

Is There a New World Order?

ROBERT COOPER

Introduction

1989 marks a break in European history.

What happened in 1989, with the democratic revolutions in Eastern Europe and the collapse of the Warsaw Pact, was not just the end of the Cold War but also the end of the balance of power system in Europe. Historically the right point of comparison is 1648, the end of the Thirty Years War when the modern European state system emerged at the Peace of Westphalia.[1]

In a curious symmetry this change has come about following a second thirty years war: 1919–1945. The First and Second World Wars brought a level of destruction which Europe had not seen since the first Thirty Years War. Thereafter the Cold War offered the possibility of devastation on a scale without historical precedent. A change in the state system in Europe was clearly required: if the existing system was producing such unacceptable levels of actual and potential destruction, it was not performing its function.

Thinking about foreign affairs – like any other kind of thinking – requires a conceptual map which, as maps do, simplifies the landscape and focuses on the main features. Before 1648 the key concept was Christendom; after, it was the balance of power. If Europe has now moved beyond the balance of power, we need to understand what new system has become the basis of our security.

A particular problem in understanding the international system – as opposed to the European system – is that it has become less unified since the end of the Cold War. In the Cold War most foreign policy issues could be viewed in the light of a single overwhelming question: how did it affect the East-West balance of power. With the end of the Cold War this rather artificial unity has been lost. While Europe is developing a new and more orderly security system, other parts of the world are becoming more disorderly.

How We Got Here: the Old Order

Until 1989 international order was based either on hegemony or on balance. Hegemony came first in the shape of *Pax Romana* or of the Mongol or Turkish Empires. The choice for the ancient and medieval worlds was between empire and chaos. The image of peace and order through a single hegemonic power centre has remained powerful ever since, in dreams of the restoration of Christendom or in proposals for world government.

Europe's world leadership came out of that uniquely European contribution, the small state. In Europe, after 1648, a third way was found between the stasis of chaos and the stasis of empire. The diversity of the small European states created competition, often in the form of war. This was a source of progress; but war risked getting out of control.

The solution to this, the essential problem of a small state system, was the balance of power. But, while this preserved pluralism among states, it had an inherent instability. It was a system in which a war was always waiting to happen.

The end of the system came about as a result of three factors. The first was German unification in 1871. Here for the first time was a state that was too powerful to be contained within the traditional European system.

The second factor was the change in technology in the late nineteenth century which brought the industrial revolution on to the battlefield, raising the price of war to levels which could no longer be afforded. The balance of power was a system which depended on periodic wars taking place. In the industrial era this was no longer sustainable.

Third, the mass society and the democratic politics meant that war and peace could no longer be left to the judgements of the internationally oriented elite who had managed balance of power politics. The mistakes of Versailles for example were partly the result of democratic pressures. More sustainable balance of power type settlements such as that reached at the Congress of Vienna no longer fitted a democratic age.

If the European state system was one of the balance of power, the world system was one of empires. Since balance in Europe prevented expansion there, it was natural for that expansion to take place overseas.

How We Got Here: the Cold War Order

The wars of 1914 to 1945 destroyed both the traditional European balance of power, and also the European empires. What happened after 1945 was however not so much a new system as the concentration and culmination of the old one. The empires became spheres of influence of the super powers. And the old multilateral balance of power in Europe became a bilateral balance of terror worldwide.

The Cold War represented the final simplification of the balance of power; what has replaced it then as the basis of security in Europe? The answer is contained in three treaties.

The first two treaties are the Treaty of Washington (1949) and the Treaty of Rome (1957). These have been the basis of peace in Western Europe since the 1950s. The Treaty of Washington began a system of unprecedented integration in defence. Joint force planning, training and exercising, brought together the forces of countries who for the previous 300 years or more had been fighting each other. NATO was a creation of the Cold War, operating under American leadership and the Soviet threat. It is none the less remarkable for that.

The Treaty of Rome, though also a child of the Cold War, was a more conscious attempt to overcome the balance of power which had ceased to work, and the nation-state which had taken nationalism to destructive extremes.

Both of these innovative treaties worked nevertheless within the framework of the Cold War balance. The third treaty which marks the end of the Cold War balance system is therefore the most remarkable of the three. This is the Treaty on Conventional Forces in Europe (1990). This Treaty is an extraordinary document.

Parties to the Treaty have to notify the other parties of the location of their heavy weapons (which are in any case limited by the Treaty) and allow challenge inspections. Under this treaty so far, more than 40,000 items of heavy military equipment – tanks, artillery, helicopters, etc. – have been destroyed by mutual agreement, surely an unprecedented event.[2]

It is important to realize what a revolution this is. The normal behaviour of armed forces is to conceal their strength from potential enemies. Treaties to regulate such matters are an absurdity in strategic logic. In the first place you do not reach agreements with enemies, since if they are enemies they cannot be trusted. In the second place you do not let the enemy visit your territory to check whether you are observing the treaty.

What is it that has brought about this apparently illogical behaviour? The answer is that behind the paradox of the CFE Treaty lies the equal and opposite paradox of the nuclear age: that in order to defend yourself you had to be prepared to destroy yourself. The shared interest of European countries in avoiding a nuclear catastrophe has proved enough to overcome the normal strategic logic of hostility and suspicion, and to create the beginnings of a new state system. The mutual vulnerability that provided stability in the nuclear age has now been extended to the conventional end of the spectrum where it becomes mutual transparency. (The Cold War nuclear stalemate already contained some elements of transparency. For deterrence to work it has to be visible.) The path towards this Treaty was laid through one of the few real innovations in diplomacy – confidence building measures. Late in the day the Cold War states, some forty years after confrontation first began and through the fog of mistrust, started to understand that the other side might not, in fact, be planning to attack them. Out of this grew measures to prevent war through miscalculation – observation of manoeuvres for example.[3] The progression has proceeded logically from there to observation of weapons systems, and to limitations on them. The solution to the prisoners' dilemma lies in ending mutual secrecy.

In one respect the CFE Treaty has already collapsed under the weight of its own contradictions. As originally designed the Treaty embodied the idea of balance between two opposite blocs. The underlying assumption was one of enmity: balance was required to make it unlikely that either side would take the risk of an attack. Transparency was required to make sure that there was really a balance. But by the time you have achieved balance and transparency it is difficult to retain enmity. The result is that transparency remains but enmity and balance (and one of the blocs) have effectively gone.

In post-Cold War Europe security rests therefore not on balance but on armed transparency – not the same thing as trust, though it might one day grow into this. With this new concept of security goes a concept of the state that is at least modified. The state, which in Weber's definition had the legitimate monopoly on force, is now prepared to see that monopoly subject to constraint and supervision.

Each of the three treaties mentioned represents a step away from the classical sovereign independent state of the days of the balance of power: NATO's integration of forces and openness in defence planning, the European Union's extensive interference in areas traditionally considered to be domestic affairs, and the CFE Treaty with its key concepts of intrusive verification and challenge inspection. These of course all represent different degrees of transparency, the Treaty of Rome being the most far reaching and the CFE Treaty the most limited.

Out of this one may begin to discern the outline of a new kind of state system, which I shall call the postmodern. In this system security is based not on the balance of power but on mutual openness and mutual vulnerability. The absolute sovereignty of states established in 1648 has thus given way to a high degree of transparency, permeability, and mutual interference.

This security system deals with the problems identified earlier that made the balance of power unworkable. By aiming to avoid war it takes account of the horrors of war which modern technology represents: indeed, it depends to a degree on the technology and on the horrors. It is also more compatible with democratic societies: the open society domestically is reflected in a more open international order. And finally, since security no longer depends on balance, it is able to incorporate large and potentially powerful states. The peaceful reunification of Germany is in itself a proof that the system has changed.

What is the origin of this change? The fundamental point is that a large number of the most powerful states no longer want to fight or to conquer. Acquiring territory is no longer of interest. Acquiring subject populations would for most states be a nightmare.

This is not altogether a novelty. Imperialism has been dying slowly for a long time. What is, however, completely new is that Europe should consist more or less entirely of states which are no longer governed by the territorial imperative.

With so much changed in Europe what has happened in the rest of the world? The answer is that the end of the Cold War, which in Europe meant the end of the balance of power, has elsewhere meant the end of empire – the Cold War blocs being the last vestige of 'the white man's burden'. In some parts of the world the modern state system established by European imperialists will survive; in others it will not. The result is something like a three-part division of the world.

The New World: the Premodern

First there is a premodern world, the prestate, postimperial chaos. Examples of this are Somalia, Afghanistan, Liberia, parts of the former Soviet Union. Here the state no longer fulfils Weber's criterion of having the legitimate monopoly on the use of force. This may come about because the state lost its legitimacy. Or, given the easy availability of conventional weapons today, it may have lost the monopoly.

What is different today is that the imperial urge is dead in the countries most capable of imperialism. Land and natural resources (with the exception of oil), are no longer a source of power for the most technologically advanced countries. No one today wants to pay the costs of saving distant countries from ruin. The premodern world belongs, at it were, in a different time zone: here, as in the ancient world, the choice is again between empire or chaos. But today, because none of us see the use of empires, we have chosen chaos.

The New World: the Modern

The second part of the world is the modern. This is where most of the world belongs. Here the classical state system remains intact. States retain the monopoly of force and may be prepared to use it against each other. If there is order in this part of the system it is because of a balance of power or because of the presence of hegemonic states which see an interest in maintaining the status quo. The modern world is for the most part orderly but it remains full of risks.

This is still a world in which the ultimate guarantor of security is force, a world in which, in theory at least, borders can be changed by force. It is not that, in the modern order, might is right so much as that right is not particularly relevant. In international relations this is the world of the calculus of interests and forces described by Machiavelli and by Clausewitz.

The United Nations as originally conceived belongs to this universe. It is an attempt to establish law and order within the modern state system. The UN Charter emphasizes state sovereignty on the one hand and aims to maintain order by force. The veto power is a device to ensure that the UN system does not take on more than it can handle by attacking the interests of the great powers. The UN was thus conceived to stabilize the order of states and not to create a fundamentally new order. This is not the whole story, since the United Nations has developed since its inception; but in conception the collective security element of the UN Charter represents an attempt to throw the weight of the international system behind the status quo, so that the international community as a whole would become the balancing factor in the balance of power system.

Before passing on to the third element in the world system it is worth noting that the modern order contains some worrying problems. The most notable feature is the lack of a real balance of power in many areas of the world. In the Gulf we have already seen the consequences of that. But elsewhere there are also powerful states – China, India, Brazil, Indonesia to name only a few – which might under certain circumstances become destabilizing factors.

The Postmodern

And thirdly the postmodern world, described above. Who belongs to this system outside Europe?

Canada certainly; the USA up to a point perhaps. The USA is the more doubtful case since it is not clear that the US Government or Congress accepts either the necessity and desirability of interdependence, or its corollaries of openness, mutual surveillance and mutual interference to the same extent as most European governments now do.

As the most powerful country in the world the USA has no reason to fear any other country or to accept the idea of security based on mutual vulnerability. The exception is the nuclear field, where the USA is unavoidably vulnerable. Hence one piece of postmodern diplomacy in an otherwise rather uncompromising insistence on sovereignty: START and all the other nuclear treaties with Russia – not least the anti-ABM Treaty which is designed to preserve mutual vulnerability.

Of non-European countries Japan is by inclination a postmodern state. It is not interested in acquiring territory, nor in using force. It would probably be willing to accept intrusive verification. Were it on the other side of the world it would be a natural member of organizations such as the CSCE or the EU. Unfortunately for Japan it is a lone postmodern country surrounded by states firmly locked into an earlier age: postmodernism in one country is possible only up to a point. If China develops in an unpromising fashion (either modern or premodern) Japan could be forced to revert to defensive modernism.

And elsewhere? What in Europe has become a reality is in many other parts of the world an aspiration. ASEAN, NAFTA, MERCOSUR, even the OAU suggest at least the desire for a postmodern environment. This wish is unlikely to be realized quickly. Most developing countries are too unsure of their own identity to allow much interference in domestic affairs. Nevertheless, imitation is easier than invention and perhaps rapid postmodernization could follow the rapid industrialization that is already underway in many parts of the world. Europe's military power may have declined; but the power of example remains. Perhaps that is the postmodern equivalent of imperialism.

Within Europe most of the EU countries clearly belong in the postmodern world though not all of them recognize or understand this. On the one hand some still use balance of power language about Western Europe; on the other there are those who seem to aim for a single European state –

the hegemonic solution to security problems. Both of these approaches miss the fact that Western Europe, and perhaps even Europe as a whole, has found a third route to security.

Whether a postmodern security system can be consolidated depends above all on Russia. Is it going to be a premodern, modern or postmodern state? It embodies all three possibilities. A collapse into premodernism is perhaps the least likely: the urbanized and industrialized society of Russia has a low tolerance for disorder. (A rural society like France in 1789 or Russia in 1917 survives chaos better since most people live on the land. A breakdown in Russia which affected food transport or urban heating systems would bring unacceptable levels of hardship.) The risk is more of the state becoming too powerful than of it disappearing altogether. But there are also postmodern elements in Russia trying to get out. And Russian acceptance of the CFE Treaty and of OSCE observers in Chechnya suggests that it is not wholly lost to the doctrine of openness.

A beginning has been made. The Soviet Union/Russia has given up its empire, joining the rest of Europe as a postimperial state. The last details of this transition remain to be settled – and this will take a long time. Nevertheless, there is at least a chance that Russia will abandon imperialist gains and imperialist ambitions altogether. This is important for West European countries. No country can feel safe while their neighbour is under enemy occupation or a regime imposed from the outside. This is why the revolutions of 1989 were a precondition of the new state system. In the postmodern world security is indivisible.

Security and the Three Orders

A three-part world requires a three-part security policy.

In the postmodern world that policy will rest on transparency, mutual surveillance and multinational institutions, even ultimately on the rule of international law. Dealing with the modern world, the world of ambitious states, requires a different approach. The Gulf War provides an illustration both of the dangers and of how they should be dealt with. One ambitious state attacks another, threatening vital Western interests. In the case of the Gulf War, there were two interests at stake: first, the maintenance of a plurality of states in an area of the world containing vital oil supplies; second, to ensure that a dangerous and ambitious state did not get its hands on weapons that could ultimately threaten the West itself.

The Western response was precisely as it should be: build the most powerful coalition possible, reverse the aggression, punish the aggressor, deal with the weapons programmes. These limited goals required limited means. They did not imply that Iraq should be invaded or occupied or that Saddam Hussein should be removed from power (attractive as that idea undoubtedly is). The reference point for a war of this nature is the eighteenth or nineteenth century, not the twentieth-century wars of absolutes. The Gulf War was a war of interests, not a clash of ideologies.

The reason for fighting this war was not that Iraq had violated the norms of international behaviour. Some mistook the Gulf War for a war for principles or a collective security action – and indeed the political rhetoric at the time fostered this impression. In fact, it was a collective defence of shared interests by the West. The Gulf War was fought to protect an old order, not to create a new one.

For the postmodern state there is, therefore, a difficulty. We need to get used to the idea of double standards. Among ourselves we operate on the basis of laws and open cooperative security. But when dealing with more old-fashioned kinds of state we need to revert to the rougher methods of an earlier era – force, pre-emptive attack, deception, whatever is necessary to deal with those who still live in the nineteenth-century world of every state for itself.

This is not easy for us. We have grown up with the legacy of the Enlightenment. We want to believe in a single global order, in universal rights and in a universal law. These are desirable goals, but we must deal with the world as it is, not as we want it to be. That means recognizing that different rules apply in different parts of the world: in some parts there are legal rights; in others there is nothing but power. Retaining the psychological flexibility to react appropriately in different areas will be a challenge. The first step is for governments to be honest with their people, to explain policy in all its complexities and not to rely on simplifying slogans.

What of the premodern? How should we deal with that? On the basis of a rational calculation of interest, the answer should be: as little as possible. Chaos does not represent a threat, at least not the kind that requires a conventional military response. One may need to bar one's door against its by-products – drugs, disease, refugees – but these are not threats to vital interests that call for armed intervention. To become involved in a zone of chaos is risky; if the intervention is prolonged it may become unsustainable with public opinion; if the intervention is unsuccessful it may be damaging to the government that ordered it. Somalia showed what happens when a small intervention goes wrong; Vietnam showed the same thing on a larger scale.

Besides, what form should intervention take? The most logical way to deal with chaos is by colonization (e.g. hegemony). But this is unacceptable to postmodern states. If the goal is not colonization what should it be? Usually the answer will be that the goals are ambiguous.

The risk of 'mission creep' is therefore considerable. Those who become involved in the premodern world run the risk that ultimately they will be there because they are there. All the conventional wisdom, and all realistic doctrines of international affairs counsel against involvement in the premodern world.

And yet such 'realistic' doctrines, for all their intellectual coherence, are not realistic. They do not take account of the postmodern state. As the state itself becomes less dominating, state interest becomes a less determining factor in foreign policy. The media, popular emotion, the interests of particular groups or regions, all come into play. The post-Cold War, postmodern environment, is one where foreign policy will be driven by domestic politics and by conscience as much as by interest. We no longer live in the world of pure national interest. Human rights and concern for our fellow human beings now inevitably play an important part in our policy-making.

This essay is intended to say many things, but especially to say one big thing. That there is no New World Order is a commonplace. It is less widely understood that there is a new European order: new in that it is historically unprecedented and also new because it is based on new concepts.

Indeed the order has preceded the concepts. In a recent speech Henry Kissinger said: 'In a world of players of operationally more or less equal strength, there are only two roads to stability. One is hegemony and the other is equilibrium'. This was the choice in the past: but today it no longer works. Balance is too dangerous; hegemony is no longer acceptable in a liberal world.

Now there is a third possibility. In fact there have been three successive sets of alternatives: first came the choice between chaos and empire. Then it was a choice between empire and nationalism. Finally, today we have a choice between nationalism and integration. Chaos is tamed by empire; empires are broken up by nationalism; nationalism gives way – we hope – to internationalism. At the end of the process is the freedom of the individual; first protected by the state and later protected from the state.

It may be that in Western Europe the era of the strong state – 1648 to 1989 – has now passed, and we are moving towards a system of overlapping roles and responsibilities, with governments, international institutions and the private sector all involved but none of them entirely in control.

22

After Social Democracy

JOHN GRAY

Social democrats have failed to perceive that Thatcherism was a modernizing project with profound and irreversible consequences for political life in Britain. The question cannot now be, How are the remains of social democracy to be salvaged from the ruins of Thatcherism?, but instead, What is Thatcherism's successor?

Like wet Tories, social democrats did not grasp the radicalism of the Thatcher project in sweeping away old class deferences and hierarchies. Many of them still view it as a blip on the screen of history, to be followed by a return to the 'normal politics' of pre-Thatcher times. This is a disabling illusion, especially for the left. The Thatcher project of fostering an American-style economic individualism in Britain has irrevocably foundered, and the political energy by which it was animated in the early 1980s has evaporated, leaving only the dreary and unmeaning formulae of new right ideology. Nevertheless Thatcherism has permanently changed the terms of political trade in Britain in ways that rule out any return either to traditional conservatism on the right – One Nation Toryism, say – or to the social democracy – Crosland or Owen, perhaps – on the left. Perhaps only a handful of observers have grasped the paradoxical nature of Thatcherism, as a project which failed in all of its positive agenda but which – in conjunction with trends in the world economy which no government directs or controls – transformed British society and public culture so as to render these earlier political projects, along with Thatcherism itself, anachronistic and redundant.

In many respects Thatcherism was a self-undermining project. Those who formulated it did not perceive that the freeing up of markets that drastically diminished the power of organized labour in Britain would have the unintended consequence, over time, of undermining economic security among the social groups who were Thatcherism's initial beneficiaries. It thereby worked to dissolve the electoral coalition of interests that had enabled it to come to power. The aspirational working-class people who perceived in Thatcherite policies the chance of upward social mobility into the middle classes, if they were successful in making the transition, discovered that the life of Middle England had been transformed beyond recognition. They emerged not in the sunlit uplands of bourgeois security but on to a desolate plateau of middle-class pauperdom. The poignant irony of Essex man and woman struggling up the economic escalator only to meet the bedraggled figures of the professional middle classes staggering down it is a narrative of our times that has yet to be properly written. Thatcherism could not act as an instrument of social mobility for its initial supporters because it undid the class structure in terms of which they had framed their aspirations. Thatcherism's capacity to alter the British social landscape profoundly, unpredictably and irreversibly, is only a particularly dramatic illustration of the power of unfettered markets to unravel traditional forms of social life.

For all these reasons, those on the new right who see political salvation – for themselves, if not for Britain – in reviving its lost verities are merely deluding themselves. In our circumstances, a return to Ur-Thatcherism is precluded both by the impact which the policies of the Thatcher and Major governments have had on its initial coalition of supporters and by changes in the public culture of Britain – such as changes in its class culture, encompassing a marked decline in public legitimacy of the House of Windsor, the disappearance of any vestiges of the culture of deference by which the elite groups that once constituted a recognizable 'Establishment' in Britain used to be supported – for which Thatcherism was itself partly responsible. But to see that we must go beyond Thatcherism is also to see that there is no going back to social democracy.

It is a paradox of British political life that, at a moment in history when social democracy is in retreat everywhere, we are very nearly all social democrats now. In all parties, most of us have converged on a sensible and pragmatic middle ground which in crucial respects already trails behind events. Social democracy was a political project whose stability and even identity depended on the geostrategic environment of the Cold War. It defined its socialist content by opposition to Soviet communism and sometimes, also, to American individualism. The Soviet collapse has removed this environment and denuded social democracy of the identity a bipolar world conferred on it. The new realities which spell ruin for the social democratic project are the billions of industrious and skilled workers released on to the global market by the communist collapse and the disappearance of any effective barriers to the global mobility of capital. In this changed historical circumstance the central economic programme of social democracy is unworkable and social democracy itself a bankrupt project.

It is true that the new social democratic consensus in Britain represents a real advance on the sterile and atavistic debate between the old left and the new right. Yet it is also a backward-looking perspective that will prove a poor guide to understanding the present and preparing for the future. My aim is to clarify and explore the emerging social democratic consensus in British public discourse. My purpose in so doing is not to endorse it. On the contrary it is to question it. Among the irreversible consequences of the Thatcherite project and its failure in Britain one of the most neglected is the impossibility of any return to the policies and institutions of social democracy. In part my argument is an historical one. Insofar as it was embodied in a labour movement which technological and economic change together with over a decade and a half of neoliberal policy has undermined, social democracy is now a political project without an historical agent. The class base of social democratic parties, not only in Britain but throughout Europe, has been eaten away by economic change, at the same time that the powers of national governments, which were the levers of social democratic policy, have been steadily reduced. Though this is a hard truth, which practising politicians inevitably find difficult to acknowledge, the new global freedom of financial capital so hems in national governments as to limit severely, or to rule out altogether, traditional social democratic full employment policies. There is an irony in the formation of a social democratic consensus just at the moment when both its class base and its political vehicle have been marginalized.

The risk of the emerging consensus is the hardening into a conventional wisdom of a set of assumptions which is as anachronistic as Thatcherism itself. The failure of neoliberal reforms of the welfare state either to diminish poverty or to control expenditure – both of which have risen inexorably[1] – encourages, as a decent and natural but misguided and unrealistic reaction, the belief that the old British welfare state can be reinvented in another guise, and the hard choices of real welfare reform avoided. Neoliberal tolerance of long-term unemployment evokes the illusion that postwar full employment policies can be revived and made effective. The crudity and failure of neoliberal policies to reduce the size of government – which arose in part because the impact of long-term unemployment on public expenditure was under-estimated – obscures the unsustainability of a large and growing state in a period in which neither taxpayers nor lenders can be relied upon to finance public deficits. The absurdity and inhumanity of neoliberal policies to trim the size of government have produced a social democratic complacency about its growth that is no less costly and dangerous.

The key test of whether we have yet formulated a

genuinely post-Thatcherite political outlook is our ability to perceive that, even as it undermined the conditions of its own political viability, Thatcherism at the same time destroyed other political projects which had once been its rivals. The end of Thatcherism – which occurred, not suddenly with a bang when Thatcher herself was toppled in 1990, but slowly and with a whimper, during the long interregnum of the Major years – marked not only the political collapse of neoliberalism in Britain but also the closing of an era in its public culture. Neoliberal policies of privatization – of railways and civil service recruitment, for example – rolled on inertly, and the nationalist wing of the Tory party exercised an effective veto over John Major's European policy; but public support for Thatcherite policies had palpably collapsed, along with the intellectual credentials of the new right ideology that formulated and legitimated such policies in the early 1980s.

The modernizing tendencies in both major parties need to run very fast simply to avoid being left far behind by events. My aim is to sketch a pattern of ideas whose chief merit may be that it is less removed from present circumstances than most of the ideas which inform political discourse. I advance a communitarian liberal perspective,[2] in the belief that it can aid thought on the central dilemma of the age, which is how revolutionary changes in technology and the economy can be reconciled with the enduring human needs for security and for forms of common life. Communitarian liberalism affirms, firstly, that individual autonomy presupposes a strong public culture in which choice and responsibility go together, and is realizable only as a common good; secondly, that market exchange makes no inherent contribution to autonomy, and market competition must be limited in contexts – such as broadcasting and urban development – where its impact on individual autonomy may be disabling rather than enhancing; and thirdly, that fairness demands the distribution of goods and responsibilities according to their common social meanings in particular contexts, thereby excluding market forces from their domains – the public provision of health care and education, for example, where it violates such common understandings.

These three claims express the distinctive communitarian political morality in which neither libertarian nor egalitarian principles are fundamental but rather the renewal and creation of worthwhile social forms. The central insight of communitarian philosophy is that conceptions of autonomy and fairness are not embodiments of universal principles – principles of justice or rights, say – but instead local understandings, grounded in particular forms of common life and liberty. In contrast with social democracy, which has extended to social welfare rights the supposedly unconditional claims of negative liberal rights, the communitarian view affirms the dependency of individual autonomy on a strong network of reciprocal obligations.

A fundamental implication of this communitarian liberal perspective is that market institutions are not freestanding but come embedded in the matrices of particular cultures and their histories. Market institutions will be politically legitimate only insofar as they respect and reflect the norms and traditions, including the sense of fairness, of the cultures whose needs they exist to serve. Legitimating the market requires that it be curbed or removed in institutions and areas of social life where common understandings demand that goods be distributed in accord with ethical norms that the market, of necessity, disregards. Public acceptance of a dynamic market economy requires that the ethos of market exchange be excluded from important contexts – contexts in which nonmarket institutions and practices are protected as a matter of public policy.

The key task we confront today is that of preserving, and extending, forms of common life, which highly individualist market institutions threaten to undermine or corrode. A connected task is that of developing common institutions in which practitioners of different cultural traditions can coexist. In both of these cases, we will face conflicts of values, uncombinable goods and choices among evils, which are unavoidable.

These conflicts of values compel revisions of some standard positions, liberal, social democratic and communitarian – revisions for which the emerging British consensus, which is shy of admitting radical conflict between fundamental values, is ill prepared. Any species of 'back to basics' communitarianism, which seeks a return to 'traditional values' or a restoration of vanished or dying forms of family or communal life, must be rejected as a form of nostalgia, whose fate in political life is likely to be no less farcical than that of the Tory 'back to basics' campaign. We cannot, and should not, hope to revive a 'traditional' form of family life that scarcely any longer exists, and which is in any case only one among a variety of kinds of families our society presently contains; but nor can we reasonably adopt the fashionable liberal ideal in which government is silent, or neutral, on the central issues of family life. A pluralist state can have few core ethical commitments; but a commitment to the family – in all its legitimate diversity – must be one of them. Government must have, and act upon, a view as to the 'thin' culture of obligations and responsibilities that family life in all its forms presupposes, even as it acts to nurture diversity in the kinds of family a pluralist society properly cultivates. Similarly, any form of social democracy which seeks across-the-board equality and denies or evades the reality of conflicts among equalities – such as that between achievable equality of opportunity and social mobility and unachievable educational equality which prohibits meritocratic selection in state schools – will in practice leave the class structure intact.

Three broad policy applications of the communitarian liberal view may be worth noting. Firstly, the claim that fairness is local and contextual and has to do with distributing goods according to their common social meanings has a cutting edge on policy in health, where it will be invoked to condemn the commercialization of the National Health Service, and in education, where it supports the argument that forms of meritocratic selection can and should be reintroduced in state schools. Such policies, which restrict or exclude market exchange in the particular contexts of specific institutions and goods, are also mandated by the fundamental insight that, contrary to neoliberalism, markets make no inherent contribution to individual autonomy. Secondly, the insight that market institutions unavoidably and desirably reflect and express particular cultures and their histories, which is central in the communitarian liberal perspective, tells against common social democratic proposals for the wholesale grafting on to British economic life of practices which have been successful in other cultural and political contexts, such as those of Germany and Japan, and against the federalist project for European institutions. Thirdly, the historical claim that the traditional social democratic commitment to full employment cannot now be implemented compels urgent consideration of policies in which the human interests that full employment protected can be promoted by other means. In each of these three policy areas, the goal is to protect in new ways the human interests once served by social democracy, and to do so without allowing the task of mediating conflicts among these interests to be distorted by the classical social democratic commitment to overall equality as an end-state desirable in itself.

The sphere of life in which such unavoidable conflicts are negotiated and, always provisionally, resolved, is that of *politics*. The illusion of standard Anglo-American liberal philosophy, according to which conflicts among rival human interests and among divergent conceptions of the good and their associated forms of common life can be arbitrated by appeal to a Rawls-style theory of justice or rights,[3] finds expression in contemporary social democratic demands for a constitutional revolution in Britain. In the communitarian liberal view I advance, constitutional reform is desirable and even indispensable, insofar as it protects fundamental freedoms by incorporating the European Convention into British law, makes accountable the new magistracy of the Quango

State and devolves power to Scotland and Wales. These important measures of constitutional reform can be achieved, however, through existing institutions of parliamentary government in an unfixed constitution, as aspects of the new *political* settlement Britain needs. Of course, national government is not the only, nor always the most important domain of political life; it is imperative that political initiative be devolved, to lower levels of government and to nongovernmental institutions. But this is, or should be, done as a dispersion of political power and an enhancement of political accountability, not as an attempt to remove issues of public policy from political life and transfer them to the jurisdiction of the courts, as has been tried, with predictably ruinous consequences, in the American culture of legalism.

The most important measure facilitating such a new political settlement is not constitutional but electoral reform. On the pluralist and communitarian view defended here, one of the principal weaknesses of social democratic thought is the illusion that the construction of legal institutions can remove the necessity for recurrent political renegotiation of a balance among competing human interests and of the political pursuit of a *modus vivendi* among different communities. After all necessary constitutional reforms, the real task is the political task of searching for the elusive thread of common life through the labyrinth of intractably conflicting interests and ideals.

It is a presupposition of my argument that, for us, individualism is an historical fact, which we can hope to temper, but not to overcome. As against both the New Right project and conservative forms of communitarianism, there is no going back to the old moral world we have lost – even if such a reversion were desirable. Equally, it is not reasonable to hope to put the social democratic project back on the road. It belonged within an historical niche that has gone beyond hope of recovery. There will be no renaissance of collectivist sentiment arising from the failures of neoliberal individualism. To imagine that there might be such a recovery is entirely to misread the lessons of the 1980s, which all point to the overwhelming power and urgency within our culture of the demand for individual autonomy. If we are humbler in our hopes, we will no more return to the collectivist dreams of the past than we will strive to resurrect the vanished folk ways of earlier generations. We will seek ways to make our economic culture friendlier to the needs of the people it exists to serve. We will aim to contrive institutions and policies which moderate its risks for them, and which make it less difficult to them to reconcile in their lives the need for enduring relationships with the imperatives of economic survival. We will strive for a fairer distribution of skills and opportunities. We can hope in these ways to make our individualism less possessive and more convivial.

There is no single reform of policy that can work as a panacea for our economic culture. Many of the ills of our society can be cured only slowly and in part, since they arise from sources in our culture which governments can certainly aggravate by their policies, but over which their leverage is otherwise strictly limited. Our economic life is only one aspect of our flawed and fractured late modern culture. Yet unless they are reformed so as to make their workings more humanly tolerable, liberal market institutions will lose political legitimacy. This is no small point, since it is an implication of the communitarian liberal view I have developed that – at least for us, as inheritors of a late modern individualist culture – there is no sustainable alternative to the institutions of liberal capitalism, however reformed.

The first duty of political thought, if it is to be other than an exercise in intellectual history or academic cross-quotation, is to understand the present. The danger of the new social democratic consensus is that it tracks a world which many of us are old enough to have lived in but which has now disappeared irretrievably. Would it not be another of history's ironies if we were to rid ourselves of the errors of the 1980s without perceiving that, in concert with the silent forces that shape events, they have transformed our world irreversibly?

BUSINESS, TECHNOLOGY AND THE FUTURE

The sectors which are changing fastest today seem to be those furthest away from traditional politics. The real legislators of the contemporary world are often the transnational firms, the technological laboratories or the financial markets rather than the parliaments and courts.

In this section we explore some of the ways in which technology and business are changing, and what lessons can be learnt. Bob Tyrrell describes the means that have been used over the last thirty years to understand the future, so as to help either governments or businesses to plan better. He shows how successive techniques such as strategic planning, scenarios, and even organizing through chaos, have been succeeded by an understanding that the most successful firms help to create their environment through clarity and force of purpose rather than just responding to it.

John Ashworth and Helena Cronin and Samuel Brittan set out how the new technologies and new understandings arising from the explosion of knowledge about genetics are set to transform our thinking not only about human nature, but also about everything from crime to education to economics and political economy.

James Woudhuysen describes the complexities of the information society, and Charles Hampden-Turner shows how the idea of the game gives an invaluable insight into the differences between how some Western businesses think about competition and how the East does. He argues that 'infinite games' in which competitors do not seek to wipe each other out may have advantages over the finite game in which one winner takes all. Douglas Hague shows how the very nature of professional work is changing as new technologies bypass older demarcations and organize knowledge in radically new ways. James Woudhuysen puts contemporary waves of hype about technology into their proper historical perspective, and Geoff Mulgan and Ivan Briscoe explain why new 'networked' organizations like the Internet and Visa have proven so successful and why they may turn out to be models for the information economy of the next century.

23

The Society of Networks

A New Form of Organization for the Information Age

GEOFF MULGAN and IVAN BRISCOE

Technologies transform the nature of organizational forms. Sometimes they make new organizational forms necessary. The car, for example, required a new infrastructure of garages and service stations and, as Alfred Chandler wrote brilliantly in 'The Visible Hand', the railways impelled the invention of the modern corporation to keep track of a far more complex logistical system. At other times technologies make new organizational forms possible: the telephone, for example, made it viable to manage dispersed operations in real time, while the car made possible the suburb and the supermarket.

Today a new wave of technologies is once again transforming the nature of organizations. Virtual companies are being established without an office and in some cases without even any staff. Small software companies are emerging as if from nowhere to become corporate titans. Traders are now dealing on world markets from remote cottages.

Given the extraordinary level of innovation in organizational forms it is remarkable that most commentators take it for granted that the age of cyberspace will be based on the classic organizational models of the twentieth century. There is no shortage of imagination about the technologies and uses of the information superhighway, but it is still widely assumed that the networks of the twenty-first century will be organized in the same way as the infrastructures of the past, either as publicly owned corporations or as regulated private ones.

The organizational forms which have dominated this century were designed for an age of materially based industry, for economies based on hardware, and for relatively uneducated workforces. Their characteristics have tended to be uniformity, standardization, clear and pyramidal lines of management and unified ownership. Within the organization the norm has been to have hierarchical command structures exercising control over dispersed production processes, flows of goods, and over labour, much of which has been devoted to precisely definable repetitive tasks, whether in the factory or the classroom, the government office or the hospital.

The information age has posed fundamental challenges to these models of behaviour and production in two ways. The first is that it tends to favour difference rather than uniformity. Employees in classic industrial occupations have to perform their tasks consistently and predictably. Autonomy and variation threaten the smooth running of the machine. Where information and knowledge are concerned, by contrast, the value the employee adds is less predictable, concerned with creativity, with reshaping information for new uses. The second major difference is that far faster flows of information make it possible to organize in far more complex ways, with networks or flotillas of organizations joined together loosely, rather than depending on integrated command structures.

These differences are particularly evident in the case of infrastructures. Where the classic infrastructure provided a largely undifferentiated product (such as gas, electricity or water), or an undifferentiated carrying capacity (like a motorway), in the information age what is required is a far more varied set of services, ranging from mobile communications to databases. And where the classic firm and the classic infrastructure could be vertically integrated, those of the information age seem to work best by articulating diverse types of service supply and diverse types of use.

Unfortunately few of the key organizations in the information industry reflect this new reality. The great majority are organized on traditional principles, and are little different from firms in manufacturing or banking, retailing or trade. Yet it is a striking fact that those that have designed their organizational shape to reflect the nature of information have, on the whole, proven far more successful than those that have stuck to older models.

One of these is the Internet, the fastest growing medium in human history. The Internet is not owned by anyone, but makes use of leased lines to interconnect different public and private networks. There is no substantial physical body underlying the whole operation – which is why the term 'cyberspace' was coined to describe the virtual realm inhabited by 'netsurfers'. Central to the popularity of this 'network of networks' is its distribution of intelligence and innovative capacity throughout the system. The Internet is essentially a 'bottom-up' structure. Innovations on the Net have generally come from users and niche software companies: the World Wide Web, for instance, was invented by a computer scientist in Switzerland, while the companies which enable connection to the Net are small operations, almost all under five years old.[1]

From complexity and network chaos has emerged something like order, and a slow but very useful system of knowledge and communication. As large telecom companies have lumbered into broadband technology, this initially low-key and highly technical medium for communication has become an extraordinary success. Yet its performance has owed nothing to advertising or corporate brainstorming; it has been the system's adaptability, the freedoms it gives users, which have given it its edge.

The second model of an information age organization is Visa, in financial services. Instead of offering a credit card supported by the resources of one bank or a consortium of banks – like the failed experiments run by American banks in the 1960s – Visa operates a credit card service which is owned by the large number of financial institutions (more than 20,000) which offer its cards and services. Visa itself is only a skeletal 'overseeing administrative organization',[2] linking the operations of its members into a cohesive and efficient whole. It is, in short, an organization which enables. By doing this, it has succeeded in making over 7 billion transactions per annum, worth over $650 billion. This is, according to Visa's founding Chief Executive Dee Hock, 'the largest single block of consumer purchasing power in the world economy.'[3]

What is interesting about both these new forms of organization is the way in which they operate broad infrastructures incorporating diversity, competition and multiple lines of power. It is no coincidence that the areas in which they have thrived are markets for information – markets in which the number of transactions, exchanges and communications handled would bemuse many more centrally directed organizations. Instead of being paralysed by this complexity, they have flourished upon it. Consumers have been drawn to Visa by the ease of using the card anywhere in the world; constant innovations, like cheap voice transmission, broaden the appeal of the Internet each year.

New theoretical accounts of the organization have trailed in the wake of the information age. Dee Hock has advocated the development of more 'chaordic' organizations such as Visa, which would avoid the institutional sclerosis experienced by hierarchical, 'command-and-control' organizations. By distributing ownership and power, according to Hock, an organization or infrastructure can embrace huge complexity, and like the human mind, evolve into an extremely effective organism able to withstand shocks and constantly incorporate new ideas. This biological motif is also prominent in the work of Internet expert Kevin Kelly, who champions evolutionary models for complex systems of information exchange (and many other types of coordinated networks or systems). He argues that our fixation with mechanical design is damaging – and likely to retard innovations in a huge number of scientific and informational fields: 'a neo-biological technology is far more rewarding than a world of clocks, gears and predictable simplicity.'[4]

Many organizations are ill-suited to this type of organic structure: the form of their product, or the nature of their markets make evolutionary, fragmented designs inappropriate. Railway networks would fall apart in such a loosely coordinated, haphazard environment (although the most imaginative thinking in transport is concentrating on how information and connections between different forms of transport can reduce journey times and waiting times, in contrast with the traditional emphasis on capacity – high-speed rail links or new roads).

The new systems also have their faults. The Internet is currently plagued by public concerns about the on-line distribution of pornography and racist or even terrorist propaganda. Freedom for users does not always translate into moral rectitude. And so far it has proven hard to adapt the Internet into a genuine market, able to sustain financial transactions.

But there are important lessons to be drawn about how the infrastructures of the next century might be better organized. The current debate sees the choice as one between monopolistic public utilities and competitive (large) private firms. The wider public interest is conceived in terms of a set of social obligations to be imposed on these firms by a regulator – such as the obligation to connect schools and hospitals, or externally imposed controls on pricing.

This faith in regulation as the key to a successful information society rests on the successes of the 1980s. Pricing controls and regulatory rules encouraged greater competition, lower prices and a wider range of services. Regulated competitive markets proved more innovative and more efficient than earlier models of state monopoly. But recent developments have shown up the limits of regulation. Regulators have found it hard to understand the technological trends and cost structures of the firms they are regulating. Despite competition, erstwhile monopolists remain overwhelmingly dominant and, more importantly, it has proven far harder than many expected to open up networks to a multiplicity of service providers. In part this is because vertically integrated dominant companies, like BT in Britain and Deutsche Telekom in Germany, are involved both in providing services themselves and in carrying the services of others. Moreover because these large telecom companies have their origins in an engineering based culture, and the more traditional job of providing an undifferentiated service, their cultures may be ill-suited to the far more customer-oriented task of cultivating a myriad of new services, ranging from teleshopping to education, video-on-demand to home alarm systems.

If the information superhighway is to become anything like a supermarket of options, then something has to be done to guarantee open access and diverse content.

The alternative model, what we call a 'Society of Networks', draws on the approach taken by Visa, and is deliberately designed to suit the nature of an informational infrastructure. Instead of having the superhighway run either by a single network operator, or by a small group of competing private companies, all service providers (including in the British case BT and Mercury, Ionica and Energis) would have a share of ownership in an open, profit-making association governing the main network infrastructure. As with Visa, rather than being a closed cartel, membership would be open to any service provider able to meet the set criteria.

There would still be strong incentives to improve the network and the technology used. But unlike current models, there would also be an incentive to minimize the cost of access, since service providers will naturally want to maximize the market for their services. This would not be a model of monopoly. Indeed it should have, and would need, no formal privileges. Any competing network provider would be free to set up in competition. But the odds are that most service providers would want to remain part of the 'Society'.

This vision of the broadband network would achieve many

of the goals that liberalization and deregulation have found elusive. It would ensure open access to the core network, incentives to maximize usage and keep prices low, and provide permanent competitive pressures. By building both competition and cooperation into the very heart of the organization, it would enable regulation to be more focused and more effective. Complexity could be managed in something resembling the 'distributed control'[5] of Kelly's predictions.

Looking further ahead, the 'Society of networks' model suggests how businesses could evolve in the future. Instead of developing internally, either through growth or acquisition by a single organizational entity, the key issues in the future business environment may come to concern their interfaces: the means by which different units interconnect. In the case of the Internet and Visa these are clearcut rules governing such things as transactions and technical standards. In other types of organization they might include shared commitments to principles, or rules governing the exchange of knowledge. These would become the glues of federations that both compete and cooperate, federations whose elements are both autonomous and interdependent.

Structures of this kind seem to defy the logic of organizations in the industrial age. In place of the industrial model of organizations defined by their boundaries, according to this view the most important characteristic of any organization is its range and number of points of connection to the outside environment: its connectedness. This is the virtue of the Society of Networks model. The fact that the Internet is the fastest growing medium, and Visa the highest turnover business enterprise the world has ever seen, is proof that these models are more than abstract ideas. They have a capacity to grow and to adapt that no other organizational form can match.

24

'Darwinism' and the Social Sciences

HELENA CRONIN and JOHN ASHWORTH

The dissolution of the Soviet Union and consequent worldwide repudiation of Marxist political systems have had momentous effects which are far from complete. But no less complete, and possibly even more far reaching, has been the collapse of Marxism as a philosophical system that claimed to provide a basis for most, if not all, of the social sciences.

Marx believed himself to be a scientist and his followers certainly thought of themselves as constructing a 'science'. Many of the habits of mind and attitudes thus created spilled over into the social sciences as they developed over the past century and were adopted more or less unconsciously by many of those who would rightly have rejected any attempt to label them as 'Marxists'. It is not proving easy to disentangle the useful and the helpful from the discredited in this complicated intellectual legacy and in the meantime, there is a real hunger for something to take the place of the old framework. If classes, at least as defined in economic terms, and the class struggle no longer have the explanatory power that they once did, what might?

Into this debate have come, triumphantly, those from the political right with individualistic philosophies espousing the view that there is no such thing as 'Society'. More diffidently have come those from the 'communitarian' or 'new' left, who are well aware of the lack of any real theoretical underpinnings to their pragmatic reworking of socialist thought. More tentative yet have come those who have suggested that modern evolutionary theories, which predict that organisms may apparently act 'altruistically' whilst still containing 'selfish' genes, can perhaps account for why both the political right and the 'new' left seem to have only partial insights. Perhaps, the suggestion is, evolutionary theories might succeed where both individualistic and group- (or class-) based explanations of behaviour have proved unsatisfactory.

The tentativeness of the biologists would have been very familiar to Darwin, whose illnesses might well have been partly caused by his all-too-conscious appreciation of the potential effect of his theories on human society. Indeed, at the end of the nineteenth century, the premature application of Darwin's theory of natural selection by Herbert Spencer and others (all of whom misunderstood it) provided for some an apparently 'scientific' basis for slavery, racial discrimination and other such notions which Darwin himself rejected with abhorrence. Worse, 'Survival of the Fittest', a phrase Spencer, not Darwin, coined, was taken as a new justification for war, conquest and the physical elimination of those held to be 'unfit'. Here Spencer, a pacifist, was as horrified as Darwin would have been by the ends to which 'Social Darwinism' was put, especially since G. E. Moore had shown conclusively in 1903 that the attempt to draw moral values from evolutionary theories (the 'naturalistic fallacy', as he termed it) was doomed from the start. But the damage had been done and most biologists and social scientists agreed to cease the dialogue that Spencer had started so enthusiastically.

This self-denying ordinance was tested a few times in the next seventy years or so. One of the real difficulties with Darwin's original hypothesis – which he well recognized – was that he had no secure theory of inheritance to account for the generation of the diversity amongst natural populations on which selection then operated. This problem was solved, at least in principle, by Mendel; and the combination of Mendelian genetics with Darwinian natural selection in the 1920s led to neo-Darwinism – an intellectually much more satisfactory theory. The application of neo-Darwinism to the social sciences was attempted more cautiously than in Spencer's time – to a great extent because of the all too evident, then contemporary, political consequences of simplistic beliefs in the biological basis of human races.

The social sciences were also better developed (thanks, in part, to Marx) and those developing them sensed, rightly, that the neo-Darwinist biologists were not yet in a position to contribute much of substance to any putative dialogue. Still, there were some brave attempts, not least the establishment by William Beveridge, when Director of the LSE, of a chair in 'Social Biology' to which Lancelot Hogben was appointed. The close contact thus engendered between some of the founding fathers of British social science and Hogben's toads (*Xenopus laevis*) created a fair amount of distaste and generated a certain quantity of intellectual heat without at the same time shedding very much light. The sad truth was that although neo-Darwinism was a better theory than Darwinism could ever have been, it still lacked two crucial features – a satisfactory account of the evolution of behaviour, especially apparently altruistic behaviour – and a description of the nature of genetic information.

Molecular biology and DNA, of course, now provide the latter whilst the solution to the first of these difficulties came, ironically, from the LSE, through the work of a PhD student – William Hamilton – in the 1960s, though there is no evidence that any of his LSE contemporaries had any idea of the significance of what he was doing.

So, armed with a new Darwinian paradigm, should the evolutionary biologists and the social scientists try for a third time to see if they have anything fruitful to say to one another? The first attempts in the 1970s, under the banner of 'sociobiology', by E. O. Wilson, were not encouraging. Wilson's self-confident and assertive tone was too reminiscent of Spencer's and many reacted, not to the new synthesis that Wilson was attempting to popularize, but rather to the previous attempts of Spencer and the social biologists of the 1930s. The passions and antipathies raised, not without reason, by those previous attempts at dialogue were still so strong that few non-biologists really stopped to notice that a new paradigm, not a rehash of the old ones, was being used. Most biologists, accepting the charges of – at best – insensitivity and tactlessness, decided to keep their heads down and few would now wish to be called 'sociobiologists'. But under various descriptions such as 'evolutionary psychology', 'behavioural ecology' or 'Darwinian anthropology', the implications of the new insights have gradually been explored and, more recently, in books such as *The Red Queen* by Matt Ridley (1993) and *The Moral Animal* by Robert Wright (1994), accessible and sensitive accounts of the results have been published in a form that might now lead to something other than a dialogue of the deaf.

Two rather different kinds of outcome might be expected from any such dialogue. The first is a change in emphasis, a shake of the intellectual kaleidoscope, as it were, rather than the addition of a new, brightly coloured piece of knowledge. Such changes can already be seen in many areas of medical research and health care and delivery, with the introduction of the idea (now common elsewhere in modern biology) that it is necessary, in order to understand a phenomenon such as 'disease', to explain why and, if possible, how, it evolved. The notion that treating the symptoms of a disease such as fever might prolong the underlying cause has surprised many medical practitioners and similarly the idea that some apparent disorders like early morning sickness in pregnancy or mild 'anxiety' might have (or have had) survival value may also lead to changes in the nature of treatments offered by medical practitioners. However, here, as in most other areas, it would be foolish in the extreme to leap too readily from a plausible, not to say beguiling, evolutionary explanation to changes in practice. The development of 'Darwinian Medicine' – as the application of evolutionary thought to classical medical practice is called – is bound to be protracted since there is not yet any firm agreement on what are medically acceptable standards of evidence for an evolutionary explanation.

To take a more everyday example: What could be more familiar than parent/offspring conflict? It is universal, has characteristic features, it seems, well, natural. But why does it happen? Robert Trivers, in the 1970s, showed that Darwinian theory provides a satisfactory answer. A parent must be judicious about the resources it puts into an individual offspring. After all, any individual child carries only half of that parent's genes; and what's more, only represents a fraction of the parent's total reproductive potential or opportunity. But from the child's point of view, it is far more precious and deserving of resources; after all, this is the only chance it will get. So there is an inherent, unavoidable imbalance at the heart of the parent/offspring relationship: it is inevitable that the offspring will always want more than the parent is prepared to give. We see this in the conflicts over weaning; in sibling jealousy; in attention-seeking tantrums and so on. All very familiar and now all very comprehensible.

But as well as these changes of view on familiar problems – the shaking of the intellectual kaleidoscope – we should also reasonably expect some brightly coloured bits of genuinely new knowledge. Typical of what should be expected are the startling insights provided by Martin Daly and Margo Wilson's studies on infanticide in the USA. Although conflict between parents and offspring is intrinsic, nevertheless altruism, love and solicitude are intrinsic too. After all, offspring and other close relatives are the only means any particular gene has of insinuating itself into future generations. It pays genes to make sure that those carrying them protect and care for those others who might also be carrying other copies of them – hence the Darwinian explanation of apparently 'altruistic' behaviour. And yet sociologists have told us that the family is a dangerous place to be. The criminologists' statistics seem to support this. But, as Daly and Wilson showed, this is only true if a very un-Darwinian notion of the 'family' is accepted. The likelihood of a child being killed by its parents is more than a hundred times greater when those parents are not biological kin – a socially appalling fact that had been obscured by the FBI's insistence on treating non-kin and kin alike in the homicide statistics. Infanticide is an extreme form of child abuse and, as we have come to realize, there is the same need in less extreme forms to keep a careful distinction between kin and non-kin. All those warnings about step-parents in fairy stories were very well based in Darwinian theory. And, by the way, much family violence is, of course, husband against wife (who are not 'family' in the Darwinian sense at all) and male and female mammals have very different, though both very rational (in terms of genetic behaviour), reproductive strategies – another helpful insight from evolutionary theory.

Indeed the list of those areas of social and cultural behaviour as well as medical practice where fruitful dialogue is happening or might be expected are growing rapidly: mate selection strategy; the nature and purpose of differences in male and female display techniques and hence the definition of 'beauty'; crime and the way it is distributed among different genders and ages; language and how/why we have (over) developed it; the size of group with which we can associate or within which we feel comfortable; even why we have moral values and a culturally very similar sense of 'natural' justice. The list is long and growing and we need to make sure that this time around, the dialogue is indeed as productive as that list is long.

25

Before We Rush to Declare a New Era

JAMES WOUDHUYSEN

In America, a new kind of kaleidoscope is being built. A user, on the move, can pull it from his pocket, look through its magnifying glass and read incoming faxes as if they were sheets of A4. The pager of the future, we are told, will be an extra eye. In America a new kind of portable video camera is being built that digitizes scenes, memorizes them on a hard drive, then plays them, ready for direct manipulation, on home PCs. With this extra eye, the user is not just a cameraman, but a film editor too.

To many users of Information Technology (IT) – that is, computers and telecommunications – extra eyes could be just as important as information superhighways. Certainly highways represent merely one application of IT among many. Before we rush to declare that humanity stands on the brink of a new era based on them we should pause for thought. After all, other IT breakthroughs have also been the subject of high hopes in the past.

Right up to the early 1990s, many commentators still felt that factory IT heralded a new era of 'flexible specialization' in manufacturing. Assisted by robots, even relatively small firms could for the first time profitably exploit low-volume, niche markets. Robots, helped by barcode scanners at retail checkouts, would enable firms to respond flexibly to market changes. By churning out only popular lines, or by assembling new models themselves based on computer-aided designs, robots and all the rest of IT would broadly allow the 'mass production of individualized products'.[1] In fact the robots are crawling, not coming. By the year 2000, human beings will still outnumber the world's industrial robots by 6000 to 1.[2] Yet the worst thing about robots is not their modest penetration, but what they tell us about technological determinism in its contemporary guise. High hopes in highways represent a narrowing of horizons.

Memories, so large in chips nowadays, are short in society. People forget how many times we have been here before with IT. For thirty years, the *technical potential* of IT has often, if not always, been undeniable. As a result, IT has frequently chalked up impressive achievements – from Telstar to the VCR. However, while information superhighways will undoubtedly have some impact, the realization of their true potential could well be frustrated by wider social and economic constraints.

To encourage the stock markets, technology and entertainment suppliers have already talked up hopes with hype. The public has been more sceptical. But there is still an undercurrent of public approval for computers, and thus, we may suspect, for superhighways.

The problem with highways, then, is not 'technofear'. The problem is that hype about highways reveals a very narrow set of horizons about the future of society.

One of the major postwar applications of IT was to put a man on the moon. By contrast, video on demand, one of the major applications of superhighways, is designed to obviate the short walk to Blockbuster Video. In the 1980s, an era was foreseen in which consumers might eventually design their own durables. In the more recessionary 1990s, expectations have come down. All that is held out to us by apostles of information technology is a world where we can stare at screens all day, communicating, computing and indulging in 'edutainment': not making things, but 'cruising' the 'Net' instead.

So even in IT there has grown up a complacent culture of

diminished ambitions – a culture of limits. The media tells us to celebrate, or to fear:

– couch potatoes who shop by remote control and are always in when, magically enough, the home delivery boy arrives on time;

– energetic cyberpunks who reply to mass junk e-mail ('spam') with abusive e-mail ('Flames');

– computer games named *Chaos Engine, Colonization, Dark Forces, Doom, Hell Cab, Quarantine;*

– computer nerds in anoraks; on-line gamblers; international pornographers; electronic voters; unseemly viruses, and dangerous invaders of personal privacy, commercial secrecy or national security.

Ironically enough, then, hype about the highway misses out on 'user-friendliness'. In practice, it denigrates human beings and their talent to change things substantially.

Illusions about information run deep. Charles Handy seriously believes that in business, Information, when multiplied by Intelligence and Ideas, amounts to Added Value: I^3 = AV. The Tofflers also believe that a world of neatly defined nation-states is being replaced by a kind of 'global "motherboard" running with three different "clock speeds"'.[3] Yet all this is hardly news. Opposite are some of the major fanfares about information since the birth of the integrated circuit in 1959.

IT does not herald a new social system. In the long view, IT is but a development of inventions first prompted by the growth of the world economy in the late nineteenth century. Then, in what Harvard's James Beniger dubs the Control Revolution, typewriters and telegraphs came into their own because of the need to control the accelerated flow of goods brought about by steam-powered factories and locomotives. IT also grew up as a symptom of changes on the demand side too. Since modern mass production first took over the Industrial Revolution, firms have needed IT to guide them

Just a small selection of post-war theories of the future

Date of publication	Author	Key concept
1962	Machlup MacLuhan	Knowledge economy Global village
1969	Drucker	Knowledge economy
1971	Touraine; Bell Toffler	Post-industrial society Superindustrial society
1977	Evans Porat	Electronics revolution Information economy
1980	Toffler	Third wave
1982	Kahn Naisbitt	Post-industrial economy Information society
1989	Zuboff Feigenbaum et al	Age of smart machine Expert company
1990	Gilder	Global quantum economy
1994	Business Week	Information revolution

Source: Beniger (1989), The Henley Centre Media Futures study 1994/5

through markets ever more competitive, changeable, diverse and distended.

As the telegraph has given way to the tickertape, telex and videoconference, so new critics have discovered that IT, in its different forms, is the key source of modern wealth. Indeed IT is now assumed by many experts to be almost omnipotent. With the end of the Cold War and the decline of orthodox economics, the roles assigned to capital and labour in traditional accounts of economic growth are no more. Instead, the comfortably neutral framework of knowledge, information and IT comes to dominate informed opinion.

That framework has some distinctly irrational components to it. The mystical aura that now surrounds superhighways contradicts the reality of straitened consumer and corporate markets for them.

Looking at IT-based services in the home first, penetration is modest. America, for instance, barely uses on-line services to conduct transactions such as home-shopping or banking. In Britain, the popularity of computer games is a useful index of the mass-market potential for superhighways, and is mainly limited to youth, and to youngish parents. Until youthful users of computers grow up, most people will, for most of the time, be unable to use Britain's installed base of IT to the full. Even regular users of IT are, after all, often unaware of the complete range of functions on the machines in front of them. Meanwhile there is an ageing, often female population of *non-users* of IT. Just as young boys play with computer games more than young girls, so taking money out of simple cashpoint machines is a minority pursuit among older people, and especially among older women.

Alongside age as a constraint on the use of IT, there is income. In the past it was the working class which first bought monochrome TVs, colour TVs and VCRs in volume. However, differentiation by income has for the past decade been on the increase. In the uncertain economic environment of the future, the market for superhighways may well never exceed 40 per cent – roughly equal to the penetration of CD players in British households.[4]

Like mobile phones and multimedia now and Virtual Reality some years hence, superhighways may meet corporate demand before they reach the consumer sector. With teleshopping and information services, the executive user looks like a safer commercial bet for highway suppliers than do people at their leisure. It is notable too that private satellite and cable-based 'business TV' networks won adherents as varied as Wal-Mart in the USA and National Power in Britain. Indeed in Europe there has been a conspicuous spread of teleports.

However, the jury is still out on the precise productivity benefits of superhighways. US government statisticians at the Bureau of Labor Statistics believe that the USA is experiencing a boom in productivity because of IT. But there is counter-evidence from the Department of Commerce for these sources to consider:

– since early 1991, US outlays on business equipment, in current dollars, are up only 34 per cent – the lowest amount for any US recovery since 1960;

– because PCs are scrapped rapidly, net investment as a share of America's GDP is way down on the levels achieved in the 1960s;

– US government statisticians insist on treating PCs and laptops as equal, in power, to twenty-four-hour number-crunching mainframe computers – when in practice they are used less frequently, and then often for simple word-processing applications.

In short, the corporate sector could well find that superhighways offer dubious advantages for still considerable purchasing costs. In particular small firms, nowadays subject to large economic expectations, may turn their attentions elsewhere. A highway is one thing; a £400 colour inkjet printer, with which to make old-fashioned hard-copy invoices, could be a much better investment.

Of course, through repeated rounds of IT-assisted Business Process Reengineering, a term coined by James Champy and Michael Hammer[5], productivity at the screen can be made to rise. But then, as the eminent Swiss ergonomist Etienne Grandjean has observed, 'human labour is intensified'.[6] The superhighway, being global, will make for longer working hours, as firms increase their exposure to international time zones. Companies will anyway want to realize their highway investments quickly, and so will have them used as much as possible.

Again and again since the early 1960s, management writers have looked forward to organizations being more flexible, because less vertical in their internal structure, processes and mentality. Yet hopes have not been fulfilled. For employees in the PC-based, decentralized office of the 1990s, autonomy, flexibility, 'empowerment' and even team-based working have often meant having to take on new and/or more complicated tasks, as well as having to make more decisions per minute. The performance of employees with such tasks and decisions is also supervised more intently – and, through IT, more easily – than ever before. Superhighways, then, could *add* to stress at work. Note, for instance, that piling up a stack of hostile e-mail memos on a colleague's screen has emerged as an excellent way of conducting office politics nowadays.

Talk of 'convergence' between consumer electronics, computing, telecommunications and entertainment is nearly twenty years old, and may very well be no more than a chimera.[7] In that time, progress has been grindingly slow. For example, Multimedia, in the form of PCs equipped with CD-ROM drives, has taken a decade to reach mass sales in America.

Why does convergence proceed so slowly? In terms of IT suppliers, the consumer electronics and computer industries are unregulated, while telecommunications firms, though operating in more liberalized commercial environments, are still regulated. Joint ventures with telecommunications companies as partners, therefore, often come apart in a clash of corporate cultures, the pace and direction of change in computing often lays even specialist computer manufacturers low. To combine successfully, in one organization, both computing and telecommunications skills may prove an impossible feat.

The vertical integration between consumer electronics firms and entertainment providers – between Sony and Columbia Pictures, or between Matsushita and MCA – has not been a conspicuous success. Like the consumer electronics and computer industries, telecommunications firms are under pressure on prices and margins. For them, investment in high-band capacity width networks remains a big, risky bet. The precise services which would be compelling and profitable enough to justify such a network are still far from defined. Meanwhile, even mixing optical fibre with coaxial cable means that wiring up 1.5 million Californian homes for superhighways would cost $800 each. That is cheaper than a fibre-only connection, but still expensive when compared with cable TV and conventional telecommunications links.

Apart from economic impediments, there are also barriers to convergence as a result of conflicting technical standards. 'Standards' in computing revolve around no fewer than fifty different hardware platforms, operating systems and graphical user interfaces. Companies and countries use technical standards as a competitive weapon. One supplier firm or nation and its standard can be on the up for a time, but not for ever – competition will see to that. Given, too, the scale of investment already made in distinctive IT systems, neither client firm nor client nation likes to go over to new standards in a hurry.

Even in multimedia and in games there are standards wars. Standards function as an obstacle to convergence. As far as users are concerned, they make incompatibility a way of life. The promise of superhighways is universal access to a seamless garment of world information. Whether highways indeed prove to be so simple remains to be seen.

Great claims have long been made for IT. Now they are being made for superhighways. They may, however, never be realized. Demand constraints at home and in the office, together with industrial, economic and technical constraints among IT suppliers, could see to that.

26

Masters of the Infinite Game

CHARLES M. HAMPDEN-TURNER

You do not have to be in Southeast Asia long to sense that this is a different world. Superficially they are capitalist and all the rhetoric about free markets, getting close to customers, working in teams, making profits and developing the economy, are very similar to Western discourse. Indeed original utterances – original ideas and insights into business practices – are as scarce or scarcer than among our own managers, consultants and captains of industry. The terms managers in Southeast Asia use are mostly borrowed from the same small clan of Western phrase-makers whose observations pass for profundity in Britain and the USA. Visitors should not expect to be startled by new concepts. They think in different ways and that makes all the difference to rates of economic development. Thailand grew at 11.8 per cent annually over the last six years. China grew at 10.6 per cent on average, with some southern provinces reaching 30 per cent to 40 per cent and some northern provinces standing still. Singapore grew at 8.8 per cent, Malaysia at 9.3 per cent, South Korea at 8.9 per cent, Taiwan at 6.9 per cent. These are not brief spurts achieved at the top of a boom. These are averages sustained over the last seven years, and in the case of China even longer. In the history of economic development we have not seen anything like this before. Britain, in her Industrial Revolution, is estimated to have grown between 0.5 and 1.5 per cent per year. Germany, France and much of continental Europe also 'came from behind' in the nineteenth century and after the Second World

War, with industrial models in the USA and the UK and with extant products which could be re-engineered. But we did not see these kinds of growth. If these trends continue the world's economic centre of gravity will swing decisively eastwards. Several Asian nations will have surpassed America's per capita GNP by the year 2010. Britain will find itself very much in the second division. The whole game is changing.

Business is often conceived of as a game, being less than an outright physical assault upon contestants with the purpose of winning. You do not have to be around business people for long to discover how all-pervasive is the game metaphor. We hear about 'level playing fields', 'picking winners', 'regulating or deregulating play', 'winning strategies', 'brilliant plays', 'even breaks', 'moving the goal posts', 'coaching players', 'world leagues' and so on. The game metaphor is useful because it suggests non lethal conflict. Animals have signals to each other which communicate 'this fight is not a fight but play'. Both will contract their claws and rehearse hunting and killing. Likewise, business looks like it is to become 'the moral equivalent of war' which the American psychologist William James called for early in this century. The world needs something with the excitement, challenges, idealism of war, said James, but without its cruelty and destructiveness. Suppose we did 'beat' the Germans and Japanese in commerce, what then would they buy from us?

Or if they 'won', what would they sell to us? 'Victory' in business and 'brilliant strategy' are clearly metaphors borrowed from the battlefield with only limited applications to commerce. And here is where the subtle differences between the West and burgeoning Southeast Asia come in. They are using different metaphors to organize experience. The terms may be wearily familiar but the context is astoundingly new to us. Here I have followed some of the contrasts offered by American philosopher James P. Carse, who speaks of finite vs infinite games. Here I can cover just four contrasts.

* * *

One is the distinction between the belief that the rules of the game cannot change and the belief that the rules of the game *must* keep changing. Huge amounts of American money are being spent on litigation, on trying to fix capitalism into a standard American mould, like a game invented and patented by Parker Brothers and conducted forever more on a 'level playing field'. Of course the courts are too slow. The market is lost before we 'win' the case. Customers buy in millions from the 'cheat', currently defined by GATT rules as 'daring' to accept less than 6 per cent profit margin. Southeast Asia countries like to 'buy' market share with wafer-thin profits. The truth emerging in Southeast Asia is that the 'game' changes all the time. It is like evolution or like coevolution, greatly speeded up with new forms finding new fits. Rules are invented by the parties themselves. Contracts change because relationships change and skills develop. A top American company I consult to won a large contract from Toshiba because it had got its defect rate on semiconductors below thirty in one million. When the third delivery met the specifications the Americans were proud, but Toshiba was vexed. 'When are you going to improve?' they asked. The point is not to keep within the rules but to surpass them, not to deliver as promised but to transcend your promise.

Another key distinction is between those who aim to win the infinite game and those whose aim is to continue long-term playing and learning in an infinite game. You cannot browse long on a business bookshelf without being exhorted 'to win'. 'Winning isn't everything; it's the only thing,' said an American football coach, whose name I have thankfully forgotten. The problem with winning is simply stated: the game comes to an end. Suppose Rupert Murdoch, who recently dropped the price of *The Times* to 20p, 'won' and the *Independent* or the *Guardian* folded as a result. Would there be more competition or less? So while Murdoch is certainly 'competing', he is doing so in a way designed to reduce diversity and competition in the longer run. He does not want the present number of quality papers 'to go on playing'. He does not want too many voices to contend. He wants his own to dominate.

> P. Y. Lai was the Chinese managing director of Intel's Malaysian subsidiary in Penang when I spoke to him. He had created a free bus service for employees, obliging other employers to go along. He had created a kindergarten for employees' children in an idyllic flower garden near the head office. Workers' children were educated free. Managers paid full fees, skilled technicians half fees. Parents spent work breaks with their children. All learned English. But Li was proudest of two other initiatives. He had started an in-company store, then used the profits to start a credit union. He had the union invest its funds in several low and medium tech companies in the Free Trade Zone. Any worker who could not master the mathematics needed to manufacture the pentium chip was outplaced in a company partly owned by the credit union. 'No one here has left without a job to go to.'

The above contrasts strongly with the contradiction at the heart of the finite game, which brings to a swift conclusion that which we claim to value, namely competing. When the hostile takeover is launched, the merger concluded, the corporation acquired, then there are fewer players in the game. The oligopoly or duopoly is closer and market power has increased. Out of the wings and on to the stage stalks the regulator, to the usual boos and hisses. (Down with statism!) But the threat to competition is real enough, as are the obscene salaries brought by down-sizing, so that tens of thousands of employees are not playing any longer either. A close look at the Chinese, Japanese or 'tiger' economies shows a much larger number of competing companies. China has more than a hundred pharmaceutical companies. Is this simply a prelude to the major shakedowns we witness in the West? Probably not, since Japan has eight automobile companies, for a population of only 120 million, twenty fork-lift truck companies, forty machine-tool makers and so on, in contrast with the UK, with no nationally owned car company remaining (unless one counts the Robin Reliant) and two forklift truck makers. The merger of Glaxo with Welcome may save on distribution costs, but will probably halve the number of ideas. Nor do most economies in Southeast Asia tolerate hostile takeovers. Why? Because the ideal is to go on playing with as much variety and novel input as possible. As Akio Morita of Sony pointed out, 'You do not break another man's rice bowl'.[1] When your opponent is on the ropes, you stand back to let him recover. You do this because the ongoing process of competing is more important than the interim results. You do not let the results harm or impoverish the process. The company who lost round three may win round six as did Yamaha after being once humbled by Honda. What is important is for an economy to keep coming up with the best ideas and for that you need multiple players, who learn from their mistakes without trauma or dislocation. If we look at Asian martial arts, especially words ending in 'o', *bushido, aikido, judo, sumo,* they all mean 'the way of', e.g. *bushido,* 'the way of swords'. In all cases these are disciplines to be perfected and only incidentally contests to be won. By competing you improve the ongoing process, the infinite game. But it is stupid to kill, to knock the other person out of the game itself. This is for the same reason that in evolution it would be stupid for one stag to kill another. If you have ten stags with stag one stronger than stag two and the weak-est being stag ten, then you need several mock fights between these stags in order that the top six or seven pass on their genes to the next generation while the bottom three or four desist from breeding. Lethal fights could lead the best to kill the second best, or the second to kill the third, or stags wounded but not killed to lose subsequent bouts. Only non-lethal contests which end before the loser is injured allow the better to breed. Only nontraumatic competing allows information to be passed on to the next generation of products and allows even losers to learn, round by round.

A further distinction is between the attempt to play the capitalist game within boundaries, with the environment, for example, as an 'externality', as opposed to the habit of playing with boundaries, to turn pollution control and photovoltaics into valuable markets. 'Externality' is a favourite word of Western economists. It refers to all those things and most values worth living for, which are deemed outside the realm of economics, i.e. the environment, health, welfare, education, culture. Moreover, making money for shareholders is often thought to marginalize other stakeholders, i.e. customers, suppliers, the community, banks, partners, employees. Top managers claiming to represent shareholders have the right to get rid of most employees if necessary, demand 'give-backs' from unions, pressure suppliers into lowering their prices, pay contractors late and float on their credit and obtain as much bank debt as possible or junk bonds to leverage shareholders' funds. Southeast Asian business draws boundaries far wider. Banks, contractors and suppliers hold shares in the company. Even where laws confine contracts to one year, custom decrees long-term relationships with employment security. The aim is not to make the company profitable at the supplier's expense, but to make that supply chain more profitable than other chains for all members – what is called 'shared destiny'. These ever more inclusive boundaries form what Michael Porter calls 'clusters'. Individuals do not grow rich by themselves. Less and less do companies grow by themselves. What develops are clusters of company, subcontractors, suppliers, partners, banks, customers and information infrastructures. You 'play with the boundaries' to include valuable assets within these, just as Victor bested Sony by including more Hollywood films in its rental videos. The Japanese *keiretsu* is the cluster formalized. It is also obvious that the finite game is short-term by definition. The ideal is 'to make a quick buck', to inflict defeat in the shortest possible time, while the infinite game is long-term. Persist as did North Vietnam. Outwait your opponent. Make profits so scarce for both of you that he gives up while you stay in. Your goals are infinite, 'change the world through fax communication'. His are finite. 'Meet the City's profit forecast for the next half year, or Wall Street's for the next quarter.'[2] It is obvious, given these values, who is going to win. For here is the central irony, 'the infinite game includes many finite plays.' In contrast the finite game wrecks the infinite game by bringing it to a premature conclusion. Any masterful player of an infinite game has the power to knock out an opponent and sometimes he will do so, especially if the player is a foreigner or Westerner. Once you have learned powerful plays you are potentially lethal to opponents, yet ironically this power has come from sparing opponents, not from eliminating them. You have gone many rounds with them to learn. Many Asian economies treat domestic opponents as friendly opponents, or fellow stags, while treating foreign opponents as creatures to be impaled if they attack. This is what is meant by 'playing with boundaries'. You can join them or beat them, include them or exclude them, yet the overall tendency is to include, to draw boundaries ever wider so as to gain knowledge and information.

The final distinction is between competition for its own sake, which is believed to elevate the character and eliminate the unfit, and competition as one phase of a learning process, with the second phase being the cooperative sharing of the winning ideas among as many players as possible. They continue to play. In finite games competition becomes an end in itself. Our victory can only be secured by another's defeat. Like a Demolition Derby we smash into rival cars, then cannibalize their spare parts for our own use, a process of 'resource allocation' praised by classical economists. The autoparts are passing from poor managers to better ones, from bad drivers to good ones. Unfortunately a company destroyed hurts and

27

Darwinian Psychology, Political Economy and the Problem of Groups

SAMUEL BRITTAN

Introduction

There are several reasons for my interest in recent attempts to extend Darwinism into a more comprehensive explanation of human behaviour and psychology. Over the years I have been put off by being told that various disputes depended on one's view of the 'Nature of Man'. I used to be a very occasional participant at a seminar held in Interlaken, where the Swiss-American Karl Brunner tried to win German social scientists away from what he called a sociological view of human beings toward an economic one. My own reaction was that the nature of Man was a biological question to be investigated empirically and not a matter for profound armchair theorizing. The same applies to the different views of our species held by all the eighteenth- and nineteenth-century social theorists brought so vividly to life in the works of Isaiah Berlin.

My interest goes back even earlier. I did once contemplate becoming a professional psychologist, no doubt out of a naive desire to better the human condition and a less naive suspicion that this was unlikely to come about through conventional political action. If I had not been dissuaded from this course by my elders (but not necessarily betters), I would have joined a pretty fragmented discipline. Today's new

Darwinian psychology, although still controversial, provides a chance for a more unified point of view.

That is not all. As a matter of temperament, I have been attracted both to individualism and to reductionism. In positive terms this means analysing the behaviour of groups as far as possible in terms of their constituent units. Ethically, it means judging the goals of public policy in terms of their effects on individuals rather than collective abstractions such as 'England', 'national morale', 'the army' or the welfare of a corporate body. Although economic reporting is largely in terms of abstract concepts such as gross national product, unemployment rates, price levels, exchange rates and so on, that is an unavoidable vulgarization. The core of neoclassical economic analysis is in terms of individuals and not societies, however embarrassing many British practitioners find this fact. Neo-Darwinism is even more reductive, conducting its analysis at the level of the gene.

The Neoclassical Economic Model

The most thoughtful recent discussion I know of neoclassical economic assumptions is that of Gerard Radnitzky, a German philosopher of science. 'Human beings,' he writes, 'are rational maximisers throughout the whole, or at least a very broad range, of their social interactions.'[1] He also refers to a whole string of nouns: scarcity, opportunities, preferences, costs, benefits, competition, rationality, optimality and equilibrium. Behind these formal concepts is the behavioural assumption that Man makes efforts to better his condition. Brunner used to speak of 'Resourceful, evaluating, maximising Man – REMM'.

The weakness of the economic model is the uncertainty about what is being maximized. To say 'material wellbeing' is too narrow and not always true. Radnitzky emphasizes 'the great variety of concrete psychological motivations'. On the other hand, the most comprehensive notion of utility makes the whole exercise circular and drives the subject into an empty mathematical formalism. In practice economists who bother about such matters assume that most human beings are chiefly concerned with the wellbeing of their closest family and associates, with some margin for more generalized benevolence. But other goals, such as hierarchy and power, do not fit in too easily. Neither do moral goals or constraints which both limit and modify the pursuit of self-chosen interests.

It is not an accident that Radnitzky's analysis comes at the beginning of a book he edited, *Universal Economics*. This is one of the latest attempts to present economic theory as a general theory of all human behaviour, explaining not only the financial pages of the newspaper, but every other page as well. Less friendly critics have called it 'economic imperialism'. The movement seems to me well past its zenith. Its most lasting legacy is that the better economists discuss not only what an ideal policy would be, but what might make governments and other agents actually follow such a policy. For instance there has been a switch of emphasis from specific policy advice to institutional structures like independent central banks or supranational currencies and also to constitutional procedures and voting methods, which are no longer left to traditional political analysts alone.

Paradigms Compared

The Darwinian and neoclassical economic models are ranged together against the prevailing sociological model, which emphasizes groups such as nations, classes, or occupational interests rather than individuals. The sociological view also plays down innate human characteristics in favour of the assumption that environmental forces – above all human institutions which are open to change – are the dominant force in determining behaviour.

Links between evolutionary biology and economics were strong in the mid-nineteenth century. Darwin paid tribute to Malthus's population theory as an inspiration for his own

Struggle for Existence. It is known that he had been reading other classical economists, including Adam Smith, when he first formulated the basic ideas later to appear in *The Origin of Species*. An interesting similarity between today's Darwinism and neoclassical economics remains the postulate of a spontaneous order. Market relations allow a great advance in the division of labour without any central planning mind. Similarly, one of Darwin's great achievements was to show how the animal and plant world could develop without the deliberate designer which the theologian William Paley believed to be necessary.

A spontaneous order is not a perfect one. A more subtle contribution of evolutionary theory is to show that change is more likely to be successful through a series of discrete trial-and-error steps than through an attempt at one great leap forward. This discovery and error correction is also something on which the 'Austrian' school of economists has insisted upon – although it can be lost to sight in general equilibrium models.

One obvious difference between many neo-Darwinians and the neoclassical economic research paradigm is that the fundamental unit is the gene in one case and the individual human being in the other. Yet for some purposes it makes no difference. The sort of person who is shocked by the remark 'There is no such thing as society; there are only individuals and their families' would be equally shocked if it concluded instead 'There are only genes and their carriers'. Those who can see the point of the remark can equally operate at either level.

A more basic difference is that a gene is not conscious of its activities and reference to it as 'selfish' or talk of its struggle to reproduce is metaphorical. A human economic agent, on the other hand, has some consciousness of what he or she is doing. The Chicago school, and especially Milton Friedman, are adamant that it does not matter whether people consciously follow their assumptions. They do not worry whether a businessman is consciously maximizing his profits or his utility, so long as his behaviour is best predicted on such assumptions. Indeed Friedman refers to the differential survival of the businessman who does maximize.

Nevertheless the economic agent is conscious of something. It is silly to throw away information on why real businessmen think they are saving, investing or not taking on more workers – even if we afterwards reinterpret this information in different terms. Not even the most hard boiled of economic positivists would want to throw away the surveys of business intentions which contribute so much to macroeconomic investigation.

Another difference is that neoclassical economists theorise about optimality conditions. A lot of high-grade mathematical effort has gone into defining the conditions in which a competitive market equilibrium would yield a social optimum. Evolutionary biologists talk in non-evaluative terms about survival and reproduction. The nearest they approach to the economists' optimality is the notion of an *evolutionary stable* strategy.

In their full rigour the economic conditions for optimality are extremely unlikely to occur; and this fact has been used by a subset of general equilibrium theorists to discredit efforts to liberalize markets. But such general equilibrium theorists do not suggest any alternative direction for policy and are in my view near a dead-end. The 'Austrian' economists, who see markets as a discovery technique in a world where tastes and techniques are changing and information is scarce and expensive, are much nearer to the evolutionary paradigm.

There is some reason to regard the biological paradigm as the primary one. The neoclassical economist thinks of human motivation in terms of material gain or at least the maximization of choice or utility. The political theorist thinks of power over others. But both power and money may be further analysed as means towards reproductive success. Indeed wealth and power have often been judged by the number of wives, concubines and children a man could have – said to run into many thousands in the case of some east African sultans.

Thus the things that the economic agent is said to maximize – whether wealth or utility – may be a side effect of pursuing fundamental biological goals.

Neither the economic nor the Darwinian model amounts to a falsifiable theory. Both are open to the charge that almost anything that happens can be interpreted in their terms and that it is difficult to think of any phenomena that they rule out. For instance, Darwinians have no difficulty in coping with species of birds where the father is bogged down sitting on the egg and then rearing the chicks while the females go out to compete for mates.

But the absence of strict falsifiability does not make either model useless. Popper described evolutionary theory as a metaphysical research programme.[2,3] This was not meant to be a criticism. On the contrary, he regarded such programmes as a source for a great many more specific lower level theories which were indeed falsifiable. The zoological example to which I have referred can be explained by evolutionary theory only in conjunction with specific facts and hypotheses about the species concerned. And to leap over to economics: phenomena such as the rise and demise of the gold standard fit in with the general economic model of Man, but could not have been predicted from the model alone.

The Neo-Darwinian Approach

So far, the resemblance between modern Darwinism and market-oriented political economy is a general one. The two disciplines nowadays have little contact with each other and make little use of each other's techniques. The most successful economic application of the evolutionary metaphor has been in areas such as the rise and fall of business firms. Much less use has been made of it in macroeconomics or the analysis of economic policy. I shall therefore continue to discuss Darwinian thinking without worrying too much about an economic application at every juncture.

A good introduction to Darwinian thinking comes in a

quotation from Professor Steve Jones, who is a mainline geneticist: 'Natural selection takes advantage of the fact that in each generation, inheritance makes mistakes. Because some are better at coping with what life throws at them, they copy themselves more successfully. Darwin's mechanism sorts out the best from what mutation supplies. It gives a direction to evolution and allows a living system to escape from the inevitability of extinction. This is as true for humans as for any other creature.' Or as an economist might put it: agents maximize their chances of reproductive success.

'Survival of the fittest' is a misconception. (In any case the phrase is Herbert Spencer's, not Darwin's.) Natural selection is concerned with differential *reproductive* success. Furthermore, selection acts not on an organism but on genes. As Samuel Butler once put it: 'A hen is only an egg's way of making another egg.'

A key term is 'adaptation'. The idea is that physical – and by extension psychological – characteristics are to be explained by the need to adapt to changes in the environment, including the behaviour of other creatures. It seems to me that there are still some puzzles here. For Darwinians do not claim that every creature is perfectly adapted; and I am never sure when to try to explain the utility of certain developments – such as the woodpecker's beak – or when to regard them as relics no longer required, as in the vestigial human tail. Not to speak of maladaptations. Of course Darwinians have guidelines for separating out such cases – just as economists have guidelines for telling us when pegging the exchange rate of one currency to a more stable one will fail to work. But how many economists actually predicted the 1995 Mexican crisis or Britain's exit from the ERM?

Modern Darwinism rejects group selection. Maxims such as 'Nature cares for the species but not for the individual' are now known to be wrong. The species is of interest only to the extent that providing for its welfare helps the gene to reproduce. This leaves room for at least two kinds of altruism: kinship altruism and reciprocal altruism. The first occurs when an organism reduces or sacrifices its own chances of reproduction for the sake of other organisms with which it has some relevant genes in common. J.B.S. Haldane is supposed to have said that he would be prepared to give his life to save two brothers or sisters or eight cousins (though actually he should have been indifferent). Reciprocal altruism is more complicated. The point is that some degree of self sacrifice for the sake of reciprocal advantage is programmed into the behaviour of many organisms on the basis that, if others do the same, their own reproductive chances are maximized.

One notable conclusion is that racial differences are trivial, because the different races have separated from each other too recently on the evolutionary timescale. On the other hand, sex differences are fundamental because of the different role of the two sexes in the reproductive process. Because of the length of pregnancy and later care of offspring, a female human has far fewer possibilities of producing offspring than the male – as demonstrated by the prevalance of polygamy in tribal societies. The desire to produce as many offspring as possible accounts for phenomena as diverse as the development of peacock's tails to attract the maximum number of peahens and the aggressive behaviour of young human males which stems from the battle to possess desirable females.*

The struggle to exist seems to leave many options open. An equilibrium might be anything from a stable community of a few dozen individuals – such as certain giant lizards – to

* I have no intention of getting diverted into feminist issues. But as a matter of logic, one must emphasize that different does not mean inferior. Socialists of an earlier generation, such as Douglas Jay, used to stress that they thought that human beings were worthy of equal respect – which did not mean that they had equal abilities. It was only with the later degeneration of these ideas that egalitarianism was taken to require the denial of human differences of which every mother on earth is aware. Similarly, emphasis on male and female differences does not mean that one sex is superior or inferior to the other. Nor does it mean that every male or female will exhibit characteristics typical of the sex. It is more that the frequency distribution of characteristics will be around *different means*. If I dare invoke what was once a neutral technical term: the bell curves will be in different places.

billions of fellow creatures covering the surface of the earth. Where in between is the definition of success? Perhaps we should follow Matt Ridley in regarding evolution as a zero sum game. Creatures do not progress. They have to change if they are to keep up, not merely with competition from other creatures, but from competition with their fellows of the same species.

The contribution of some of the most recent popular Darwinian books seems to me to be primarily in the realm of psychology. Earlier evolutionary biologists concentrated on physical features and on behaviour. Some modern writers also discuss the accompanying thoughts and feelings, which harks back to some interests of Darwin himself. The idea of human nature has been revived, especially by Matt Ridley in *The Red Queen*.[4] This emphasis on psychology is also the hallmark of Robert Wright's *The Moral Animal*.

Let me mention two striking applications. First, the vast majority of murders are committed by young men – not women – an instance of the struggle to fertilize as many ova as possible. Secondly, instances of child abuse and neglect are far more common among step-parents than natural ones, illustrating the effects of the absence of any genetic relationship. This example confirms the wicked stepmother syndrome, which some may have regarded as a feature of fairy tales or unconscious infantile fears. One implication is that the presumption in favour of the mother having custody of children in divorce cases might be re-examined if the father is prepared to bring up the children himself and if the mother has acquired a new partner. (In Joanna Trollope's *The Choir*, the boy hit on the solution of staying with his maternal grandfather.)

There is however no hope of avoiding controversy by moving from economics to theoretical biology. For instance there are respectable biologists (such as Professor Michael Ghiselin, who appears in the Radnitzky volume) who still deny that the primary unit is the gene, or who regard the concept of human nature as outmoded.

After Eugenics

There are already many practical applications of the new biology to disciplines such as plant and animal breeding and medical science. How far these could have been accomplished by genetics alone and how far the specifically Darwinian element enters, I am not competent to judge. But what application is there for either or both in broader questions about the management of human affairs?

It is not surprising that early attempts to improve the human race should have given the whole idea a bad name. Steve Jones, a geneticist who is highly critical of the eugenics movement, has given numerous unfortunate examples in the book based on his Reith Lectures.[5] Francis Galton started the eugenics movement in part to 'check the birth rate of the unfit and improve the race by furthering the activity of the fit by early marriage of the best stock'. Winston Churchill expressed similar sentiments when he was Home Secretary in 1910, but they were not made public until 1992. It is notorious that Hitler carried such thinking to the extent of concentration camps and to experiments on living people. Elisabeth Nietzsche, the sister of the philosopher, chose what she regarded as especially splendid German volunteers to start a community in Paraguay in 1886 that would be the beginning of a new race of supermen and women. In the late twentieth century, the remaining survivors of Nueva Germania have been found to be 'poor, inbred and diseased'.

Such enthusiasms were by no means confined to the political right. The central theme of Bernard Shaw's *Man and Superman* was the admission that contemporary men and women were not equipped to make a go of socialism, but to conclude that the species must be improved until they could. This becomes very clear in the appendix entitled 'The Revolutionist's Handbook'. He writes: 'The only fundamental and possible socialism is the socialization of the selective breeding of Man; in other terms of human evolution. We must eliminate the Yahoo or his vote will wreck the Commonwealth . . . that may mean that we must establish a State Department of Evolution, with a seat in the Cabinet for its chief, and a revenue to defray the cost of direct state experiments and provide inducements to private persons to achieve successful results.'

These examples show not only that schemes for genetic improvement are peculiarly liable to manipulation by evil people. They also show the danger of jumping the gun, that is, of acting before knowledge in this highly emotive area is really secure. We must therefore be grateful that Shaw and Galton – who were far from evil men – were not able to give full rein to their fancies.

But we cannot retreat forever from ideas because they have been misunderstood and interpreted in absurd ways. The fact that a certain form of behaviour has genetic roots does not mean that it has to be modified genetically. Different results will be produced by the same genetic material under different environmental conditions. Caution suggests that the overwhelming emphasis of any attempts at improvement deriving from Darwinian psychology should be directed at the institutional environment which interacts with innate tendencies.

But can we be sure that this will always be enough? Can we honestly and forever rule out a more directly genetic approach? This is already a central feature of discussions about preventing the most dreadful inborn diseases. But would it not be a gain to have human beings whose innate programming made them less likely to indulge in actions like ethnic cleansing?

It should not be controversial to say that there are many profoundly distasteful aspects of the behaviour of the human species. One need only to point to events in central Africa, the Caucasus, former Yugoslavia or the numerous horrifying examples of child cruelty and child neglect nearer to home. Such events crop up in so many forms throughout human history and so far seem impervious to modification by the various forms of political organization under which people have lived. Their roots must run pretty deep in the nature of the species; and any attempts at improvement would have to be carried out by members of the same species.

The 'Moral Animal'

Most recent attempts to apply neo-Darwinism to current problems have been in areas like human mating. Characteristic titles of recent papers have been on 'the evolution of desire' and 'monogamy, polygamy and serial divorce'. The avoidance of headline prescriptions for national and international policy reflects a healthy caution after the experiences of the eugenics movement and after the fierce hostility (whether merited or not) which greeted E. O. Wilson's attempt to launch 'sociobiology' in the mid 1970s.

But I doubt if I would ever be taken seriously as an adviser on mating problems. I have been chiefly interested in what neo-Darwinism might contribute to politics, political economy and political philosophy. It was for this reason that I leapt at Robert Wright's *The Moral Animal,*[6] which touched off the present essay. Wright's willingness to try to draw some practical conclusions from recent work attracted me. His overwhelming emphasis, however, is still on sexual rather than political problems – and properly so if, as he might want to argue, sexual battle is at the heart of the wider political struggle.

Philosophical critics of the book have objected to the use of words like hypocrisy to describe apparently noble attitudes which can be traced to basic survival strategies, like kin altruism and reciprocal altruism. As a matter of logic the critics are right: a man who jumps into a raging torrent to save a child is not a hypocrite, whether his actions spring from genetic programming, the effects of events in his early infancy or anything else. But if we are interested in promoting such acts or minimizing other anti-social ones, the more we can learn about their origins the better.

The Bogey of Determinism

Any attempt at a scientific or semi-scientific explanation of human behaviour – whether Darwinian, Freudian or anything else – comes up against the charge of determinism. If our actions are determined by some combination of genetic endowment plus environment, does not free will go out of the window; and what becomes of traditional notions of blame and punishment?

Wright is quite willing to say that he is a biological determinist. Everyone is a product not of genes, but of genes and environment together: knobs and tunings. A stereo set has no more control over its tunings than of the knobs it was born with. There is no sense in which the stereo is to blame for the music it produces. Any act is a combined product of genes and environment.

Many people feel that without free will there would be no case for personal or political freedom. Wrong. My freedom to travel to Iceland means that no one will stop me. It is not affected by whether some scientist with enough data about my genetic constitution and all past events in my life could predict whether I chose to make the journey. The opposite of freedom is coercion, not determinism.

Wright argues that determinism is a humane doctrine which substitutes understanding for judgement and limits punishment to where it is unavoidable as a deterrent. It is those who go on about free will and responsibility who are most inclined to clamour for retributive justice. This last statement may turn out to be empirically true. Maybe everyone is a robot and no one 'deserves' to be punished. On that case, universal forgiveness brought by understanding would undermine punishment and retaliation.

Wright may, however, be making a logical mistake which unnecessarily weakens his own case. The view that behaviour can be entirely accounted for by heredity and environment is part of a metaphysical research programme. But let us suppose that, however far science advances, there will continue to be a random element in behaviour not predictable from prior information. Does that reintroduce free will? Surely not. Free will, for those who believe in it, is not randomness but conscious control over one's destiny. The same applies to the indeterminate elements in modern quantum mechanics. If an electron unpredictably jumps from one circuit to another, or if it is impossible to measure precisely the mass of a particle together with its velocity, the particles in question still do not exhibit anything in the least like the power to choose between good and evil that God supposedly gave to human beings. Someone who is inclined to doubt whether anyone is ever to 'blame' is on equally strong ground whatever the proportions of predictability and randomness in human affairs.

Wright may be on the right track when he speculates that the illusion about free will could be an adaptation. In practice a person is said to have free will if anticipations of punishment can influence him – or, an economist might say, if he responds to incentives. If no praise or blame or sanctions have the slightest chance of affecting a person's actions, courts are likely to accept that his crime was committed as a result of some psychotic disorder. The court decision does not imply an absence of genetic and environmental causality, but merely that the accused criminal is not affected by normal human incentives. Free will and its absence are convenient legal distinctions, as is the doctrine that anyone ever deserves anything. In Wright's words, we have to live with 'the intellectual groundlessness of blame and the practical use for it'.

A Digression on Utilitarianism

No 'ought' assertion can be derived from an 'is' statement. Therefore modern Darwinism does not commit one to any particular set of moral beliefs. At most, it can warn that some beliefs may be impossible to observe in practice and hint at more and less successful methods of implementing the beliefs one may hold for independent reasons. It is nevertheless understandable that Wright should put in a plea for utilitarianism in the closing chapters of his book. He espouses it in the simple form that happiness should be the guide to moral conduct and that everyone's happiness should be of equal importance to all of us.

The temptation arises because Charles Darwin himself was pretty much a utilitarian and corresponded with John Stuart Mill, whom he admired. The difficulty they both encountered is that evolution seems designed for anything but the happiness of the individual, which when it occurs is a passing means to the reproduction of his or her genes. As Mill observed: 'If there are any marks at all of special design in creation, one of the things most evidently designed is that a large proportion of animals should pass their existence in tormenting and devouring other animals.' Darwin was characteristically more specific: 'I cannot persuade myself that a beneficent and omnipotent God would have designedly created the Ichneumonidae [parasitic wasps] with the express intention of their feeding within the living bodies of caterpillars, or that a cat should play with mice.'[7] Or as Wright puts it: 'To ponder natural selection is to be staggered by the amount of suffering and death which must be the price for a single, slight advance in organic design.' Such an advance might be longer, sharper, canine teeth in male chimpanzees to make other animals suffer or die more surely.

Wright does not deal with the weaknesses that some have seen in ulititarianism. Nor does he discuss the shift from maximizing happiness to maximizing choice that some utilitarians, influenced by economic theory, have made. He does however make the acceptance of utilitarianism more difficult by insisting that our actions should be directed equally to the welfare of all the inhabitants of the world – to which many philosophers in this camp would add the welfare of the yet unborn. He even cites (I hope ironically) the maxim that one should prefer to rescue an unknown bishop rather than the washerwoman, even if the washerwoman is one's mother.

The argument is that the bishop would have more opportunities for doing good in the future.

A more plausible version is that form of 'rule utilitarianism' which accepts that we are most likely to promote the general welfare by doing most for those with whom we have the closest ties – for instance if mothers look after their own children rather than striving impartially for the welfare of millions of others. This version too would accord much better with human psychology as Wright himself describes it.

I have discussed utilitarianism extensively elsewhere.[8] My own view is that it can only be supported as a special case of a wider system of political morality. But in many cases this wider system will lead to much the same results. Indeed we are much more likely to fall short of utilitarianism than improve upon it, both in our personal and in public contexts.

Wright's own main point is that, far from embracing the values that might seem to be implicit in evolution, we should reject them and that Man is the first evolutionary product capable of so doing. Richard Dawkins said something very similar in *The Selfish Gene*;[9] and so does Daniel Dennett in his more recent book.[10] What I had hoped for was a much more detailed confrontation of utilitarianism (or any other humane ethical system) with the difficulties put in its path by inborn patterns of behaviour and – most important of all – an exploration of the most promising ways of overcoming them.

Problems of Groups

Finally, let me note, without trying to solve, what has struck me again and again as the most difficult problem posed by human evolution. During 98 per cent of its past existence the human species is said to have lived in small bands of around 100–150 hunter gatherers, usually closely related to each other. The nature of this group is illuminated by the colourful idea of a tribal chief who would periodically be killed by a younger male who would then take on the role of leadership himself, a primordial Oedipal event of which there are, according to some Freudians, still traces in the modern adult human mind. The impact of these early groups has been pondered over by thinkers as different as Sigmund Freud[11] and Friedrich Hayek. They both contrast the requirements of life in such primal groups with those of the Great Society (a term invented by an LSE professor, Graham Wallas, for the spontaneous order involving the interaction of millions of individuals).

It is extremely unlikely that the behaviour that emerged through natural selection in the population of hunter gatherers would in all respects be suitable for today's Great Society. The good side of group solidarity is obvious enough: family affection, patriotism, mutual help, doing one's duty and all the communitarian virtues. So, alas, is the bad side: intolerance of the outsider, willingness to go to war for trivial reasons, ethnic cleansing, football hooliganism and much else.

The syndrome is often much discussed under the heading of nationalism or xenophobia. But that is to understate it. People of the most diverse nationalities sacrificed their lives for the British Empire, the Hapsburg Empire and many others. When there are no genuine national differences or rival crowns, religious differences will do instead. Indeed the most trivial distinction will divide people into ferociously hostile factions. In medieval Constantinople a completely artificial distinction between blues and greens, factions at the circus, divided the population into groups whose hostility could lead to murder and worse.

There is another aspect to in-group feelings of which honesty compels a mention. That is the hostility to any reward system depending on the luck of the market rather than face-to-face evaluation. This can do untold damage to the reward and incentive structure on which the market depends. To protect my flank, I must point out there it may be possible to redistribute income via the tax and transfer system to those ill-favoured by the market. The harm that is done is in the resistance to equilibrium rates of pay, so that some people are priced out of work while other types of worker are in short supply.

Market-inclined economists often say their opponents want to pay according to supposed 'merit' or are overinfluenced by egalitarianism. But this may not be quite right. People in face to face groups do not look for either equality or moral merit in scales of pay. They look for a known and agreed hierarchy which does not change too quickly. Is it possible that these responses reflect the hunter-gatherer group, which had agreed rules for the sharing of prey? What is more difficult to explain is why very large prizes which depend completely on luck – such as those distributed in the national lottery – or mostly on luck – as in the case of popular entertainers and sportsmen – are nevertheless acceptable.

Conclusion

The two problems of group mentality – (a) resistance to the market rewards which emerge from the Great Society and (b) the enormously powerful drive of such groups to make war on, or otherwise oppress, other groups – have haunted me for a long time. Both kinds of behaviour are examples of people thinking that they are rising above self-interest when they are actually falling below it, and produce results which are worse than the pursuit of genuine self-interest constrained by a framework of rules and customary inhibitions. In the time-honoured tradition of suggesting work for other people to do, I hope that the next popular Darwinian book will go into detail on this tribal legacy and make specific suggestions on how we can either modify it or live with it without blowing ourselves to pieces.

28

The Shapers of Things to Come

BOB TYRRELL

Images of the future have always played a central role in human affairs. The nature of these images has differed substantially over time and in different cultures, but individuals, organizations and states have always needed *some* image of the future, whether that image presents the future as something that happens to them or as something that they can actively create.

The common element in thinking about the future is always a desire in some way to increase control. Peter Schwarz, President of the Global Business Network, puts this very directly in the first paragraph of his recent book *The Art of the Long View*. 'This book,' he writes, 'is about freedom.' What he means is that without an understanding or an *exploration* (a distinction which is central in this essay) of what the future might hold we lack the freedom to make the most of our opportunities and to control our destinies.

Yet in modern times the history of planning has been intimately tied up with communist regimes, which liberals have characterized as seeking to usurp the prerogative of nature and of God to control our destinies by substituting planning, backed up by the power of science.

Interestingly, the communist model of planning could still be said to take a cue from God. If the assumption was that God (or, even more abstractly, history) has purpose and design (in corporate speak, a 'strategy'), the advance made by Marx, with appropriate acknowledgements to Hegel, was to crack that design and to describe how to facilitate its realization. The common assumption was that the future was determinate. The advance was to determine what the conditions in the system were and from these to predict the end state.

Liberal regimes and philosophies have always resisted these views and seen planning as being in opposition to the free market. The philosophy of the free market is premised on the complexity of nature, the freedom and autonomy of individuals and the consequent need for the devolution of decision-making. There may or may not be a pattern to be discerned, but either way such a project is beyond ordinary mortals' capacity either to know or to control.

For the extreme exponents of this view planning and its implicit objective of control is eschewed not only at the level of markets and economies but at the level of the firm too. For example, Tom Peters has seriously suggested that attempts to plan and to understand how corporations work (and, by extension, to control their evolution) is not only foolish but dangerous. He argues about the corporation by analogy with national economies. No one understands how the US economy works, yet it works very well. The Soviets 'understood' how their economy worked and it was a disaster. His prescription is for chaos and 'crazy organizations for crazy times'. More generally there is a good deal of evidence of the triumph of the 'liberal' approach to planning in corporations, one that relies less on the rational, analytic and passive and more on the inspirational and emotional.

How did we get here? Within firms the development of formal strategic planning methods in organizations can be traced back to the 1950s when large firms such as ICI in the UK or Boeing in the US began to adopt the vocabulary of military strategy and to assimilate the experience of planning gained by governments during the war. With the social sciences, and economics in particular, also strongly deterministic in stance, there was an additional and critical conditioning factor in the shape that corporate strategic planning took. At this time it was still possible to look to the example of the

Soviet Union as testimony to the power of science, techno-cratic knowledge and managerialism to solve social problems and create 'progress'.

It was against this background that the early management theorists of planning (such as Igor Ansoff and Henry Mintz-berg) began to emerge in the 1960s. They prescribed a highly structured and quantitative approach to planning. The organ-ization was depicted as a passive agent operating in an environment that was complex and uncertain but still, in principle, one that could be fathomed and predicted. The environment was typically categorized under a number of headings, such as the social, technological, economic and political (known, unsurprisingly, as the STEP approach). 'Models' were developed to characterize these environments and used to predict their course and the impact of specific events or 'shocks' to the system. In the case of the economy the models were typically quantitative, in the other areas they were more often intuitive or judgemental. The theory was that organizations should relate different parts of their operations to the operating environments and 'read off' the implications for corporate action of the changes predicted by the models.

By the 1970s, the limitations of this approach were begin-ning to be evident. One problem was that it was not all that easy to read implications off in the way suggested. More seriously, there were doubts about the single point, determin-istic approach to describing the future. The answer that came back was 'scenarios'. These became serious currency in the USA which had already seen the development of a large and respectable 'futures' industry in the 1960s. In the UK scenario planning found its most enthusiastic practitioners in the Shell company.

The Shell experience was widely disseminated, especially in the wake of the 1974 oil price explosion. In one of its scenarios the company had described a large increase in oil prices. As a result the company was said to have been better able to adapt to the dramatically different conditions that prevailed. The Shell precedent was widely discussed and large numbers of other companies started to do their own scenario planning.

Unqualified enthusiasm for scenario planning did not last long. The main difficulty was that executives still needed to take decisions on the basis of a single point of view. Whilst exploring alternative futures could make you more flexible in your attitude to change and more responsive and adaptable, this was often judged to be of insufficient value when set against the costs in time and other resources required to generate and assimilate the scenarios.

More seriously, the uncertainties in the 1980s seemed to be multiplying. Things started to happen that no one had anticipated in any scenarios. In economics the breakdown of the postwar welfare consensus and the rise of Thatcherism and Reagonomics turned old assumptions on their heads. Analysis could tell you that cutting taxes could raise revenue . . . or, maybe, lower revenue. Logic alone could no longer discriminate between possible outcomes. The threat this posed to the confidence of Enlightenment thinking cannot be overstated and has still to see its full repercussions work through. The breakdown of the certainties of the Cold War added to this sense of a chaotic world. Anything seemed possible and if anything was possible what was the point of trying to anticipate the future?

Corporate priorities were also changing in the 1980s as the attention in companies turned to internal rather than external imperatives. Competitive strategy, competitor benchmarking, focusing on core competencies, re-engineering the business around these competencies and financial restructuring became the new management mantras.

As an alternative to planning, if anything could happen, then you had to prepare for anything. Infinite flexibility became the goal. Change was not now something that happened to things, it was a phenomenon in its own right and the ability to respond to change became itself a source of competitive advantage. In a survey of 100 chief executives and main board directors in 1990 the Henley Centre found this to be their top rated attribute of successful companies.

The parallel recent history of national planning in the liberal democracies is varied and plagued by at least as many of the difficulties as those encountered in corporate planning. In continental Europe, France with its system of 'indicative planning' was frequently held up as an example of the best of both worlds, fusing free markets with the potential for enhanced rationality that planning always, in theory, offered.

In the UK the Wilson-led Labour government set up its own Department of Economic Affairs in 1964 and within a little over a year inaugurated its first Five Year Plan. The National Economic Development Office was also set up, along with 'little neddies' for key industry sectors. These were designed to facilitate the discussion and dissemination of planning assumptions within the key (corporate, trade union and government) parties to the planning process. The aim was to ensure a systematic cascading of implications from the macro to the micro level.

But almost as soon as the plan was published it was blown off course. The fatal flaw was the failure to attain the critical macroeconomic prediction/premise of a 3 per cent p.a. growth rate. On this hinged many other elements of the plan and it was the cue industry was supposed to take for its own plans and actions. To many this experience demonstrated not only that planning was impossible and a waste of time but, insofar as it misguided investment plans, that it was actually damaging.

Attempts were made to sustain the process, but other problems distracted the government and when the Tories were returned to power in 1970 macro planning was shelved. By this time the benefits of the French planning experience were also being questioned and, in the ceaseless quest to find a model on which we could base our own industrial revival, Japan became the new paragon of virtue. The role attributed to the industrial strategy of MITI (the Ministry of International Trade and Industry) in Japan's industrial success encouraged a continuation of the practice of 'picking industry winners'.

There were further attempts to sustain an active industrial strategy in the second Wilson government that won power in the two elections of 1974, mainly centred around Tony Benn. However, this government's experience instead foreshadowed what was, in the 1980s, to become an ideology of 'powerless government'. Keynesian economics was being progressively discredited as economies ran into the problems of 'stagflation' and without Keynes, governments discovered that they had lost their macroeconomic steering wheel.

The link between the decline in the efficacy of planning and the decline in the efficacy of the nation-state is unmistakeable. Planning implies objectives and the ability to control. Whereas governments were previously seen as the regulators or even the creators of markets, today the markets are the new gold standard by which governments are to be disciplined. The new mental model is clearly illustrated by this quote from an *Economist* magazine survey on the global economy in October 1995:[1]

> One thing is sure: plenty more clashes between global markets and national governments lie ahead. The danger is that some governments will be tempted to respond to market excesses by trying to force the global capital market back into a straitjacket. But they would be bound to fail. Governments would do better to rethink the way they conduct policy to avoid destabilizing market expectations, and ensure that markets are better informed *so that they can become stricter disciplinarians* [italics added].

At a more philosophical level the demise of planning is also linked to the 'end of history' and the 'postmodern' condition in which the narratives to explain the human condition and of progress are lost.

Postmodern Corporate Planning

But even though some nations have given up planning and the purposeful pursuit of objectives, this is not the case in corporations. I left the corporate story at the point where 'flexibility' was being seen as the substitute for planning – but this is not the end of the story. The current corporate chapter on planning contains some extremely interesting twists in the plot. A recently published best-seller from Gary Hamel and C. K. Prahalad, entitled *Competing for the Future*,[2] is significant in this respect. This series of short passages from their book indicates the direction in which corporate planning in some companies may be starting to move:

> We are standing on the verge of a revolution ... the environmental revolution, the genetic revolution, the materials revolution, the digital revolution and, most of all, the information revolution ... Existing industries – education, health care, transportation, banking, publishing ... will be profoundly transformed ... Thus the question of which companies and countries *create the future* is far from academic ... The wealth of a firm, and of each nation in which it operates, largely depends on its role in *creating tomorrow's markets*... in emerging opportunity arenas ... the rules are waiting to be written. In existing industries the rules are waiting to be rewritten [italics added].

The key change is one from planning as a process to generate understanding, to planning as exploration and creation. If you haven't a clue what's going to happen and infinite flexibility is neither attainable nor consonant with human and corporate nature, then all you have left is to articulate your vision and strive to realize it. Clearly that vision has to be intelligent and rational but, for example, is it the vision of the future of the information society of Bill Gates of Microsoft, Jim Clark of Netscape or Eckhard Pfeiffer of Compaq that is correct? The answer is, in substantial part, dependent on who has the strongest vision and drive behind that vision. The coming corporate mantra is that winners will be those who have discovered the strongest sense of purpose. The injunction is to decide who you are, believe in it with a passion . . . and things should start to happen for you.

What this approach starts from is a recognition that we live in extraordinarily fluid times. In many, if not most, situations today there is a much greater range of possible futures. However, there will still only be one actual outcome, and an enhanced power in determining that outcome will be influenced by the relative strength of purpose of the agents in any situation. In this context the agent is the corporation and the corporate will is revealed in and energized by the corporate plan. In other words, the planning causality is beginning to be reversed. Now it's not just 'how should the corporation adapt to the environment' but rather 'how does the corporation need to adapt the environment in order to achieve its objectives?' The emphasis in corporations on envisioning the future, the role of mission statements, the use of 'positive thinking' techniques under a range of guises such as neuro-linguistic programming all testify amply to this change.

Other, more circumstantial, contemporary evidence also supports the argument. For example the current merger and acquisition boom is patently different from the one that preceded it in the late 1980s. This time the overriding goal of most mergers and acquisitions is category or market dominance. The view this reflects is: If you can't control or predict your operating environment, then own it.

This development from a passive to an active mode of planning has its analogue in the social sciences. Many social and natural scientists are moving away from deterministic and reductionist stances for their disciplines. They are accepting that the future is plural and that outcomes are not even in principle determined independently of the actions of agents.

Conclusion: the Case for and the Possibility of National 'Planning'

The potential dangers of the contemporary corporate planning philosophy cannot be ignored in an unregulated environment where the countervailing power of governments has declined. In his book, *When Corporations Rule the World,* David Korten gives a chilling account of these dangers. But, for practical purposes, what can governments do?

I stressed earlier that there are two conditions necessary for the successful execution of a planning process. First, a set of objectives and second, some ability to control outcomes. In extraordinarily fluid times, outcomes are not determined by the logic of situations, but by the strength of purpose of the agents in any situation. If business planning has become, in part, a case of identity affirmation then perhaps it is not too simplistic to say that one of the responses of governments should be to 'affirm' back! National 'stories' have to be developed and, the 'liberal' resistance to contriving an identity and a sense of direction has to be overcome. Governments and global corporations are now much more nearly equals in power to control events. If the further accretion of corporate power is to be contained, then a necessary condition of that containment is that we need a matching level of political purpose.

This question of purpose is also important in the relationships between governments. Nowhere is this more clearly borne out at the moment than in the battle over EMU. The question is not 'will EMU happen or won't it?', but rather 'who is going to make what happen?' 'Events' are clearly relevant to the outcome (look at the problems in realizing their purpose of the German and French governments), but the fluidity of this (and many other) situations today is such that the balance between agents and events has altered. Waiting to see what the logic of events dictates is less sensible today that it might previously have been.

Given the more singular purpose for which corporations

exist (to maximize shareholder wealth) the corporate precedent has to be taken with caution. Government represents all the 'stakeholders' in society, the interests and objectives of which are much more numerous, more diverse and, perhaps, more difficult to reconcile. It is possible, too, that today's extraordinary fluidity will not persist forever – in which case the arguments for the more analytic and 'passive' approach to corporate and national planning might once again be more persuasive.

In the meantime, increasing numbers of companies are recognizing that the times in which we live make it imperative to have a clear sense of identity and direction as the centrepiece of their planning methods and strategies. Given that corporations cannot ever seriously and fairly represent the other stakeholder interests in society – especially those yet to be born, there is, perhaps more than ever, a duty on governments to reconcile and to represent these potentially conflicting stakeholder interests within a coherent, farsighted and energizing sense of national identity and purpose.

CONTRIBUTORS

Andrew Adonis

Andrew Adonis is a political analyst at the *Observer*. He was formerly a Fellow of Nuffield College, Oxford and has served as a local councillor. His books include *Failure in British Government: the Politics of the Poll Tax*, with David Butler and Tony Travers.

John Ashworth

John Ashworth is Chairman of the British Library and was previously Director of the London School of Economics. He is a member of the Demos advisory council.

Zygmunt Bauman

Zygmunt Bauman is Emeritus Professor of Sociology at Leeds University. His recent books include *Modernity and the Holocaust, Morality, Immorality and Other Life Strategies* and *Post-Modern Ethics*.

Ivan Briscoe

Ivan Briscoe was a researcher at Demos until 1996. He is now based in Argentina.

Samuel Brittan

Sir Samuel Brittan is an Assistant Editor of the *Financial Times*. He is an Honorary Fellow of Jesus College, Cambridge, an Honorary Doctor of Letters (Heriot-Watt University, Edinburgh) and a Chevalier de la Légion d'Honneur. He has been a Visiting Professor at the Chicago Law School, a Visiting Fellow of Nuffield College, Oxford and an Honorary Professor of Politics at Warwick University. He was a member of the Peacock Committee on the Finance of the BBC (1985–6).

Vincent Cable

Vincent Cable was educated at Cambridge and Glasgow University, and is currently Chief Economist at Shell International Petroleum Company Ltd. He is also Senior Research Fellow on the International Economics Programme, Royal Institute of International Affairs.

David Cannon

David Cannon is a Research Fellow at the London Business School and a Research Associate at Demos.

Robert Cooper

Robert Cooper is a member of the British Diplomatic Service and was previously Head of the Policy Planning Staff at the Foreign and Commonwealth Office.

Helena Cronin

Helena Cronin works at the Centre for the Philosophy of the Natural and Social Sciences at the London School of Economics and is the author of *The Ant and the Peacock.*

Philip Dodd

Philip Dodd is the Editor of *Sight and Sound* and a writer and broadcaster who has published widely on questions of national identity within Britain. Formerly Deputy Editor of the *New Statesman*, consultant to BBC Television for several years and an academic for more than ten, his books include *Englishness, Politics and Culture 1880–1920.*

Amitai Etzioni

Dr Amitai Etzioni served as Senior Adviser in the White House from 1979 to 1980 and is now the first University Professor of the George Washington University. He founded and was the first president of the international Society for the Advancement of Socio-Economics and is now an Honorary Fellow. He is editor of *The Responsive Community: Rights and Responsibilities*, a communitarian quarterly.

Howard Gardner

Howard Gardner is Professor of Education and Adjunct Professor of Psychology at Harvard University, and Co-Director of Harvard Project Zero. He is best known in educational circles for his theory of multiple intelligences. He has most recently published *Leading Minds: an Anatomy of Leadership*.

John Gray

Dr John Gray is a Fellow of Jesus College, Oxford. He has lectured in Eastern and Western Europe, North America, Australia and East Asia, and contributes regularly to the *Guardian*.

Liz Greenhalgh

Liz Greenhalgh has been researching in the fields of cultural policy and urban policy for the past eight years. Last year she published with Ken Worpole and Charles Landry, *Libraries in a World of Cultural Change* and with Ken Worpole, *Park Life: Urban Parks and Social Renewal*.

Sir Douglas Hague

Sir Douglas Hague is an Associate Fellow of Templeton College, Oxford, where he chairs the College's Strategic Leadership Programme. He is also a visiting Professor at the Manchester Business School, of which he was a founder. Sir Douglas was an economic adviser to Mrs Thatcher from 1967 to 1979 and an adviser to the Prime Minister's Policy Unit at Number 10 Downing Street from 1979 to 1983. He was Chairman of the Economic and Social Research Council from 1983 to 1987, and remains a non-executive director of the CRT Group plc. He is a trustee of Demos.

Charles Hampden-Turner

Charles Hampden-Turner is based at the Judge Institute of Management Studies, at Cambridge University, and is the author of *Seven Cultures of Capitalism*.

David H. Hargreaves

David H. Hargreaves is Professor of Education at the University of Cambridge. He was the Chief Inspector of the Inner London Education Authority and is now Chairman of the Committee on the Training and Development of University Teachers.

Charles Leadbeater

Charles Leadbeater was Industrial Editor and Tokyo Editor of the *Financial Times* and Assistant Editor of the *Independent*. He is now a Research Associate at Demos.

Geoff Mulgan

Geoff Mulgan is Director of Demos and the author of *Communication and Control* and *Politics in an Antipolitical Age*.

Robin Murray

Robin Murray was employed until recently by the Government of Ontario and is now working with Demos on a range of projects concerning recycling and job creation in the United Kingdom.

Perri 6

Perri 6 is Research Director at Demos. He was previously Lecturer in European Social Policy at the University of Bath and is a former parliamentary lobbyist. During the 1980s he wrote widely on housing law, legal services and public policy.

Michael Power

Michael Power is Professor of Accounting at the London School of Economics. After obtaining a Doctorate in Philosophy at Cambridge he subsequently qualified as a chartered accountant before joining the LSE in 1987. He is an associate member of the Institute of Taxation.

Roger Scruton

Roger Scruton is a writer and philosopher, and was formerly a professor at Birkbeck College, London, and Boston University, Massachusetts. He now lives as a freelance writer in Wiltshire.

Peter Singer

Peter Singer was the founding President of the International Association of Bioethics, and is now the President of the Australian and New Zealand Federation of Animal Societies. He is currently Professor of Philosophy and Deputy Director of the Centre for Human Bioethics at Monash University, Melbourne.

Bob Tyrrell

Bob Tyrrell is Chairman of the Henley Centre for Forecasting.

Helen Wilkinson

Helen Wilkinson is Project Director at Demos. She has previously worked at the BBC, the House of Commons and the US Congress, and at the National Consumer Council. Her book, *The Age of Androgyny* is published in 1997.

Ken Worpole

Ken Worpole is a writer and researcher who has worked closely with Demos since its inception, notably on the study of urban parks undertaken jointly with Comedia. He specializes in issues of urban and cultural policy and has worked and lectured in many countries. His most recent book *Staying Close to the River: reflections on travel and politics* was published in 1995.

James Woudhysen

Since 1995 James Woudhysen has been Manager of worldwide market intelligence at Philips Sound and Vision, Eindhoven.

Previously he has been editor of *Design* magazine, a director of the international design consultants Fitch, and head of consulting in information technology at the Henley Centre for Forecasting, of which he remains a Fellow. He is also Professor of Design Management at De Montfort University.

NOTES

2. Identity Politics

1 Gardels, N., 'Two concepts of nationalism: an interview with Isaiah Berlin', *New York Review of Books* (November 1991).
2 Ignatieff, M., *Blood and Belonging* (BBC/Chatto, London, 1993).
3 Albert, M., *Capitalisme contre Capitalisme* (Editions du Seuil, Paris, 1992).
4 O'Brien, R., *Global Financial Integration: The End of Geography* (RIIA, Chatham House/Pinter, London, 1992).
5 Hirst, P. and Thompson, G., *Globalisation in Question* (Polity, Oxford, 1996).
6 Hampden-Turner, C. and Trompenaarrs, A., *The Seven Cultures of Capitalism* (Doubleday, New York, 1993).
7 Brittan, S., *Capitalism with a Human Face* (Edward Elgar, Hampshire, 1995).
8 Galbraith, J. K., *The Culture of Contentment* (Penguin, London, 1992).

3. No Turning Back

1 Popular culture has best captured these shifts in films like *Falling Down* and *Disclosure* but even the BBC has got in on the act with its 'The Trouble With Men' series on BBC 2 in spring 1996.
2 Statistics cited in: Wilkinson, H., *No Turning Back: Generations and the Genderquake* (Demos, London, 1994).
3 Harkness, S., Machin, S., and Waldfogel, J., *Evaluating the Pin Money Hypothesis: The Relationship Between Women's Labour Market Activity, Family Income and Poverty in Britain* (Discussion Paper No. WSP/108, Welfare State Programme, Centre for Economic Performance, London School of Economics 1995), 16.
4 For more details of this research see Wilkinson, H. and Mulgan, G., *Freedom's Children: Work, Relationships and Politics for 18–34 Year Olds in Britain today* (Demos, London, 1995).
5 For more on this see: Wilkinson, *No Turning Back* and also *Management in the Next Millennium* (Institute of Management, London, 1995).
6 For TV role models see: British Broadcasting Council, *Perspectives of*

Women on TV (Research Working Paper IX, British Broadcasting Council, London, 1994).

7 For more on this see: Wilkinson, H., 'She's raw, she's rough, she's our new icon', *Independent* (16 June 1995).

8 A MORI poll reported on in 'Who's winning the battle of the sexes?', *Mail on Sunday* (25 June 1995), 39. This poll found that 71 per cent of the women interviewed felt positively about feminism and 49 per cent thought that it had been good for both men and women.

9 There are numerous studies which confirm this cohort effect see: Wilkinson, *No Turning Back*; Wilkinson, H., Mattinson, D., and Cooke, V., *Continuity and Change Amongst 18–34 Year Olds* (Working Paper Nine, Demos, London, 1995); Wilkinson, H. and Mulgan, G., *Freedom's Children*, and Siann, Dr G., and Wilkinson, H., *Gender, Feminism and the Future* (Working Paper Three, Demos, London, 1995) for a review of research in this field. 'What women really think', *Guardian* (7 March 1991). This survey found that 58 per cent of women interviewed would call themselves feminist some of the time and self-proclaimed feminists were more likely to be under thirty-five years of age. Pilcher, J., 'I'm not a feminist but . . .', *Sociology Review* (November 1993) 4–6. This qualitative research study found a similar cohort effect. Siann, Dr G., *Gender, Sex and Sexuality* (Taylor & Francis, London, 1994). In a study of four Scottish Universities 63 per cent of female students and 39 per cent of male students said that they were very or quite sympathetic to feminism.

10 For more on detail on the value shifts see: Wilkinson, *No Turning Back*.

11 National Council of Women, *Superwoman Keeps Going: Understanding the Female Web: A Survey of Women's Lives and Expectations* (National Council of Women of Great Britain, London, 1992).

12 This prediction was made in the *Family Policy Studies Centre Bulletin* (April 1995).

13 For these survey results see: Wilkinson and Mulgan, *Freedom's Children*.

14 Balding, J., *Young People in 1993* (University of Exeter, Exeter, 1994). Cited in: Wilkinson, *No Turning Back*.

15 For details of this see: Wilkinson, *No Turning Back*.

16 The limits of conventional polling in the case of

women is well-documented by feminists and others who recognize that whilst women have historically been less party political than men, they are involved in a wide range of community politics – campaigning against the closure of a hospital for example. See for example: Nelson, B. and Chowdhury, N., *Women and Politics Worldwide* (University Press, 1994). This 42-country-wide study concluded that the notion that women are not political is undermined by evidence of their role in community action groups and volunteer organizations. The book concluded that women's activism is alive and well; it is simply not reflected in the party political process.

17 Figures cited in: Wilkinson, *No Turning Back*. This is less of a problem for the Conservative Party membership which has traditionally been dependent on women but is a particular issue for the Labour Party whose membership base has traditionally been male dominated.

18 This was on the grounds that politics is all talk and no action, political meetings are boring, that politics is dominated by men and that people's motives for going into politics are self-serving. Cited in: *Women and Politics* (MORI, London, 1993). This was confirmed in our analysis of the MORI *Socioconsult* survey. For survey evidence see: Wilkinson and Mulgan, *Freedom's Children*. See Park, A., 'Chapter 3: Teenagers and their Politics', in *British Social Attitudes 12th report* (Dartmouth Publishing, Aldershot, 1995). This study found that girls were considerably more likely than boys to be lacking in political knowledge.

19 For more details on experience from abroad and on the debate around quotas in the Labour Party see: Lovenduski, J., 'Will quotas make Labour more "woman friendly"?' *Renewal* (Vol. 2, No. 1, January 1994); Lovenduski, J. and Norris, P. (eds), *Gender and Party Politics* (Sage, London, 1993).

20 Wolf, N., *Fire With Fire: The New Female Power and How It Will Change the 21st Century* (Chatto & Windus, London, 1993), 6–7.

21 The experience of quotas in the British Labour Party is a case in point. We also found much resistance from younger women to forcing

change through targets in the workplace and quotas in politics with many saying they wanted to be treated as an individual first rather than as a woman. See: Wilkinson, H., Mattinson, D. and Cooke, V., *Continuity and Change Amongst 18–34 Year Olds: A Qualitative Research Study* (Working Paper Nine, Demos, London, 1995).

22 For a wealth of survey evidence on this phenomenon and a discussion of its significance see: Denfeld, R., 'Introduction', *New Victorians: A Young Woman's Challenge to the Old Feminist Order* (Simon & Schuster, London, 1995). See also: *Women's Voices: A Polling Report* (Ms Foundation for Women and Centre for Policy Alternatives, 1992), 10–31. 62 per cent viewed the women's movement favourably but were distanced from the term feminist. The report concluded that the women's movement 'needs to build coalitions with organizations where 65 per cent of women are already active: their religious institutions, parent groups and community organizations.'

23 For research evidence on this phenomenon see: Griffin, C., 'I'm Not a Women's Libber But . . .', Skevington, S. and Baker, D., *The Social Identity of Women* (Sage, London, 1989); Pilcher, J., 'I'm not a feminist, but . . .', *Sociology Review*, 1993), 4–6; Siann, Dr G., *Gender, Sex and Sexuality: Contemporary Psychological Perspectives* (Taylor and Francis London, 1994); Wilkinson, Cooke, and Mattinson, *Continuity and Change Amongst 18–34 Year Olds*. For poll data on this see: 'The age of post feminist woman', *Mail on Sunday* (May 1988). In this poll 28 per cent of women aged between 18 and 34 said that they would never describe themselves as feminist and 24 per cent said they found feminism alienating. It also showed however that although 63 per cent would call themselves feminist sometimes, only 9 per cent would do so all the time; 'What women really think', *Guardian* (7 March 1991). This survey of 1100 women found that only 9 per cent of respondents viewed feminism positively and only 13 per cent belonged to a women's group despite the fact that 51 per cent of those in management positions thought that they were discriminated against and that 58 per cent of women

thought that there was still discrimination against women in the workplace; poll cited in Wolf, *Fire with Fire* (Chatto and Windus, London, 1993). For more of an explanation of this phenomenon see: Siann and Wilkinson, *Gender, Feminism and the Future*. For the role of young women in women's organizations see: Grant, J., *Where Have All the Women Gone?: The Experience of Women Aged Between 18–34 In Women's Organisations* (Working Paper Six, Demos, London, 1995).

24 For individualism see: Wilkinson, H., *No Turning Back*; Cannon, D., *Generation X and the New Work Ethic* (Working Paper One, Demos, London, 1994); Grant, *Where Have All the Women Gone?: The Experience of Women Aged Between 18–34 in Women's Organisations*; Samms, C., *Global Generation X: Values and Attitudes in Different Countries* (Working Paper Eight, Demos, London, 1995); Wilkinson and Mulgan, *Freedom's Children: Work, Relationships and Politics For 18–34 Year Olds in Britain Today*.

25 For more on this phenomenon see: Grant, *Where Have All the Women Gone? The Experience of Women Aged Between 18–34 in Women's Organisations*. This study suggested that in some ways younger women were more individualistic and less willing to be as selfless as women in the past. See also: Kelly and Breilinger, *Involvement in Women's Groups and Campaigns: Why Women Do or Don't Get Involved* (Birkbeck College, London University, 1995), 6. They conclude that 'younger women seem less likely to see the need for or benefit of women's groups and do not seem to feel as strongly about the need for social change in the area of gender'. See also: Wilkinson, Mattinson, and Cooke, *Continuity and Change Amongst 18–34 Year Olds: A Qualitative Research Study*.

26 Ibid. In Demos's qualitative research study this was the case even amongst those women impatient for change.

27 There are similar trends on the other side of the Atlantic. See: Wolf, *Fire With Fire*.

28 This shift can best be highlighted in terms of a tension between sexual politics and a focus on more 'bread and butter' issues. This is the main critique of American feminism to be found in: Denfeld, R., *The*

New Victorians (Simon & Schuster, London, 1995). See also: *Women's Voices: A Polling Report*, Ms Foundation for Women and Centre for Policy Alternatives, New York, 1992. This noted a lack of emphasis on bread and butter issues amongst certain feminist groups.

29 Faludi, S., *The Undeclared War Against Women* (Chatto & Windus, London, 1992); French, M., *War Against Women* (Hamish Hamilton, 1993).

30 Wariness about the label does seem to be linked to the fact that feminists have a poor image. It is also associated with being too extreme which jars with people's perceptions of feminine behaviour. See: Wilkinson, Mattinson, and Cooke, *Continuity and Change Amongst 18–34 Year Olds: a Qualitative Research Study* Siann, *Gender, Sex and Sexuality: Contemporary Psychological Perspectives*. See also: Siann, and Wilkinson, *Gender, Feminism and the Future* and other poll evidence previously cited.

31 For a more general discussion about femininity see: Siann, and Wilkinson, *Gender, Feminism and the Future* Siann, *Gender, Sex and Sexuality: Contemporary Psychological Perspectives*.

32 Wolf, *Fire With Fire*. She draws a distinction between two types of feminism – the dominant tradition of victim feminism which relies on a language of oppression – and power feminism which focuses on women's capacity to bring about change. Wolf would also argue that one of the main explanations for women's lack of activism is less connected to an organized backlash against women than the fact that women have made more progress than ever before, and therefore have more to lose from challenging the system. She calls this process 'economic silencing'.

33 Farrell, W., *The Myth of Male Power* (4th Estate, London, 1994).

34 In 1995 the Equal Opportunities Commission found a firm guilty of reserving jobs for women and the EOC also admitted that it now receives more complaints from men about job advertisements and employers' preferences. For more on male discrimination see: Wilkinson, *No Turning Back*, and also: Wilkinson, and Mulgan, *Freedom's Children*.

35 Crichton, M., *Disclosure* (Arrow, London, 1994).

36 Thomas, D., *Not Guilty –*

Men: The Case for the Defence (Weidenfeld & Nicolson, 1992) and Lyndon, N., *No More Sex Wars* (Sinclair Stevenson, London, 1992).

37 There have been various programmes and books drawing attention to these issues. See for example, 'Male victims of domestic violence', *First Sight* (BBC TV, 1994) and also 'Mother Love', BBC2 (May 1994); Elliott, Dr M., *Female Sexual Abuse: The Ultimate Taboo* (Longman, London, 1993).

38 For details on 'masculine values' and rising attachment to violence see: Wilkinson and Mulgan, *Freedom's Children.*

39 This is also leading to a revised view of the backlash with many feminists now concluding that male resentment, the heightening of gender tension in the workplace, and even the growth of an antifeminist 'men's movement' is something to be expected: that men could never be expected to relinquish power gracefully and are simply shouting in the transitional phase of a power-shift. Indeed it is significant that for all that Wolf has been attacked by many feminists for her revisionism, she herself is quite clear that nothing less than a gender war is underway. Power feminism is thus a means to an end in this gender war which women must mobilize in order to mount one final assault on the crumbling masculine order. See Wolf, *Fire With Fire.*

40 See for example, Kimbrell, A., 'A time for men to pull together: A manifesto for the new politics of masculinity', *Utne Reader* (No. 45, USA) 1991. Our research evidence suggests that younger men in particular are less attached to the old order.

41 Reproductive control was once seen as a woman's issue but with the advent of medical technology and the development of the male pill this is fast becoming an issue for men as much as women.

4. The Postmodern Work Ethic

1 Hall, E. T., *Beyond Culture* (Doubleday, New York, 1976).

2 This article is based on a qualitative study of young people between the ages of 18 and 30 conducted by the author in the UK, Canada and the USA between 1984 and 1996. The sample (n = 1248) is predominantly university students with a minority of subjects having no higher education. Gender and ethnic mix were

representative of the population. Depth interviews and focus groups were used to collect the data.

3 Davis, S. M., *Future Perfect* (Addison Wesley, New York, 1987).

4 Geiser, A., 'Japan's changing work ethic', *Review – The Journal of the International Business Forum* (Issue VII, 1994/5).

7. Wellbeing and Time

1 Bruce Williams estimated a decline from 154,000 hours in 1881 to 88,000 in 1981, 'Shorter hours, increased employment', paper for OECD, 1984.

2 See *International Social Attitudes* (SCPR, London, 1994).

3 Sahlins, M., *Stone Age Economics*,

4 Howse, D., *Greenwich Time and the Discovery of Longitude* (OUP, Oxford, 1980) and Kern, S. *The Culture of Time and Space 1880–1918* (Harvard, 1983).

5 The sources for these and other facts contained in this piece can be found in 'Time Facts' in *The Time Squeeze, Demos Quarterly* 5 (1995) 48–50.

6 Mumford, Lewis *Technics and Civilisation* (The Freedom Press, London, 1986).

7 Thompson E. P., 'Time, work-discipline and industrial capitalism', *Past and Present*, 36: 52–97.

8 Bell, Daniel, *The Cultural Contradictions of Capitalism*, (Heinemann, Oxford, 1979).

9 Adam, Barbara, *Time and Social Theory* (Polity Cambridge, 1990) provides an impressive overview of recent thinking.

10 Linder, Staffan, *The Harried Leisure Class* (Columbia UP, New York, 1970).

11 Research by the Henley Centre for Demos, contained in *The Time Squeeze, Demos Quarterly* 5 (1995), 48–50.

12 *Fortune* (14 June 1993) 70.

13 *Planning for Social Change*, Henley Centre, 1994/5.

14 Schor, Juliet, *The Overworked American: the unexpected decline of leisure* (Basic Books, New York, 1993).

15 *Planning for Social Change*, Henley Centre, 1994/5.

16 Hillman, Mayer, *One False Move* (Policy Studies Institute, 1991).

17 See Franco Bianchini, 'The 24-Hour City' in *The Time Squeeze, Demos Quarterly* 5 (1995) 48–50.

18 *Futures . . .*, Vol. 25 (Butterworth-Heinemann, Oxford, 1993).

19 *The Changing Workforce*

(Work Families Institute, Vol. 1, 1993).

20 Csikszentmihalyi, Mihaly *Flow: Psychology of Happiness* (Rider, London, 1992).

21 Jahoda et al in *Die Arbeitslosen von Marienthal* in 1932 was one pioneer, more recently followed by many studies of time experience.

22 For those living alone and not members of a church, Sunday morning is the lowest point of the week: without any external task, people feel lost and depressed.

8. The Battle over Britain

1 The best resource on the Thatcher years, particularly on her speeches, is Hugo Young, *One of Us. A Biography of Margaret Thatcher*, Final Edition (Macmillan, London, 1993).

2 Newspapers are, at the time of writing, rife with articles which assume that the Tories will lose the next election and which speculate about either mass defections by the Eurosceptic factions or even the breakup of the Party. For example, see the *Independent on Sunday* (5 May 1996), reporting after the heavy defeat of the Tories in the May Local Authority elections.

3 Newman, Gerald, *The Rise of English Nationalism: A Cultural History 1740–1830* (Weidenfeld and Nicolson, London, 1987), *passim*, is useful on the defining of Britain in terms of its superiority to its loathsome neighbours.

4 Tony Benn is the standard bearer of this position: see 'The Pentonville Five', *Daily Mirror* (3 August 1972), reprinted in Benn, *Speeches by Tony Benn* (Spokesman Books with the Bertrand Russell Peace Foundation Nottingham, 1974), p. 38. The 'national' question does not divide people on normal party lines. For instance Eric Hobsbawm (1996) has recently argued that Labour needs to use the words 'Great Britain', 'the nation', and 'patriotism' in order to recover the national spirit: *New Statesman and Society* (3 May 1996), 14. Neal Ascherson (1996), also from the left, takes a very different view, supporting Euro-federalism as a solution to ugly English nationalism. See *What Needs to Change: New Visions of Britain*, Giles Radice (ed.) (London, HarperCollins, 1996), 82–95.

5 See Nicholas Tate (Chief Executive of the School

Curriculum and Assessment Authority), 'The role of history in the formation of national identity, a talk given to a Council of Europe Conference, York, 18 September 1995.

6 See Patrick Wright, 'Re-enchanting the Nation: Prince Charles and Architecture', *Modern Painters* 2 iii (1989), 26–35.

7 See editorial of the *Independent* (23 June 1994), quoting the 1992 British Crime Survey which estimates there were 140,000 racial incidents in 1992, only one in twenty of which is reported to the police.

8 On Henry VIII, see Alan G. R. Smith, *The Emergence of a Nation-State: The Commonwealth of England 1529–1660* (Longman, London and New York, 1984); on the late seventeenth-century Protestant settlement see Bruce Lenman (1996), 'Prudence, Liberty, and Property, an aspect of English thought in the era of the Glorious Revolution', in Dale Hoak and Mordechai Feingold (eds), *The World of William and Mary, Anglo Dutch Perspectives on the Revolution of 1688–89* (Stanford University Press, Stanford, Calif.) and Geoffrey Holmes, *The Making of a Great Power. Late Stuart and early Georgian Britain 1609–1722* (Longman, London and New York, 1993); on patriotism during the wars with France see Perry Anderson, *Arguments within English Marxism* (NLB and Verso, London, 1980), 36–7; on 1880–1920 see Robert Colls and Philip Dodd (eds), *Englishness: Politics and Culture 1880–1920* (Croom Helm, London, 1986).

9 For an account of the irreducible internal conflicts within Britain during the Second World War, see Angus Calder, *The People's War 1939–45* (Cape, London, 1969), *passim*.

10 Benedict Anderson claims that all nations must be imaginatively constructed; only a tiny fraction of the people who belong to a national community can possibly know one another, yet people are able to maintain an 'image of their communion' through such constructions. See *Imagined Communities. Reflections on the Origin and Spread of Nationalism* (Verso, London, 1983), 15.

11 See Paul Gilroy, *The Black Atlantic: Modernity and Double Consciousness* (Verso, London and New York, 1993).

12 See Linda Colley, *Britons:*

Forging the Nation 1707–1837 (Yale University Press, New Haven and London, 1992), 39–40. On nineteenth-century migration patterns see N. J. G. Pounds, *An Historical Geography of Europe* (Cambridge University Press, Cambridge, 1990), table 11.3, 361. On contemporary British migration see Eurostat, *Migration Statistics* (Office of Official Publications of the European Communities, Luxembourg, 1995), Table A3, 9.

13 See Hugo Young, *One Of Us*, 372.

14 On the formation of England and Englishness and the 'threat' of the Jew, see James Shapiro, *Shakespeare and the Jews: Immigrants and Minorities in British Society* (George Allen and Unwin, London, 1978), 117; for the anti-Semitism in liberal and socialist 'Little England' thinking around the turn of the nineteenth century, see W. D. Rubinstein, *A History of the Jews in the English Speaking World: Great Britain* (Macmillan Press, Basingstoke, 1996), 109–123; on recent British national identity and the black communities, see Paul Gilroy *'There Ain't No Black in the Union Jack'. The Cultural Politics of Race and Nation* (Hutchinson Education, London, 1987).

15 Quoted in Alan Smith, *The Emergence of the Nation-State*, 88.

16 Linda Colley, *Britons*, 1–9; Hugo Young, *One Of Us*, 372.

17 David Starkey, 'Daze of Empire', *Guardian* (11 January 1995).

18 Gwyn A. Williams, *When Was Wales? A History of the Welsh* (Penguin, London, 1985), 114.

19 On race and nation see Paul Gilroy, *'There Ain't No Black in the Union Jack'*; on the Thatcher years in relation to these issues see John Solomos, 'The politics of immigration since 1945' in Solomos (ed.), *Racism and Antiracism: Inequalities, Opportunities and Politics* (Sage, London, 1992), 7–29.

20 See Philip Dodd (1995), 'A Mongrel Nation', *New Statesman and Society* (24 February 1995), 26–7.

21 Tom Nairn's reflections on the 1996 Culloden commemorations and his summary of the television debate between Alex Salmond of the SNP and Labour MP George Galloway are a useful summary of this strand of thinking: 'Diary', *London Review of Books* (9 May 1996).

22 Gwynn A. Williams, *When Was Wales*, 236.

23 Victor Kiernan, 'Britons Old and New' in *Immigrants and Minorities in British Society* (George Allen and Unwin, London, 1978), 151.
24 Colley, *Britons*, 55.
25 Colley, *Britons*, 373.

10. Transforming the Dinosaurs

1 For a stimulating but idiosyncratic introduction to organizational cultures, see Handy, C., *Gods of Management* (Pan Books, London, 1985).
2 I know how difficult the position of a newcomer can be. I was asked by junior minister Jeremy Bray to join the North Western Gas Board in the 1960s to try to push them more quickly into using modern management thinking and methods – a thankless task, since I was greatly outnumbered.
3 See Senge, P. M., *The Fifth Discipline* (Century Business, London, 1992), especially chapter 1. Inevitably, because it is a new concept, there is much dispute over precisely what a learning organization can learn and how. This book gives a good, mainstream account of what a learning organization is and does. Chapter 1 sets out the basic concepts, which are explored and applied in the remainder of the volume, although the systems model is very simplistic when compared with that of Stafford Beer, see note 4.
4 See Beer, S., *The Heart of Enterprise* (Wiley, Chichester, 1979, 1994), especially chapters 2 to 4. *The Heart of Enterprise* is essential reading for anyone who wishes to understand how complex systems, especially businesses and other organizations, can remain viable. Those who lead organizations do so best if they can master the art of systems thinking and Beer's book provides what is, in my view, the most helpful introduction to that. It is a weighty volume in all senses of the word, but will repay careful study by those who persist. Stafford Beer begins with an explanation of what a system is (chapter 1) and, in chapters 2 to 4, proceeds to set out the essential characteristics which a system must have if it is to be viable. The notion of variety reduction, dealt with in chapters 2 and 4, is a very useful concept for managers, which is inadequately understood and used.
5 See Morgan, G., *Images of Organisation* (Sage Publications, Beverly Hills, California, 1986). In a remarkable book, which

has received wide acclaim, Gareth Morgan has pulled together virtually all that matters in recent writings on organization theory in an imaginative and practical way. He believes that good managers and professionals become skilled at 'reading' the situations they have to handle and this book seeks to make such a skill accessible to the rest of us. The author uses a series of metaphors – or images – each of which throws light on the characteristics of a particular type of organization or a particular aspect of a number of organizations. The images use familiar notions so that organizations are likened to machines, organisms, brains, political systems, psychic prisons, instruments of domination, etc. Chapter 2 which considers the organization as a machine therefore looks at bureaucracies, like the civil service. Readers will find chapters 4 and 5, on organizations as brains, and on organizations as cultures, very useful. Those interested in obtaining a splendid insight into this field are encouraged to read the whole book. A more recent publication by the same author is *Imaginization* (Sage Publications, London, 1993). It will not appeal to everyone, being laced with somewhat humorous illustrations to make it more accessible. Charts like that on p. 95 are, however, helpful in showing how Morgan's metaphors can be used to analyse real-world problems.

6 I hasten to make my peace with those government departments which do use mathematics and diagrams. I think especially of the Treasury, whose large model of the UK economy is used extensively and well, despite jibes to the contrary from outside. I would, however, make two points. First, the Treasury is unusual among civil service departments in being so nonliterary. Second, even the Treasury model follows standard macroeconomic practice in using monetary amounts to report on very complex socio/technical/ economic phenomena. GDP is a good example. This does not 'make sense' of complex systems but avoids the problem of doing so by reducing them to sums of money, as all macroeconomics does. It is variety reduction of a very high order.

7 I have myself argued that 'however academic and business thinking on managerial issues changes, the civil service machine

goes on operating in time-honoured ways. It does so because civil servants spend too little of their time thinking and learning about organizational processes and because those who do think about them are rarely promoted to the interesting or glamorous positions in the service.' This quotation is taken from 'Can scientists manage science?' in Douglas Hague (ed.), *The Management of Science* (Macmillan, Basingstoke and London, 1991).

8 Gardner, H., *Frames of Mind*, (Fontana Press, London, 1993). See especially chapter 13.

9 *The Mosaic of Learning* (Demos, 1994), 12.

10 Gardner, H., *The Unschooled Mind* (Fontana Press, London, 1993). See especially, chapter 13.

11 Bruer, T., *Schools for Thought* (Massachusetts Institute of Technology, Mass., 1994).

12 Bruer, *Schools for Thought*, 7.

13 Bruer, *Schools for Thought*, 290.

14 Hargreaves, D., *The Mosaic of Learning* (Demos, London, 1994), 47.

15 See pp. 148–9 below.

16 Despite being a 'professional' subject, medicine is different. It holds a powerful position in (almost) every British university with a faculty of medicine. Perhaps it is because the study of medicine began very early in university history; perhaps because medicine is relatively well funded; or perhaps medical scholarship and skills really *are* superior to those in other 'professions'.

17 Jenkins, S., *Accountable to None* (Hamish Hamilton, London, 1995), 153.

18 Laurillard, D., *Rethinking University Education* (Routledge, London, 1993), 2.

19 Ibid.

20 The significance of this is that if a top executive is dismissed the amount of 'compensation for loss of office' often depends on the length of the contract not yet served, whether or not the recipient has performed well in the job – something which is rarely easy to prove.

21 See Douglas Hague, *The Management of Science*.

22 It is encouraging to see that Michael Bichard has moved from local government to become Permanent Secretary of the Department for Education and Employment – the first appointee to a top civil service job advertised nationally. At the same time, one can hope there

will in future be similar moves from outside the public sector altogether.

23 See pp. 148–9 below.

24 Hague, D., *Beyond Universities* (Hobart Paper 115, Institute of Economic Affairs, London, 1991). See especially pp. 80–1.

25 Schon, D. A., *Beyond the Stable State* (Random House, New York), 163. Although now somewhat dated, this is a pithy and well-written account of the kind of issue – e.g. organizational conservatism and learning – dealt with in this paper. Chapter 5, on 'Government as a learning system', raises important issues in a transatlantic context.

26 Schon, *Beyond the Stable State*, 175.

11. Education

1 Drucker, P. F., *Post-capitalist Society* (Butterworth Heinemann, 1993), 48.

2 The nearest thing to an official estimate is that in HM Chief Inspector of Schools Annual Report 1994–5 (HMSO, 1996), 36. Extrapolated from inspections of a sample of schools, it is said that nearly 15,000 teachers in schools (primary and secondary) are unsatisfactory and should not remain in the profession. It is also extrapolated that almost 50,000 teachers are first-rate.

3 Handy, C., *The Age of Unreason* (Business Books, London, 1989).

4 Handy, C., *The Empty Raincoat* (Hutchinson, London, 1994).

5 Sacks, J., *The Persistence of Faith* (Weidenfeld & Nicholson, 1991), 66.

6 NOP poll reported in the *Independent* (6 September 1993).

7 Fuller, T. (ed.), *Voice of Liberal Learning, Michael Oakeshott on Education* (Yale University Press, London, 1990).

8 Gardner, H., 'Opening minds', *Demos Quarterly* Issue 1 (Winter 1993), 1–5.

9 Illich, Ivan D., *De-schooling Society* (Calder and Boyars, London, 1971).

10 Cuban, L., 'Computers meet classroom: classroom wins', *Teachers' College Record*, vol. 95, 2 (1993) 185–209.

12. The Convivial City

1 Martin J. Weiner, *English Culture and the Decline of the Industrial Spirit* (Cambridge University Press, 1981).

2 Greenhalgh, L. and Worpole, K., *Park Life: Urban Parks and Social Renewal* (Comedia & Demos, London, 1995).

3 *Leisure Landscapes: Leisure, Culture and the English Countryside* (London, CPRE, 1994).
4 *Anxieties about crime* (findings from the 1994 British Crime Survey, Home Office, London, 1996).
5 Mike Davies, *City of Quartz*, (Vintage, London, 1992).
6 *Independent* (2 November 1994).
7 Lola Young, *Soundings* (Autumn 1995). Environmental images and imaginary landscapes.
8 In our study of public libraries, we came across a number of people who said that they stopped noticing time when they were absorbed in browsing or reading in the public library. See Liz Greenhalgh and Ken Worpole, with Charles Landry, *Libraries in a world of cultural change*, (UCL Press, London, 1995).
9 Brian Robson *et al*, *Assessing the Impact of Urban Policy* (HMSO, London, 1994).
10 Andrew Lovatt with Justin O'Connor, John Montgomery and Paul Owens (eds), *The 24 Hour City*, Selected Papers from the First National Conference on the Night-Time Economy (Manchester Institute for Popular Culture, Manchester, 1994).
11 Jan Gehl, *Places for People* (Melbourne City Council Melbourne, 1994).

13. The End of Unemployment

1 Charles Handy, *The Empty Raincoat* (Hutchinson, London, 1994).
2 Anyone still in any doubt about the connections between crime and unemployment should read David Dickinson of the Dept of Applied Economics at Cambridge, *Crime and Unemployment* (IPPR, London, 1995).which provides a detailed assessment of the evidence and concludes that there is 'a close association between unemployment and offending rates of young men . . .'.
3 For these and other figures we are indebted to John Wells of Cambridge University.
4 Department of Employment, 1993.
5 Many have simply been encouraged to go off the unemployment register and on to invalidity benefits. Since 1978/9 the numbers on invalidity benefit have risen from 600,000 to 1.6 million.
6 In a Henley Centre survey in 1992 the two groups least secure in their jobs represented both ends of the spectrum: professionals in

management and government, and workers in manufacturing.

7 *International Social Attitudes* (SCPR, London, 1995).

8 According to the International Labour Office.

9 According to a 1994 Mintel survey four out of ten men and women say that how well they do in their job is central to self-esteem. An even higher proportion would carry on working even if they did not need the money.

10 For an extensive survey of analyses of the work experience and learning see Robert Lane's magisterial *The Market Experience* (Cambridge University Press, 1991).

11 This is evidenced in the recent *International Social Attitudes Survey* (SCPR, London, 1993).

12 Drucker, P., *Aspen Quarterly,* Winter 1994.

13 If schooling is not improved it may be too late. What is in effect remedial training in low-level vocational qualifications for those over sixteen brings very poor returns. Research by the LSE team in *Paying for Learning* and *Learning Should Pay,* published in 1992 and 1993 shows this clearly.

14 Many of these ideas are explored in Hague, D., *Transforming the Dinosaurs* (Demos, London, 1993).

15 Adapted from 'The view from the 1990s: how the global economy is reshaping corporate power and careers', afterword to *Men and Women of the Corporation* (Basic Books, London, 1993 edn).

16 The more detailed case for reform of taxation and spending mechanisms was made in Mulgan, G. and Murray, G. R., *Reconnecting Taxation* (Demos, London, 1993).

17 A good recent analysis of what this can mean is contained in O'Regan, F. and Conway, M., *From the bottom up: toward a strategy for income and employment generation among the disadvantaged* (Aspen Institute, 1993).

18 Quoted in Lane, R., *The Market Experience* (C.V.P., Cambridge, 1991).

19 Smith, A., *The Wealth of Nations* (Pickering and Chatto, London, 1995).

14. The Parenting Deficit

1 *Current Population Survey* (Bureau of Labor Statistics, unpublished tabulations, 1991).

2 According to a *Wall Street Journal* article 20 May 1994, Sec. A, 5E, the number of latchkey children exceeds 1.6 million, with more than

500,000 children under the age of twelve.

3 Gill, R. T., Glazer N., Thernstrom, S. A., *Our Changing Population* (Prentice-Hall, New Jersey, 1992) 278.

4 Gill *et al., Our Changing Population,* 49.

5 Baydar, N. and Brooks-Gunn, J., 'Effects of maternal employment and child care arrangements on preschoolers' cognitive and behavioral outcomes: evidence from the children of the National Longitudinal Survey of Youth', *Developmental Psychology* 27 (November 1991): 932–46. Belsky, J. and Rovine, M. J., 'Non-maternal care in the first year of life and the security of infant-parent attachment', *Child Development* 59 (February 1988), 157–67. Brazelton, T. B., 'Issues for working parents', *American Journal of Orthopsychiatry* 56 (1986), 14–25. Belsky, J. and Eggebeen, D., 'Early and extensive maternal employment in young children's socioemotional development: children of the National Longitudinal Survey of Youth', *Journal of Marriage and Family* 53 (November 1991), 1083–110. Vaughn, B. E., Deane, K. E. and Waters, E., 'The impact of out-of-home care on child-mother attachment quality: another look at some enduring questions', in I. Bretherton and E. Water, (eds), *Growing Points of Attachment Theory and Research. Monographs for the Society for Research in Child Development,* 50 (1985): 1–2, serial No. 209. Some studies have found that the effects of child care are not different from parental care. For example, see Clarke-Stewart, K. A. and Fein, G. G., 'Early childhood programs', 917–99, in P. H. Mussen (ed.), *Handbook of Child Psychology,* vol. 2 (Wiley, New York, 1983). And a few studies show that child care rather than parental care is more effective for the intellectual development of poor children. For example, see Jay Belsky, 'Two waves of day care research: developmental effects and conditions of quality' in R. C. Ainslie (ed.), *The Child and the Day Care Setting: Qualitative Variations and Development* (Praeger, New York, 1984), 1–34.

6 Lowe Vandell, D. and Corasaniti, M. A., 'The relationship between third-graders' after-school care and social, academic, and emotional functioning', *Child Development* 59 (August 1988), 874.

7 For more information on

family role differentiation see Zelditch, M., 'Role differentiation in the nuclear family: a comparative study' in Parsons, T. and Bales, R. F., *Family, Socialization and Interaction Process* (Free Press, Glencoe, Illinois; 1955).

8 American Enterprise Institute, 1990.

9 William R. Mattox, Jr., 'The Parent Trap', *Policy Review*, No. 5 (Winter 1991), 6–13.

10 'Virtually all adults want children, but many of the reasons are intangible', *The Gallup Poll Monthly* (June 1990), 22.

11 The study appeared in the July 1993 issue of *Pediatrics* (vol. 82, No. 1), 32–8. Richardson's colleagues were Barbara Radziszewski, Clyde W. Dent and Brian R. Flay.

15. Freedom's Children and the Rise of Generational Politics

1 Wilkinson, H. and Mulgan, G., *Freedom's Children: Work, Relationship and Politics for 18–34 Year Olds in Britain Today* (Demos, London, 1995), 109.

2 Directorate-General V; Employment, Industrial Relations and Social Affairs, *The demographic situation in the European Union* (European Commission, Brussels, 1995).

3 Northcott, J., *Britain in 2010: The PSI Report* (Policy Studies Institute, Demos, London, 1991).

4 Cited in Walker, A., 'Whither the social contract? Intergenerational solidarity in income and employment', in Hobman, D. (ed.), *Uniting Generations: Studies in Conflicts and Cooperation* (Age Concern, London, 1993).

5 For poll details see: Etzioni, A. and Brodbeck, L., *The Intergenerational Covenant: Rights and Responsibilities* (A Communitarian Working Paper, The Communitarian Network, Washington, 1995), 21. Cited in: Wilkinson, and Mulgan, *Freedom's Children* 110.

6 *The Boston Globe Magazine* (28 November 1993).

7 Lead or Leave claims some twenty thousand members and is supported by Ross Perot. See *Boston Globe Magazine* (28 November 1993) and also *US News and World Report* (22 February 1993).

8 *Economist* (22 May 1995).

9 Daniel Callaghan is quoted in Etzioni and Brodbeck, *The Intergenerational Covenant: Rights and Responsibilities*, 21. Cited in Wilkinson, and Mulgan, 110.

10 Thompson, D., 'The welfare state and the generation conflict: winners and losers', Johnson, P. *et al.*, *Workers Versus Pensioners: Intergenerational Justice in an Ageing World* (Centre for Economic Policy Research, Manchester University Press, 1989), 33–56.
11 See Caplan, B., 'Working welfare', *The Age of Asia: Learning From the Sunrise Societies*, Quarterly, Issue 6, Demos (1995), 31. The proportion of Singapore's population aged over sixty will rise from 8.5 per cent in 1990 to 29.4 per cent in 2030.
12 Walker, A., *Age and Attitudes*, Commission of the European Communities (1993), 15–20.
13 Henley Centre for Forecasting, *Planning for Social Change*, vol. 2, Planning for Social Change, 24.
14 Henley Centre for Forecasting, *Planning for Social Change*, vol. 2, Planning for Social Change, London, 1995.
15 Henley Centre for Forecasting, *Planning for Social Change*, vol. 2, Planning for Social Change, London, 1995, 24
16 Johnson, P. and Falkingham, J., 'Intergenerational transfers and public expenditure on the elderly in modern Britain', *Ageing and Society* (1988) 8.
17 Hills, J., *Does Britain have a Welfare Generation? An Empirical Analysis of Intergenerational Equity* (Welfare State Programme, No. WSP/76). In this study Hills makes the point that each five-year generation gets back at least 90 per cent of what it puts in. He recognizes however that any attempt to abolish or substantially scale down the welfare state would lead to younger generations losing heavily and having to invest for their own private provisions as they continue to fund those who have not already done so. In addition, if social security payments continued to be price- rather than income-linked over the next fifty years, the picture would deteriorate for those born after 1921.
18 For more on this see: Cannon, D., *Generation X And the New Work Ethic* (Working Paper One, Demos, London, 1994).
19 See Wilkinson and Mulgan, 'Reconnecting politics' in *Freedom's Children* (1995).
20 For more on the international trends see Wilkinson, and Mulgan, *op. cit.*
21 For survey results on young people and politics see ibid.
22 For an analysis of what is

happening in terms of retirement age in various Western countries see Briscoe, I., 'Time rights in the 1990s: An international survey', *The Time Squeeze Demos Quarterly*. (Issue 5, Demos, London, 1995), 38.

23 Kotlikoff, L. J., *Generational Accounting: Knowing Who Pays, and When, for What We Spend* (Free Press, New York, 1992).

24 *Older People in the United Kingdom* (Age Concern Factsheet, London, 1995).

25 Figures provided by the House of Commons Library Service, 1995.

26 *Older People in the United Kingdom* (Age Concern Factsheet, London, 1995).

27 *Campaigns and Elections* (USA 1989). Cited in; Wilkinson and Mulgan, *Freedom's Children*.

28 It is significant in Australia that compulsory voting is a nonissue amongst youth organizations and is not seen by the public at large as an invasion of civil liberties.

16. Back to Greece

1 Fishkin's article in the *Independent* (9 May 1994) on the case for deliberative polling summarizes his book.

2 Heath, A. *et al.*, *Understanding Political Change* (Pergamon, Oxon, 1991), 165–6.

3 Cmnd 9797, vol. 1, 63.

4 See Wilson, J. Q., *The Moral Sense* (Free Press, New York, 1993) for a fascinating account of the consistent nature of morality in modern life.

5 See Aristotle's *Politics*, especially Bks. 3 and 4.

6 This and later references to Tocqueville draw especially on Larry Siedentop, *Tocqueville* (Oxford University Press, 1984), especially chapter 3.

7 See Meadowcroft, J. and Taylor, M. W., 'Liberalism and the Referendum in British Political Thought', in *Twentieth Century British History* (1990).

8 Had local rates referendums been implemented in 1981, the poll tax would probably not have followed. See Butler, D., Adonis, A. and Travers, T., *Failure in British Government: The Politics of the Poll Tax* (Clarendon Press, Oxford).

9 Butler, D. and Ranney, A. (eds), *Referendums* (Macmillan, Basingstoke, 1994).

10 Zander, M., *Cases and Materials on the English Legal System* (Weidenfeld and Nicolson, London, 1992, 6th edn.), 468–9.

11 McCabe, S. and Purves, R., *The Shadowy Jury at Work* (Blackwell, Oxford, 1974).

12 For one balanced discussion, see Abrahamson, J. B. *et al.*, *The Electronic Commonwealth* (Basic Books, New York, 1988).

13 The authors are grateful for background material from William Dutton of the Annenberg School for Communication and PICT in the UK.

18. Governing by Cultures

1 In this chapter, when I speak of cultures, I mean nothing more sophisticated than those sets of beliefs and behaviours, aspirations, expectations, values, senses of duty and right, those ways of evaluating what is prudent and legitimate and so forth, that inform the decisions of politicians, bureaucrats, organizations, the users of services or the public at large. I also use 'government' and 'the state' interchangeably, as is the popular use, to mean the whole apparatus of public sector organizations the operations of which are backed ultimately by the force of law and the legitimate right of force.

2 In economics, the rational expectations school argues that individuals and firms will have taken into account almost everything government does and will be able to undermine its intentions. Incentives, therefore, are likely not to be effective. Public choice theorists of the new right, such as W. A. Niskanen, *Bureaucracy and the Representative* (Aldine-Atherton, Chicago, 1971), have argued that bureaucratic action is always vitiated by the self-interest and aggrandizement of the bureaucrats. Many have argued that legislation is the object of a political competition between interest groups to secure law in their own interest. D. Mueller, *Public Choice II* (Cambridge University Press, Cambridge, 1989), and F. von Hayek, *Law, Legislation, and Liberty: a New Statement of the Liberal Principles of Justice and Political Economy* (Routledge and Kegan Paul, London, 1973–82), took the argument further by arguing that the information problems in legislating make laws produced by legislatures blunt instruments, by comparison with the cybernetically superior mechanism of common law development. That regulators are usually captured by the regulated is a well-known argument

against regulation, except where absolutely necessary: see M. Bishop, 'Regulation: an owner's manual', *Missionary Government, Demos Quarterly* 7 (1995). More generally, writers on 'globalization' often write as though the nation-state were too small any longer to be effective in anything it does: see K. Ohmae, *The End of the Nation State: The Rise of Regional Economies* (Free Press, New York, 1995).

3 In this category, we may put libertarians such as F. von Hayek, *Law, Legislation and Liberty: a New Statement of the Liberal Principles of Justice and Political Economy* (Routledge and Kegan Paul, London, 1973–1982); R. Nozick, *Anarchy, State and Utopia* (Polity, Cambridge, with Blackwell, Oxford 1974); and the novelist Ayn Rand, *Atlas Shrugged* (Random House, New York, 1957).

4 Friedman, M., *Capitalism and Freedom* (University of Chicago, Chicago, 1962): p. 201, quoting Dicey, acknowledged the enormous weight of expectations that run against the libertarian case. Nozick, R., *Anarchy, State and Utopia* (Policy, Cambridge, with Blackwell, Oxford, 1974), professed himself shocked at the radicalism of his own arguments. Rand, A., *Atlas Shrugged* (Random House, New York, 1957), continually stressed that hers was a philosophy for heroes.

5 See for example Jowell, R., *British Social Attitudes*, SCPR (Dartmouth Publishing Company, Vermont, 1995).

6 See for example Rhodes, R. A. W. and Marsh, D. (eds), *Implementing Thatcherite Policies: Audit of an Era* (Open University Press, Buckingham, 1992).

7 For example, the columnist Janet Daley, formerly of *The Times*, and now of the *Daily Telegraph*, has frequently argued on Radio 4's *The Moral Maze* that the rehabilitation of offenders smacks of totalitarianism, and that only retributive and deterrent styles of punishment are consistent with freedom.

8 Adonis, A. and Hames, T. (eds), *A Conservative Revolution? The Thatcher-Reagan Decade in Perspective* (Manchester University Press, Manchester, 1994).

9 Jowell, R., *British Social Attitudes*, SCPR (Dartmouth Publishing Company, Vermont, 1995), 290.

10 This is even true of Hayek, who claimed to be a sort of utilitarian: see Kukathas,

C., *Hayek and Modern Liberalism* (Oxford University Press, Oxford, 1992) and Friedman, M., *Capitalism and Freedom* (University of Chicago Press, Chicago, 1962).

11 Herbert Spencer was the leading nineteenth-century advocate of the minimal state: see Spencer, H., *The Man versus the State* (Caxton, Ohio, 1960).

12 Duncan, A. and Hobson, D., *Saturn's children: how the State devours Liberty, Prosperity and Virtue* (Sinclair-Stevenson, London, 1995), 36, 54.

13 Gingrich, N., *To Renew America* (HarperCollins, New York, 1995).

14 Duncan and Hobson, *Saturn's children: how the State devours Liberty, Prosperity and Virtue*

15 Galbraith, J. K., *The Culture of Contentment* (Sinclair-Stevenson, New York, 1992): ch. 15.

16 Field, F., *Making Welfare Work: Reconstructing Welfare for the Millenium* (Institute for Community Studies, London, 1992).

17 Kooiman, J. (ed.), *Modern Governance: New Government-Society Interactions* (Sage, London, 1992); Eliassen, K. and Kooiman, J. (eds), *Managing Public Organisations*, 2nd edn (Sage, London, 1992).

18 Osborne, D. and Gaebler, T., *Reinventing Government: how the Entrepreneurial Spirit is Transforming the Public Sector* (Plume [Penguin], New York, 1991).

19 Ormand, D. and Blume, D., 'Global watch: retooling governments', *Missionary Government, Demos Quarterly* 7 (1995), 24–7.

20 Metcalfe, L. and Richards, S., *Improving Public Management*, 2nd edn (Sage, London, 1993); Dunleavy, P., 'The globalisation of public services production: can government be "best in world"?', *Public Policy and Administration* (1994), 9, 2, 36–65.

21 Klein, R., *The New Politics of the National Health Service*, 3rd edn (Longman, Harlow, 1995). Ham, C., *Management and Competition in the New NHS*, National Association of Health Authorities and Trusts (Birmingham, 1994).

22 Carnaghan, R. and Bracewell-Milnes, B., *Testing the Market: Competitive Tendering for Government Services in Britain and Abroad* (Institute of Economic Affairs, London, 1992); Walsh, K., *Public Services and Market Mechanisms: Competition, Contracting and the New Public Management* (Macmillan, Basingstoke, 1995); Cochrane, A., *Whatever Happened to Local*

Government (Open University Press, Buckingham, 1993).

23 Pyper, R., *The British Civil Service*, (Prentice-Hall and Harvester Wheatsheaf, Hemel Hempstead, 1995).

24 Majone, G. (ed.), *De-regulation or Re-regulation? Regulatory Reform in Europe and the United States* (Pinter, London, 1990); Wright, V., 'Public administration, regulation, deregulation and reregulation', in Eliassen and Kooiman (eds), *Managing*, 244–61.

25 Klein, R. and Day, P., *Home Rules: Regulation and Accountability in Social Housing* (Joseph Rowntree Foundation, York, 1993).

26 Kemp, P., *Beyond Next Steps: a Civil Service for the 21st century* (Social Market Foundation, London, 1993); Greer, P., *Transforming Central Government: the Next Steps Initiative* (Open University Press, Buckingham, 1994).

27 Walsh, *Public Services and Market Mechanisms: Competition, Contracting and the New Public Management.*

28 Harden, I., *The Contract State* (Open University Press, Buckingham, 1993).

29 Power, M., *The Audit Explosion* (Demos, London, 1994).

30 OECD, 1994.

31 Marriott, R. and Jones, A., 'The economics of charitable giving and taxation policy', *Non-Profit Studies*, 1, 1 (1996).

32 NCVO, 1995.

33 Gore, A., *Creating a Government that Works Better and Costs Less: report of the National Performance Review* (Times/Random House, New York, 1993).

34 Zifcak, S., *New Managerialism: administrative reform in Whitehall and Canberra* (Open University Press, Buckingham, 1994).

35 DiJulio, J. J., jnr., *Deregulating the Public Service: Can Government be Improved?* (Brookings Institution, Washington D.C., 1993); DiJulio, J. J., jnr. Garvey, G. and Kettl, D. F., *Improving Government Performance: an Owner's Manual*, (Brookings Institution, Washington D.C, 1994).

36 Cochrane, A., *Whatever Happened to Local Government* (Open University Press, Buckingham, 1993); Lund, B., 'The enabling role: local authorities, social integration and the housing market', *Political Quarterly*, (1994) 65, 3: pp. 326–36.

37 See, MORI, *Survey of public standing of occupational groups* (MORI, London, 1993).

38 Henley Centre, 1995, private communication.

39 House of Commons Public Accounts Committee, *The proper conduct of public services*, paper 154, 1993–4 session (HMSO, London, 1994).
40 Zifcak, S., *New Managerialism: Administrative Reform in Whitehall and Canberra* (Open University Press, Buckingham, 1994); Pollitt, C., *Managerialism and the Public Services: Cuts or Cultural Change in the 1990s?*, 2nd edn (Blackwell, Oxford, 1993).
41 Jowell, R., *British Social Attitudes*, SCPR (Dartmouth Publishing Company, Vermont, 1995), 290; MORI, *Citizens' satisfaction with various services* (MORI, London, 1995).
42 Demos (eds), 'Lean democracy', *Demos Quarterly* 3 (1994).
43 Kooiman, J. (ed.), *Modern Governance: New Government-Society Interactions* (Sage, London, 1992).
44 Alexander, A., *Managing the Fragmented Authority* (Local Government Management Board, Luton, 1993).
45 Walsh, *Public Services and Market Mechanisms: Competitition, Contracting and the New Public Management*; Gronbjerg, K. A., *Understanding Nonprofit Funding* (Jossey-Bass, San Francisco, 1993).
46 The British Conservative administration has recently had to announce initiatives to trim the swelling numbers of managers in the NHS.
47 Demos, 'Liberation technology', *Demos Quarterly* 4 (1994).
48 6, P., and Briscoe, I., *On the Cards: privacy, identity and trust in the age of smart technologies* (Demos, London, 1996).
49 Goldblatt, D., 'The paradox of power: globalisation and national government', *Missionary Government, Demos Quarterly* 7 (1995), 28–9; Hirst, P., and Thompson, G., *Globalization in Question* (Polity, Cambridge, with Blackwell, Oxford, 1995).
50 Margetts, H. and Dunleavy, P., 'Public services on the world markets', *Missionary Government, Demos Quarterly* 7 (1995), 30–32.
51 Wilkinson, H., *No Turning Back: Generations and the Genderquake* (Demos, London, 1994); Wilkinson, H. and Mulgan, G., *Freedom's Children: Work, Relationships and Politics for 18–34 year olds in Britain today* (Demos, London, 1995).
52 Woudhuysen, J., 'More to learn from business', *Missionary Government, Demos Quarterly* 7 (1995), 33–8.

53 Hammer, M. and Champy, J., *Re-engineering the Corporation: a Manifesto for Business Revolution* (HarperCollins, New York, 1993).

54 Fukuyama, F., *Trust: the Social Virtues and the Creation of Prosperity* (Hamish Hamilton, New York, 1995); Putnam, R. D., with Leonardi, R. and Nanetti, R. Y., *Making Democracy Work: Civic Traditions in Modern Italy* (Princeton University Press, Princeton, New Jersey, 1993); Hampden-Turner, C., and Trompenaars, F., *The Seven Cultures of Capitalism* (Piatkus, London, 1994); Gambetta, D., *Trust: Making and Breaking Co-operative Relations* (Cambridge University Press, Cambridge, 1988).

55 Putnam *et al*, *Making Democracy Work: Civic Traditions in Modern Italy*; Fukuyama, *Trust: the social virtues and the creation of prosperity*; Hampden-Turner and Trompenaars, *The Seven Cultures of Capitalism*; Gambetta, *Trust: Making and Breaking Co-operative Relations*; Granovetter M.S., 'Economic action and social structure: the problem of embeddedness', *American Journal of Sociology*, 91(1985), 481–510; reprinted in Granovetter, M. S. and Swedberg, R. (eds), *The Sociology of Economic Life* (Westview Press, Boulder, Colorado, 1992) 53–81.; Zucker, L. G., 'Institutionalisation and cultural persistence', *American Sociological Review*, 42, 5 (1977), 726–43; repr. in Powell, W.W., and DiMaggio, P.J. (eds), *The New Institutionalism in Organisational Analysis*, (University of Chicago Press, Chicago, 1991), 83–107.

56 Jencks, C., *The Homeless* (Harvard University Press, Cambridge, Massachusetts, 1994).

57 Mott, J., Mirlees-Black, C., *Self-reported Drug Misuse in England and Wales: findings from the 1992 British crime survey* (Home Office, London, 1994).

58 Hayek's 1973–82 position is that government power should be limited only to a negative agenda of freedom, in which such projects of transformation would be constitutionally ruled out.

59 6, P, and Brown, C., 'Whither private rented housing after deregulation?' (Demos, London, 1996).

60 Plant, M., and Plant, M., *Risk-takers: Alcohol, Drugs, Sex, and Youth* (Tavistock Routledge, London, 1992), ch.12.

61 Banks, J., Blundell, J. and Dilnot, A., 'Tax-based initiatives in the UK', seminar paper (Institute for Fiscal Studies, London, 1994).

62 Fox, A., *Beyond Contract: Work, Power and Trust Relations* (Faber and Faber, London, 1994); Fukuyama, *Trust: the Social Virtues and the Creation of Prosperity.*

63 Fox, *Beyond Contract: Work, Power and Trust Relations.*

64 Putnam *et al.*, *Making Democracy Work: Civic Traditions in Modern Italy*; Fukuyama, *Trust: the Social Virtues and the Creation of Prosperity.*

65 As Duncan, A., and Hobson, D., *Saturn's Children: how the State devours Liberty, Prosperity and Virtue* (Sinclair-Stevenson, London, 1995), ch.1 seem to think.

66 Fukuyama, *Trust: the Social Virtues and the Creation of Prosperity.*

67 The distinction between effectors and detectors was introduced by C. C. Hood, *The Tools of Government* (Macmillan, Basingstoke, 1983). I have found it helpful to add the two additional categories, collectors and selectors. L. M. Salmon, *Beyond Privatisation: the Tools of Government Action* (Urban Institute Press, Washington D.C., 1989), offers a slightly different approach to classifying the tools of government.

68 Dunleavy, P., 'The globalisation of public services production: can government be "best in world"?' *Public Policy and Administration*, 9, 2, (1994), 36–65.

69 Bishop, M., 'Regulation: an owner's manual', *Missionary Government, Demos Quarterly* 7 (1995), 46–8.

70 Carter, N., Klein, R. and Day, P., *How Organisations Measure Success: the use of Performance Indicators in Government* (Routledge, London, 1992).

71 Such things can, in principle, be measured. See, for example, T. Bentley and R. Stanley, 'Governing by numbers', *Missionary Government, Demos Quarterly* 7 (1995), 52–4, suggest that it would be possible to use methods of measuring culture developed by such writers as J. Hampton, 'Giving the grid/group dimensions an operational definition', in Douglas, M. (ed.), *Essays in the Sociology of Perception* (Routledge and Kegan Paul, London, 1982); 64–83, and R. P. Boyle, and R. M. Coughlin, 'Conceptualising and operationalising cultural theory', in Coyle, D. J. and Ellis, R. J. (eds),

Policy, Politics and Culture (Westview Press, Boulder, Colorado, 1994).

72 'Communitarianism' is, of course, a protean idea. However, we can perhaps identify a continuum from, at one extreme, A. Etzioni, *The Spirit of Community* (Fontana Press, London, 1995), whose work combines insistence on personal morality with family duties and a larger role for nonprofit bodies conceived as appropriate organizational expressions of morality, and at the other extreme, F. Fukuyama, *Trust: the Social Virtues and the Creation of Prosperity* (Hamish Hamilton, New York, 1995), who is more concerned with the variety of organizational forms that sustain social capital. The work of R. D. Putnam *et al* *Making Democracy Work: Civic Traditions in Modern Italy*, sits somewhere between in privileging voluntary action as an indicator of social capital, but placing less stress on personal and family morality. I have criticized elsewhere the tendency to romanticize the value of voluntary action as a distinctive organizational activity or the repository of social capital and values, See Perri 6, 'Conclusion: will anyone talk about the "third sector" in ten years' time?' in 6, P. and Vidal, I. (eds), *Delivering welfare: repositioning non-profit and co-operative action in western European welfare states* (Centre d'Iniciatives de l'Economia Social, Barcelona, 1994), 401–9.

73 Thompson, M., Ellis, R. J. and Wildavsky, A., *Cultural Theory* (Westview Press. Boulder, Colorado, 1990).

74 Zucker, L. G., 'Institutionalisation and cultural persistence', *American Sociological Review*, 42, 5 (1977), 726–43; repr. in Powell and DiMaggio (eds), *The New Institutionalism in Organisational Analysis*, 83–107.

75 Hague, D., *Transforming the Dinosaurs: how organisations learn* (Demos, London, 1993), 3–4.

76 Pollitt, C. and Bouckaert, G. (eds), *Quality Improvement in European Public Services: Concepts, Cases and Commentary* (Sage, London, 1995); Zifcak, S., *New Managerialism: Administrative Reform in Whitehall and Canberra* (Open University Press, Buckingham, 1994).

77 Pollitt, and Bouckaert (eds.), *op. cit.*

78 Pollitt, C., *Managerialism and the Public Services: Cuts or Cultural Change in the*

1990s?, 2nd edn, (Blackwell, Oxford, 1993).

79 Mayo, E., *The Social Problems of an Industrial Civilisation* (Routledge, London, 1949).

80 Reynolds, D., 'Why are Asians so good at learning?', *The Age of Asia: learning from the sunrise societies, Demos Quarterly* 6 (1995), 35–6 and Goodman, R., 'Chasing illusions: the real lessons from Japanese schools', *The Age of Asia: learning from the sunrise societies, Demos Quarterly* 6 (1995), 37–8.

81 Börsch-Supan, A., 'Savings in Germany – part I: incentives', in Poterba, J. M. (ed.), *Public Policies and Household Saving* (University of Chicago Press, Chicago, 1994), 81–2; Ito, T. and Kitamura, J., 'Public policies and household savings in Japan', in Poterba (ed.), *op. cit.*, 134.

82 Jupp, B., 'The grey and the good: government ethics around the world', *Missionary Government, Demos Quarterly* 7 (1995), 50–51; Jackson, M. W., 'How can ethics be taught?', in Chapman, R. A. (ed.), 1993, 31–42; more generally on cultural change in government ethics, see H. G. Frederickson (ed.), *Ethics and Public Administration* (M. E. Sharpe, Armonk, New York, 1993) and R. A. Chapman (ed.), *Ethics in Public Service* (University of Edinburgh Press, Edinburgh, 1993).

83 Gardner, H., with E. Laskin, *Leading Minds: anatomy of leadership* (HarperCollins, London, 1995).

84 The British Deputy Prime Minister Michael Heseltine recently got into political difficulties by making the unguarded suggestion that late payment was a perfectly respectable business practice.

85 Kendall and 6. 1994.

86 Hague, 1993.

87 Coyle and Ellis, 1994.

88 Duncan and Hobson, 1995.

19. The Audit Explosion

1 It has also been brought to my attention that the terms 'audit' and 'auditor' have for many years played a central role in the ideas of the Church of Scientology.

2 This essay is based in part upon, 'The Audit Society', in Anthony Hopwood and Peter Miller (eds.), *Accounting as Social and Institutional Practice* (Cambridge University Press, Cambridge, 1994).

3 See Carol Jones, 'Auditing Criminal Justice', *British Journal of Criminology*, vol. 33, No. 2 (Spring 1993), 187–202.

4 See, *Working for Patients* (HMSO, London, 1989).

5 The HEFC advertised for a number of posts in early 1994, including quality auditors on a part-time basis. The job description was interesting because management experience in relation to education is preferred but is not regarded as essential.

6 See 'UK prospects in the booming global environmental market', *ENDS Report* 212 (September 1992).

7 See 'Environmental consultants ride out recession', *ENDS Report* 213 (October 1992).

8 See, 'NACCB to be accreditation body for BS7750 and EC Eco-Audit', *ENDS Report* (November 1993), 36–7.

9 See, *University Statistics 1991–92* (HMSO, London, 1993), 64–5.

10 For evidence of the burden on small companies, see 'Unloved expense', *Financial Times* (2 February 1993).

11 Of nearly 13,500 charities registered with the Charity Commission, only 11 per cent submitted accounts to them in the early 1990s. See 'Act of charity brings audit day of reckoning', *Financial Times* (19 November 1992).

12 A new journal entitled *Accountability in Research: Policies and Quality Assurance* (Gordon & Breach), was launched in 1989.

13 See, for example, the white paper, *Realising our potential: A strategy for science, engineering and technology* (HMSO, London, 1993). The new public management of science is discussed in Brad Sherman, 'Governing Science: Patents and Public Sector Research', *Science in Context*, vol. 7, No. 3 (1994).

14 See Adrian Gain and Jonathan Rosenhead, 'Problem structuring for medical quality assurance', *LSE Working Papers in Operational Research* (November 1993). This empirical study reports on various ways to generate consensus and shared objectives around the audit process. However, in the design of audit arrangements the tensions between clinical and managerial resource-based judgements proved the most intractable, with clinicians having considerable anxiety about the coopting of audit processes for disciplinary purposes.

15 For an exploration of this see Brunsson, N., 'Ideas and Action: Justification and Hypocrisy as Alternatives to Control',

Accounting, Organizations and Society, vol. 18, No. 6 (1993), 489–506.

16 These comments draw heavily from Cohen, S., *Visions of Social Control* (Polity Press, Cambridge, 1985), 155–60.

17 It would be easy to regard the audit explosion as extending rationalization in Weber's sense. Certainly it creates its own bureaucratic machinery and can be regarded as a form of rationalization. But its instrumentality is problematic and often obscure. One therefore has a puzzle which escapes Weber's framework: widespread investment in a practice with ambiguous functional credentials.

18 See Beck, U., *Risk Society* (Sage, London, 1992).

19 See 'The Special Intelligence Agency', *Times Higher Educational Supplement* (24 September 1993), 16–17. This article contains a cartoon which epitomizes the essential structure of the audit society. It depicts a large quality assurance inspector checking over the shoulder of another smaller official who is in turn checking the work of another even smaller individual whose identity as lecturer or student is not made clear. The quality assurance inspector is remote from the first order activity. His or her role is that of control of control.

20 Critics, such as the Labour Party MP Austen Mitchell, regard independence as the underlying problem. They argue that financial auditors are too close to the interests of management who control their remuneration. Accordingly the objectivity of auditors is systematically impaired and can only be improved by institutional change. These critics suggest that a new body, such as a general audit council, could provide the necessary oversight and effective discipline. Others see the problem in terms of the expectations which audit creates among consumers and the 'gap' between them and auditors' own conception of their mission. Initial responses to this problem have been conceived in terms of educating consumers of audit services to have the 'correct' expectations. Now there is an, albeit cautious, mood for a different response – to bring the audit product into line with these expectations (see Humphrey, C., Moizer, P. and Turley, S., *The Audit Expectations Gap in the United Kingdom* (Institute of

Chartered Accountants in England and Wales, London, 1991)). While practitioners can be precise about the costs of audit, its benefits in terms of providing assurance to other parties about the quality of financial statements have consistently defied precision, despite attempts to integrate statistical techniques into audit programmes.

21 This crisis has different faces. Firstly, financial audit practitioners are facing a mature market experiencing competition with a vengeance. Secondly, they are also facing a growth in litigation (not yet evident in other fields of auditing) which is increasing the risk they face (see 'Auditors turn cold as legal claims hot up', *Financial Times* (11 October 1993)). Thirdly, they are experiencing an erosion of reputation as the consuming public begins to doubt the value of this statutory product. Under these circumstances it is to be expected that audit firms would seek to diversify into markets for other services, including audits in other areas.

22 I would not necessarily concede that 'democracy' and 'communications audits' are exceptions to my claim since the mechanics of audit, even if designed with style B in mind, has the potential to drift towards style A. See Beetham, D., *Auditing Democracy in Britain* (Charter 88 Trust Publications, London, 1992); Booth, A., *Communications Audit: A Guide for Managers* (Gower, London, 1988).

23 See 'Auditing the Accountants', *Political Quarterly* vol. 64, No.3, (1993), 270.

24 In the context of the United States, Johnson and Kaplan have argued that auditing has seriously inhibited the evolution of management accounting systems with damaging effects on competitiveness. See Johnson, T. and Kaplan, R., *Relevance Lost – The Rise and Fall of Management Accounting* (Harvard Business School, Harvard, 1987).

20. Reconnecting Taxation

1 For a discussion of the current UK situation see Glennerster, H., *Paying for Welfare: Issues for the Nineties* (LSE Welfare State Working Programme, Discussion paper No. 82, December 1992).

2 Attitudes are summarized

in 'What do citizens think about taxes', Peters, B. G., *The Politics of Taxation* (Blackwell, Oxford, 1991), which gathers together and critically assesses a very wide range of surveys and studies.

3 On the history of tax see Ardant, Gabriel, *Histoire de l'Impot* (Fayard, Paris, 1971). The second volume covers the period from the eighteenth century to the present. Published on the eve of the oil price rise and the first major postwar slump, Ardant had no sense of the profound fiscal changes which were to come, save for being an early exponent of environmental taxes. See also Webber,Carolyn and Wildavsky, Aaron, *A History of Taxation and Expenditure in the Western World* (Touchstone, Exmouth, 1986).

4 For Britain see Sabine, B. E. V., *A History of Income Tax* (Allen and Unwin, London, 1966).

5 This attitude was embodied in successive pieces of legislation and has only begun to be tackled in the 1990s. The 1842 Finance Act stated that 'the profits of any married woman living with her husband shall be deemed the profits of her husband'. The 1918 Act introduced the 'married man's allowance' and the 1970 Income and Corporation Taxes Act 1970 stated that 'a woman's income shall be deemed for income tax purposes to be his income and not to be her income'. *Income Tax and Sex Discrimination* (Equal Opportunities Commission, Manchester, 1979).

6 All sides of the political spectrum have been guilty in this respect. The same tax scare technique which was used by the Conservatives to defeat the UK Labour Party in the 1992 election was used by the Australian Labour Party to win re-election in 1993. In neither case did the electoral argument bear much relation to the real choices facing each nation.

7 Changes to tax could be an even more important cause of disconnection in the future. Much of the logic of recent reforms has been towards a simpler system, perhaps with a single rate for all income whether personal or corporate. In New Zealand, the Labour Finance Minister Roger Douglas introduced a 10 per cent goods and services tax with a very wide base, and a widened scope for income tax, as a deliberate and radical step in this direction. At first glance this seems attractive. But its great danger is that it would

simply make the whole system of spending even more opaque and incomprehensible and would further the loss of connection between taxes and services.

8 Colbert, Louis XIV's finance minister, said that the art of taxation consisted in 'so plucking the goose as to obtain the largest amount of feathers with the smallest possible amount of hissing'.

9 Hague, D., *A Target for Public Expenditure* (unpublished mimeograph 1992).

10 In California, which has often led the world in this area, some authorities estimate that the ratio of taxpayers to tax-beneficiaries has fallen from eight to three since the 1950s.

11 This remains a contested topic. For a detailed econometric survey which suggests the importance of lower average tax rates to productivity growth, and which also shows that the UK failed to reverse economic decline in part because of the Thatcher government's failure to lower average rates, see Newell, A. and Symons, J., 'Macroeconomic consequences of taxation in the 1980s' (Working Paper 113, Centre for Economic Performance, LSE, 1991).

12 The concept of representative democracy was developed by the utilitarians as a way of preserving this top-down model while extending the franchise, and was later accepted by the left who saw the resultant state as an instrument which, once captured, could be used progressively.

13 Such as Emanuel Mounier and Jacques Maritain.

14 A full list is provided in Bracewell-Milnes, B., 'Earmarking in Britain: Theory and Practice', *The Case for Earmarked Taxes* (Institute of Economic Affairs, London, 1991), 57 ff.

15 The case for hypothecation never wholly disappeared. James Buchanan argued in the early 1960s that tax decisions and expenditure decisions should be relinked so as to better reflect individual preferences. See Buchanan, J., 'The economics of earmarked taxes', *Journal of Political Economy* (October 1963), 457–69. There have also been studies showing that hypothecation can improve compliance, since voters will have more confidence that their money is spent on useful outcomes. See for example Deran, E., 'Earmarking and expenditures: a survey and a new test', *National Tax Journal* (December 1965).

However ideas of this kind never made much headway against the prevailing conventional wisdom.

16 Hypothecation of this kind seems to fit better with public attitudes than pooled taxation. Contrary to the assumptions of the majority of economists who have influenced tax theory, most people see different goods and services such as transport, land, water, justice or schooling as different in kind, and consequently believe that it is quite appropriate to reflect these differences in tax policy. This is one reason why there is far stronger support for a more equal distribution of health care, justice and education than there is for an egalitarian distribution of money. In this respect Michael Walzer's approach is considerably more useful than those of more abstract political philosophers and economists. See *Spheres of Justice* (Harvard, Cambridge MA, 1983).

17 The Swiss motorway charge is also an interesting example of a tax that is precisely designed to fall more heavily on foreigners who use Swiss roads.

18 See for example the excellent survey of insurance systems, markets and informational failures in Barr, N., 'Economic Theory and the Welfare State', *Journal of Economic Literature*, XXX (June 1992).

19 The insurance system could dovetail with a reformed education system. There is a lively debate beginning about whether everyone should be given the right to a number of years of tertiary education at some point in their life: like a modified insurance system it would encourage a more efficient and equitable use of time.

20 Interestingly, a more direct involvement by electorates in tax policy would tend to reinsert morality. This is both a question of desert and need for people and a question of how different goods are taxed. Most people recognize that goods bring with them very different levels of risk and danger, both external and personal. This is not well-represented by tax neutrality. A strong public sense of good and bad (and not just price inelasticity) lies behind the long history of 'sin' taxes on products such as alcohol and tobacco, or gambling, and, conversely, the tax exemption of books and newspapers. A public that is becoming rapidly more attuned to risk in fields such as food, cars and

cosmetics may well seek a more differentiated tax system to reflect this.

21 For the first time government would have to show the local and regional impacts of decisions, and whether, for example, subsidies to depressed industrial areas are of the same order of magnitude as indirect subsidies through the defence budget, or mortgage tax relief to the southeast.

22 There is conflicting evidence about how electorates would react, whether to packages offering specific action on poverty or to a broader programme of redistribution. David Miller suggests that a democratically determined distribution of incomes, to the extent that it is conceivable, would be 'substantially inegalitarian, but at the same time a good deal less inegalitarian than that which currently obtains'. It would reflect a widely shared belief that different abilities and work should be differentially rewarded and an equally widely shared belief that the existing system often rewards the wrong people. Miller's survey also demonstrates the weakness of popular support for familiar notions of social justice. Miller, D., 'Distributive justice: what the people think', *Ethics*, 102 (April 1992), 566.

21. Is There a New World Order?

1 The Peace of Westphalia is the name given to the Treaties of Münster and Osnabrück: there were separate negotiations and separate treaties because the Swedes refused to talk to the Papal Representative. These treaties established the principle that the states of Europe were sovereign and independent, i.e. that they were no longer part of a hierarchical order headed by the Pope and the Holy Roman Emperor.

2 Destruction is regulated in detail and has to meet agreed criteria. For example, in the case of aircraft the tail must be sawn off, in the case of tanks *inter alia* the barrel of the gun must be cut and the turret ring broken, etc. Parties to the treaty have a right to observe destruction.

3 This process was pursued through the CSCE, 'Helsinki' process. The Stockholm Conference of 1968 was especially important in agreeing a range of far-reaching confidence-building measures.

22. After Social Democracy

1 Public expenditure under the Thatcher administration never fell below 38 per cent of GNP, and touched that level only very briefly, before returning to the pre-Thatcher norm of just over 40 per cent, where it has stayed.

2 I find the central elements of communitarian liberalism in the work of Isaiah Berlin and Joseph Raz. I discuss Berlin's thought in my book, *Berlin* (Fontana Press, London, 1995). Raz's thought is discussed in the Postscript to my book, *Mill on Liberty: a Defence*, 2nd edn, (Routledge, London and New York, 1996). I do not claim that my understanding of communitarian liberalism would be endorsed by either Berlin or Raz.

3 I have criticized Rawlsian legalism in my book, *Enlightenment's Wake: Politics and Culture at the Close of the Modern Age* (Routledge, London and New York, 1996), Chapters 1, 6, 8 and 9.

23. The Society of Networks

1 *Economist* (1 July 1995).

2 *Visa International: the Management of Change* (Harvard Business School, 1981), 2.

3 Hock, D., 'The chaordic organization: out of control and into order', *World Business Academy Perspectives*, vol. 9, No. 1 (1995).

4 Kelly, K., *Out of Control* (Fourth Estate, London, 1994), 607.

5 Kelly, *op. cit.*, p. 58.

25. Before We Rush to Declare a New Era

1 Dertouzos, M. L., 'Communications, computers and networks', *Scientific American* (September 1991), 30, 36. See also Malone T. W. and Rockart, J. F., 'Computers, networks and the corporation', *Scientific American, op. cit.* For 'post-Fordist' theories, see Aglietta, M., *A Theory of Capitalist Regulation* (New Left Books, London, 1979); Alain Lipietz, *Mirages and Miracles: the crises of global Fordism* (Verso, London, 1987), and Stuart Hall and Martin Jacques, *New Times: The Changing Face of Politics in the 1990s* (Lawrence & Wishart, London, 1990). The classic text of flexible specialization, whose fondness for the textile firms of northern Italy is still popular, is Piore, M. J. and Sabel, C. F., *The Second Industrial Divide* (Basic Books, New York, 1984).

2 Figure derived from United Nations, *World Industrial Robots 1994: Statistics 1983–93 and Forecasts to 1997* (October 1994).
3 Toffler A. and Toffler, H., *War and Anti-War* (Little Brown, London, 1994), 247–8.
4 BMRB, *TGI*, 1995.
5 Champy, J. and Hammer, M., *Reengineering the Corporation*, (Brealey, London, 1993).
6 Etienne Grandjean, 'Ergonomics at the interface between man and machine', in Barbacetto, G. (ed.), *Design Interface* (Arcadia Edizioni, 1987).
7 Two French authors elided telecommunications and 'informatics' (computers) into the neologism telematics. See Nora, S. and Minc, A., *The computerization of society: a report to the President of France* (MIT, 1980, first published in 1978).

26. Masters of the Infinite Game

1 Porter, M., *The Competitive Advantage of Nations* (Free Press, New York, 1990); Akio Morita, *Japan Inc.* (Signet, New York, 1986).
2 Carse, J.P., *Finite and Infinite Games* (Ballentine Books, New York, 1992).
3 Porter, M. *The Neoclassical Advantage of Nations* (Macmillan, Basingstoke, 1990).

27. Darwinian Psychology, Political Economy and the Problem of Groups

1 Radnitzky, G. (ed.), *Universal Economics* (Pergamon House, New York, 1992).
2 Popper, K. R., *Unended Quest* (Fontana, London, 1976).
3 Popper, K. R., *Objective Knowledge* (Oxford University Press, Oxford, 1974).
4 Ridley, M., *The Red Queen* (Penguin, London, 1994).
5 Jones, S., *The Language of the Genes* (HarperCollins, London, 1994).
6 Wright, R., *The Moral Animal* (Little Brown, London, 1995).
7 Cronin, H., *The Ant and the Peacock* (Cambridge University Press, Cambridge, 1991).
8 Brittan, S., *Capitalism with a Human Face* (Edward Elgar, Hampshire, 1995).
9 Dawkins, R., *The Selfish Gene* (Oxford University Press, Oxford, revised edition, 1989).
10 Dennett, D., *Darwin's Dangerous Idea* (Penguin, London, 1995).
11 Badcock, C., *PsychoDarwinism* (HarperCollins, London, 1994).

INDEX